THE RUSSIAN ANARCHISTS

THE RUSSIAN ANARCHISTS

Paul Avrich

AK Press
Edinburgh, Oakland, West Virginia

This edition copyright © 2005 AK Press

First published in 1967 by Princeton University Press

The Russian Anarchists

ISBN 1 904859 48 8
ISBN13 9781904859482
Library of Congress Control Number: 2005905989

AK Press	AK Press
674 A 23rd Street	PO Box 12766
Oakland CA	Edinburgh, Scotland
94612-1163 USA	EH8 9YE
www.akpress.org	www.akuk.com

For a dollar, a pound or a few IRC's, the above addresses would be delighted to provide you with the latest complete AK Press catalog.

Cover design by
John Yates

ACKNOWLEDGMENTS

I wish to express my sincere gratitude to Geroid Tanquary Robinson, Seth Low Professor Emeritus of History, Columbia University, who guided and encouraged my study of modern Russian history. I am also indebted to James Joll, Sub-Warden of St. Anthony's College, Oxford, and Professor Alexander Erlich of the Russian Institute, Columbia University, who read this work in manuscript form and offered constructive criticisms and suggestions. In addition, Max Nomad read most of the manuscript and kindly allowed me to see documents and rare publications in his possession. My thanks are due also to Princess Alexandra Kropotkin, Boris Yelensky, and the editors of the *Freie Arbeiter Stimme* in New York City, Isidore Wisotsky, Morris Shutz, and the late Leibush Frumkin, who gave me the benefit of their personal recollections of the men and events discussed herein; and to Judith Maltz, the late Rose Pesotta, Senya Fleshin, John Cherney, and Irving Abrams, who were good enough to answer my inquiries and to place at my disposal literature and photographs that could not be obtained elsewhere. Needless to say, however, the sole responsibility for this volume remains my own.

For their expert assistance in finding pertinent materials, I am indebted to Lev Magerovsky of Columbia University's Archive of Russian and East European History and Culture; Hillel Kempinski and Lola Szafran of the Bund Archives of the Jewish Labor Movement; Edward Weber and Marjorie Putnam of the Labadie Collection; Rudolf de Jong and L. J. van Rossum of the International Institute of Social History; and the staffs of the Hoover, Columbia, and Harvard Libraries, the New York Public Library, the Library of Congress, the Yivo Institute of Jewish Research, the Tamiment Library, the British Museum, and the Lenin and Saltykov-Shchedrin Libraries in the Soviet Union. Finally, I am deeply grateful to the American Philosophical Society, the American Council of Learned Societies, the Social Science Research Council, the Ford Foundation, and the City University of New York for making my visits to these archives and libraries possible.

NOTE: In the spelling of Russian names, I have adhered, by and large, to the transliteration system of the Library of Congress, without the soft sign and diacritical marks. Exceptions have been made (a) when other spellings have become more or less conventional (Peter Kropotkin, Leo Tolstoy, Alexander Herzen, Angelica Balabanoff, Trotsky, and Gorky), (b) in two cases where the persons involved spent most of their careers in the West and themselves used a different spelling in the Latin script (Alexander Schapiro and Boris Yelensky), and (c) in a few diminutive names (Fanya, Senya, Sanya).

CONTENTS

ILLUSTRATIONS
Following page 214

THE RUSSIAN ANARCHISTS

INTRODUCTION

Although the idea of a stateless society can be traced back to ancient times, anarchism as an organized movement of social protest is a comparatively recent phenomenon. Emerging in Europe during the nineteenth and early twentieth centuries, it was, like liberalism and socialism, primarily a response to the quickening pace of political and economic centralization brought on by the industrial revolution. The anarchists shared with the liberals a common hostility to centralized government, and with the socialists they shared a deep hatred of the capitalist system. But they held no brief for the "reformism, parliamentarism, and unrelieved doctrinairism" of their competitors; nothing less than a clean sweep of "bourgeois civilization," with its growing regimentation and callous indifference to human suffering, could satisfy their "thirst for the absolute."[1] Focusing their attack on the state and on capitalism as the chief institutions of domination and exploitation, the anarchists called for a social revolution that would abolish all political and economic authority and usher in a decentralized society based on the voluntary cooperation of free individuals.

In Russia at the turn of the century, as in Western Europe several decades earlier, it was the arrival of the industrial revolution and the social dislocation it produced that called a militant anarchist movement into being. It is not surprising, then, that the Russian anarchists should have found themselves debating many of the same questions that had long been preoccupying their comrades in the West, notably the relationship between the anarchist movement and the newly emergent working class and the place of terrorism in the impending revolution. Yet however much Russian anarchism owed its predecessors in Western Europe, it was deeply rooted in a long tradition of native radicalism stretching back to the peasant revolts of Stenka Razin and Emelian Pugachev, a tradition which was shortly to reach a climax in the Revolutions of 1905 and 1917. The social creed propagated by the Russian anarchists was itself a curious

[1] Victor Serge, *Mémoires d'un révolutionnaire* (Paris, 1951), pp. 18-19.

3

blend of western and indigenous elements; originating in the West with Godwin, Stirner, and Proudhon, it subsequently filtered through the prisms of Bakuninism, Kropotkinism, and native Populism, thus acquiring a distinctive Russian hue. The character of Russian anarchism, moreover, was shaped by the repressive political environment into which it had been born. Tsar Nicholas II, by thwarting all efforts by enlightened members of Russian society to reform the autocracy and alleviate social and economic distress, drove his opponents to seek redress in a frenzy of terrorism and violence.

Anarchism in Russia flourished and waned with the fortunes of the revolutionary movement as a whole. When rebellion erupted in 1905, the anarchists jubilantly hailed it as the spontaneous mass upheaval forecast by Bakunin a generation before, and they threw themselves into the fray with bombs and pistols in hand. However, failing to build up a coherent organization or to penetrate the expanding labor movement on any significant scale, they remained a loose collection of obstreperous little groups whose activities had a relatively minor impact on the course of the uprising. The episodic character of the opening section of this book is, in part at least, a reflection of the disarray within the anarchist movement during its formative years. After the 1905 revolt was suppressed, the movement fell dormant until the First World War set the stage for a new uprising. Then, in 1917, the sudden collapse of the monarchy and the breakdown of political and economic authority which followed convinced the anarchists that the millennium had indeed arrived, and they applied themselves to the task of sweeping away what remained of the state and transferring the land and factories to the common people.

The Russian anarchists have long been ignored by those who regard all history through the eyes of the victors. Political success, however, is by no means the sole measure of the worth of a movement; the belief that triumphant causes alone should interest the historian leads, as James Joll recently observed, to the neglect of much in the past that is valuable and curious, and narrows our view of the world.[2] Thus if one is to appreciate the true range and complexity of the Revolution of 1917 and the

[2] James Joll, *The Anarchists* (London, 1964), p. 11.

events that followed in its wake, the role played by the anarchists must be taken into account. In the turmoil of insurrection and civil war, the anarchists attempted to carry out their program of "direct action"—workers' control of production, the creation of free rural and urban communes, partisan warfare against the enemies of a libertarian society. They acted as the gadfly of total rebellion, brooking no compromise with the annihilation of government and private property, refusing to accept anything but the Golden Age of full liberty and equality. In the end, however, a new despotism arose upon the ruins of the old, and the anarchist movement was stamped out. The few who survived, though they suffered the melancholy of defeat, nevertheless clung to the belief that ultimately their vision of a stateless utopia would triumph. "Bolshevism is of the past," Alexander Berkman could write in 1925, when his Russian comrades were in prison or exile. "The future belongs to man and his liberty."[3]

[3] Alexander Berkman, *The "Anti-Climax": The Concluding Chapter of My Russian Diary "The Bolshevik Myth"* (Berlin, 1925), p. 29.

PART I · 1905

1 · THE STORMY PETREL

The time has come, an enormous thing is moving
down on us all, a mighty, wholesome storm is
gathering; it is approaching, is already near, and
soon will cleanse from our society its indolence,
indifference, prejudice against work,
and foul ennui.

BARON TUZENBAKH, CHEKHOV'S
The Three Sisters

At the beginning of the twentieth century, the Russian Empire was entering a time of troubles, a cataclysmic period of war and revolution destined to leave the old order in ruins. Opponents of the autocracy had long been forecasting the approach of a destructive tempest. Decades before Nicholas II ascended the throne, Mikhail Bakunin had sensed that the atmosphere in Russia was growing heavy with storms of devastating power, and Alexander Herzen more than once had thought he could hear the moan and grumble of an impending debacle.[1] The reforms of Alexander II cleared the air momentarily, but after the emperor's assassination in 1881 the dark clouds of reaction enshrouded the country once more. By the turn of the century, few could escape the conviction that the old regime was on the eve of a great upheaval. The air seemed full of portents and forebodings. In a poem that was on many lips, Maksim Gorky predicted that a stormy petrel would appear "like black lightning" in the heavens, the harbinger of an immense storm soon to burst upon the Russian land.[2] The stormy petrel became a symbol for Russians of all backgrounds—for some the symbol of approaching calamity, for others of imminent salvation.

But Nicholas II firmly refused to heed the danger signals. He remained unshakeable in his determination to preserve the au-

---

[1] M. A. Bakunin, *Sobranie sochinenii i pisem, 1828-1876*, ed. Iu. M. Steklov (4 vols., Moscow, 1934-1936), III, 148; A. I. Herzen, *"Kolokol": izbrannye stat'i A. I. Gertsena, 1857-1869* (Geneva, 1887), p. 299.

[2] M. Gorky, "Pesnia o burevestnike," *Antologiia russkoi sovetskoi poezii* (2 vols., Moscow, 1957), I, 9-10.

tocracy as his father had done before him. Under the spell of his reactionary advisor Konstantin Pobedonostsev, the Procurator of the Holy Synod, the Tsar stifled every constitutional impulse of the enlightened members of society. Dismissing as "senseless dreams" their desperate petitions for a larger political role, he placed his trust in an unwieldy bureaucracy, a large but ill-equipped army, and a stultifying network of secret police.

The greatest threat to the *ancien régime* came from the peasantry. A catastrophic famine in 1891 had reawakened Russian society to the misery that pervaded the countryside. Overpopulation and stagnation in the villages persisted even after the Emancipation. As the peasants multiplied (from fifty to eighty millions in a single generation), the average size of their already inadequate family holdings steadily shrank, so that most villagers could no longer support themselves without earning additional income as hired hands in agriculture or in manufacture. The peasants hungered for more land and struggled under the crushing burden of taxes and redemption payments. They remained paralyzed by the restrictions of communal tenure long years after the Tsar had proclaimed them free men. In most places, the widely scattered strips of farmland were still redistributed every few years, and antiquated methods of cultivation had not yet given way to modern agricultural techniques. The muzhiks continued to live out their primitive lives in one-room wooden huts with earthen floors, sharing them perhaps with their pigs and goats, and subsisting on bread, cabbage soup, and vodka.

The black-earth provinces of central Russia, once the bulwark of serfdom, had changed but little since the great Emancipation of February 1861. In this overcrowded region, where "beggarly allotments" of land abounded, the impoverished peasants managed to avoid starvation only by carrying on their long-established cottage manufacture of nails, sacking, cutlery, and other small items. By the close of the century, however, handicrafts production had entered a steep decline, hard pressed by the competition of efficient factories in the burgeoning industrial towns to the north and west. The villagers, thrust into the darkness of despair, took to casting sullen and baleful looks at their former masters, whose land they now coveted more than ever before. In 1901, a landowner of Voronezh province fancied he could see a bloody mist crawling over his estate, and noted that breathing and living had lately become more difficult, "as before a storm."[3] In the autumn of that year, the central and southern agricultural regions yielded disastrously meager harvests, and the following spring the peasants of Poltava and Kharkov provinces resorted once again to the ugly weapons of Stenka Razin and Emelian Pugachev—axe, pitchfork, and torch—seizing grain wherever any could be found, and plundering the manor houses of their districts until government troops arrived to restore order.[4]

The wretched condition of the peasantry was matched by that of the growing class of industrial workers. Serfs only yesterday, the workers found themselves uprooted from their native villages and crowded into the squalid factory dormitories of the big towns. Victimized by callous foremen and factory directors, their paltry wages habitually reduced for petty infractions of workshop rules and without any legal means of communicating their grievances, the workmen could adjust to their new mode of life only with the greatest difficulty.[5]

Laborers in the factories, moreover, were afflicted with a crisis of identity. Powerful magnets pulled them in two directions, one leading back to their traditional villages, the other towards a strange new world beyond their comprehension. At the beginning of the new century, a large majority of factory workers—especially those in the textile mills of north-central Russia—were still legally classified as peasants. As such, they retained at least nominal possession of some allotment land and were liable to certain regulations of the commune, such as the issuance of work permits for factory employment. These worker-

[3] Bertram D. Wolfe, *Three Who Made a Revolution* (New York, 1948), p. 265.

[4] *Krest'ianskoe dvizhenie 1902 goda* (Moscow and Petrograd, 1923), pp. 17-128; P. P. Maslov, *Agrarnyi vopros v Rossii* (2 vols., St. Petersburg, 1908), II, 104-129.

[5] K. A. Pazhitnov, *Polozhenie rabochego klassa v Rossii* (St. Petersburg, 1906), pp. 92-161; Theodore H. Von Laue, "Factory Inspection under the Witte System, 1892-1903," *American Slavic and East European Review*, XIX (October 1960), 347-362; Von Laue, "Russian Peasants in the Factory, 1892-1904," *Journal of Economic History*, XXI (March 1961), 76-80; Gaston V. Rimlinger, "The Management of Labor Protest in Tsarist Russia, 1870-1905," *International Review of Social History*, V (1960), 226-248; Rimlinger, "Autocracy and the Factory Order in Early Russian Industrialization," *Journal of Economic History*, XX (March 1960), 67-92.

peasants often left their wives and children in the village, returning for the harvest season, or in times of sickness or old age. Their peasant mentality was evidenced in their sporadic outbursts against the harassments of the factory, more akin to the jacqueries of an earlier age than to the organized strikes of a more mature proletariat.[6]

Yet, at the same time, the workers were loosening their ties with the countryside. The heavy concentration of labor in Russian enterprises helped give the factory hands a sense of collectivity that more and more replaced the old loyalties of the village.[7] The odd form of social schizophrenia that plagued the emerging working class was beginning to heal. The workingmen were breaking with past traditions and beliefs and taking on a single new identity as a social group distinct from the peasantry from which they sprang.[8]

The turn of the century brought the embryonic Russian working class an economic jolt as severe as the crop failures that shook the peasants in the central rural districts. In 1899, after a prolonged period of industrial growth, the Empire of the Tsars entered a depression from which it took nearly a decade to recover. The depression first struck a glancing blow at the textile industry of the northern and western provinces, then moved rapidly southward, enveloping factories, mines, oil fields, and ports, and bringing serious labor disturbances in its train. During the summer of 1903, the oil workers of Baku and Batum engaged in bloody skirmishes with the police, and walkouts in Odessa broadened into a general strike which swiftly spread to all the centers of heavy industry in the Ukraine, striking with particular force in Kiev, Kharkov, Nikolaev, and Ekaterinoslav.[9]

[6] M. I. Tugan-Baranovskii, *Russkaia fabrika v proshlom i nastoiashchem* (3 edn., St. Petersburg, 1907), pp. 446-447; Maslov, *Agrarnyi vopros v Rossii*, I, 376-377.

[7] A. G. Rashin, *Formirovanie promyshlennogo proletariata v Rossii* (Moscow, 1940), pp. 169-184.

[8] P. N. Liashchenko, *Istoriia narodnogo khoziaistva SSSR* (2 vols., Leningrad, 1947-1948), II, 168-171; Von Laue, *Journal of Economic History*, XXI, 61-71; Maslov, *Agrarnyi vopros v Rossii*, I, 378-382.

[9] *Vseobshchaia stachka na iuge Rossii v 1903 godu: sbornik dokumentov* (Moscow, 1938); D. Shlossberg, "Vseobshchaia stachka 1903 g. na Ukraine," *Istoriia Proletariata SSSR*, VII (1931), 52-85; D. Kol'tsov, "Rabochie v 1890-1904 gg.," in *Obshchestvennoe dvizhenie v Rossii v nachale XX-go veka*, ed. L. Martov, P. Maslov, and A. N. Potresov (4 vols., St. Petersburg, 1909-1914), I, 224-229.

A noteworthy characteristic of the turbulence in Russia was the tendency of disaffected social elements to combine with one another to form highly inflammable mixtures. Factory workers, for example, acting as conduits for the radical ideas they absorbed in the cities, disrupted the isolation of their native villages. In a similar vein, a significant feature of the industrial strikes in the south was the frequent appearance of university students alongside the workmen in mass meetings, street demonstrations, and clashes with the authorities.

The years of economic decline coincided with a period of student unrest on an unprecedented scale in Russia's history. Many of the students felt as estranged from the existing social order as the pauperized peasants and their semi-proletarianized cousins in the factories. Quite commonly, university students led impecunious lives in dreary lodgings, embittered by the injustice of the tsarist regime and disheartened by the inevitable prospect of a minor post in the bureaucratic machinery. Even those who came from the wealthier nobility found it difficult to tolerate the highhanded policies of the government or the obscurantism of the Tsar's advisors, who obstinately refused to make any concessions to constitutional principles. The students deeply resented the university statute of 1884, which had dissolved their clubs and societies, banished liberal professors to obscure locations in the provinces, and destroyed all semblance of university autonomy and academic freedom.[10]

In February 1899, students at St. Petersburg University, indignant because the authorities had cautioned them against rowdy behavior during their annual college celebrations, created a small disturbance, whereupon mounted policemen dispersed them with whips. In reprisal, the furious students organized strikes and obstructed the attendance of lectures. Sympathetic demonstrations swept the other universities of European Russia, disrupting normal academic life for several months. The situation was tantamount to a general strike in higher education, to which the government responded by expelling hundreds of insubordinate students and drafting many of them into the

[10] Thomas Darlington, *Education in Russia*, volume 23 of Great Britain, Board of Education, *Special Reports on Educational Subjects* (London, 1909), pp. 134-136, 433-449; William H. E. Johnson, *Russia's Educational Heritage* (Pittsburgh, 1950), pp. 153-154.

army.[11] One of the expelled young men, Karpovich by name, vented his outrage by assassinating the Minister of Education, N. P. Bogolepov, whom he blamed for the government's harsh measures against the students. Recalling to everyone's mind the murder of Tsar Alexander II, carried out twenty years earlier by the group of young Populists known as the People's Will, Bogolepov's death touched off a rash of terrorist acts directed at high state officials. In March 1901, a month after Bogolepov was killed, a terrorist shot at Pobedonostsev, but missed his quarry. The following year, a disgruntled student mortally wounded the Minister of the Interior, D. S. Sipiagin, and a workman made an unsuccessful attempt on the life of the Governor of Kharkov. In May 1903, another worker with truer aim shot and killed the Governor of Ufa, who had ordered his troops to fire on a group of unarmed strikers.

In the midst of this violence, Russia hovered between two worlds, one dying and the other powerless to be born. The embitterment of the peasants, workers, and students could not be assuaged peacefully, for there were no legitimate outlets for their mounting frustrations, nor was the Tsar willing to introduce any reforms from above. There was a growing tendency among the insulted and injured to seek extreme solutions to their accumulating difficulties, especially after the depression dealt its body blow to the economy.

The signs of imminent upheaval were most noticeable in the provinces located along the periphery of the Empire, where social disquiet was intensified by national and religious persecution.[12] During four centuries of continuous expansion, Russia had extended its dominion over Finns, Estonians, Latvians, Lithuanians, Poles, Georgians, Armenians, Azerbaijanis, and many other nationalities. Indeed, at the close of the century, non-Russians constituted a majority of the total population of the Empire. Living mostly in the border areas, they could plainly hear the reverberations of nationalism in central Europe. Yet,

[11] Darlington, *Education in Russia*, pp. 153-155; Johnson, *Russia's Educational Heritage*, pp. 176-179; N. Cherevanin, "Dvizhenie intelligentsii," in *Obshchestvennoe dvizhenie v Rossii*, I, 273-283; Nicholas Hans, *History of Russian Educational Policy, 1701-1917* (London, 1931), pp. 169-174.

[12] Z. Lenskii, "Natsional'noe dvizhenie," in *Obshchestvennoe dvizhenie v Rossii*, I, 349-371.

paradoxically, national consciousness among the minority peoples received an even stronger stimulus from the Russian government itself. Inspired by Pobedonostsev, whose political philosophy pervaded the era of the last Romanovs, Alexander III and his son Nicholas embarked upon a program of Russification, an attempt to force the restless inhabitants of the frontier provinces to suppress their own national traditions and recognize the supremacy of Russian culture. Intended somehow to curb national and social discontent, Russification only aggravated such problems in a multinational empire. The ethnic question played an important part in the strikes among the Transcaucasian oil workers in 1902 and 1903; and in 1904, after Nicholas II extended Russification to loyal Finland, which had been enjoying constitutional privileges since 1809, the son of a Finnish senator murdered the Russian Governor-General, N. I. Bobrikov.

No national or religious minority suffered more from the harsh policies of the government than the Jews. At the opening of the twentieth century, five million Jews resided in the Empire, mainly in the Pale of Settlement, which extended along the western borderlands from the Baltic to the Black Sea. They had fared comparatively well during the moderate reign of Alexander II. In his program of reforms, the Tsar had permitted prosperous Jewish merchants, skilled craftsmen, former soldiers, and holders of university diplomas to live and work outside the Pale. But Alexander's violent death in March 1881 abruptly ended this period of calm and relative prosperity for the Jews. Easter time marked the outbreak of an ugly rash of pogroms, which spread through more than one hundred districts in the southwestern provinces. Although the least show of force was sufficient to stop a pogrom at once, the local authorities as a rule looked the other way before the rapine and plunder, and in some cases even encouraged the pogromists.[13] On top of these depredations by the local populace, the government issued a series of obnoxious decrees affecting every vital aspect of Jewish life. "Temporary regulations" prohibited the Jews from settling in rural communities, even within the Pale, and although these rules applied only to new settlers, many old residents were expelled from the villages of their birth and forced to live in the

[13] S. M. Dubnow, *History of the Jews in Russia and Poland* (3 vols., Philadelphia, 1916-1920), II, 247-258.

15

larger towns. Movement from village to village was restricted and searches were conducted for Jews residing illegally outside the borders of the Pale, which was reduced somewhat in size. The Ministry of Education introduced quotas limiting the number of Jewish students in secondary schools and universities to 10 per cent of the student body inside the Pale and 5 per cent outside, except in St. Petersburg and Moscow, where the figure was fixed at 3 per cent. Jewish doctors could no longer find public employment, and their service in the army medical corps was curtailed. Admission to the bar for "non-Christians" was made subject to the approval of the Minister of Justice, who rarely granted entry to Jewish candidates. Jews could no longer participate in the *zemstva* (rural assemblies) or in the city councils. Furthermore, in 1891, the authorities evicted twenty thousand Jewish merchants and artisans from Moscow, where Alexander II had allowed them to settle in 1865, and three years later the introduction of a state monopoly on alcohol deprived many Jewish innkeepers of a livelihood.[14]

These pernicious regulations remained in force with little modification throughout the reign of Nicholas II. The plight of the Jews grew desperate. Crowded into ghettos, subjected to religious persecution, largely barred from higher education and professional careers, their traditional occupations increasingly circumscribed, the Jews faced the total collapse of their economic and social structure. After the depression struck in 1899, the vast majority were compelled to live on the margin of pauperism. Lacking modern equipment and cheap credit, the small entrepreneurs characteristic of the Pale were threatened with ruin by rising competition from large-scale industry. Artisans, abandoning forever their cherished dream of becoming independent manufacturers, joined the ranks of the factory wage earners or, if less fortunate, the swelling army of *luftmenshn*—men without any employment, who lived precariously "off the air."

Matters were brought to a head soon after Viacheslav Pleve succeeded the slain Sipiagin as Minister of the Interior in 1902. A former director of the security police and an ardent agent of Russification, Pleve was an inveterate Jew-baiter and a re-

[14] *Ibid.*, ɪɪ, 309-312, 336-357, 399-413; Louis Greenberg, *The Jews in Russia* (2 vols., New Haven, 1944-1951), ɪɪ, 19-54.

actionary bureaucrat of the worst stamp. It was Pleve who, in 1904, was to advocate saving the autocracy by instigating a "small victorious war" against the Japanese. The same motive now led him to divert popular discontent against the Jews. By stigmatizing the revolutionary movement as "the work of Jewish hands," he hoped to drown the revolution in Jewish blood.[15]

Pleve's strategy gave encouragement to P. A. Krushevan, the publisher of an anti-Semitic newspaper in Kishinev, the capital of Bessarabia. Launching a campaign of invective against the Jews, Krushevan accused them of revolutionary plots and ritual murders and called upon the Christian population to take revenge on their Jewish exploiters. On Easter Day of 1903, the horrible Kishinev pogrom erupted. For two days the police stood aside as hoodlums massacred scores of Jews, injured hundreds more, and ransacked their shops and dwellings. Many Jewish families were left homeless and destitute, utterly ruined by the attack, which ceased the moment the authorities intervened. A few months later, a tide of pogroms swept through the Pale, ravaging Rovno, Kiev, Mogilev, and Gomel.[16]

It was here in the borderlands of the west and the southwest, and chiefly in the Jewish towns, that the Russian anarchist movement was born. In these areas, economic distress combined with intense national oppression to nourish a strong nihilist sentiment among the workers, students, and peasants, driving many of them to the outermost fringe of radicalism. Ever since the very first years of reaction under Alexander III, artisans, intellectuals, and factory workers of the frontier provinces had been forming clandestine circles devoted mainly to self-education and radical propaganda. The great famine of 1891 stimulated the growth of such organizations, and throughout Russia they multiplied very rapidly, becoming the nuclei around which the two major socialist parties—the Marxian Social Democrats and the neo-Populist Socialist Revolutionaries—took shape at the end of the century. Yet by the spring of 1903, the year of the pogroms, a

[15] Dubnow, *History of the Jews*, III, 69. Cf. S. Iu. Witte, *Vospominaniia* (2 vols., Berlin, 1922), I, 193; and S. D. Urussov, *Memoirs of a Russian Governor* (London, 1908), pp. 9, 15.

[16] S. M. Dubnov (Dubnow) and G. Ia. Krasnyi-Admoni, eds., *Materialy dlia istorii antievreiskikh pogromov v Rossii* (2 vols., Petrograd, 1919-1923), I, 130-295; Dubnow, *History of the Jews*, III, 72-104; Greenberg, *The Jews in Russia*, II, 50-52.

considerable number of young workers and students in Bialystok, a center of the radical labor movement in the Pale, were already finding serious shortcomings in the socialist parties and were abandoning the Bund (the organization of Jewish Social Democrats), the Socialist Revolutionaries, and the PPS (the Polish Socialist party, whose socialist creed was wedded to a powerful desire for national independence) for the more extreme doctrines of anarchism.[17]

The new anarchist recruits defected from the Social Democratic Bund for a number of reasons, not the least of which was the organization's firm stricture against acts of terrorism; such deeds, argued the Bund's leaders, would only demoralize the workers and lead to the degeneration of the labor movement.[18] Defying this ban on violence, small groups of young rank-and-file Bundists formed a radical "opposition" within the movement and proclaimed a program of "direct action" against the state and private property. They obtained revolvers and dynamite, attacked government officials, manufacturers, policemen, and *agents provocateurs*, and carried out "expropriations" in banks, post offices, stores, factory offices, and private homes.[19] These activities provoked a heavy barrage of criticism from the Bund leadership, causing many of the young terrorists to abandon Social Democracy for a brand of anarchism that favored violent exploits of every sort.[20]

The anarchists felt also that Marx's disciples included too many intellectuals who seemed bent on drowning the will to act in a mighty torrent of words; ideological debates and struggles for political leadership were exhausting their strength before the battle with the Tsar had even commenced. In the summer of

[17] In the Ukrainian provinces, the RUP (Revolutionary Ukrainian Party) also lost some of its members to the anarchists.

[18] *Di Geshikhte fun Bund*, ed. G. Aronson *et al.* (2 vols., New York, 1962), II, 92; H. Frank, *Natsionale un politishe bavegungen bay Yidn in Bialystok* (New York, 1951), p. 53; A. S. Hershberg, *Pinkos Bialystok* (2 vols., New York, 1950), II, 103.

[19] M. Rafes, *Ocherki po istorii "Bunda"* (Moscow, 1923), pp. 81-89; A. Litvak, *Vos geven* (Vilna, 1925), pp. 188-190; R. Abramovitch, *In tsvey revolutsies* (2 vols., New York, 1944), I, 202-203; N. A. Bukhbinder, *Istoriia evreiskogo rabochego dvizheniia v Rossii* (Leningrad, 1925), pp. 253-264.

[20] H. Frank, "Di Bialystok tkufe fun der ruslendisher anarkhistisher bavegung," *Geklibene shriftn* (New York, 1954), pp. 388ff.

1903, a number of nascent anarchists from Bialystok attended the second congress of the Social Democratic party, a disillusioning spectacle of organizational squabbles and theoretical hairsplitting that ended in the schism of the Marxist movement into two irreconcilable factions, Mensheviks and Bolsheviks. For all their ideological armor, declared the anarchists, the Social Democrats lacked "revolutionary scope" and intensity.[21] Instead of idle chatter, the *enragés* of Bialystok craved direct action to eliminate the tyrannical state, which they regarded as the embodiment of evil and the source of all the suffering in Russia.

Furthermore, the anarchists were determined to rid themselves of the state at once, while the followers of Marx insisted that the intermediate stages of parliamentary democracy and the "dictatorship of the proletariat" were necessary predecessors of the stateless society. This convinced the impatient anarchists that the socialist intellectuals meant to defer the attainment of a workers' paradise indefinitely, in order to satisfy their own political ambitions. According to the anarchists, moreover, the Social Democrats relied too exclusively on the organized forces of skilled labor to emancipate Russia, and neglected the masses of peasants as well as the unskilled and unemployed castaways of society.

The anarchists found equally serious drawbacks in the programs of the SR party and the PPS. Although they admired the SR campaign of terror against government officials, the anarchists wished to wage "economic terror" as well, to extend violent activities to their employers and to property owners in general. In addition, they objected to the preoccupation of the SR's with the agrarian question; nor did they share the nationalist objectives of the PPS or, for that matter, the belief of all socialists in the necessity of some form of government.

In short, the anarchists accused all the socialist groups of temporizing with the existing social system. The old order was rotten, they argued; salvation could be achieved only by destroying it root and branch. Gradualism or reformism in any shape was utterly futile. Impatient for the immediate realization of their stateless utopia, the youthful anarchists had only withering contempt for intermediate historical stages, partial achievements,

[21] *Al'manakh: sbornik po istorii anarkhicheskogo dvizheniia v Rossii* (Paris, 1909), p. 6.

and palliatives or compromises of any sort. They turned away from the Marxists and SR's and looked instead to Bakunin and Kropotkin for new inspiration. If the stormy petrel was soon to appear in Russia, they were convinced it was coming as the herald of the anarchist millennium.[22]

The young anarchists found the personality of Mikhail Aleksandrovich Bakunin as electric as his creed. Born into the landed gentry and trained as an army officer, Bakunin abandoned his noble heritage for a career as a professional revolutionist; in 1840, at the age of twenty-six, he left Russia and dedicated his life to a relentless struggle against tyranny in all its forms. Not one to sit in libraries, studying and writing about predetermined revolutions, Bakunin threw himself into the uprisings of 1848 with irrepressible exuberance, a Promethean figure moving with the tide of revolt from Paris to the barricades of Austria and Germany. Arrested during the Dresden insurrection of 1849, he spent the next eight years in prison, six of them in the darkest dungeons of Tsarist Russia, the fortresses of Peter-Paul and Schlüsselburg. His sentence was commuted to a lifetime of Siberian exile, but Bakunin escaped his warders and embarked on a sensational odyssey that encircled the globe and made his name a legend and an object of worship in radical groups all over Europe.[23]

Bakunin's broad magnanimity and childlike enthusiasm, his burning passion for liberty and equality, and his volcanic on-

[22] On the origins of the anarchist movement in the border provinces, see also *Khleb i Volia*, No. 11, September 1904, pp. 3-4; No. 12-13, October-November 1904, p. 8; *Chernoe Znamia*, No. 1, December 1905, pp. 6-8; *Burevestnik*, No. 8, November 1907, pp. 9-12; "Di anarkhistishe bevegung in Rusland," *Der Arbayter Fraynd*, 27 October, 3 November, and 10 November 1905; B. I. Gorev, *Anarkhizm v Rossii* (Moscow, 1930), pp. 58-69; L. Kulczycki, *Anarkhizm v Rossii* (St. Petersburg, 1907), pp. 74ff; V. Zalezhskii, *Anarkhisty v Rossii* (Moscow, 1930), pp. 20-22; and Peter Kropotkin, *Der Anarchismus in Russland* (Berlin, 1905).

[23] For accounts of Bakunin's life, see Edward Hallett Carr, *Michael Bakunin* (London, 1937); H.-E. Kaminski, *Michel Bakounine: la vie d'un révolutionnaire* (Paris, 1938); Iu. M. Steklov, *Mikhail Aleksandrovich Bakunin: ego zhizn' i deiatel'nost'* (4 vols., Moscow and Leningrad, 1926-1927); and Max Nettlau, "Michael Bakunin: eine Biographie" (manuscript, 3 vols., London, 1896-1900).

slaughts against privilege and injustice, all gave him enormous human appeal in libertarian circles. "What struck me most," wrote Peter Kropotkin in his memoirs, "was that Bakunin's influence was felt much less as the influence of an intellectual authority than as the influence of a moral personality."[24] As an active force in history, Bakunin exerted a personal attraction that Marx never could rival. He won a unique place among the adventurers and martyrs of the revolutionary tradition.

Yet it was not Bakunin's personal magnetism alone that drew the raw youths of Bialystok away from Marxism and into the anarchist camp. There were also fundamental doctrinal differences between Bakunin and Marx, foreshadowing the disputes that were to arise in Russia a generation later between the anarchists and the Social Democrats. These differences centered around the nature of the approaching revolution and the form of society that would arise from its wake. In Marx's philosophy of dialectical materialism, revolutions were predetermined by historical laws; they were the inevitable product of ripened economic forces. Bakunin, on the other hand, considered himself a revolutionist of the deed, "not a philosopher and not an inventor of systems, like Marx."[25] He adamantly refused to recognize the existence of any "*a priori* ideas or preordained, preconceived laws."[26] Bakunin rejected the view that social change depended on the gradual maturation of "objective" historical conditions. On the contrary, he believed that men shaped their own destinies, that their lives could not be squeezed into a Procrustean bed of abstract sociological formulas. "No theory, no ready-made system, no book that has ever been written will save the world," Bakunin declared. "I cleave to no system, I am a true seeker."[27] Mankind was not compelled to wait patiently as the fabric of history unfolded in the fullness of time. By teaching the working masses theories, Marx would only succeed in stifling the revolutionary ardor every man already possessed—"the impulse to liberty, the passion for equality, the holy instinct of

[24] Peter Kropotkin, *Memoirs of a Revolutionist* (Boston, 1899), p. 288.
[25] Steklov, *Mikhail Aleksandrovich Bakunin*, III, 112.
[26] Michel Bakounine (Bakunin), *Oeuvres* (6 vols., Paris, 1895-1913), I, 91.
[27] Carr, *Michael Bakunin*, p. 167.

revolt."[28] Unlike Marx's "scientific" socialism, his own socialism, Bakunin asserted, was "purely instinctive."[29]

In sharp contrast with Marx, who had a rationalist's scorn for the more primitive elements of society, Bakunin never deprecated the revolutionary capacities of nonworkers. He accepted the notion of a class struggle, it is true, but one that would not confine itself to the proletariat and bourgeoisie, since the instinct of rebellion was the common property of all the oppressed classes of the population. Bakunin shared the Populist faith in the latent forces of violence in the Russian countryside, with its long tradition of blind and pitiless uprisings. His vision was of an "all-embracing" revolution, a great rising both in town and country, a true revolt of the downtrodden masses, including, besides the working class, the darkest elements of society—the primitive peasantry, the *Lumpenproletariat* of the urban slums, the unemployed, the vagrants and outlaws—all pitted against those who thrived on the misery and enslavement of their fellow creatures.[30]

Bakunin's conception of an all-encompassing class war made room for still another unorganized and fragmented element of society for which Marx had only disdain. Bakunin assigned a major role to the disaffected students and intellectuals, alienated from the existing social order and from the uneducated masses as well. In Marx's view, these intellectuals did not comprise a class of their own, nor were they an integral component of the bourgeoisie; they were merely "the dregs" of the middle class, "a bunch of *déclassés*"—lawyers without clients, doctors without patients, petty journalists, impecunious students, and their ilk —with no vital role to play in the historical process of class conflict.[31] For Bakunin, on the other hand, the intellectuals were

[28] Bakunin, *Oeuvres*, II, 399.

[29] Steklov, *Mikhail Aleksandrovich Bakunin*, I, 189.

[30] M. A. Bakunin, *Izbrannye sochineniia* (5 vols., Petrograd and Moscow, 1919-1922), v, 202; *Gesammelte Werke* (3 vols., Berlin, 1921-1924), III, 52; *Pis'ma M. A. Bakunin k A. I. Gertsenu i N. P. Ogarevu*, ed. M. P. Dragomanov (Geneva, 1896), pp. 497-498.

[31] Friedrich Engels, Paul Lafargue, and Karl Marx, *L'Alliance de la Démocratie Socialiste et l'Association Internationale des Travailleurs* (London, 1873), chapter 5; quoted in Max Nomad, *Apostles of Revolution* (Boston, 1939), p. 127.

a valuable revolutionary force, "fervent, energetic youths, totally *déclassé*, with no career or way out."[32] In the bitter struggle between Marx and Bakunin for supremacy in the European revolutionary movement, the *déclassé* intellectuals, as Bakunin saw it, were bound to join his side, for they had no stake whatever in things as they were and saw no prospect for improvement except through an immediate revolution that would demolish the present system. The part the intellectuals were to play in the overthrow of the old order was crucial: they would ignite the dormant rebelliousness of the people into a bonfire of destruction.

Such a philosophy of immediate revolution inevitably attracted its largest following in the relatively backward regions of Europe, in those countries still groping towards modern industrialism, countries where the hopes of the *déclassés* were dim, where the peasantry remained large and impoverished, and where the workers were unskilled and unorganized. In such circumstances, the abject and illiterate populace could scarcely respond to the "gradualism" or to the theoretical intricacies of Marxism. Whereas Marx foresaw the revolt of a mature proletariat in the most advanced industrial nations, Bakunin insisted that the revolutionary impulse was strongest where the people truly had nothing to lose but their chains. This meant that the universal upheaval would start in the south of Europe, rather than in more disciplined and prosperous countries like Germany.[33] Consequently, in the feverish contest for mastery in the International Working Men's Association (the First International), the Bakuninists succeeded in creating vigorous branches in Italy and Spain, lands in which the Marxists never managed to secure a significant following.

While entrusting the intellectuals with a critical role in the forthcoming revolution, Bakunin at the same time cautioned them against attempting to seize political power on their own, in the manner of the Jacobins or their eager disciple Auguste Blanqui.[34] On this point Bakunin was most emphatic. The very idea that a tiny band of conspirators could execute a *coup d'état* for the benefit of the people was, in his derisive words, a "heresy

---

[32] Bakunin, *Gesammelte Werke*, III, 120-121.
[33] Bakunin, *Oeuvres*, IV, 381.
[34] Bakunin, *Izbrannye sochineniia*, IV, 175; *Gesammelte Werke*, III, 87.

against common sense and historical experience."[35] These strictures were aimed as much at Marx as at Blanqui. For both Marx and Bakunin, the ultimate goal of the revolution was a stateless society of men liberated from the bonds of oppression, a new world in which the free development of each was the condition for the free development of all. But where Marx envisioned an intervening proletarian dictatorship that would eliminate the last vestiges of the bourgeois order, Bakunin was bent on abolishing the state outright. The cardinal error committed by all revolutions of the past, in Bakunin's judgment, was that one government was turned out only to be replaced by another. The true revolution, then, would not capture political power; it would be a *social* revolution, ridding the world of the state itself.

Bakunin perceived the authoritarianism inherent in a so-called dictatorship of the proletariat. The state, he insisted, however popular in form, would always serve as a weapon of exploitation and enslavement.[36] He predicted the inevitable formation of a new "privileged minority" of savants and experts, whose superior knowledge would enable them to use the state as an instrument to rule over the uneducated manual laborers in the fields and factories. The citizens of the new people's state would be rudely awakened from their self-delusion to discover that they had become "the slaves, the playthings, and the victims of a new group of ambitious men."[37] The only way the common people could escape this lamentable fate was to make the revolution themselves, total and universal, ruthless and chaotic, elemental and unrestrained. "It is necessary to abolish completely in principle and in practice, everything that may be called political power," Bakunin concluded, "for as long as political power exists, there will always be rulers and ruled, masters and slaves, exploiters and exploited."[38] And yet, for all his vehement assaults on revolutionary oligarchies, Bakunin nevertheless was determined to create his own "secret society" of conspirators, whose members would be subjected to the "strictest discipline" and subordinated to a small revolutionary directorate. This clandestine organization, moreover, would remain intact even after the revolution had

[35] V. A. Polonskii, *Materialy dlia biografii M. Bakunina* (3 vols., Moscow and Leningrad, 1923-1933), III, 375.
[36] Bakunin, *Izbrannye sochineniia*, V, 20.
[37] *Ibid.*, I, 234; *Oeuvres*, IV, 376.
[38] Bakunin, *Oeuvres*, II, 39.

been accomplished, in order to forestall the establishment of any "official dictatorship."[39] Bakunin's most famous successors, above all Kropotkin, were to find this strange and contradictory feature of their mentor's revolutionary strategy untenable and, it will be seen, would hasten to jettison it.

In Bakunin's theoretical framework, the popular rebellion that would erase all governments from the face of the earth did not lack a constructive side. Indeed, the most famous sentence ever to issue from his pen proclaimed that "the urge to destroy is also a creative urge."[40] But the constructive side was exceedingly nebulous. Once the state was abolished, it was to be replaced by "the organization of productive forces and economic services."[41] The tools of production were not to be nationalized by a workers' state, as Marx desired, but were to be transferred instead to a free federation of autonomous producers' associations, organized on a worldwide basis "from the bottom up."[42] In the new society, everyone except the aged or infirm would be expected to perform manual work and each was to be rewarded in proportion to his labor.[43] Beyond this extremely vague picture Bakunin was not willing to venture. Contemptuous as he was of all rational speculation, he refused to draw up a detailed blueprint of the future,[44] preferring to rely on the creative powers the masses would display once they had been freed from the shackles of private property and the state.

At bottom, Bakunin's philosophy of anarchism was an ardent protest against all forms of centralized power, political and economic alike. Bakunin was not only an enemy of capitalism, like Marx, but an intransigent opponent of any concentration of industrial might, whether in private hands or public. Deeply rooted in French "utopian" socialism and in the Russian Populist tradition, Bakunin's anarchist doctrines repudiated large scale industry as artificial, unspontaneous, and corrosive of genuinely human values. Through the creative spirit of ordinary men and women, aided by certain critically thinking individuals, the backward countries of eastern and southern Europe could

[39] Bakunin, *Gesammelte Werke*, III, 35-38, 82.
[40] Bakunin, *Sobranie sochinenii i pisem*, III, 148.
[41] Bakunin, *Oeuvres*, II, 39.
[42] *Ibid.*, v, 75.   [43] *Ibid.*, I, 55.
[44] Steklov, *Mikhail Aleksandrovich Bakunin*, III, 454-455.

avoid the "fate of capitalism"; these lands were not predestined to suffer the agonies of exploitation from any centralized authority, nor were their inhabitants foredoomed to undergo conversion into a dehumanized army of robots. The decentralized, libertarian society of the future, with its loose federation of workers' cooperatives and agricultural communes (purged of their ancient patriarchal authoritarianism), would accomplish a total reconstruction of social values and a regeneration of humanity. To Marx, whose ideology suited the temper of industrialism far better than it did the mood of pre-industrial societies, these anarchist images were romantic, unscientific, utopian, and altogether removed from the unalterable path of modern history. In Bakunin's judgment, however, Marx may have known how to construct rational systems, but he lacked the vital instinct of human freedom. As a German and a Jew, Marx was "an authoritarian from head to foot."[45]

Peter Kropotkin, Bakunin's outstanding disciple, was, like his predecessor, a scion of the landed nobility, reared in a nest of gentlefolk even more illustrious than the estate in Tver province where Bakunin spent his boyhood. Kropotkin's ancestors had been grand princes of Smolensk in medieval Russia, descended from a branch of the Rurik clan, which had ruled in Muscovy before the advent of the Romanovs. Educated in the exclusive Corps of Pages in St. Petersburg, Kropotkin served with great devotion as a *page de chambre* of Emperor Alexander II and later as an army officer in Siberia, attached to the Cossack regiment of the Amur. Like Bakunin before him, Kropotkin renounced his aristocratic heritage for a life spent largely in prisons and in exile. He too was forced to flee from Tsarist Russia in extremely dramatic circumstances, escaping in 1876—the year of Bakunin's death—from a prison hospital near the capital, and then through Finland to the West, where he remained until, at the age of seventy-five, the February Revolution enabled him to return to his native country.[46]

Although Kropotkin embraced some of the principal tenets

[45] *Ibid.*, I, 192-193.

[46] For the events of Kropotkin's life, see his *Memoirs of a Revolutionist*; George Woodcock and Ivan Avakumovic, *The Anarchist Prince* (London, 1950); and N. K. Lebedev, *P. A. Kropotkin* (Moscow, 1925).

of the Bakuninist creed, from the moment he took up the torch of anarchism, it burned with a gentler flame. Kropotkin's nature was singularly mild and benevolent. He lacked completely Bakunin's violent temperament, titanic urge to destroy, and irrepressible will to dominate; nor did he possess Bakunin's anti-Semitic streak or display the hints of derangement that sometimes appeared in Bakunin's words and actions. With his courtly manner and high qualities of character and intellect, Kropotkin was the very picture of reasonableness. His scientific training and optimistic outlook gave to anarchist theory a constructive aspect which stood in sharp contrast with the spirit of blind negation that permeated Bakunin's works.

For all his saintly qualities, however, Kropotkin by no means offered blanket opposition to the use of violence. He upheld the assassination of tyrants if the perpetrators were impelled by noble motives, though his acceptance of bloodshed in such instances was inspired by compassion for the oppressed rather than by any personal hatred of the ruling despots. Kropotkin believed that acts of terror were among the very few means of resistance available to the enchained masses; they were useful as "propaganda by the deed," calculated to supplement oral and written propaganda in awakening the rebellious instincts of the people. Nor did Kropotkin shrink from revolution itself, for he hardly expected the propertied classes to give up their privileges and possessions without a fight. Like Bakunin, he anticipated an upheaval that would demolish capitalism and the state for all time. Nevertheless, he earnestly hoped the rebellion would be a tame one, with "the smallest number of victims, and a minimum of embitterment."[47] Kropotkin's revolution was to be speedy and humane—quite unlike Bakunin's demonic visions of fire and brimstone.[48]

Again in contrast with Bakunin, Kropotkin deplored the use of putschist methods in preparing the revolution. As a member of the Chaikovskii circle in St. Petersburg during the early 1870's, Kropotkin had been sharply critical of the shadowy

[47] Kropotkin, *Memoirs*, pp. 290-291.
[48] Bakunin, too, once expressed the wish that the revolution should claim as few lives as possible, but added the ominous footnote that one must not be greatly surprised if the people did kill many of their oppressors. Bakunin, *Gesammelte Werke*, III, 86.

intrigues surrounding the personage of Sergei Nechaev, Bakunin's fanatical young admirer, whose mania for secret organizations exceeded even that of his master. The Chaikovskii circle concentrated its efforts on spreading propaganda among the factory workers of the capital, and denounced Nechaev, as Kropotkin put it, for resorting to "the ways of old conspirators, without recoiling even before deceit when he wanted to force his associates to follow his lead."[49] Kropotkin had little use for secret associations of "professional revolutionists," with their clandestine schemes, ruling committees, and iron discipline. The proper function of the intellectuals was to disseminate propaganda among the plain folk in order to hasten the latter's own spontaneous rising. All self-contained conspiratorial groups, divorced from the people, carried the malignant germ of authoritarianism. No less vehemently than Bakunin, Kropotkin insisted that the revolution was not to be "a simple change of governors," but a "social" revolution—not the capture of political power by a tiny group of Jacobins or Blanquists, but "the collective work of the masses."[50] And yet, while Kropotkin never explicitly directed his animadversions at his teacher's own secret society of revolutionists, it was nonetheless clear that his rejection of every potential dictatorship was meant to include Bakunin's "invisible" one.

Kropotkin's unyielding determination to protect the spontaneous and egalitarian nature of the revolution was reflected in his conception of the new society that would emerge from the ruins of the old. Although he accepted Bakunin's vision of autonomous producers' associations loosely united in a free federation, he dissented on one fundamental point. Under Bakunin's "anarchist collectivism," each member of the local workers' cooperative was obliged to perform manual work and was to receive payment in proportion to his "direct contribution of labor."[51] In other words, the criterion of distribution, as under the proletarian dictatorship of the Marxists, was performance rather than need. Kropotkin, on the other hand, regarded any system of rewards based on the individual's capacity to produce

---

[49] Kropotkin, *Memoirs*, p. 305.
[50] Peter Kropotkin, "Revolutionary Government," in *Kropotkin's Revolutionary Pamphlets*, ed. Roger N. Baldwin (New York, 1927), pp. 246-248; *Modern Science and Anarchism* (New York, 1908), p. 86.
[51] Bakunin, *Oeuvres*, I, 55.

as just another form of wage slavery. By drawing a distinction between superior and inferior labor, and between what is mine and what is yours, a collectivist economy rendered itself incompatible with the ideals of pure anarchism. Collectivism, moreover, necessitated some authority within the workers' association to measure individual performance and to supervise the distribution of goods and services accordingly. Consequently, like the conspiratorial organizations that Kropotkin eschewed, a collectivist order contained the seeds of inequality and domination. It was impossible to evaluate each person's part in the production of social wealth, declared Kropotkin in *The Conquest of Bread*, for millions of human beings had toiled to create the present riches of the world.[52] Every acre of soil had been watered with the sweat of generations, and every mile of railroad had received its share of human blood. Indeed, there was not even a thought or an invention that was not the common inheritance of all mankind. "Each discovery, each advance, each increase in the sum of human riches owes its being to the physical and mental travail of the past and present," Kropotkin continued. "By what right then can anyone whatever appropriate the least morsel of this immense whole and say—This is mine, not yours?"[53]

Kropotkin considered his own theory of "anarchist communism" the very antithesis of the wage system in all its forms.[54] No center of authority would compel any individual to work, though everyone would willingly labor "to the full extent of his capacities."[55] For the principle of wages, Kropotkin substituted the principle of needs: each person would be the judge of his own requirements, taking from the common storehouse whatever he deemed necessary, whether or not he contributed a share of the labor. Kropotkin's benign optimism led him to assume that once political power and economic exploitation had been eliminated, all men would work of their own free will, without any compulsion whatsoever, and take from the communal warehouse no more than they required for a comfortable existence. Anarchist

[52] P. Kropotkin, *La Conquête du pain* (Paris, 1892), p. 14.
[53] *Ibid.*, pp. 5-9.
[54] *Ibid.*, pp. 33-34, 74.
[55] Kropotkin, "Anarchist Communism: Its Basis and Principles," in *Kropotkin's Revolutionary Pamphlets*, p. 59.

communism would put an end, at long last, to every manner of coercion and privilege, ushering in a Golden Age of liberty, equality, and brotherhood among men.

An eminent geographer and naturalist, Kropotkin believed—no less than Marx—that his own social theories rested on a scientific basis. During his five years of government service in Siberia, Kropotkin came to reject the emphasis which Darwin's followers (T. H. Huxley, in particular) placed on competition and struggle in the evolution of biological species. His study of animal life in the eastern regions of Siberia[56] led him to question the widely accepted picture of the natural world as a savage jungle, red in tooth and claw, in which the fittest members of each species are the ultimate survivors. His own observations indicated that, in the process of natural selection, spontaneous cooperation among animals was far more important than ferocious competition, and that "those animals which acquire habits of mutual aid are undoubtedly the fittest" to survive.[57] By no means did Kropotkin deny the existence of struggle within the animal kingdom,[58] but he was confident that mutual dependence played a much larger role—indeed, mutual aid was "the chief factor of progressive evolution."[59]

Kropotkin saw no reason why the principle of mutual aid should not apply with the same validity to Homo sapiens as to the other species of the animal world. In his boyhood, he had come to believe heart and soul in the fraternal spirit of the Russian peasantry.[60] Some years later, while serving in the Siberian wilderness, the successful cooperation he observed among the Dukhobor colonies and the native tribes was a flood of light that illuminated his later thinking. It was during his Siberian sojourn that Kropotkin shed all hope that the state could act as a vehicle of social reform. His gaze turned instead to the spontaneous creativity of small anarchist communities.[61] His favorable impressions of uncorrupted communal life were reinforced in 1872, when he visited the watchmaking communities of the Jura Mountains in Switzerland. He was drawn at once to their voluntary

[56] Peter Kropotkin, *Mutual Aid: a Factor of Evolution* (London, 1902), pp. 46-49.
[57] *Ibid.*, p. 6.   [58] *Ibid.*, p. 57.
[59] Kropotkin, *Modern Science and Anarchism*, p. 44.
[60] Kropotkin, *Memoirs*, pp. 105-106.
[61] *Ibid.*, pp. 216-217.

associations of mutual aid and to the absence among them of political ambitions or of any distinction between leaders and subordinates. Their mixture of manual and mental labor as well as the integration in their mountain villages of domestic manufacture and agricultural work likewise won his warm admiration.

Kropotkin found what he considered scientific confirmation of these pleasant observations in his scrutiny of the annals of human history. Throughout the past, he maintained, men had displayed a marked propensity to work together in a spirit of solidarity and brotherhood. Mutual aid among human beings had been far more potent a force than the egoistic will to dominate others. Mankind, in fact, owed its very survival to mutual aid.[62] The theories of Hegel, Marx, and Darwin notwithstanding, Kropotkin held that cooperation rather than conflict lay at the root of the historical process. Furthermore, he refuted Hobbes' conception of man's natural condition as a war of each against all.[63] In every period of history, he declared, mutual aid associations of diverse kinds had appeared, reaching a high point in the guilds and communes of medieval Europe.[64] Kropotkin considered the rise of the centralized state from the sixteenth through the nineteenth centuries merely a transitory aberration from the normal pattern of western civilization. In spite of the state's appearance, voluntary associations had continued to play a key role in human affairs, he believed, and the spirit of mutual aid was reasserting itself "even in our modern society, and claims its right to be, as it has always been, the chief leader towards further progress."[65] The predominant trends of modern history were pointing back towards decentralized, nonpolitical cooperative societies, in which men could develop their creative faculties freely, without the machinations of kings, priests, or soldiers. Everywhere the artificial state was abdicating its "holy functions" in favor of natural voluntary groups.[66]

Kropotkin's study of human history, together with his first-

[62] Kropotkin, *Modern Science and Anarchism*, p. 48.

[63] *Ibid.*, p. 45; *Mutual Aid*, pp. 77-78.

[64] Kropotkin, *Mutual Aid*, pp. 153-222. As a prisoner in the fortress of Peter-Paul, Kropotkin relished perusing the chronicles of Pskov, the republican city-state of medieval Russia. *Memoirs*, p. 351.

[65] Kropotkin, *Mutual Aid*, p. 292.

[66] Kropotkin, *La Conquête du pain*, pp. 40, 188; "Anarchist Communism," *Kropotkin's Revolutionary Pamphlets*, pp. 51-53, 59-61.

hand experiences in Siberia and among the Jura watchmakers, nourished his deeply rooted conviction that men were happiest in communities small enough to permit the natural instincts of solidarity and mutual aid to flourish. At the close of the century, Kropotkin sketched a new society in which "industry [was] combined with agriculture and brain work with manual work," as he succinctly described it in the subtitle of one of his best-known books.[67] Men and women in the localities, joined by the natural bonds of cooperative effort, would rid themselves of the artificiality of centralized states and massive industrial complexes. Not that Kropotkin had any aversion to modern technology in itself. "I fully understand," he remarked at one point in his memoirs, "the pleasure that man can derive from the might of his machine, the intelligent character of its work, the gracefulness of its movements, and the correctness of what it is doing."[68] Placed in small voluntary workshops, machinery would rescue human beings from the drudgery and monotony of capitalist enterprise, and the stamp of inferiority once borne by manual work would disappear forever.[69] Members of the community would work from their twenties to their forties, four or five hours of labor a day sufficing for a comfortable life. The division of labor, including the invidious separation between mental and manual tasks, would yield to a variety of pleasant jobs, resulting in a reintegrated, organic existence, such as prevailed in the medieval city.[70]

In this serene portrait of the future, Kropotkin's nostalgic yearning for a simpler but fuller life led him to idealize the autonomous social units of bygone years—the manor and guild, the *obshchina* and *artel'*. In the face of the ever-growing concentration of economic and political power in nineteenth-century Europe, he looked backward to a blissful world as yet undefiled by the intrusion of capitalism and the modern state, and forward to a similar world liberated from the straitjackets constricting the natural impulses of humanity.

To the new anarchists of Bialystok, the theories of Bakunin

[67] Peter Kropotkin, *Fields, Factories, and Workshops* (London, 1899).
[68] Kropotkin, *Memoirs*, p. 119.
[69] Kropotkin, *La Conquête du pain*, pp. 194-195.
[70] Kropotkin, *Fields, Factories, and Workshops*, pp. 184-212.

and Kropotkin appeared singularly applicable to the highly centralized and oppressive Russian state. The appalling misery of
the peasants and workers, the alienation of the students and
intelligentsia from government and society, the recurring instances of violence and terrorism, and the outrageous persecution of national and religious minorities—all compounded by
the economic depression—darkened the atmosphere with frus-
tration and despair. According to Bakunin's teachings, Russia,
as a relatively backward country, should have been ripe for revolt. At the beginning of the twentieth century, Russia was in
great flux, having recently begun a fitful and jarring transition
from rural to urban life, a transition which tore at the vital roots
of tradition and stability. The Juggernaut of industrialism was
leaving by the wayside a mound of human debris—the *Lumpenproletariat* and other shattered elements of society, bereft
of the least bit of security in a hostile and changing world. These
wretched outcasts might well have been expected to respond to
the anarchist appeal for the annihilation of the existing regime
and the subsequent inauguration of a Golden Age. And, indeed,
a good many of them did join the first anarchist circles in 1903
and 1904.

Yet, even in these troubled times, when the spirit of nihilism
was abroad in the land, comparatively few citizens of the Empire
entered the anarchist movement. The explanation lies partly in
the fact that the political consciousness of the masses was still
on a very low level—indeed, the membership rolls even of the
two major socialist parties which had emerged at the turn of the
century contained but a tiny fraction of the peasant and proletarian populations. The few peasants who did have an interest
in political questions commonly joined the Socialist Revolutionaries, whose programs were closely tailored to the aspirations of
the rural folk. As for the workingmen, the doctrines of anarchism
appealed most either to displaced artisans, who yearned with
Peter Kropotkin for a passing age of crafts manufacture, or to
the unskilled, unorganized, and unemployed castaways of the
urban slums. Many members of these two groups, however,
found an outlet for their violent propensities in the terrorist
wing of the SR's or in the PPS. Between the artisans and the slum
proletariat stood a growing class of steadily employed factory
workers who were beginning to find a place in the evolving in-

dustrial economy; they looked to the Social Democrats—if to any political party at all—for the protection of their interests.

Still another reason for the failure of anarchism to attract a larger following was the reluctance of most Russians, even those in the lowest depths of despair, to accept either the ultra-fanaticism of Bakunin or the seemingly naive romanticism of Kropotkin as a plausible solution to their pressing difficulties. The socialist parties of Russia, in contrast to those of Western Europe with their strong reformist taint, were sufficiently militant to accommodate all but the most passionate and idealistic young students and craftsmen and the rootless drifters of the city underworld. Finally, the very nature of the anarchist creed, with its bitter hostility toward hierarchical organizations of any sort, impeded the growth of a formal movement. The Social Democrats, by contrast, not only shared much of the revolutionary spirit of anarchism, but were able to bolster it with an effective organizational underpinning.

For these reasons, throughout the quarter-century of their existence the Russian anarchists were to remain a varied assortment of independent groups, without a party program or a measure of effective coordination. Nevertheless, events were to show that anarchism, so closely attuned to the "maximalist" mood of revolutionary Russia, would exert an influence in the opening decades of the new century quite out of proportion to the number of its adherents.

2 · THE TERRORISTS

We will set the world aflame,
Bitter woe to all bourzhooy,
With blood will set the world aflame—
Good lord, give us thy blessing.

ALEKSANDR BLOK

The anarchist movement which emerged in the Romanov Empire at the beginning of the twentieth century had antecedents in the Russian past. Over the centuries, the Russian borderlands had been the scene of wild popular uprisings with strong anarchic overtones. Although the rebellious peasants had reserved their venom for the landlords and officials, and had continued to venerate the Tsar or some false pretender, this heritage of mass revolts, from Bolotnikov and Stenka Razin to Bulavin and Pugachev, was a rich source of inspiration to Bakunin, Kropotkin, and their anarchist disciples.

The anarchistic religious sects which abounded in Russia also made a deep impression on the leaders of the revolutionary anarchist movement, despite the fact that the sectarians were devout pacifists who placed their faith in a personal communion with Christ rather than in violent social action. The sects adamantly rejected all external coercion, whether religious or secular. Their adherents spurned the official hierarchy of the Russian Orthodox Church, and they often avoided paying taxes and refused to take oaths or bear arms. "The children of God," proclaimed members of the Dukhobor sect imprisoned in 1791, "have no need either of tsars or ruling powers or of any human laws whatever."[1]

This same Christian quietism was a basic tenet of Leo Tolstoy and his followers, who began to form anarchistic groups during the 1880's in Tula, Orel, and Samara provinces, and in the city of Moscow.[2] By the turn of the century, Tolstoyan missionaries had spread the gospel of Christian anarchism with considerable effect throughout the black-earth provinces and had founded

[1] Quoted in Geroid T. Robinson, *Rural Russia under the Old Regime* (New York, 1957), p. 46.
[2] A. Dunin, "Graf L. N. Tolstoi i tolstovtsy v Samarskoi gubernii," *Russkaia Mysl'*, 1912, No. 11, p. 159.

colonies as far south as the Caucasus Mountains.[3] The Tolstoyans, while condemning the state as a wicked instrument of oppression, shunned revolutionary activity as a breeder of hatred and violence. Society, they believed, could never be improved through bloodshed, but only when men had learned Christian love. The revolutionary anarchists, of course, held no brief for Tolstoy's doctrine of nonresistance to evil; however, they admired his castigation of state discipline and institutionalized religion, his revulsion against patriotism and war, and his deep compassion for the "unspoiled" peasantry.[4]

Another source of anarchist ideas, though an indirect one, was the Petrashevskii circle in St. Petersburg, which transmitted Fourier's "utopian" socialism to Russia during the 1840's. It was in part from Fourier that Bakunin and Kropotkin and their followers derived their faith in small voluntary communities, as well as their romantic conviction that men could live in harmony once the artificial restraints imposed by governments had been removed. Similar views were drawn from the Russian Slavophiles of the mid-nineteenth century, particularly Konstantin Aksakov, for whom the centralized, bureaucratic state was "evil in principle." Aksakov was thoroughly at home with the writings of Proudhon and Stirner as well as Fourier, and his idealized vision of the peasant commune strongly influenced Bakunin and his successors.[5] Finally, the anarchists learned much from the libertarian socialism of Alexander Herzen, a progenitor of the Populist movement, who firmly refused to sacrifice individual freedom to the tyranny of abstract theories, whether advanced by parliamentary liberals or by authoritarian socialists.[6]

[3] A. S. Prugavin, *O L've Tolstom i o tolstovtsakh* (Moscow, 1911), pp. 193-200.
[4] The leading apostle of Tolstoyanism during the first years of the twentieth century was Vladimir Grigorievich Chertkov, editor of the periodical *Svobodnoe Slovo* (The Free Word) in Christchurch, England. Besides this journal (published in 1901-1905), see V. G. Chertkov, *Protiv vlasti* (Christchurch, 1905).
[5] See N. N. Rusov, "Anarkhicheskie elementy v slavianofil'stve," in A. A. Borovoi, ed., *Mikhailu Bakuninu, 1876-1926: ocherk istorii anarkhicheskogo dvizheniia v Rossii* (Moscow, 1926), pp. 37-43; and E. Lampert, *Studies in Rebellion* (London, 1957), pp. 155-157.
[6] See Isaiah Berlin, "Herzen and Bakunin on Individual Liberty," in Ernest J. Simmons, ed., *Continuity and Change in Russian and Soviet Thought* (Cambridge, Mass., 1955), pp. 473-499; and Martin Malia,

Notwithstanding this rich legacy left by the peasant revolts, the religious sects and Tolstoyan groups, the *Petrashevtsy* and Slavophiles, and Alexander Herzen, no revolutionary anarchist movement arose in Russia before the twentieth century—not even in the heyday of Bakunin during the late 1860's and early 1870's. It is true that Bakunin won over a handful of young Russian émigrés, who collaborated with him in publishing two short-lived journals in Geneva (*Narodnoe Delo* and *Rabotnik*) and in organizing (in 1872) an ephemeral circle in Zurich known as the Russian Brotherhood; and it is true, also, that he cast his unique spell over many of the student Populists who "went to the people" during the 1870's, and that his influence was felt within the clandestine groups of factory workers which began to appear at that time in Petersburg, Moscow, Kiev, and Odessa. Nevertheless, no genuine Bakuninist organization was founded on Russian soil during his lifetime.[7]

Bakunin's principal followers in Switzerland were N. I. Zhukovskii, M. P. Sazhin ("Armand Ross"), and a young rebel of Rumanian descent named Z. K. Ralli. In 1873, Ralli helped create a small group in Geneva called the Revolutionary Commune of Russian Anarchists, which, like the Zurich Brotherhood, disseminated Bakunin's ideas among the radical exiles.[8] Bakunin's most dramatic disciple inside Russia, however, the bizarre figure of Sergei Gennadievich Nechaev, was less a genuine anarchist than an apostle of revolutionary dictatorship, far more concerned with the means of conspiracy and terror than with the lofty goal of a stateless society. The true revolutionist, according to Nechaev, was a man who had broken completely with the existing order, an implacable enemy of the contemporary world, ready to use even the most repugnant methods—including the dagger, the rope, and every manner of deception

---

Alexander Herzen and the Birth of Russian Socialism, 1812-1855 (Cambridge, Mass., 1961), pp. 376-382.

[7] Franco Venturi, *Roots of Revolution* (New York, 1960), pp. 429-468.

[8] See J. M. Meijer, *Knowledge and Revolution: the Russian Colony in Zuerich (1870-1873)* (Assen, 1955); M. P. Sazhin, "Russkie v Tsiurikhe (1870-1873)," *Katorga i Ssylka*, 1932, No. 10 (95), pp. 25-78; and A. A. Karelin, "Russkie bakunisty za granitsei," in *Mikhailu Bakuninu*, pp. 181-187.

and perfidy—in the name of the "people's vengeance."[9] This image of the ruthless underground conspirator was to grip the imagination of more than a few anarchist youths during the stormy months of both 1905 and 1917.

The quarter-century following Bakunin's death in 1876 was a period of dark reaction in the Tsarist Empire. Only the prolific pen of Peter Kropotkin, who was living in West European exile, kept the dream of an anarchist movement alive. Then, in 1892, probably stirred into action by the great famine that afflicted their homeland, a group of Russian students in Geneva established an anarchist propaganda circle, the first since Ralli's Revolutionary Commune of 1873. Led by Aleksandr Atabekian, a young Armenian doctor and disciple of Kropotkin, the new group, which called itself the Anarchist Library (*Anarkhicheskaia Biblioteka*), printed a few pamphlets by Bakunin and Kropotkin, and by the noted Italian anarchists, Errico Malatesta and Saverio Merlino. Atabekian's efforts to smuggle the literature into Russia appear to have met with little success, but the work of his Anarchist Library was taken up again towards the end of the 'nineties by another propaganda circle, known simply as the Geneva Group of Anarchists. On the press of a sympathetic Swiss printer named Émile Held, the Geneva group turned out more pamphlets by Kropotkin and works by such celebrated West European anarchists as Jean Grave, Élisée Reclus, and Johann Most. In 1902, a group of Kropotkin's followers in London issued a Russian translation of *The Conquest of Bread* under the ringing title of *Khleb i Volia* (Bread and Liberty), which immediately entered the armory of anarchist slogans.

Not until 1903, when the rising ferment in Russia indicated that a full-scale revolution might be in the offing, was a lasting anarchist movement inaugurated both inside the Tsarist Empire and in the émigré colonies of Western Europe. In the spring of that year, the first anarchists appeared in Bialystok and organized the *Bor'ba* (Struggle) group, with about a dozen mem-

[9] On the strange history of Nechaev, see Carr, *Michael Bakunin*, chapter 28; Venturi, *Roots of Revolution*, pp. 354-388; Nomad, *Apostles of Revolution*, pp. 215-255; and Michael Prawdin, *The Unmentionable Nechaev: A Key to Bolshevism* (London, 1961), pp. 13-107.

bers.[10] At the same time, a small circle of young Kropotkinites in Geneva founded a monthly anarchist journal (printed by Émile Held) which they christened *Khleb i Volia*, after their mentor's famous book. The leaders of the new Geneva group were K. Orgeiani, a Georgian whose real name was G. Gogeliia, his wife Lidiia, and a former student named Maria Korn (née Goldsmit), whose mother had once been a follower of the eminent Populist, Petr Lavrov, and whose father had published a Positivist journal in St. Petersburg.[11] Kropotkin, from his London residence, gave *Khleb i Volia* his enthusiastic support, contributing many of the articles and editorials. Bakunin's famous dictum, "The urge to destroy is also a creative urge," was chosen to adorn the masthead. The first issue, appearing in August 1903, contained the exultant proclamation that Russia was "on the eve" of a great revolution.[12] Smuggled across the borders of Poland and the Ukraine, *Khleb i Volia* was greeted with intense excitement by the Bialystok anarchists, who passed the precious copies among their fellow students and workmen until the paper disintegrated.

The *Khleb i Volia* group was soon deluged with appeals for more literature. In response, they issued additional pamphlets by Bakunin and Kropotkin, and Russian translations of works by Grave, Malatesta, and Élisée Reclus, among others. Varlaam Nikolaevich Cherkezov, a Georgian of princely blood and Kropotkin's best-known associate in London, contributed a critical analysis of Marxist doctrine,[13] and Orgeiani produced an account of the tragic Haymarket Square riot of 1886, which had ended in the martyrdom of four Chicago anarchists.[14] In addition

[10] Frank, *Geklibene shriftn*, p. 390.

[11] *P. A. Kropotkin i ego uchenie: internatsional'nyi sbornik posviashchennyi desiatoi godovshchine smerti P. A. Kropotkina*, ed. G. P. Maksimov (Chicago, 1931), pp. 328, 333; I. Knizhnik, "Vospominaniia o P. A. Kropotkine i ob odnoi anarkhistskoi emigrantskoi gruppe," *Krasnaia Letopis'*, 1922, No. 4, p. 32; "Pis'ma P. A. Kropotkina k V. N. Cherkezovu," *Katorga i Ssylka*, 1926, No. 4 (25), p. 25; G. Maksimov, in *Delo Truda*, No. 75, March-April 1933, pp. 6-11; Max Nettlau, "A Memorial Tribute to Marie Goldsmith and Her Mother," *Freedom* (New York), 18 March 1933, p. 2.

[12] *Khleb i Volia*, No. 1, August 1903, p. 3.

[13] V. N. Cherkezov, *Doktriny marksizma: nauka-li eto?* (Geneva, 1903).

[14] K. Iliashvili (pseudonym for Gogeliia-Orgeiani), *Pamiati chikag-*

to these works in Russian, a few copies of the Yiddish periodicals *Der Arbayter Fraynd* and *Zsherminal*, published by Jewish anarchists in London's East End,[15] managed to reach the ghettos of the Pale.[16] Before very long, the Bialystok circle was hectographing handwritten copies of articles from the anarchist journals in the West,[17] and turning out its own leaflets, proclamations, and manifestoes,[18] which were sent in large batches to nearby communities, as well as to such distant points as Odessa and Nezhin (in Chernigov province), where anarchist groups arose toward the end of 1903.[19] A few copies of *Khleb i Volia* even reached the industrial centers of the remote Ural Mountains, and in 1904 a handful of anarchist propagandists were circulating them in the ancient and dilapidated factories of Ekaterinburg.[20]

In 1905, the long-awaited storm burst upon Russia at last. Popular discontent had been greatly exacerbated by the war with Japan that had broken out in February 1904. Totally unprepared for the conflict, the Russian colossus suffered a series of humiliating defeats, which the population naturally blamed on the blun-

---

skikh muchenikov (Geneva, 1905). On the Haymarket incident, see Henry David, *The History of the Haymarket Affair* (New York, 1936).

[15] The Federation of Jewish Anarchists, located in the Whitechapel and Mile End districts of London, consisted largely of artisans who had emigrated from Russia during the 1880's and 1890's. At the turn of the century, their leader and the editor of their publications was Rudolf Rocker, a remarkable German of Christian ancestry, who had mastered the Yiddish language after joining the London group. Kropotkin and Cherkezov frequently spoke at the Federation's club on Jubilee Street. See Rocker's *The London Years* (London, 1956).

[16] Still circulating within the Pale was an early piece of anarchist literature which *Der Arbayter Fraynd* had published in 1886 in London but labeled "Vilna" to deceive the tsarist police. In the form of a Passover *Hagadah*, or prayerbook, the pamphlet set forth the traditional "Four Questions," which begin, "Wherefore is this night of Passover different from all other nights in the year?" but gave them a radical twist: "Wherefore are we different from Shmuel the factory owner, Meier the banker, Zorekh the moneylender, and Reb Todres the rabbi?" *Hagadah shol Peysakh* (Vilna [London], 1886), p. 6, Bund Archives.

[17] For example, a handwritten leaflet in the Columbia Russian Archive, "Nuzhen-li anarkhizm v Rossii?," was copied from *Khleb i Volia*, No. 10, July 1904, pp. 1-3.

[18] *Al'manakh*, p. 6; *Khleb i Volia*, No. 10, pp. 3-4; *Burevestnik*, No. 8, November 1907, p. 10.

[19] *Al'manakh*, p. 7; *Burevestnik*, No. 10-11, March-April 1908, p. 27.

[20] *Burevestnik*, No. 13, October 1908, p. 18.

dering policies of the government. By the beginning of 1905, the situation in St. Petersburg was extremely tense. The dismissal of a few workmen from the huge Putilov metal works touched off a chain of strikes in the capital, culminating on 9 January in the gruesome episode known as Bloody Sunday.*

That day, workers from the factory suburbs poured into the center of the city and formed a mammoth procession that filled several streets. Led by Georgii Gapon, a histrionic priest of the Orthodox Church, the procession, bearing holy icons and portraits of the Tsar, and singing religious and patriotic hymns, converged on the Winter Palace. The unarmed crowds of workmen and their families carried a dramatic petition begging their sovereign to put an end to the war, to summon a constituent assembly, to grant the workers an eight-hour day and the right to organize unions, to abolish the redemption payments of the peasantry, and to endow all citizens with personal inviolability and equality before the law. Government troops greeted the marchers with point-blank fire, leaving hundreds lying dead or wounded in the streets.

In an instant, the ancient bond between Tsar and people was severed; from that day forward, in Father Gapon's words, the monarch and his subjects were separated by "a river of blood."[21] Revolution immediately flared up all over the country. Strikes, especially violent in the non-Russian cities, broke out in every major industrial center; nearly half a million workers left their machines and went into the streets. Soon afterwards, the Baltic provinces and the black-soil regions of central Russia were ablaze with rebellion, the peasants burning and looting as in the time of Pugachev. By mid-October, waves of strikes, emanating from Moscow and St. Petersburg, had paralyzed the entire railway network and had brought industrial production to a near standstill. The rising number of peasant disturbances in the countryside, the October general strike in the cities, and the sudden appearance of a Soviet of Workers' Deputies at the head of the Petersburg strike movement frightened Nicholas into signing the Manifesto of 17 October, which guaranteed full civil

---

* All dates are given according to the Julian calendar (thirteen days behind the western calendar in the twentieth century), which was used in Russia until February 1918.

[21] Quoted in V. I. Lenin, *Sochineniia* (2nd edn., 31 vols., Moscow, 1930-1935), VII, 80.

liberties to the population and pledged that no law would become effective without the consent of the State Duma.[22] Denied any satisfaction of their economic demands, however, and carried forward by the momentum of the revolution, the peasants and workers continued to riot.

In December, the revolution reached a climax. In Moscow, strikes and street demonstrations swelled into an armed insurrection, chiefly the work of the Bolsheviks, but in which anarchists and other left-wing groups took an active part. Barricades went up in the working-class quarter of Presnia. After more than a week of fighting, the uprising was put down by government troops, most of whom proved loyal to the Tsar despite sporadic mutinies earlier in the year. Fierce battles also raged for a short time in Odessa, Kharkov, and Ekaterinoslav, but the army and police succeeded in suppressing the rebels.

The outbursts of popular indignation touched off by Bloody Sunday gave a powerful boost to the inchoate radical movements in Russia. During the Revolution of 1905, as Iuda Roshchin, a leading participant in Bialystok recalled, anarchist groups "sprang up like mushrooms after a rain."[23] Before 1905, there had been a mere twelve or fifteen active anarchists in Bialystok, but by the spring of that year five circles were in existence, composed largely of former Bundists and Socialist Revolutionaries and totaling about sixty members. In the month of May, according to a reliable source, the entire "agitation section" of the Bialystok SR's went over to the anarchists.[24] When the movement reached its peak the following year, there were perhaps a dozen circles united in a loose federation.[25] Roshchin estimates that the Bialystok anarchists, at their greatest strength, numbered about 300,[26] but that figure seems too generous; the total num-

[22] For the text of the October Manifesto, see Bernard Pares, *The Fall of the Russian Monarchy* (London, 1939), pp. 503-504; and Sidney Harcave, *First Blood: The Russian Revolution of 1905* (New York, 1964), pp. 195-196.

[23] I. Grossman-Roshchin, "Dumy o bylom (iz istorii belostotskogo anarkhicheskogo 'chernoznamenskogo' dvizheniia," *Byloe*, 1924, No. 27-28, p. 176.

[24] Frank, *Geklibene shriftn*, p. 393.

[25] *Burevestnik*, No. 9, February 1908, p. 11; *Al'manakh*, p. 9; *Khleb i Volia*, No. 10, July 1904, p. 3; M. Ivanovich, "Anarkhizm v Rossii," *Sotsialist-Revoliutsioner*, 1911, No. 3, pp. 81-82.

[26] Grossman-Roshchin, *Byloe*, 1924, No. 27-28, p. 177.

ber of active anarchists probably did not exceed 200 (factory workers, artisans, and intellectuals), though hundreds more regularly read their literature and sympathized with their views.

In the western provinces, the organization of anarchist groups spread from Bialystok to Warsaw, Vilna, Minsk, Riga, and also to such smaller cities as Grodno, Kovno, and Gomel. Eventually, even the little *shtetls* (market towns) that dotted the Jewish Pale had tiny anarchist groups containing from two to a dozen members, who received literature from the larger towns and weapons to use against the government and property owners.[27] In the south, anarchist groups sprouted first in Odessa and Ekaterinoslav, branching out to Kiev and Kharkov in the Ukraine as well as to the major cities of the Caucasus and the Crimean Peninsula.[28]

Everywhere the pattern was the same: a handful of disaffected Social Democrats or Socialist Revolutionaries formed a small anarchist circle; literature was smuggled in from the West or brought by envoys from Riga, Bialystok, Ekaterinoslav, Odessa, or some other propaganda center, and distributed among the workers and students in the area; other circles sprang up and, before long, federations were organized which plunged into radical activity of every sort—agitation, demonstrations, strikes, robberies, and assassinations. As the revolution gathered momentum, the anarchist tide began to move centripetally, sweeping into Moscow and St. Petersburg, the political centers of imperial Russia, though the movement in the twin capitals assumed a mild form in comparison with the violence in the peripheries.[29]

[27] Hershberg, *Pinkos Bialystok*, II, 103; A. Trus and J. Cohen, *Breynsk* (New York, 1948), p. 125; *Sefer Biale-Podlaske* (Tel Aviv, 1961), pp. 222-223. The *shtetl* of Breynsk was located in Grodno province, and Biala-Podlaska between Warsaw and Brest-Litovsk.

[28] On the spread of anarchism in the outlying areas of the Empire during 1905, see *Khleb i Volia*, No. 16, April 1905, p. 4; No. 21-22, August-September 1905, p. 8; *Buntar'*, No. 1, 1 December 1906, p. 30; *Chernoe Znamia*, No. 1, December 1905, pp. 6-7; *Listki "Khleb i Volia,"* No. 1, 30 October 1906, pp. 9-12; No. 3, 28 November 1906, p. 4; *Burevestnik*, No. 4, 30 October 1906, pp. 14-16; No. 6-7, September-October 1907, pp. 4-16; No. 8, November 1907, p. 10; No. 9, February 1908, pp. 9-13; No. 15, March 1909, pp. 18-19; and *Anarkhist*, No. 1, 10 October 1907, pp. 28-31. Orgeiani has left a detailed account of the movement in Georgia: *Al'manakh*, pp. 82-111.

[29] *Al'manakh*, pp. 47-61; *Burevestnik*, No. 3, 30 September 1906,

The common object of the new anarchist organizations was the total destruction of capitalism and the state, in order to clear the way for the libertarian society of the future. There was little agreement, however, as to how this was to be accomplished. The most heated disputes centered on the place of terror in the revolution. On one side stood two similar groups, *Chernoe Znamia* and *Beznachalie*, which advocated a campaign of unmitigated terrorism against the world of the bourgeoisie. *Chernoe Znamia* (The Black Banner—the anarchist emblem), easily the largest body of anarchist terrorists in the Empire, considered itself an Anarchist-Communist organization, that is, one which espoused Kropotkin's goal of a free communal society in which each person would be rewarded according to his needs. Its immediate tactics of conspiracy and violence, however, were inspired by Bakunin. *Chernoe Znamia* attracted its greatest following in the frontier provinces of the west and south. Students, artisans, and factory workers predominated, but there were also a few peasants from villages located near the larger towns, as well as a sprinkling of unemployed laborers, vagabonds, professional thieves, and self-styled Nietzschean supermen. Although many of the members were of Polish, Ukrainian, and Great Russian nationality, Jewish recruits were in the majority. A striking feature of the *Chernoe Znamia* organization was the extreme youth of its adherents, nineteen or twenty being the typical age. Some of the most active *Chernoznamentsy* were only fifteen or sixteen.

Nearly all the anarchists in Bialystok were members of *Chernoe Znamia*. The history of these youths was marked by reckless fanaticism and uninterrupted violence. Theirs was the first anarchist group to inaugurate a deliberate policy of terror against the established order. Gathering in their circles of ten or twelve members, they plotted vengeance upon ruler and boss. Their *"Anarkhiia"* (Anarchy) printing press poured forth a veritable torrent of inflammatory proclamations and manifestoes expressing a violent hatred of existing society and calling for its immediate destruction. Typical of these was a leaflet addressed to "All

---

pp. 12-14; No. 10-11, March-April 1908, pp. 28-30; No. 13, October 1908, pp. 17-18; *Listki "Khleb i Volia,"* No. 17, 21 June 1907, p. 4; Ivanovich, *Sotsialist-Revoliutsioner*, 1911, No. 3, pp. 87-88.

the Workers" of Bialystok, 2,000 copies of which were distributed in the factories during the summer of 1905, shortly before the conclusion of peace with Japan. The air was filled with anguish and despair, it began. Thousands of lives had been wasted in the Far East, and thousands more were dying at home, victims of the capitalist exploiters. The true enemies of the people were not the Japanese, but the institutions of the state and private property; the time had come to destroy them. The leaflet warned the Bialystok workers not to be diverted from their revolutionary mission by the alluring promises of parliamentary reform put forward by many Social Democrats and SR's. Parliamentary democracy was nothing but a shameless fraud, a clever instrument which the middle class would use to dominate the working masses. Do not be fooled, declared the leaflet, by the "scientific smoke-screen" of the socialist intellectuals. Let life alone be your leader and teacher. The sole path to freedom is "a violent class struggle for anarchist communes, which will have neither master nor ruler but true equality." Workers, peasants, and the unemployed must hold aloft the Black Banner of anarchy and march forward in a true social revolution. "DOWN WITH PRIVATE PROPERTY AND THE STATE! DOWN WITH DEMOCRACY! LONG LIVE THE SOCIAL REVOLUTION! LONG LIVE ANARCHY!"[30]

Although their usual meeting places were workshops or private dwellings, the *Chernoznamentsy* of Bialystok often assembled in cemeteries, under the pretense of mourning the dead,[31] or in the woods on the outskirts of town, posting guards to warn of approaching danger. During the summer of 1903, socialist and anarchist workmen had held a series of forest meetings to plan their strategy against the rising number of layoffs in the textile mills. When one of these gatherings was dispersed with needless brutality by a contingent of gendarmes, the anarchists, in reprisal, shot and wounded the Bialystok chief of police. Thus began a vendetta which was to continue without interruption for the next four years.[32]

The situation in the factories continued to deteriorate. Finally,

[30] "Ko vsem rabochim" (leaflet, Bialystok Group of Anarchist-Communists, July 1905), Columbia Russian Archive.
[31] Grossman-Roshchin, *Byloe*, 1924, No. 27-28, p. 177.
[32] Frank, *Geklibene shriftn*, pp. 390-391.

in the summer of 1904, the weavers went out on strike. The owner of a large spinning mill, Avraam Kogan, retaliated by bringing strikebreakers onto the scene, with bloody skirmishes as the result. This provoked an eighteen-year-old *Chernoznamenets* named Nisan Farber to seek revenge on behalf of his fellow workers. On the Jewish Day of Atonement (*Yom Kippur*), he attacked Kogan on the steps of the synagogue, gravely wounding him with a dagger. A few days later, another forest meeting was held to consider further action against the textile manufacturers. Several hundred workmen attended—anarchists, Bundists, SR's, and Zionists. They made bristling speeches and sang revolutionary songs. As shouts of "Hail Anarchy!" and "Long live Social Democracy!" pierced the air, the police descended on the all too boisterous assembly, wounding and arresting dozens of men. Once again Nisan Farber sought vengeance. After testing his home-made "Macedonian" bombs in a local park, he threw one of them through the entrance of police headquarters, injuring a few officers inside. Farber himself was killed by the explosion.[33]

Nisan Farber's name soon became a legend among the *Chernoznamentsy* of the borderlands. After the outbreak of the revolution in January 1905, they began to follow his example of unbridled terrorism. To obtain weapons, bands of anarchists raided gun shops, police stations, and arsenals; the Mausers and Brownings thus acquired became their most cherished possessions. Once armed with pistols and with crude bombs produced in makeshift laboratories, the terrorist gangs proceeded to carry out indiscriminate murders and "expropriations" of money and valuables from banks, post offices, factories, stores, and the private residences of the nobility and middle class.

Attacks on employers and their enterprises—acts of "economic terror"—were daily occurrences throughout the revolutionary period. In Bialystok, sticks of dynamite were tossed into the factories and apartments of the most loathed manufacturers.[34] Anarchist agitators in one leather factory provoked

[33] "Pokushenie v Belostoke" (*Listok No. 5*, Russian Anarchist-Communists, 1904?), Bund Archives; *Khleb i Volia*, No. 23, October 1905, pp. 7-8; *Chernoe Znamia*, No. 1, December 1905, pp. 8-9; *Al'manakh*, pp. 179-181.

[34] "Di anarkhisten bay der arbayt," *Folk-Tsaytung* (Vilna), 24 May

the workers into attacking the boss, who jumped out of a window
to escape his assailants.[35] In Warsaw, partisans of the Black
Banner robbed and dynamited factories and sabotaged bakeries
by blowing up ovens and pouring kerosene into the dough.[36] The
Chernoznamentsy of Vilna issued "an open declaration" in Yiddish to the factory workers, warning them against company spies
who had been planted among them to ferret out terrorists.
"Down with *provocateurs* and spies! Down with the bourgeoisie
and the tyrants! Long live terror against bourgeois society!
Long live the anarchist commune!"[37]

Incidents of violence were most numerous in the south. The
Chernoznamentsy of Ekaterinoslav, Odessa, Sevastopol, and
Baku organized "battle detachments" of terrorists, who set up
bomb laboratories, perpetrated countless murders and holdups,
bombed factories, and fought in gory engagements with the de-
tectives who raided their hideouts.[38] On occasion, even mer-
chant vessels docked in the port of Odessa were targets of anarchist "ex's," as the "expropriations" were called, and businessmen, doctors, and lawyers were forced to "contribute" money
to the anarchist cause under penalty of death.[39]

A case history of a typical terrorist was that of Pavel Golman,
a young worker in Ekaterinoslav. Son of a village policeman, he
was employed in the Ekaterinoslav Railroad Workshop. In 1905,
having passed through the ranks of the SR's and Social Democrats, he joined *Chernoe Znamia*. "It was not the orators who
won me over to anarchism," he explained, "but life itself."
Golman served on the strike committee in his factory and fought

1906, p. 5; 28 May, 1906, p. 6; *Mikhailu Bakuninu*, p. 292; Hershberg,
Pinkos Bialystok, II, 104-108; Frank, *Geklibene shriftn*, pp. 398-400.

[35] S. Dubnov-Erlikh, *Garber-bund un bershter-bund* (Warsaw, 1937),
pp. 114-115.

[36] *Burevestnik*, No. 9, February 1908, pp. 16-17; B. I. Gorev, "Apoliticheskie i antiparlamentskie gruppy (anarkhisty, maksimalisty, makhaevtsy)," in *Obshchestvennoe dvizhenie v Rossii*, III, 489.

[37] "Ayn efentlikhe erklerung" (leaflet, Vilna Group of Anarchist-
Communists, 1905), Columbia Russian Archive.

[38] *Khleb i Volia*, No. 24, November 1905, pp. 5-8; *Chernoe Znamia*,
No. 1, December 1905, pp. 6-7; *Burevestnik*, No. 6-7, September-October
1907, p. 6; S. Anisimov, "Sud i rasprava nad anarkhistami kommu-
nistami," *Katorga i Ssylka*, 1932, No. 10 (95), pp. 129-142; P. A.
Arshinov, *Dva pobega (iz vospominanii anarkhista 1906-9 gg.)* (Paris,
1929); *Mikhailu Bakuninu*, pp. 307-313.

[39] *Al'manakh*, p. 151; *Mikhailu Bakuninu*, pp. 258-259, 268.

behind the barricades during the October general strike. Soon he was taking part in "ex's" and sabotaging the railway system in the vicinity of Ekaterinoslav. Wounded by one of his own bombs, he was captured and sent to a hospital under guard. When his companions failed in a daring attempt to free him, Golman shot himself to death. He was then twenty years old.[40]

In the eyes of the *Chernoznamentsy*, every deed of violence, however rash and senseless it might seem to the general public, had the merit of stimulating the lust of the great unwashed for vengeance against their tormentors. They needed no special provocation to throw a bomb into a theater or restaurant; it was enough to know that only prosperous citizens could congregate in such places. A member of *Chernoe Znamia* in Odessa explained this concept of "motiveless" (*bezmotivnyi*) terror to the judges officiating at his trial:

We recognize isolated expropriations only to acquire money for our revolutionary deeds. If we get the money, we do not kill the person we are expropriating. But this does not mean that he, the property owner, has bought us off. No! We will find him in the various cafés, restaurants, theaters, balls, concerts, and the like. Death to the bourgeois! Always, wherever he may be, he will be overtaken by an anarchist's bomb or bullet.[41]

A dissenting group within the Black Banner organization, headed by Vladimir Striga (Lapidus), was convinced that random forays against the bourgeoisie did not go far enough, and called for a mass uprising to convert Bialystok into a "second Paris Commune."[42] These *kommunary* (Communards), as they were known to their fellow *Chernoznamentsy*, did not reject deeds of violence, but simply wished to take the further step of mass revolutionary action to inaugurate the stateless society without delay. Their strategy, however, failed to win much support. At a conference held in Kishinev in January 1906, the *bezmotivniki*, who argued that isolated acts of terrorism constituted the most effective weapon against the old order, easily prevailed over their

[40] *Burevestnik*, No. 3, 30 September 1906, pp. 14-16.
[41] *Ibid.*, No. 5, 30 April 1907, p. 14.
[42] Frank, *Geklibene shriftn*, p. 403.

kommunary associates.[43] For the *bezmotivniki* had just achieved two dramatic successes: in November and December 1905, they had exploded bombs in the Hotel Bristol in Warsaw and the Café Libman in Odessa,[44] gaining considerable notoriety and sending shudders through the respectable citizenry. Exhilarated by these accomplishments, the *bezmotivniki* now laid even more magnificent plans of destruction, unaware that their triumphant moment of violence was soon to be succeeded by a much longer interval of cruel retribution.

Just as fanatical as *Chernoe Znamia* was a smaller group of militant anarchists centered in St. Petersburg called *Beznachalie* (Without Authority). Operating largely outside the Pale of Settlement (though small circles did exist in Warsaw, Minsk, and Kiev), *Beznachalie*, unlike the Black Banner organization, contained few Jewish members. The proportion of students in its ranks was very high, even higher than in *Chernoe Znamia*, with unskilled workers and unemployed drifters comprising only a small fraction of the membership. Like the *Chernoznamentsy*, the *Beznachal'tsy* claimed to be Anarchist-Communists, since their ultimate goal was the establishment of a free federation of territorial communes. Yet they had much in common with the individualist anarchists, the epigoni of Max Stirner, Benjamin Tucker, and Friedrich Nietzsche, who exalted the individual ego over and above the claims of collective entities. And in their passion for revolutionary conspiracy and their extreme hostility towards intellectuals—despite the fact that, for the most part, they were intellectuals themselves—the *Beznachal'tsy* bore the stamp of Sergei Nechaev and his forerunners, the ultra-radical Ishutin circle which had operated in St. Petersburg during the 1860's.[45]

Like their cousins of the Black Banner association, the *Beznachalie* rebels were ardent exponents of "motiveless" terror. Every blow dealt to government officials, policemen, or property holders was considered a progressive action because

[43] *Buntar'*, No. 1, 1 December 1906, pp. 20-24; *Al'manakh*, p. 23.

[44] See O. I. Taratuta, "Kievskaia Luk'ianovskaia katorzhnaia tiur'ma," *Volna*, No. 57, September 1924, pp. 39-40. The author was a participant in the Odessa bombing.

[45] On the Ishutin circle, see Venturi, *Roots of Revolution*, pp. 331-353.

it sowed "class discord" between the submerged multitudes and their privileged masters.[46] "Death to the bourgeoisie!" was their battle cry, for "the death of the bourgeoisie is the life of the workers."[47]

The *Beznachalie* group was founded in 1905 by a young intellectual who went by the name of Bidbei. His real name, by an odd coincidence, was Nikolai Romanov, the same as the Tsar's. Born the son of a prosperous landowner, Romanov was small and lithe, and possessed an impetuous nature and a sharp wit. He enrolled as a student in the St. Petersburg Mining Institute at the beginning of the century, but was dismissed for participating in student demonstrations. When the director of the Institute sent him a letter of expulsion, Romanov returned it with the inscription, "*Prochël s udovol'stviem* ("I read it with pleasure"), *Nikolai Romanov*," which the Emperor often wrote on documents submitted for his approval.[48] His dismissal thus sealed, young Romanov left for Paris, an underground man with a new identity. In a startling pamphlet composed there on the eve of the 1905 Revolution, Bidbei conjured up a demonic image of the debacle just beyond the horizon: "A terrible night! Terrible scenes. . . . Not the innocent pranks of 'the revolutionists.' But that *Walpurgisnacht* of revolution, when on Lucifer's call the Spartacuses, the Razins, and the heroes of the bloody boot will fly down to earth. The uprising of Lucifer himself!"[49]

Some weeks after the outbreak of the revolution, Bidbei enlisted the help of two fellow exiles[50] in printing an ultra-radical journal called the *Listok gruppy Beznachalie* (Leaflet of the *Beznachalie* Group), which appeared twice during the spring and summer of 1905. The first issue set forth the credo of *Beznachalie*, a curious mixture of Bakunin's faith in society's

[46] T. Rostovtsev, *Nasha taktika* (Geneva, 1907), pp. 7ff.

[47] *Listki "Khleb i Volia,"* No. 8, 15 February 1907, pp. 3-5; *Buntar'*, No. 1, 1 December 1906, p. 29.

[48] I. Genkin, "Anarkhisty: iz vospominanii politicheskogo katorzhanina," *Byloe*, 1918, No. 9, pp. 168-169; Genkin, *Po tiur'mam i etapam* (Petrograd, 1922), pp. 283-284; Max Nomad, *Dreamers, Dynamiters, and Demagogues* (New York, 1964), pp. 77-78.

[49] A. Bidbei, *O Liutsifere, velikom dukhe vozmushcheniia, "nesoznatel'nosti," anarkhii i beznachaliia* (n.p. [Paris?], 1904), p. 28.

[50] Ekaterina Litvina and Mikhail Sushchinskii. See *Probuzhdenie*, No. 80-81, March-April 1937, p. 26.

castaways, Nechaev's demand for bloody vengeance against the privileged classes, Marx's concepts of class struggle and permanent revolution, and Kropotkin's vision of a free federation of communes. Bidbei and his confederates declared a "partisan war" on contemporary society, in which terror of every sort—individual terror, mass terror, economic terror—would be sanctioned. Since the "bourgeois" world was corrupt to the roots, parliamentary reforms were of no use. It was necessary to wage a broad class struggle, an "armed uprising of the people: peasants, workers, and every person in rags . . . open street fighting of every possible type and in the fiercest possible form . . . a revolution *en permanence*, that is, a whole series of popular uprisings until a decisive victory of the poor is achieved." In a Nechaevist spirit (Bidbei was fond of quoting or paraphrasing Nechaev, whom he keenly admired), the *Beznachalie* credo repudiated religion, the family, and bourgeois morality in general, and encouraged the dispossessed to attack and rob the businesses and homes of their exploiters. The revolution must be made not only by the peasant and worker, declared Bidbei, echoing Bakunin, but also by the so-called "base rabble—the unemployed, vagabonds, hoboes, and all the outcast elements and renegades of society, for they are all our brothers and comrades." Bidbei summoned them all "to a *mighty and ruthless, total and bloody, people's vengeance*" (Nechaev's famous motto). "Hail the federation of free communes and cities! Long live anarchy (*beznachalie*)!"[51]

Bidbei's horrendous visions of the revolution were shared by a small circle of *Anarkhisty-Obshchinniki* (Anarchist-Communists), who turned out a prodigious quantity of incendiary literature in St. Petersburg during 1905. The outstanding member of this group was "Tolstoy" Rostovtsev (the alias of N. V. Divnogorskii), the son of a government official in the Volga province of Saratov. About thirty years of age (Bidbei was in his early twenties), Rostovtsev had a homely but interesting face and an idealistic nature that was readily transmuted into revolutionary fanaticism. While attending Kharkov University, he became a passionate disciple of Tolstoyan nonviolence (whence his peculiar *nom de guerre*), but soon

[51] *Listok gruppy Beznachalie*, No. 1, April 1905, pp. 1-3.

swung to the opposite pole of unmitigated terrorism.[52] By 1905, Rostovtsev was writing instructions on the preparation of home-made "Macedonian" bombs (complete with diagrams) and advising the peasantry on "how to set fire to the landlords' haystacks."[53] On the cover of one of his pamphlets is a drawing of bearded peasants, scythes and pitchforks in hand, burning the church and manor house of their village. Their banner bears the motto, *"Za zemliu, za voliu, za anarkhicheskuiu doliu"* ("For land and liberty, for an anarchist future!").[54] Rostovtsev summoned the Russian people to "take up the axe and bring death to the tsarist family, the landlords, and the priests!"[55]

Rostovtsev and his fellow *Anarkhisty-Obshchinniki* addressed other leaflets to the factory workers of Petersburg, exhorting them to smash their machines, dynamite the city's power stations, throw bombs at the middle-class "hangmen," rob banks and shops, blow up the police stations, and throw open the prisons. Bloody Sunday had taught the workers what to expect from the Tsar and from the timid advocates of piecemeal reform. "Let a broad wave of mass and individual terror envelop all of Russia!" Inaugurate the stateless commune, in which each would take freely from the common warehouse and work only four hours a day to allow time for leisure and education— time to live "like a human being." Onward with "the SOCIAL REVOLUTION! HAIL THE ANARCHIST COMMUNE!"[56]

The Petersburg *Anarkhisty-Obshchinniki* and Bidbei's *Beznachalie* group in Paris clearly had a great deal in common. Many leaflets of the Petersburg group, in fact, were reprinted in Bidbei's *Listok*. It was therefore not surprising that, when Bidbei returned to the Russian capital in December 1905, the

[52] Genkin, *Byloe*, 1918, No. 9, pp. 172-173; *Po tiur'mam i etapam*, pp. 288-289.

[53] "Prigotovlenie bomb" (leaflet of the *Anarkhisty-Obshchinniki*, 1905), Columbia Russian Archive; "Kak podzhigat' pomeshch'i stoga," reprinted in *Listok gruppy Beznachalie*, No. 2-3, June-July 1905, pp. 9, 16. Though simply signed *"Anarkhisty-Obshchinniki,"* these leaflets are very probably the work of Rostovtsev. See Genkin, *Byloe*, No. 9, pp. 173-174. They are labeled "Moscow" rather than "St. Petersburg," most likely to mislead the police.

[54] T. Rostovtsev, *Za vsiu zemliu, za vsiu voliu* (n.p., n.d. [1905?]).

[55] *Listok gruppy Beznachalie*, No. 2-3, June-July 1905, pp. 3-4.

[56] "Anarkhisty-Obshchinniki" and "K rabochim g. Peterburga" (leaflets, St. Petersburg, March and April 1905), Columbia Russian Archive. The first was distributed in 2,000 copies, the second in 5,000.

Anarkhisty-Obshchinniki at once accepted him as their leader and changed their name to *Beznachalie*.

The ranks of *Beznachalie* included a female doctor, three or four *gimnaziia* pupils, Rostovtsev's wife, Marusia, and several former university students (besides Bidbei and Rostovtsev), most notably Boris Speranskii, a youth of nineteen from the provinces, and Aleksandr Kolosov (Sokolov), about twenty-six years old and the son of a priest in Tambov province. Like so many others in the revolutionary movement, Kolosov received his education in an Orthodox seminary, where he excelled in mathematics and foreign languages. He was admitted to the Spiritual Academy, but cut short a promising church career by joining an SR circle and plunging into revolutionary agitation. He then spent brief periods in a succession of Russian universities, only to return to his father's village, where he distributed propaganda among the peasants. In 1905, Kolosov came to St. Petersburg and joined Rostovtsev's circle of anarchists.[57]

Aside from Bidbei (and possibly Rostovtsev), at least one other *Beznachalets* was of noble birth. Vladimir Konstantinovich Ushakov, whose father was a government administrator (*zemskii nachal'nik*) in the province of St. Petersburg, had been brought up on the family estate near Pskov. After graduating from the *gimnaziia* at Tsarskoe Selo, where the Tsar had his summer palace, Ushakov entered St. Petersburg University, and in 1901 became involved in the student movement. Like Bidbei, he went abroad, but returned to St. Petersburg in time to witness the massacre of Bloody Sunday. Soon afterwards, he joined the *Anarkhisty-Obshchinniki*, serving as an agitator among the factory workers, to whom he was known as "the Admiral."[58]

Finally, one other member of Bidbei's circle must be mentioned, a certain Dmitriev or Dmitrii Bogoliubov, who turned out to be a police spy and brought about the group's downfall in January 1906. As the *Beznachal'tsy* were planning a major "expropriation" (so far, they had perpetrated only two acts of violence, a bombing and the shooting of a detective), the police broke into their headquarters, arrested the plotters, and seized

[57] Genkin, *Byloe*, 1918, No. 9, pp. 175-176; *Po tiur'mam i etapam*, p. 292.

[58] *Burevestnik*, No. 6-7, September-October 1907, pp. 29-30.

their printing press.[59] Only Ushakov was lucky enough to elude the authorities, escaping to the city of Lvov in Austrian Galicia.

Chernoe Znamia and *Beznachalie*, though certainly the most conspicuous, were by no means the only Anarchist-Communist organizations to spring up in revolutionary Russia. Of the rest, a few pursued the relatively moderate course of Kropotkin's *Khleb i Volia* group, content to distribute propaganda among the workers and peasants. The majority, however, adopted the sanguinary creed of Bakunin and Nechaev and embarked upon the path of terrorism. One such ultra-radical society, the International Group in the Baltic city of Riga, carried out a series of "ex's" and issued a stream of hectographed leaflets reviling moderation and gradualism of any sort. The Riga group scornfully dismissed the claim of the socialists that the 1905 upheaval was merely a "democratic revolution" and denounced them for advocating "peaceful cooperation in parliaments with all capitalist parties." The slogan of "liberty, equality, fraternity," as the European revolutions of the eighteenth and nineteenth centuries had amply demonstrated, was an empty promise of the middle class. Now "scientific" socialism aimed at a similar deception. The Marxists, with their centralized party apparatus and elaborate talk of historical stages, were no more "friends of the people" than Nicholas II. They were, rather, present-day Jacobins who aimed to use the workers to capture power for themselves. The true liberation of mankind could be accomplished only by means of a social revolution of the broad masses.[60] This impatient brand of anarchism took its most violent form in the south, where the "battle detachments" of the large cities, in an effort to coordinate their terrorist activities, joined together in a loose-knit South Russian Battle Organization.

The anarchists of Kiev and Moscow, by contrast, placed heavier emphasis on the dissemination of propaganda. The Kiev

[59] *Ibid.*, No. 3, 30 September 1906, pp. 12-13; "Nezavisimaia Sotsialisticheskaia Mysl'" (hectographed journal, Petrograd, 1924), Fleshin Archive.

[60] "Politicheskaia revoliutsiia ili Sotsial'naia?" and "Ko Vsem Iskrennim Druz'iam Naroda" (leaflets, Riga, 1905), Columbia Russian Archive.

Group of Anarchist-Communists found a strong advocate of this moderate course in a young Kropotkinite named German Borisovich Sandomirskii.[61] Moscow, however, was the more important propaganda center. Its first anarchist circle was founded in 1905, but fell apart almost immediately when the police arrested its leader, another young disciple of Kropotkin, Vladimir Ivanovich Zabrezhnev (Fedorov). The *Svoboda* (Freedom) group, which succeeded it in December 1905, acted as an entrepôt of propaganda materials, obtaining literature from Western Europe and from anarchist circles in the border provinces, and passing it on to new cells in Moscow, Nizhnii Novgorod, Tula, and other industrial towns of central Russia. During 1906, four more groups appeared in Moscow: *Svobodnaia Kommuna* (The Free Commune), *Solidarnost'* (Solidarity), and *Bezvlastie* (Anarchy), which attracted their followings in the working-class districts; and a circle of students who used the classrooms of Moscow University as revolutionary forums. Joint meetings with the SR's and Social Democrats, marked by angry debates over the merits of parliamentary government, were occasionally held in the Sparrow Hills and Sokolniki Woods on the edge of town. "Down with the Duma!" the anarchists would shout. "Down with parliamentarism! We want bread and liberty! Long live the *people's* revolution!"[62] Some of the Moscow groups added a measure of terrorism to their propaganda activities, manufacturing "Japanese" bombs and holding secret conclaves in the Donskoi Monastery to plan "expropriations." One young woman of twenty-six lost her life when a bomb she was testing exploded in her hands.[63]

[61] In 1907, Dmitrii Bogrov, who was to assassinate Prime Minister Stolypin in Kiev four years later, was a member of the Kiev Group of Anarchist-Communists while serving as an agent of the secret police. His murder of Stolypin, however, seems to have been a personal act, not directly related to his revolutionary or police associations. See George Tokmakoff, "Stolypin's Assassin," *Slavic Review*, xxiv (June 1965), 314-321; G. Sandomirskii, "Po povodu starogo spora," *Katorga i Ssylka*, 1926, No. 2, pp. 15ff.; I. Knizhnik, "Vospominaniia o Bogrove, ubiitse Stolypina," *Krasnaia Letopis'*, 1923, No. 5, p. 290; E. Lazarev, "Dmitrii Bogrov i ubiistvo Stolypina," *Volia Rossii* (Prague), 1926, No. 8-9, p. 59; A. Mushin, *Dmitrii Bogrov i ubiistvo Stolypina* (Paris, 1914), pp. 106ff.; and V. Bogrov, *Dmitrii Bogrov i ubiistvo Stolypina* (Berlin, 1931), pp. 37-48.

[62] *Burevestnik*, No. 3, 30 April 1906, pp. 13-14; *Al'manakh*, p. 56.
[63] *Al'manakh*, pp. 55-58.

Apart from the numerous Anarchist-Communist groups which appeared all over Russia during the Revolution of 1905, a second, much smaller body of anarchists, the Anarcho-Syndicalists (to be discussed later), sprang up in Odessa, and yet another variety, the Anarchist-Individualists, emerged in Moscow, St. Petersburg, and Kiev.[64] The two leading exponents of individualist anarchism, both based in Moscow, were Aleksei Alekseevich Borovoi and Lev Chernyi (Pavel Dmitrievich Turchaninov). From Nietzsche, they inherited the desire for a complete overturn of all values accepted by bourgeois society— political, moral, and cultural. Furthermore, strongly influenced by Max Stirner and Benjamin Tucker, the German and American theorists of individualist anarchism, they demanded the total liberation of the human personality from the fetters of organized society. In their view, even the voluntary communes of Peter Kropotkin might limit the freedom of the individual.[65] A number of Anarchist-Individualists found the ultimate expression of their social alienation in violence and crime, others attached themselves to avant-garde literary and artistic circles, but the majority remained "philosophical" anarchists who conducted animated parlor discussions and elaborated their individualist theories in ponderous journals and books.

While all three categories of Russian anarchism—Anarchist-Communism, Anarcho-Syndicalism, and Anarchist-Individualism—drew their adherents almost entirely from the intelligentsia and the working class, the Anarchist-Communist groups made some effort to dispense their ideas among the soldiers and peasants as well. As early as 1903, a "Group of Russian Anarchists" published a small pamphlet which called for the "disorganization, dissolution, and annihilation," of the Russian Army and its replacement by the armed masses of people.[66] After the outbreak of the Russo-Japanese War, anarchist leaflets strove to convince the soldiers that their real struggle was at

[64] See V. Zabrezhnev, *Ob individualisticheskom anarkhizme* (London, 1912); and Zabrezhnev, "Propovedniki individualisticheskogo anarkhizma v Rossii," *Burevestnik*, No. 10-11, March-April 1908, pp. 4-9.

[65] A. Borovoi, *Obshchestvennye idealy sovremennogo obshchestva* (Moscow, 1906); L. Chernyi, *Novoe napravlenie v anarkhizme: assotsiatsionnyi anarkhizm* (Moscow, 1907).

[66] *Chto nam delat' v armii?* (n.p., 1903).

home—against the government and private property.[67] Anti-militarist literature of this sort, however, was distributed in limited quantities, and it is doubtful that it made much impression on the troops.

Propaganda in the peasant villages was conducted on a larger scale, but appears to have yielded only slightly better results. In September 1903, the second number of *Khleb i Volia* endorsed "agrarian terror" as an "outstanding form of the partisan struggle" against the landlords and central government.[68] An illegal brochure published in St. Petersburg the same year assured the peasants that they needed "neither tsar nor state" but only "land and liberty." The author conjured up the myth of an idyllic age of freedom that existed in medieval Russia, when authority rested with the local town assembly (*veche*) and the village commune; to restore this libertarian society, the *narod* was urged to wage an "unrelenting war of liberation." "Peasants and workers! Scorn all authority, every uniform and priest's cassock. Love only liberty, and introduce it now."[69]

The Revolution of 1905 lent powerful impetus to propaganda of this type. "Down with the landlords, down with the wealthy," proclaimed Rostovtsev of the *Beznachalie* group, as he instigated the peasants to set fire to their masters' haylofts. "All the land belongs to us, to the entire peasant *narod*."[70] Anarchist-Communists from the cities of Odessa, Ekaterinoslav, Kiev, and Chernigov descended into the villages with "little books" containing the message of revolt, just as their Populist forebears had done thirty years earlier.[71] Leaflets with such titles as "Pull Your Plow from the Furrow" and "How the Peasants Succeed Without Authority" passed through many hands in Riazan province;[72] the latter portrayed a village commune which, having rid itself of the government, lived in freedom and harmony. "And bread, clothing, and other supplies everyone took from the com-

[67] For example, "Po povodu voiny" (*Listok No. 4*, Russian Communist-Anarchists, 1904), Bund Archives.

[68] *Khleb i Volia*, No. 2, September 1903, p. 6.

[69] *Vol'naia Volia*, 1903, No. 1.

[70] Rostovtsev, *Za vsiu zemliu*, p. 3.

[71] *Khleb i Volia*, No. 6, January 1904, p. 8; *Burevestnik*, No. 8, November 1907, pp. 9-12; No. 13, October 1908, pp. 18-19; *Al'manakh*, pp. 12-13, 76-81, 187-188.

[72] *Burevestnik*, No. 5, 30 April 1907, p. 15.

mon storehouse according to his needs."[73] In Tambov province, the *Beznachalets* Kolosov sowed the seeds of anarchism in 1905, which bore fruit three years later in the form of the *Probuzhdenie* (Awakening) group of peasant anarchists.[74] Other anarchist groups appeared in the rural districts between 1905 and 1908, but they were seldom a match for the Socialist Revolutionaries, who maintained a near monopoly on peasant radicalism throughout the revolutionary period.

During the 1905 uprising, while the *Chernoznamentsy* and *Beznachal'tsy* were waging their life-and-death struggle against the government and the propertied classes of Russia, Kropotkin and his coterie remained in the West, occupied with the less flamboyant tasks of propaganda and organization. Both extremist groups found the comparative respectability of Kropotkin's *Khleb i Volia* association exceedingly distasteful. The terrorists, risking their lives in daily acts of violence, resented what they conceived to be the passive attitude of the Kropotkinites towards the heroic epic unfolding in Russia. Already uneasy over Kropotkin's description, in 1903, of the impending Russian revolution as merely "a prologue, or even the first act of the local communalist revolution,"[75] the ultras grew more suspicious in 1905, when Kropotkin compared the tempest in Russia to the English and French revolutions,[76] which in their view had simply installed a new set of masters into power. For the *Beznachal'tsy* and *Chernoznamentsy*, 1905 was not just a timid step toward a compromising system of "liberal federalism," but the final and decisive battle, Armageddon itself.[77]

To a certain extent, perhaps, these zealots of the anarchist movement misconstrued the observations Kropotkin made in 1905. In drawing his analogy between the Russian revolution on the one side and the English and French revolutions on the other, Kropotkin specifically stated that Russia was undergoing more than just "a simple transition from autocracy to consti-

[73] S. Zaiats, *Kak muzhiki ostalis' bez nachal'stva* (Moscow, 1906), p. 16.
[74] *Burevestnik*, No. 17, July 1909, p. 10.
[75] *Khleb i Volia*, No. 1, August 1903, p. 5.
[76] P. Kropotkin, *Russkaia revoliutsiia* (Geneva, 1905), p. 3; *Khleb i Volia*, No. 15, February 1905, pp. 2-3; No. 16, April 1905, pp. 1-4.
[77] Grossman-Roshchin, *Byloe*, 1924, No. 27-28, p. 173.

tutionalism," more than a mere political transfer in which the aristocracy or the middle class would become the new rulers in place of the king.[78] What had impressed Kropotkin most in his study of the earlier upheavals in Western Europe was their all-encompassing scope and the profound changes they had wrought in human relationships. The Revolution of 1905, he believed, was Russia's "great revolution," comparable in breadth and depth to the great English and French revolutions and not just another transitory mutiny executed by a small body of insurrectionists.[79] It was "not a simple change of administration" that Russians were witnessing, but a *social* revolution that would "radically alter the conditions of economic life" and forever put an end to coercive government.[80] Indeed, the Russian revolution would prove even more sweeping than the prior revolts in the West, for it was a "people's liberation, based on true equality, true liberty, and genuine fraternity."[81]

Yet Kropotkin's continuous references to the revolutions in England and France did seem to imply something short of the immediate realization of stateless communism which the *Chernoznamentsy* and *Beznachal'tsy* so desperately craved. Moreover, in view of Kropotkin's strong antipathy towards mutinies and insurrections launched by small rebel bands, it is not surprising that the terrorist circles should have frowned upon his analysis of the 1905 uprising. Time and again, Kropotkin reiterated his opposition both to Blanquist *coups* and to campaigns of terrorist violence waged by tightly-knit conspiratorial bands in isolation from the bulk of the people.[82] Random murders and holdups, he insisted, could effect no more change in the existing social order than could the mere seizure of political power; individual "ex's" had no place in a full-scale revolt of the masses, the aim of which was not the greedy transfer of wealth from one group to another, but the total elimination of private property itself.[83] One of Kropotkin's disciples, Vladimir Zabrezhnev, likened the escapades of the Russian terrorists to the "era of dynamite" in France—the early 1890's, when the audacious exploits of Ravachol, Auguste Vaillant, and Émile

[78] Kropotkin, *Russkaia revoliutsiia*, p. 10.
[79] *Ibid.*, p. 9.   [80] *Ibid.*, p. 13.   [81] *Ibid.*, p. 15.
[82] P. Kropotkin, ed., *Russkaia revoliutsiia i anarkhizm* (London, 1907), pp. 8-9.
[83] *Ibid.*, pp. 5-7.

Henry made statesmen and businessmen tremble for their lives.[84] The endemic violence of those years, though prompted by social injustice, was little more than an outlet for personal "anger and indignation," said Zabrezhnev.[85] "It stands to reason," he concluded, "that such acts as attacking the first bourgeois or government agent one encounters, or arson or explosions in cafés, theaters, etc., in no sense represent a logical conclusion from the anarchist *Weltanschauung*; their explanation lies in the psychology of those who perpetrate them."[86] In a similar manner, Kropotkin's *Khlebovol'tsy* denounced such robber bands as *Chernyi Voron* (The Black Raven) and *Iastreb* (The Hawk) of Odessa for using the ideological cloak of anarchism to conceal the predatory nature of their activities. These "bomb-thrower-expropriators," declared the Kropotkinites, were no better than the bandits of southern Italy;[87] and their program of indiscriminate terror was a grotesque caricature of anarchist doctrine, demoralizing the movement's true adherents and discrediting anarchism in the eyes of the public.

For all these harsh words, Kropotkin and his *Khlebovol'tsy* nevertheless continued to sanction acts of violence impelled by outraged conscience or compassion for the oppressed, as well as "propaganda by the deed," specifically designed to awaken the revolutionary consciousness of the people. The *Khleb i Volia* group also approved of "defensive terror" to repulse the depredations of police units or of the Black Hundreds, the squads of hoodlums who launched frightful attacks upon Jews and intellectuals in 1905 and 1906.[88] Thus a report from Odessa printed in *Khleb i Volia* during the tumultuous summer of 1905 could declare, "Only the enemies of the people can be enemies of terror!"[89]

[84] V. Zabrezhnev, "O terrore," in *Russkaia revoliutsiia i anarkhizm*, pp. 44-47; *Listki "Khleb i Volia*," No. 3, 28 November 1906, pp. 2-4; No. 4, 13 December 1906, pp. 3-5. On the "era of dynamite," see Jean Maitron, *Histoire du mouvement anarchiste en France (1880-1914)* (Paris, 1951), pp. 189-230.

[85] Zabrezhnev, in *Russkaia revoliutsiia i anarkhizm*, p. 47.

[86] *Ibid.*, p. 54.

[87] *Burevestnik*, No. 8, November 1907, p. 11; *Anarkhist*, No. 1, 10 October 1907, p. 31; *Al'manakh*, p. 151; I. Genkin, "Sredi preemnikov Bakunina," *Krasnaia Letopis'*, 1927, No. 1, pp. 199-201.

[88] Zabrezhnev, in *Russkaia revoliutsiia i anarkhizm*, p. 43.

[89] *Khleb i Volia*, No. 19-20, July 1905, p. 11.

Of the several schools of anarchism to make their appearance in Russia during this period, the severest critics of terrorist tactics were the Anarcho-Syndicalists. Not even the comparatively moderate *Khlebovol'tsy* were spared their censure. The foremost Anarcho-Syndicalist leader inside Russia, who went under the pseudonym of Daniil Novomirskii ("man of the New World"—his real name was Iakov Kirillovskii), rebuked Kropotkin and his associates for sanctioning propaganda by the deed and other isolated forms of terrorism, which, he said, only fostered a wasteful "spirit of insurgency" among the backward and unprepared masses.[90] As for the outright terrorists of *Beznachalie* and *Chernoe Znamia*, Novomirskii compared them to the People's Will organization of the previous generation, since each group mistakenly relied on small "rebel bands" to bring about a fundamental transformation of the old order, a task which could be performed only by the broad masses of Russian people themselves.[91]

Novomirskii happened to be in the crowd which gathered outside the Café Libman after it was bombed in December 1905. The café was not a gathering place of the wealthy, he observed, but a "second-class" restaurant which catered to the petty bourgeoisie and intelligentsia. The bomb exploded in the street, producing "nothing but noise." Novomirskii noted the reaction of a workman in the crowd: "Do the revolutionaries really have nothing better to do than throw bombs into restaurants? One might think the tsarist government had already been overthrown and bourgeois power eliminated! Undoubtedly the bomb was thrown by the Black Hundreds in order to discredit the revolutionaries."[92] Should the anarchists continue to pursue these fruitless tactics and plunge into battle without readying their battalions, Novomirskii warned, their fate would be as tragic as that of the People's Will, whose leaders ended on the scaffold. The immediate mission of anarchism, he said, was to spread propaganda in the factories and organize revolutionary labor unions as vehicles of class warfare with the bourgeoisie. In

[90] D. I. Novomirskii, *Iz programmy sindikal'nogo anarkhizma* (n.p., 1907), pp. 16ff.

[91] *Ibid.*, pp. 19-20; *Novyi Mir*, No. 1, 15 October 1905, p. 10. Cf. *Bez Rulia*, No. 1, September 1908, p. 6; and the anonymous pamphlet, *Anarkhizm i khuliganstvo* (St. Petersburg, 1906).

[92] *Mikhailu Bakuninu*, p. 256.

these modern times, he added, the only effective terror was "economic terror"—strikes, boycotts, sabotage, assaults on factory managers, and the expropriation of government funds.[93] The indiscriminate forays of marauding bands, instead of raising the revolutionary consciousness of the proletariat, would only "embitter the workers and nourish coarse and bloodthirsty instincts."[94]

Ironically enough, Novomirskii's own group of Odessa Anarcho-Syndicalists itself organized a "battle detachment," which carried out a series of daring "expropriations." To fill the group's coffers, the "battle detachment" robbed a train outside Odessa, and, on another occasion, collaborated with a band of SR's in a bank holdup which netted the anarchists 25,000 rubles. (They used the money to purchase more weapons and to set up a printing press, which published Novomirskii's Anarcho-Syndicalist program and one number of a syndicalist journal, Vol'nyi Rabochii—The Free Worker.) Novomirskii's group even had a bomb laboratory, run by a Polish rebel who was nicknamed "Cake" because he and his wife liked to dance the Cake-Walk in the laboratory with bombs in hand.[95] A second anarchist leader in Odessa, Lazar Gershkovich, though he considered himself a disciple of Kropotkin, concocted a similar mixture of syndicalism and terrorism. A mechanical engineer, Gershkovich constructed his own bomb laboratory and became known as the "Kibalchich" of the Odessa movement, after the young engineer of the People's Will who had made the bombs that killed Alexander II.[96]

Novomirskii tried to justify the seemingly hypocritical maneuvers of his terrorist colleagues with the claim that they were acting for the benefit of the movement "as a whole"—quite a different matter from wanton bombthrowing or the "purely vagabond conception of expropriation."[97] Novomirskii's arguments against "motiveless" terror were echoed in Western Europe by another prominent Russian syndicalist, Maksim Raev-

[93] Novomirskii, Iz programmy sindikal'nogo anarkhizma, p. 192.

[94] Novomirskii, "Programma iuzhno-rossiiskoi gruppy Anarkhistov-Sindikalistov," Listki "Khleb i Volia," No. 5, 28 December 1906, p. 9.

[95] Mikhailu Bakuninu, pp. 263-271.

[96] Buntar', No. 1, 1 December 1906, p. 31; Al'manakh, pp. 150-151; Listki "Khleb i Volia," No. 12, 12 April 1907, p. 5.

[97] Novomirskii, Iz programmy sindikal'nogo anarkhizma, p. 161.

skii (L. Fishelev), who denounced the "Nechaevist tactics" of such conspiratorial societies as *Chernoe Znamia* and *Beznachalie*, and derided their faith in the revolutionary capacity of thieves, tramps, the *Lumpenproletariat*, and other dark elements of Russian society. It was high time, Raevskii declared, to recognize that a successful social revolution required an organized army of combatants, an army which only the labor movement could provide.[98]

In the "maximalist" atmosphere of 1905, it was perhaps inevitable that the terrorist wing of the anarchist movement should have gained the upper hand. The patient efforts of the Anarcho-Syndicalists and *Khlebovol'tsy* to disseminate propaganda in the factories and villages were eclipsed by the daring exploits of their extremist comrades. Not a day went by without newspaper accounts of sensational robberies, murders, and acts of sabotage perpetrated by bands of anarchist desperadoes. They robbed banks and shops, seized printing presses to turn out their literature, and shot down watchmen, police officers, and government officials. Reckless and frustrated youths, they satisfied their desire for excitement and self-affirmation by hurling bombs into public buildings, factory offices, theaters, and restaurants.

Lawlessness reached a climax near the close of 1905, when the *bezmotivniki* exploded their bombs in the Hotel Bristol in Warsaw and the Café Libman in Odessa, and bands of "Forest Brethren" made a Sherwood Forest of the northern woodlands from Viatka to the Baltic provinces.[99] After the suppression of the Moscow uprising, there followed a momentary lull, dur-

[98] *Burevestnik*, No. 8, November 1907, pp. 3-4. Similar criticisms of anarchist banditry came from the socialist camp. The primitive battle cry of the anarchists, according to one Social Democrat, was "Your money or your life!" At the same time, he added, the anarchists tried to win over the workers by "evoking in them golden dreams of the future paradise of the anarchist system." S. Ivanovich, *Anarkhisty i anarkhizm v Rossii* (St. Petersburg, 1907), pp. 1, 8. Thirty years later, the Bolshevik historian Emelian Iaroslavskii condemned the terrorist acts of the anarchists as "sheer banditry." E. Yaroslavsky, *History of Anarchism in Russia* (New York, 1937), p. 37. In doing so, he chose to ignore the "ex's" carried out by his own party during and after 1905. See Wolfe, *Three Who Made a Revolution*, chapter 22.

[99] *Al'manakh*, pp. 66-75; Pares, *The Fall of the Russian Monarchy*, p. 104.

ing which many revolutionaries went into hiding. But terrorism was resumed shortly afterwards. SR's and anarchists claimed more than 4,000 lives during 1906 and 1907, although they lost a comparable number of their own members (mostly SR's). The tide, however, was turning against them. P. A. Stolypin, the Tsar's new Prime Minister, initiated stern measures to "pacify" the nation. In August 1906, Stolypin's own summer house was blown up by SR Maximalists (an ultra-radical off-shoot of the Socialist Revolutionary party that demanded the immediate socialization of agriculture and industry), wounding his son and daughter and killing 32 people. By the end of the year, the Prime Minister had placed most of the Empire under a state of emergency. The gendarmes tracked the *Chernoznamentsy* and *Beznachal'tsy* to their lairs, seizing caches of weapons and ammunition, recovering stolen presses, and smashing bomb laboratories. Punishment was swift and ruthless. Field courts-martial were set up, in which preliminary investigation was waived, verdicts delivered within two days, and sentences executed at once.[100]

If the young rebels had to die, they were determined to go in their own way, rather than fall victim to "Stolypin's necktie" —the hangman's noose which was sending hundreds of revolutionaries, real and suspected, to an early grave. Death did not seem so terrible after a life spent in degradation and despair; as Kolosov of *Beznachalie* observed after his arrest, death is "the sister of liberty."[101] Thus, when cornered by the police, it was not unusual for the terrorists to turn their pistols on themselves, or if captured, to resort to the grim gesture of Russian fanatics since the Old Believers of the seventeenth century—self-immolation.[102] "Damn the masters, damn the slaves, and damn me!"—Victor Serge's characterization of the anarchist terrorists in Paris on the eve of the First World War might well have been said of these Russian youths. "It was like a collective suicide."[103]

The ranks of *Chernoe Znamia* were quickly decimated, scores

[100] *Vtoroi period revoliutsii, 1906-1907 gody* (7 vols., Moscow, 1959-1963), II, 73-84; V, 66-78.

[101] Genkin, *Byloe*, 1918, No. 9, p. 183.

[102] *Ibid.*, p. 166; Genkin, *Krasnaia Letopis'*, 1927, No. 1, pp. 181-182; *Anarkhist*, No. 5, March 1910, pp. 1-4.

[103] Serge, *Mémoires d'un révolutionnaire*, pp. 41-42.

of young men dying violent deaths. Boris Engelson, a founder of the "*Anarkhiia*" printing press in Bialystok, was arrested in Vilna in 1905, but escaped from prison and fled to Paris. When he returned to Russia two years later, he was promptly recaptured and sent to the gallows.[104] In 1906, two of the most notorious Bialystok terrorists, men who had followed in Nisan Farber's footsteps, perished during encounters with the authorities. The first, Anton Nizhborskii, a member of the Polish Socialist party before entering the anarchist movement, killed himself to avoid capture after an unsuccessful "ex" in Ekaterinoslav.[105] His comrade-in-arms, Aron Elin (alias "Gelinker"), a former SR who had established his reputation as a terrorist by assassinating a Cossack officer and tossing a bomb into a group of policemen, was shot down by soldiers while attending a workers' meeting in a Bialystok cemetery.[106] Vladimir Striga, a third Bialystok *Chernoznamenets*, the offspring of well-to-do Jewish parents and an erstwhile student and Social Democrat, died in Parisian exile the same year. "Would it make any difference which bourgeois one throws the bomb at?" Striga asked in a letter to his comrades just before his death. "It is all the same: the shareholders will still lead their depraved lives in Paris. . . . I proclaim 'Death to the bourgeoisie,' and shall pay for it with my own life."[107] Striga met his end as he was walking in the Bois de Vincennes on the outskirts of the French capital. He stumbled, setting off a bomb in his pocket, which blew him to smithereens.[108]

The Revolution of 1905 and its aftermath saw the accumulation of a "huge martyrology" of anarchists, as Nikolai Ignatievich Rogdaev (Muzil), one of Kropotkin's followers, noted in

[104] *Khleb i Volia*, No. 23, October 1905, p. 4; *Burevestnik*, No. 9, February 1908, p. 1; *Al'manakh*, pp. 156-161.

[105] *Buntar'*, No. 1, 1 December 1906, pp. 35-36; *Al'manakh*, pp. 29-32.

[106] *Burevestnik*, No. 1, 20 July 1906, p. 1; No. 8, November 1907, pp. 23-24; *Al'manakh*, pp. 33-36; Grossman-Roshchin, *Byloe*, 1924, No. 27-28, pp. 179-180.

[107] *Pis'mo Vladimira Lapidusa (Strigi)* (n.p., 1907), p. 7. The Labadie Collection.

[108] *Buntar'*, No. 1, pp. 32-34. Death by suicide or accidental explosion was extraordinarily common. For a few interesting cases, see *Al'manakh*, pp. 55, 114-116, 161-162; *Burevestnik*, No. 3, 30 September 1906, pp. 14-16; and No. 9, February 1908, pp. 20-23. An incident in London's Greenwich Park in 1894, strikingly similar to Striga's death, provided Joseph Conrad with material for his novel, *The Secret Agent*.

a report to an international congress of anarchists held in 1907.[109] Stolypin's military tribunals awaited those terrorists who managed to survive the bullets of the police and their own defective bombs. Hundreds of young men and women, many of them still in their teens, were summarily brought to trial and frequently sentenced to death or murdered by their jailers.[110] At the trials, it was common for anarchist defendants to deliver impassioned speeches upholding their cause. A *Chernoznamenets* in Vilna, arrested for carrying explosives, endeavored to convince his audience that anarchy was not, as its traducers held, tantamount to sheer chaos: "Our enemies equate anarchy with disorder. No! Anarchy is the highest order, the highest harmony. It is life without authority. Once we have dealt with the enemies with whom we are struggling, we shall have a commune—life will be social, fraternal, and just."[111] In Kiev, another typical case was that of a Ukrainian peasant girl named Matrena Prisiazhniuk, an Anarchist-Individualist convicted of taking part in a raid on a sugar factory, and of murdering a priest and attempting to kill a district police officer. After the military court pronounced the death sentence, the condemned girl was allowed to make her last remarks. "I am an Anarchist-Individualist," she began. "My ideal is the free development of the individual personality in the broadest sense of the word, and the overthrow of slavery in all its forms." She told of the poverty and hunger in her native village, "moans, suffering, and blood all around." Bourgeois morality, "official and cold—purely commercial," was the cause. Then, in a brief peroration, the girl exalted her approaching death and the deaths of two fellow anarchists convicted with her: "Proudly and bravely we shall mount the scaffold, casting a look of defiance at you. Our death, like a hot flame, will ignite many hearts. We are dying as victors. Forward, then! Our death is our triumph!"[112] Prisiazhniuk's

[109] *Burevestnik*, No. 8, p. 11.

[110] In 1906, for example, six members of the International Group in Riga were tried and executed. All were teen-agers. *Listki "Khleb i Volia,"* No. 3, 28 November 1906, p. 4.

[111] *Burevestnik*, No. 1, p. 8.

[112] *Rech' Matreny Prisiazhniuka v Kievskom voenno-okruzhnom sude 19-go iiulia 1908 goda* (New York, 1916); *Golos Truda* (New York), 1 March 1913, pp. 9-11. Also see Prisiazhniuk's letters from Kiev prison, in *Golos Ssyl'nykh i Zakliuchennykh Russkikh Anarkhistov*, No. 2, October 1914, pp. 11-12.

vision never came to pass, however, for she escaped her execu-
tioner by taking cyanide capsules smuggled into her cell after
the trial.[113]

Sometimes the defendants expressed their contempt for the
court by scornful silence or by loud and furious outbursts.
When Ignatii Muzil (Nikolai Rogdaev's brother) was brought
to trial—he was seized in the woods near Nizhnii Novgorod
with anarchist literature in his possession—he refused to recognize the court or to stand up before his questioners.[114] Similarly, a doomed terrorist in Odessa named Lev Aleshker branded
his trial a "farce" and excoriated the judges who had condemned him. "You yourselves should be sitting on the bench
of the accused," he exclaimed. "Down with all of you! Vil-
lainous hangmen! Long live anarchy!"[115] While awaiting his
execution, Aleshker drafted an eloquent testament, which prophesied the coming of the anarchist Golden Age:

> Slavery, poverty, weakness, and ignorance—the eternal fet-
> ters of man—will be broken. Man will be at the center of
> nature. The earth and its products will serve everyone duti-
> fully. Weapons will cease to be a measure of strength and
> gold a measure of wealth; the strong will be those who are
> bold and daring in the conquest of nature, and riches will
> be the things that are useful. Such a world is called "An-
> archy." It will have no castles, no place for masters and
> slaves. Life will be open to all. Everyone will take what he
> needs—this is the anarchist ideal. And when it comes about,
> men will live wisely and well. The masses must take part in
> the construction of this paradise on earth.[116]

The most spectacular of the anarchist trials involved the
Odessa *bezmotivniki* who bombed the Café Libman in December 1905, and the *Beznachalie* group of St. Petersburg, rounded

[113] Edgar Khorn, the young Anarchist-Communist who delivered the
poison, was apprehended and brought to justice. *Anarkhist*, No. 4, September 1909, p. 29.

[114] *Listki "Khleb i Volia,"* No. 4, 17 December 1906, p. 7; *Burevestnik*, No. 5, 30 April 1907, p. 15.

[115] *Al'manakh*, p. 134. Compare the courtroom scenes in Riga (*Listki
"Khleb i Volia,"* No. 3, p. 4); Nizhnii Novgorod (*Burevestnik*, No. 6-7,
pp. 30-31); Kiev (*Anarkhist*, No. 3, May 1909); and Moscow (*Burevestnik*, No. 13, pp. 21-22).

[116] *Mikhailu Bakuninu*, p. 251.

up by the police in 1906. Five young men and women were taken to court in the Libman affair. (A sixth participant, N. M. Erdelevskii, had been captured after wounding four policemen, but succeeded in escaping to Switzerland, where he helped found a *Chernoe Znamia* circle known as *Buntar'*—The Mutineer.)[117] All five were convicted in short order, three of them receiving the death penalty. Moisei Mets, twenty-one years old and a joiner by trade, refused to acknowledge any criminal guilt, though he readily admitted throwing a bomb into the café "with the aim of killing the exploiters there."[118] Mets told the court that his group demanded nothing less than the complete leveling of the existing social system. No partial reforms would do, but only "the final annihilation of eternal slavery and exploitation." The bourgeoisie, no doubt, would dance on his grave, Mets went on, but the *bezmotivniki* were only the first swallows of the approaching spring. There would be others, he declared, who would take away "your privileges and idleness, your luxuries and authority. Death and destruction to the whole bourgeois order! Hail the revolutionary class struggle of the oppressed! Long live anarchism and communism!"[119] Two weeks after the trial, Mets went to the gallows, together with two of his comrades, an eighteen-year-old boy and a girl of twenty-two.[120]

[117] One issue of a journal entitled *Buntar'* was published by the *Chernoe Znamia* exiles in Paris in December 1906, and four numbers appeared in Geneva in 1908-1909. A single number of another journal, *Chernoe Znamia*, was printed in Geneva in December 1905.

[118] *Burevestnik*, No. 5, p. 13.

[119] *Ibid.*, p. 14. The courtroom statements of the Russian terrorists often resembled the famous trial speech of the French "propagandist by the deed," Émile Henry, which had been translated into Russian by the Geneva Group of Anarchists and published by Émile Held in 1898: *Rech' Emilia Anri pered sudom*. A translation also appeared in *Vol'naia Volia*, 1903, No. 2.

[120] *Listki "Khleb i Volia,"* No. 3, p. 4; No. 4, p. 7. According to a tabulation made by an anarchist prisoner in the Odessa jail, 167 anarchists and anarchist "sympathizers" were tried in Odessa during 1906-1907. This figure included 12 Anarcho-Syndicalists, 94 *Chernoznamentsy*, 51 anarchist sympathizers, 5 members of the SR Fighting Union, and 5 members of the Anarchist Red Cross, an organization that gave aid to political prisoners and exiles. The list contains a fairly equal proportion of Russian, Ukrainian, and Jewish names. The ages were mostly nineteen to twenty-two. Of those tried, 28 were executed and 5 escaped from jail (Olga Taratuta was among them). *Burevestnik*, No. 10-11, March-April 1908, pp. 23-24. From the sketchy data available (the anarchists,

The other two defendants received long jail terms. The oldest of the group, Olga Taratuta, about thirty-five years of age, had joined the Social Democratic party in Ekaterinoslav when it was formed in 1898, then subsequently transferred her loyalty to the anarchist camp. Sentenced to seventeen years in prison, Taratuta broke out of the Odessa jail and fled to Geneva, where she entered Erdelevskii's *Buntar'* association. But the sedentary life of an émigrée proved uncongenial to Taratuta's dynamic temperament, and she soon returned to the active struggle inside Russia. Taratuta became a member of the Anarchist-Communist "battle detachment" in her native Ekaterinoslav, but was arrested in 1908 and sentenced to a long term of penal servitude. This time she did not escape.[121]

On 13 November 1906, the very day that the three Odessa *bezmotivniki* were hanged, the *Beznachalie* group stood trial in the capital. The defendants, charged with possessing explosives and "belonging to a criminal society," refused to answer any questions put to them by the magistrates. Aleksandr Kolosov declared that the court, since it obviously had made its decision in advance of the proceedings, should simply pronounce sentence so that he and his friends could thank the judges and quietly depart. Bidbei, the group's sardonic leader, would not rise when the chief magistrate called his name, explaining that he never talked to anyone "with whom he was not personally acquainted."[122] The accused were thereupon removed from the courtroom. Bidbei was sentenced to 15 years in prison. Kolosov, who received the same penalty, committed suicide 3 years later, throwing himself down a well in a Siberian penal colony.[123]

---

of course, issued no "party cards" and generally shunned formal organizational machinery), there appear to have been about 5,000 active anarchists in the Russian Empire at the peak of the movement (1905-1907), as well as thousands of sympathizers, who regularly read anarchist literature and closely followed the movement's activities without taking a direct part in them.

[121] Anisimov, *Katorga i Ssylka*, 1932, No. 10, pp. 129-176; *Anarkhist*, No. 5, March 1910, p. 24. The leaders of the Ekaterinoslav "battle detachment," Andrei Shtokman and Sergei Borisov, were hanged.

[122] *Listki "Khleb i Volia,"* No. 4, 13 December 1906, p. 8; Genkin, *Byloe*, 1918, No. 9, p. 179; *Po tiur'mam i etapam*, p. 297; Nomad, *Dreamers, Dynamiters, and Demagogues*, p. 78. Romanov-Bidbei was tried under another pseudonym, Ter-Aganesov.

[123] Genkin, *Byloe*, 1918, No. 9, p. 183.

Boris Speranskii received a lesser sentence of 10 years because of his youth (he was then twenty). He made an unsuccessful attempt to escape from the Schlüsselburg fortress, and 10 more years were added to his period of confinement. Clandestine reports from Schlüsselburg in 1908 stated that Speranskii was beaten for insulting a jailer and, on another occasion, was shot in both legs by a prison guard.[124] Of his ultimate destiny, nothing is known.

It remains to describe the fate of "Tolstoy" Rostovtsev and Vladimir Ushakov. Feigning insanity while immured in the Peter-Paul fortress, Rostovtsev was removed to a prison hospital, from which he escaped to safety in the West, just as Kropotkin had done 30 years before. Unfortunately, Rostovtsev had not left his terroristic proclivities behind in Russia. He tried to hold up a bank in Montreux, but succeeded only in killing several innocent bystanders, and had to be rescued from a lynch mob by the Swiss police. Imprisoned in Lausanne, he poured kerosene over his body and burned himself alive.[125] Ushakov, it will be recalled, had evaded the police net in St. Petersburg and had found temporary sanctuary in Lvov. Before long, he returned to Russia, first joining the Ekaterinoslav "battle detachment," then moving on to the Crimea. Captured during the "expropriation" of a bank in Yalta, Ushakov was taken to a prison in Sevastopol. He tried to escape, but as the police closed in, he put a pistol to his head and blew out his brains.[126]

During the period of "pacification" that followed the 1905 Revolution, many other well-known anarchists were sentenced to long terms in prison or in forced labor camps. Among them were Lazar Gershkovich and Daniil Novomirskii, the leaders of the anarchist movement in Odessa,[127] and German Sandomirskii of the Kiev Anarchist-Communist organization.[128] Vladimir

[124] *Burevestnik*, No. 13, October 1908, p. 22; No. 14, January 1909, pp. 18-20.

[125] "Nezavisimaia Sotsialisticheskaia Mysl'," Fleshin Archive; Genkin, *Byloe*, 1918, No. 9, pp. 182-183; *Po tiur'mam i etapam*, pp. 300-301.

[126] *Burevestnik*, No. 6-7, September-October 1907, pp. 29-30.

[127] *Listki "Khleb i Volia,"* No. 12, 12 April 1907, p. 5; *Buntar'*, No. 1, 1 December 1906, p. 31. Eight policemen were killed or seriously injured when one of them lit a match during the raid on Gershkovich's bomb laboratory. *Mikhailu Bakuninu*, pp. 255-256.

[128] *Burevestnik*, No. 16, May 1909, p. 27; *Anarkhist*, No. 3, May 1909, pp. 28-32.

Zabrezhnev and Vladimir Barmash, key figures in the Moscow movement, were arrested and imprisoned, but both managed to escape.[129] Zabrezhnev eventually found his way to Kropotkin's circle in London, where a different sort of life awaited him, a life without the dangers and derring-do of the Moscow underground, but one which nevertheless demanded tireless effort and great fortitude. It was by now apparent that 1905 had been just a prelude after all, that it was necessary to lay the groundwork for the *true* social revolution yet to come.

[129] *Al'manakh*, p. 48; Knizhnik, *Krasnaia Letopis'*, 1922, No. 4, pp. 34-35; *Buntar'*, No. 1, p. 29; *Burevestnik*, No. 13, pp. 21-22.

3 · THE SYNDICALISTS

Let every conscientious man ask himself this question: Is he ready? Is he so clear in his mind about the new organization towards which we are moving, through the medium of those vague general ideas of collective property and social solidarity? Does he know the process—apart from sheer destruction—which will accomplish the transformation of old forms into new ones?

ALEXANDER HERZEN

A second issue, closely related to the vexed question of terrorism, arose in 1905 and greatly accentuated the divisions already discernible within the anarchist movement. A class of industrial workers had been emerging in urban Russia ever since the emancipation of the serfs. During the last decade of the century alone, the number of factory workers had nearly doubled, the figure surpassing three million by the outbreak of the revolution. What attitude were the anarchists to adopt towards the infant labor movement?

The *Beznachalie* and *Chernoe Znamia* groups, for their part, were instinctively hostile to large-scale organizations of any sort and showed little patience for the wearisome distribution of pamphlets and manifestoes in the factories, except for propaganda designed to incite the workers to violence against their employers or to signal an immediate armed uprising. Rejecting the incipient trade unions as reformist institutions which only "prolonged the agony of the dying enemy" through "a series of partial victories,"[1] they tended to rely on their own militant bands as the instruments to wreck the tsarist regime. The *Khlebovol'tsy* and Anarcho-Syndicalists, on the other hand, condemned the terrorists for dissipating their forces in hit-and-run raids on the privileged classes; considering organized labor a powerful engine of revolt, they became champions of the syndicalist cause.

The doctrine of revolutionary syndicalism as it evolved in France during the 1890's was a curious blend of anarchism,

[1] *Mikhailu Bakuninu*, pp. 327-328.

Marxism, and trade unionism. From Proudhon and Bakunin, the makers of the anarchist tradition, the French syndicalists inherited an overpowering hatred of the centralized state, a sharp distrust of politicians, and a rudimentary conception of workers' control in industry. As early as the 1860's and 1870's, the followers of Proudhon and Bakunin in the First International were proposing the formation of workers' councils designed both as the weapon of class struggle against the capitalists and as the structural basis of the future libertarian society.[2] This idea was further developed by Fernand Pelloutier, a high-minded young intellectual with strong anarchist sympathies, who became the outstanding figure in the French syndicalist movement during its formative years. During the early nineties, the notorious wave of bombthrowing in Paris created widespread disillusionment with the tactics of terrorism, causing large numbers of French anarchists to enter the workers' unions. Thus imbued with a strong anarchist flavor, the majority of unions, by the end of the century, had come to regard the state with hostile eyes and to reject the conquest of political power—whether by revolutionary or parliamentary methods—as inimical to their true interests. Instead, they looked forward to a social revolution which would destroy the capitalist system and inaugurate a stateless society in which the economy would be managed by a general confederation of labor unions.

The second source of syndicalist ideas, comparable in importance to the anarchist tradition, was the legacy of Karl Marx, in particular his doctrine of class struggle. Like Marx, the proponents of syndicalism pinned their hopes of eliminating capitalism on the working class, and placed class conflict at the very center of social relationships. As they saw it, producers were pitted against parasites in a relentless battle that would ultimately end in the annihilation of the bourgeois world. The class struggle lent purpose to the otherwise dismal lives of the factory workers; it sharpened their awareness of being exploited and cemented their revolutionary solidarity. Conceiving the doctrine of class warfare to be the very essence of Marxism, the syndicalists deplored the manner in which Marx's revolu-

---

[2] James Guillaume, *L'Internationale: documents et souvenirs (1864-1878)* (4 vols., Paris, 1905-1910), I, 205; Rudolf Rocker, *Anarcho-Syndicalism* (London, 1938), pp. 71-72.

tionary teachings were being compromised by the reformists and revisionists of European socialism, who sought to alleviate social antagonisms through the procedures of parliamentary democracy.

Trade-unionism, the third wellspring of syndicalist concepts and techniques, resembled Marxism in treating the individual worker as a member of a class of producers, as an economic rather than a political animal. Accordingly, the workman's principal source of strength lay in the organized solidarity of his class. But where Marx urged the working class to unite for the political purpose of seizing the state apparatus, the "pure" trade unionists chose to concentrate on immediate economic objectives. The workers were to rely on their own power as producers, employing direct economic action to attain material benefits. Direct action usually took the form of strikes, demonstrations, boycotts, and sabotage. The last included "bad work for bad pay," loafing on the job, damaging machinery and equipment, and the literal observance of petty rules and work specifications; however, violence against foremen, engineers, and directors was generally frowned upon.

Syndicalism—simply the French word for trade unionism—assigned the labor unions (*syndicats*) a predominant role in the lives of the workingmen. Through direct action against the employers, the unions would obtain higher pay, shorter hours, and better working conditions. Legalized in France during the 1880's, the *syndicats* grouped together all the workmen of a city or district according to their trade. The local *syndicats*, in turn, were linked together in national federations, and, finally, the General Confederation of Labor (CGT), founded in 1895, embraced all the *syndicats* and their federations. After 1902, the CGT encompassed the *bourses du travail* as well. Organized along geographic rather than industrial lines, the *bourses* were local labor councils serving all the trade unions of a given area. They acted as placement bureaus, social clubs, statistical centers (gathering information on wages and employment), and cultural centers, equipped with libraries and offering evening vocational courses to train the workers for their future role as managers and technicians.

Material improvements, however, scarcely represented the ultimate goal of the revolutionary syndicalist movement in France.

Labor unions were not organized merely to achieve partial reforms or for the benevolent purpose of social reconciliation, but to combat a class enemy. Convinced that the capitalist system faced imminent collapse, the union leaders dismissed such evolutionary tactics as collective bargaining or agitation for factory legislation on the grounds that they implied the acceptance of the existing order. The pure "economism" of the reformist unions, which confined their efforts to extracting more and more material benefits from the owners, would never succeed in doing away with the entrenched system of exploitation. Such methods only dulled the edge of the class struggle. The true value of bread and butter demands, as far as the partisans of revolutionary syndicalism were concerned, lay in strengthening the position of the workingmen at the expense of their masters. The day-to-day economic struggle served to stimulate the spirit of militancy in the workers and to train them for the final showdown with capitalism and the state. Every local strike, every boycott, and every act of sabotage helped prepare the working class for the climax of direct action—the general strike.

The general strike was the supreme act of the class struggle, the dramatic instrument for wrecking the capitalist system. Beyond the mere elevation of living standards, it was the mission of the unions to become the vehicles of social revolution as well as the basic cells of the ensuing stateless society. No armed insurrection or political *coup* would be necessary. The entire proletariat would simply lay down its tools and leave the factories, thereby bringing the economy to a halt and forcing the bourgeoisie to capitulate. The spectacle of millions of workers cooperating in a universal cessation of labor would paralyze the industrialists' will to resist. Thereupon, the unions would seize the means of production and proceed to run the economy.

In the new society, the labor unions were to hold a preponderant position, supplanting both the market economy and the machinery of government. The tools of production were to become the common property of all the people, insofar as any concept of ownership could still be said to apply. In practice, the various industries would fall under the direct control of the appropriate labor unions. The CGT was to assume the responsibility of coordinating economic matters on a national scale, as well as handling public affairs and generally smoothing the operation of the entire federal system.[3]

Two of the original members of Kropotkin's *Khleb i Volia* group, Maria Korn and Gogeliia-Orgeiani, were among the earliest Russian proponents of the syndicalist creed. As émigrés in Geneva and Paris, they derived their ideas in great measure from their observation of the French model. In 1903, the first number of *Khleb i Volia* extolled the general strike as a "potent weapon" in the hands of the working class;[4] the next issue hailed the July disturbances in Baku as the first instance of a general strike in Russian history.[5] At the height of the 1905 Revolution, the journal explicitly endorsed "revolutionary syndicalism."[6] Maria Korn remarked that as recently as the beginning of the century there had been no Russian word for "sabotage," and that a Russian who used the expression "general strike" would have seemed to be speaking "in some strange, incomprehensible language."[7] But the great strikes in the south in 1903 and the general strike of October 1905 had radically altered the situation. According to Korn, Russia was beginning to learn from the revolutionary *syndicats* in France, which had been attracting the "best, most energetic, youngest, and freshest forces" of the anarchist camp.[8] Orgeiani also invoked the French example as he proposed the establishment in Russia of workers' unions, *bourses du travail* (he aptly defined a *bourse* as "a union of local unions"), and ultimately a general confederation of labor

[3] For able discussions of French syndicalism, see Louis Levine, *Syndicalism in France* (2nd edn., New York, 1914); Val R. Lorwin, *The French Labor Movement* (Cambridge, Mass., 1954), pp. 15-46; and Paul Louis, *Histoire du mouvement syndical en France* (2 vols., Paris, 1947-1948), I, 129-212.

[4] *Khleb i Volia*, No. 1, August 1903, p. 5.

[5] *Ibid.*, No. 2, September 1903, pp. 1-3. Cf. *ibid.*, No. 7, February 1904, pp. 1-4.

[6] *Ibid.*, No. 23, October 1905, pp. 1-3.

[7] M. Korn, *Revoliutsionnyi sindikalizm i anarkhizm; Bor'ba s kapitalom i vlast'iu* (Petrograd and Moscow, 1920), pp. 10n, 116. Cf. M. Korn, "Vseobshchaia stachka," *Listki "Khleb i Volia,"* No. 7, 25 January 1907, pp. 1-4; and Korn, *Bor'ba s kapitalom i vlast'iu; Nashi spornye voprosy* (London, 1912).

[8] M. Korn, "Na sovremennye temy," *Khleb i Volia* (Paris), No. 1, March 1909, p. 30. Cf. Korn, "Chto takoe nash sindikalizm?," *Rabochii Mir*, No. 1, February 1914, pp. 3-5; and *Listki "Khleb i Volia,"* No. 1, 30 October 1906, p. 8.

organizations along the lines of the CGT.[9] Such a framework for Russian labor, he believed, would not merely replace the capitalist economy and the autocratic state, but would revolutionize the psychological and moral world of the workers into the bargain. The trade unions, he said, would provide a *"milieu libre* in which, psychologically, a new world is born and which creates the psychological conditions for a new life."[10]

D. I. Novomirskii, until his arrest the leading syndicalist inside Russia, similarly placed the labor movement at the focus of anarchist efforts. From his vantage point in Odessa, however, he recognized that the French model would have to be adapted to suit Russian conditions:

What is to be done [he asked in 1907] once capitalism and the state are destroyed? When and how will the transition to the future occur? What is to be done right now? Nothing concrete can be said, even if we attempt to apply in this connection the idea of the general strike. Our literature is not geared to specific *Russian* propaganda and to *Russian* conditions, and it therefore proves to be too abstract for the workers.[11]

Nonetheless, Novomirskii's own syndicalist theories adhered very closely to the French prototype: the trade unions were to carry on the daily economic struggle while preparing the working class for the social revolution, after which the unions would become "the cells of the future workers' society."[12] No-

[9] K. Orgeiani, "Organizatsionnyi printsip revoliutsionnogo sindikalizma i anarkhizm," *Burevestnik,* No. 14, January 1909, pp. 2-7.

[10] K. Orgeiani, "O rabochikh soiuzakh," *Listki "Khleb i Volia,"* No. 14, 10 May 1907, pp. 2-4. This article was one of a series later collected as a pamphlet with the same title, *O rabochikh soiuzakh* (London, 1907). Also see Orgeiani's small book, *Kak i iz chego razvilsia Revoliutsionnyi Sindikalizm* (n.p. [London], 1909), which has an interesting preface by Kropotkin.

[11] D. N. (Novomirskii), "Pis'mo iz Rossii," *Listki "Khleb i Volia,"* No. 17, 21 June 1907, pp. 4-5. Novomirskii's group in Odessa adopted the name "Anarcho-Syndicalists" rather than the French term "revolutionary syndicalists" partly to emphasize their distinctly Russian character, partly to indicate that their members were all *anarchists* (many of the revolutionary syndicalists in France had Marxist, Blanquist, and other radical affiliations), and partly to distinguish themselves from the Anarchist-*Communists*, who were not as exclusively concerned with the labor movement as they were.

[12] Novomirskii, *Iz programmy sindikal'nogo anarkhizma*, p. 191.

vomirskii also adopted from the French syndicalists the notion that a conscious minority of farsighted workmen would be needed to galvanize the inert masses into action. Filling the role of the "revolutionary minority," Novomirskii's Anarcho-Syndicalists would not attempt to take command of their brother workers, but would serve only as "pathfinders" in the revolutionary struggle.[13] Their immediate task was to prevent the trade unions from becoming subsidiary organs of the political parties. It was essential for anarchist workers to establish clandestine cells to combat socialist "opportunism" within the existing unions. At the same time, in order to attract the unorganized and uncommitted elements of the working class, the anarchists were to form their own unions and federate them into a Revolutionary All-Russian Union of Labor, Novomirskii's version of the CGT.[14]

Between 1905 and 1907, Novomirskii's South Russian Group of Anarcho-Syndicalists attracted a considerable number of workers in the large cities of the Ukraine and New Russia, as well as intellectuals from the Social Democrats, SR's, and Anarchist-Communists. Though his claim of 5,000 adherents is highly exaggerated,[15] Novomirskii's syndicalist followers included, besides factory workers, a number of seamen and stevedores of the Odessa port districts, and bakers and tailors in Ekaterinoslav.[16] His group forged links with anarchist circles in Moscow and elsewhere, set up an "organizational commission" to coordinate the activities of the local units, and recruited a "battle detachment" to obtain funds for the movement. "I am convinced," remarked Iuda Roshchin, "that God, if he existed, must be a syndicalist—otherwise Novomirskii would not have enjoyed such great success."[17]

Apart from the Anarcho-Syndicalists, who were concentrated largely in the south, the Anarchist-Communists of the *Khleb i Volia* school also made headway in the blossoming Russian labor movement. In Moscow, anarchist agitators distrib-

[13] *Novyi Mir*, No. 1, 15 October 1905, pp. 4, 10.
[14] Novomirskii, *Iz programmy sindikal'nogo anarkhizma*, pp. 178-191; *Listki "Khleb i Volia,"* No. 5, 28 December 1906, p. 9.
[15] *Mikhailu Bakuninu*, p. 264.
[16] *Ibid.*, pp. 252ff; Gorev, *Anarkhizm v Rossii*, pp. 64-66; *Obshchestvennoe dvizhenie v Rossii*, III, 477.
[17] *Mikhailu Bakuninu*, p. 264.

uted leaflets in the factories of the Zamoskvorechie and Presnia districts and in the mills of the nearby textile towns; anarchist cells in such large enterprises as the Tsindel (Zündel) Textile Factory and the Electric Power Station organized a number of strikes and demonstrations; and the *Svobodnaia Kommuna* group, loosely associated with Novomirskii's movement despite the fact that it was an Anarchist-Communist organization, drew a substantial following within the metal workers' union as well as a lesser following among the typographers.[18] In April 1907, a Conference of Anarchist-Communist Groups in the Urals, largely sympathetic to the *Khleb i Volia* position, called for the creation of "illegal inter-party unions" and, simultaneously, for anarchist participation in the existing trade unions in order to counteract the corrupting influence of the socialist "opportunists."[19] Meanwhile, in North America, thousands of emigrants were being recruited by the Anarcho-Syndicalist Union of Russian Workers of the United States and Canada.

The Russian syndicalists both at home and in exile were enormously impressed by the tendency of the industrial workers towards self-organization, in spite of the government's unbending opposition. Clandestine unions had already been leading a precarious existence in Russia for some 30 years, in defiance of the legal ban against them, and strike committees had appeared during the great Petersburg textile strikes of 1896 and 1897. In 1903, the government permitted the formation of councils of elders (*sovety starost*) in industrial enterprises, and even though the election of elders was subject to confirmation by the employers, their mere existence constituted an important stage in the evolution of Russian workers' organizations. Many of the councils, in fact, became true representatives of labor during the heady days of 1905. The revolution also witnessed the spontaneous formation of workers' committees in the factories and workshops. These committees played a vital role in the creation of the soviets of workers' deputies, first in the textile center of Ivanovo-Voznesensk and later in St. Petersburg and other cities. The trade unions likewise made remarkable

[18] *Burevestnik*, No. 10-11, March-April 1908, pp. 28-30; *Al'manakh*, pp. 47-59; *Buntar'*, No. 1, 1 December 1906, p. 29.
[19] *Listki "Khleb i Volia*," No. 18, July 1907, p. 6.

progress in 1905, and were finally legalized in March of the following year.[20]

The revolutionary atmosphere in Russia fostered a radical spirit in these workers' organizations, more akin to the revolutionary syndicalism of France or Italy than to the evolutionary trade unionism prevalent in England or Germany. In 1905, the Russian labor movement was still weak and undisciplined, riven by factionalism and by mistrust between the manual workers and the intellectuals. Without a tradition of parliamentary democracy or of legal unionism, the Russian workers expected very little from either the state or the industrialists, and turned to the devices of direct action exercised through local militant committees. The heavy concentration of labor in large enterprises seems to have encouraged rather than hindered the growth of small workers' committees, since the bigger industrial concerns were commonly divided into numerous workshops, which proved fertile soil for radical action groups.

The events of 1905 confirmed the belief of many syndicalists in the spontaneous generation of local cooperative institutions, above all during times of acute crisis. There were those, no doubt, who saw the soviets, trade unions, and factory committees in a Kropotkinian light, as the modern expression of man's natural propensity towards mutual aid, traceable to the tribal councils and village assemblies of a more primitive age. But the partisans of syndicalism went beyond Kropotkin by reconciling the principle of mutual assistance with the Marxian doctrine of class struggle. For the syndicalists, mutual aid did not embrace humanity as a whole, but existed only within the ranks of a single class, the proletariat, enhancing its solidarity in the battle with the manufacturers. The various workers' organizations, they insisted, were combat units, not arbitration boards designed to alleviate class conflict, as liberals and reformists believed. The syndicalists regarded the soviets, for instance, as admirable versions of the *bourses du travail*, but with a revolu-

[20] Peterburzhets, *Ocherk peterburzhskogo rabochego dvizheniia 90-kh godov* (London, 1902), pp. 41-42, 61-62; A.M. Pankratova, *Fabzavkomy v Rossii v bor'be za sotsialisticheskuiu fabriku* (Moscow, 1923), pp. 94-171; *Fabzavkomy i profsoiuzy* (Moscow, 1925), pp. 21-22; Ia. Fin, *Fabrichno-zavodskie komitety v Rossii* (Moscow, 1925), p. 5; Oskar Anweiler, *Die Rätebewegung in Russland, 1905-1921* (Leiden, 1958), pp. 27-28, 45-49.

tionary function added to suit Russian conditions.[21] Open to all leftist workers regardless of specific political affiliation, the soviets were to act as nonpartisan labor councils improvised "from below" on the district and city levels with the aim of bringing down the old regime. This syndicalist conception of the soviets as nonpolitical and non-ideological battle stations of the working class was anathema to the Russian Social Democrats. Opposed to the ultra-extremism of the anti-syndicalists in the anarchist camp, and fearful of the dangerous competition of the pro-syndicalists, the socialists strove to exclude both groups from the soviets, trade unions, and workers' committees. In November 1905, after the general strike had begun to subside, the executive committee of the Petersburg Soviet voted to bar all anarchists from entering its organization;[22] this action increased the determination of the Russian syndicalists to form their own anarchist unions separate from the existing institutions of labor, contrary to the nonparty and non-ideological beliefs of the French syndicalists.

Compared with the enthusiasm of Korn and Orgeiani for the syndicalist cause, Kropotkin's attitude was at best lukewarm. He was chary of the socialist-dominated soviets and recommended anarchist participation in workers' organizations only so long as they remained nonparty vehicles of popular rebellion. An Anarchist-Communist group in Kharkov, sympathetic to Kropotkin's point of view, declared that if the soviets were to fall under the political control of the socialists, they would never fulfill their true function as "battle organizations" rallying the toilers for "the insurrectionary general strike."[23] Dominated by phrasemongering intellectuals, the revolutionary soviets would inevitably degenerate into parliamentary debating societies. As for the workers' unions, Kropotkin did not share the enchantment of his young associates, but offered only qualified support. He acknowledged that the unions were "natural organs for the direct struggle with capitalism and for the composition of the future order," and also that the general strike was "a powerful

[21] The pro-syndicalists of *Khleb i Volia* also likened the 1905 Petersburg Soviet—as a nonparty mass organization—to the central committee of the Paris Commune of 1871. *Listki "Khleb i Volia,"* No. 2, 14 November 1906, p. 5.

[22] Gorev, *Anarkhizm v Rossii*, p. 85.

[23] *Burevestnik*, No. 4, 30 October 1906, p. 13.

weapon of struggle."[24] At the same time, however, he criticized the syndicalists, as he had been criticizing the Marxists, for thinking solely in terms of the industrial proletariat to the neglect of the peasantry and its needs. Still only a small minority in predominantly rural Russia, the working class could not by itself carry out the social revolution, nor could the trade unions become the nuclei of the anarchist commonwealth.[25] In Kropotkin's estimation, the Anarchist-*Communist* vision of the future was far broader than that of the Anarcho-Syndicalists, aiming as it did at an integrated society in which all healthy aspects of human life could flourish.

To a certain extent, Kropotkin might also have been troubled by the syndicalist belief in a "conscious minority" whose function was to arouse the enthusiasm of the languid multitudes. The idea of a revolutionary vanguard—even if composed exclusively of manual laborers—had the odor of Jacobinism, Kropotkin's *bête noire*, and bore too close a resemblance to the élitist theory of Bolshevism that Lenin was elaborating at that time. It was dangerous to rely too heavily on the workers' unions for still another reason: they might seek an accommodation with the bourgeois world or, even worse, fall prey to the ambitious socialist intellectuals. The wise course, therefore, was to establish purely anarchist unions or to join only nonparty unions, with the intention of winning them over to the anarchist cause. At all events, the anarchists were adjured to keep out of any union that already had adopted a socialist platform.[26]

The acrimonious dispute over the relationship between anarchism and syndicalism was by no means confined to Russia. Indeed, it was threatening to split the anarchist movement throughout Europe into two hostile camps. The issue came to a head at an International Congress of Anarchists held in

[24] Kropotkin, ed., *Russkaia revoliutsiia i anarkhizm*, pp. 12-13.
[25] *Ibid.*, p. 14.
[26] *Listki "Khleb i Volia,"* No. 2, 14 November 1906, p. 5. The *Khleb i Volia* group discussed the question of syndicalism at two meetings in London (December 1904 and October 1906) and one in Paris (September 1905). For reports of these conferences, see Kropotkin, ed., *Russkaia revoliutsiia i anarkhizm*; Korn, *Revoliutsionnyi sindikalizm i anarkhizm; Bor'ba s kapitalom i vlast'iu;* Korn, *Revoliutsionnyi sindikalizm i sotsialisticheskie partii* (London, 1907); and *Listki "Khleb i Volia,"* No. 1, 30 October 1906, pp. 6-9.

Amsterdam during the summer of 1907.[27] The gathering heard
a lively debate between Pierre Monatte, a young French exponent of revolutionary syndicalism, and the dedicated Italian
Anarchist-Communist Errico Malatesta. Monatte presented an
extreme interpretation of labor's place in human affairs. Echoing the Charter of Amiens, a succinct statement of the syndicalist position adopted by the CGT the previous year,[28] he
assigned the trade unions the task of transforming the bourgeois order into a workers' paradise; the unions, after waging
the struggle to overthrow capitalism and the state, were to become the phalanxes of social reorganization in a world inherited by the industrial workers.[29]

In an eloquent rebuttal, Malatesta hinted strongly that the
syndicalist preoccupation with the proletariat smacked of narrow Marxism. "The fundamental error of Monatte and of
all the revolutionary syndicalists," he declared, "proceeds, in
my opinion, from a much too simplified conception of the
class struggle."[30] Malatesta reminded his audience that they
were anarchists first and foremost. As such, their goal was the
emancipation of all humanity, not of a single class alone. The
fight for liberation was the work of the abused millions from
every walk of life. It was folly, Malatesta continued, to regard
the general strike as a "panacea," precluding the necessity of
an armed rebellion of all the underprivileged and oppressed.
The bourgeoisie had accumulated large stores of food and
other necessities, but the proletariat was compelled to rely
entirely on its labor for survival. How then could the workers,
merely by folding their arms, hope to bring the employers to
their knees? Malatesta admonished the delegates to shake off
their naive fascination with the labor movement, which was
leading them to attribute extraordinary powers to the working

[27] Nikolai Rogdaev and Vladimir Zabrezhnev were among the five
Russian delegates to the Amsterdam Congress. Representing the Jewish
Anarchist Federation of London was Alexander Schapiro, who was later
to play a major part in the Russian anarchist movement.

[28] The Charter of Amiens is in Louis, *Histoire du mouvement syndical*,
I, 262-263.

[29] *Congrès anarchiste tenu à Amsterdam Août 1907* (Paris, 1908), pp.
62-71; N. Rogdaev, *Internatsional'nyi kongress anarkhistov v Amsterdame* (n.p., 1907), pp. 20-21.

[30] *Congrès anarchiste*, p. 81.

class.[31] He cautioned them against entering unions infested with socialist politicians, lest they lose sight of the ultimate goal of a classless society. Fearful that syndicalism would sink into the morass of trade-unionist reformism and "bureaucratism,"[32] Malatesta warned his anarchist comrades not to become union officials. Should they ignore this advice, he said, they would find themselves pursuing their own selfish interests, and then "Goodbye anarchism!"[33] A year and a half later, Malatesta's sympathizers completely dismissed the notion that the trade unions could act as the basic cells of the new society; the unions, as "the offspring of the capitalist system,"[34] were fated to be swept away by the social revolution.

Among the large number of Russians who shared Malatesta's anti-syndicalist views, the most trenchant critic was Abram Solomonovich Grossman, a *Chernoznamenets* known in the anarchist movement as "Aleksandr." A former Socialist Revolutionary, Grossman had spent two years in prison before the outbreak of the 1905 Revolution. After his release, he went to Paris, where he became a regular contributor to the anarchist journal *Burevestnik* (The Stormy Petrel), using the signature of "A—" (presumably for "Aleksandr"). In 1907, Grossman returned to Russia and became a leader of the Anarchist-Communist "battle detachment" in Ekaterinoslav. The following February he was cornered by the gendarmes in the Kiev railway station and shot to death while resisting arrest.[35]

In a series of articles published in *Burevestnik* in 1906 and 1907, Grossman made an unsparing assault upon the syndicalist position. He charged that the *Khlebovol'tsy* had been bewitched by the French labor movement and were falsely equating syndicalism with anarchism. French syndicalism, he maintained, was "the specific product of specific French con-

[31] *Ibid.*, pp. 82-83; Rogdaev, *Internatsional'nyi kongress anarkhistov*, p. 20.

[32] Rogdaev, *Internatsional'nyi kongress anarkhistov*, p. 18.

[33] *Congrès anarchiste*, p. 82.

[34] A. Liubomirov, "Neskol'ko slov o znachenii professional'nykh soiuzov," *Trudovaia Respublika*, No. 2, February 1909, p. 8-12.

[35] *Burevestnik*, No. 10-11, March-April 1908, pp. 1-2; No. 19, February 1910, pp. 15-16; Knizhnik, *Krasnaia Letopis'*, 1922, No. 4, p. 39; Anisimov, *Katorga i Ssylka*, 1932, No. 10, pp. 134-135.

ditions," and more often than not inapplicable to the revolutionary situation in Russia.[36] Instead of preparing for the social revolution, Grossman wrote, the French union leaders seemed far more interested in carrying on a struggle for partial reforms; the unions had abandoned their revolutionary duties and were becoming a conservative instrument for the "mutual accommodation of the proletarian and bourgeois worlds."[37] "All reforms," Grossman declared, "all partial improvements carry a threat to the revolutionary spirit of the working masses, carry the germ of political seduction."[38] What Russia needed was not the respectable and law-abiding type of labor movement found in the Western countries, he asserted, but "a *direct, illegal, revolutionary* means of warfare."[39] The French syndicalists talked endlessly about the general strike, and yet "the essence of the revolution is not a strike, but mass expropriation."[40] The doctrine of syndicalism, Grossman went on, was replete with "poetry" and "legends," the most fanciful of which portrayed the "glowing prospects" of the workers' unions in the unenslaved realm of the future.[41] Obviously, the syndicalists were forgetting that the anarchist holocaust would annihilate the existing social structure with *all* its institutions, the trade unions not excepted. "The strength of anarchism," Grossman concluded, "lies in its total and radical negation of all the foundations of the present system."[42]

After his brother's untimely death, Iuda Solomonovich Grossman (alias Roshchin) took up the anti-syndicalist banner. Writing in the Geneva journal *Buntar'*, of which he was an editor, Roshchin charged that the Russian syndicalists in West European exile had lost sight of the specific needs of the Russian labor movement. Their demands for higher wages and a shorter working day, he said, could benefit the organized

[36] A———, "Anarkhizm i revoliutsionnyi sindikalizm," *Burevestnik*, No. 6-7, September-October 1907, p. 2.
[37] *Ibid.*, p. 3.
[38] A———, "Nash sindikalizm," *ibid.*, No. 4, 30 October 1906, p. 3.
[39] *Ibid.*, p. 4.   [40] *Ibid.*, No. 6-7, pp. 4-5.
[41] *Ibid.*, pp. 5-6.
[42] *Ibid.*, p. 3. Cf. A. Ivanov, "Zametka o revoliutsionnykh sindikatakh," *ibid.*, No. 16, May 1909, pp. 6-10; and Pereval, *Bezgosudarstvennyi kommunizm i sindikalizm* (n.p., n.d. [191?]). Also see Maksim Raevskii's reply to the anti-syndicalists, "Antisindikalisty v nashikh riadakh," *Burevestnik*, No. 8, November 1907, pp. 3-6.

forces of skilled labor only, while callously neglecting the plight of the *Lumpenproletariat* and vagrants, the unskilled and unemployed. To ignore society's outcasts was, in Roshchin's view, to destroy the solidarity of the downtrodden majority.[43]

The anti-syndicalists did not all go as far as the Grossman brothers in criticizing their adversaries. A more temperate approach was taken by a young Anarchist-Communist named German Karlovich Askarov (Iakobson)[44] in a series of articles appearing between 1907 and 1909 in *Anarkhist*, a journal he edited first in Geneva and then in Paris. Writing under the pseudonym of Oskar Burrit, Askarov drew a sharp distinction between the reformist trade unions (*profsoiuzy*) of England and Germany and the revolutionary *syndicats* (*sindikaty*) of France. While the former were "striving towards a reconciliation of labor and capital," he said, the latter were carrying on the radical tradition of the First International.[45] The *syndicats* were not selfishly seeking only to improve the lot of their own members, but were bent on the total destruction of the state and private property, with the general strike as their principal weapon.[46] Nevertheless, said Askarov, the *syndicats* were falling into the same error that had earlier sealed the doom of the First International. By opening their ranks to workingmen of all political stripes rather than maintaining anarchist homogeneity, they were bound to succumb to the machinations of politicians and the blandishments of union officials.[47] In Askarov's judgment, trade unionism in any form contained the seeds of authoritarian centralism. Therefore, he urged his fel-

---

[43] "Neskol'ko slov o sindikalizme," *Buntar'*, No. 2-3, June-July 1908, pp. 12-14; Roshchin, "Pis'mo k tovarishcham" (leaflet, Geneva, November 1908), Columbia Russian Archive. Cf. A. Kolosov, "Anarkhizm ili sindikalizm?," *Anarkhist*, No. 1, 10 October 1907, p. 11. The *syndicats*, wrote Kolosov, ignored "the huge cadres of unemployed, vagrants, and unskilled workers." He added that the relatively peaceful evolution of anarchism since the era of dynamite in France was "a minus, not a plus" for the movement.

[44] His brother Nikolai, an anarchist in Kiev, was executed for terrorism in 1906. *Listki* "*Khleb i Volia*," No. 3, 28 November 1906, p. 4; *Anarkhist*, No. 1, 10 October 1907, p. 1.

[45] O. Burrit, "Anarkhizm i rabochaia organizatsiia," *Anarkhist*, No. 1, 10 October 1907, p. 5.

[46] *Ibid.*, p. 7.

[47] O. Burrit, "Professionalizm, sindikalizm i Anarkhizm," *ibid.*, No. 2, April 1908, pp. 6-7.

low anarchists to shun the "eloquent orators" of the Marxist parties and to depend solely on "the black force and power from the life of the working class." Organize underground anarchist unions, he told them, and "declare an *unrelenting war* against authority, always and everywhere."[48]

Although the controversy between the syndicalists and anti-syndicalists continued to brew for more than a decade, it was clear that the heyday of the terrorists had passed. As government reprisals against terrorism mounted, the need for organization and discipline became painfully evident. The aftermath of the revolution saw a rapid shift from the romanticism of terroristic deeds to a pragmatic strategy of mass action. More and more anarchists turned to the quiet work of dispensing propaganda in an attempt to consolidate the foothold they had gained in the labor movement in 1905. During the years between the suppression of the revolution and the outbreak of the First World War, the majority of anarchists who had fled to the West applied their energies to the practical matters of organization. Of the members of *Chernoe Znamia* and *Beznachalie* who survived the counterrevolution, the more fanatical persisted in their opposition to trade unionism, retaining their faith in the *Lumpenproletariat* and the unemployed, though there were a few, most notably Grossman-Roshchin, who moderated their position considerably. Taking a new stand which he called "critical" syndicalism, Roshchin accepted the view of the *Khlebovol'tsy* that the labor unions, if free from the manipulation of socialist politicians, constituted a valuable weapon in the revolutionary struggle. He even agreed that the anarchists might take part in the unions, so long as they endeavored to convert the other workers to anarchism.[49]

The schism in the anarchist camp caused by the thorny

[48] Burrit, *ibid.*, No. 1, p. 9. Cf. Burrit, "Printsipy trudovogo anarkhicheskogo soiuza," *ibid.*, No. 3, May 1909, pp. 8-12; and Burrit, "Po povodu odnoi stat'i," *ibid.*, No. 4, September 1909, pp. 14-18.

[49] On the debate over the question of syndicalism during the early war years, see the four numbers of *Rabochee Znamia*, an Anarchist-Communist journal published in Lausanne in 1915. Of special interest are the articles by Roshchin, Orgeiani, Aleksandr Ge, and "Rabochii Al'fa" (A. Anikst). Also see M. Raevskii, *Anarkho-sindikalizm i "kriticheskii" sindikalizm* (New York, 1919).

issues of terrorism and syndicalism was in keeping with the fissiparous tendencies displayed by every radical movement in Russia since the Decembrist revolt of 1825. Indeed, the drift from Anarchist-Communism towards Anarcho-Syndicalism resembled the defection a generation before of Plekhanov and his confederates from Populism to Marxism. Like the early Russian Marxists, the Anarcho-Syndicalists considered the rising proletariat the revolutionary wave of the future. They too placed class struggle at the center of all things, and yet—once again like the early Marxists—eschewed terrorism in favor of marshaling the workers for the approaching conflict with the bosses and the government. For these reasons, their terrorist antagonists branded the syndicalists as "legal" anarchists,[50] analogous to the "legal Marxists" of the 1890's. The label acquired a measure of validity after the Tsar's censors began allowing the syndicalists to publish large quantities of books and pamphlets, which were widely read by workers and intellectuals both inside Russia and abroad.[51]

The anti-syndicalists deplored this legal activity. In their judgment, the syndicalists were rapidly sinking into a quagmire

[50] *Al'manakh*, p. 19.

[51] Among the more important works to appear in St. Petersburg and Moscow during the post-revolutionary period were the following: Fernand Pelloutier, *Istoriia birzh truda* (*Histoire des bourses du travail*) (St. Petersburg, 1906), and *Zhizn' rabochikh vo Frantsii* (*La Vie ouvrière en France*) (St. Petersburg, 1906); Arturo Labriola, *Sindikalizm i reformizm* (St. Petersburg, 1907); Hubert Lagardelle, *Revoliutsionnyi sindikalizm* (St. Petersburg, 1906); P. Strel'skii, *Novaia sekta v riadakh sotsialistov* (Moscow, 1907), containing chapters on Labriola, Lagardelle, Paul Delesalle, and other theorists and practitioners of revolutionary syndicalism; *Svoboda i trud: anarkhizm-sindikalizm* (St. Petersburg, 1907), a collection of articles by Labriola, Lagardelle, and others; N. Kritskaia and N. Lebedev, *Istoriia sindikal'nogo dvizheniia vo Frantsii, 1789-1907* (Moscow, 1908); A. Nedrov, *Rabochii vopros* (St. Petersburg, 1906); L. S. Kozlovskii, *Ocherki sindikalizma vo Frantsii* (Moscow, 1907), and *Sotsial'noe dvizhenie v sovremennoi Frantsii* (Moscow, 1908), containing articles by Georges Sorel, Hubert Lagardelle, Édouard Berth, Émile Pouget, and others; and a series of books by the former "legal Marxist" V. A. Posse, published in St. Petersburg (1905-1906) under the general title of *Biblioteka rabochego*. In addition to these works printed inside Russia, numerous syndicalist books and pamphlets in the Russian language appeared in Western countries. Furthermore, the pro-syndicalist journals contained hundreds of passages and citations from the literature of revolutionary syndicalism, and many general studies of anarchism, appearing legally at this time, included sections on syndicalism.

of economic reform, bureaucratic organization, and quasi-Marxist ideology. The *Beznachal'tsy* and *Chernoznamentsy* felt certain they could detect in their opponents the same disdain for the simple peasantry and the unwashed *Lumpenproletariat* that Bakunin and the Populists had seen in their Marxist rivals. They continued to oppose any organization of labor on a large scale, even a loose federation of trade unions, afraid that an organized body of skilled workers, together with its "conscious minority" of leaders, might become a new ruling aristocracy. As Bakunin had taught, the social revolution had to be a true revolt of the masses, waged by *all* the oppressed elements of society rather than by the trade unions alone; the daily pressures of the syndicalists to ameliorate labor conditions merely threw cold water on the revolutionary fires of the dispossessed. According to the zealots, what was needed was the immediate demolition of the old regime amidst terror and fury of all sorts—"mere anarchy loosed upon the world." Nor would the final outcome be a society of massive industrial complexes managed by trade unions. The anti-syndicalists deprecated the unions as being integral components of the capitalist system, outmoded institutions of a dying era, hardly suitable to become the fundamental units of the anarchist utopia. They envisioned, rather, a free federation of territorial communes, embracing all categories of the common people, in which manufacture would be carried on in small workshops. In the light of these beliefs, it is understandable that the artisans and semiskilled workers of Bialystok, threatened as they were by the rapid growth of modern enterprises, were more likely to lean towards the Anarchist-Communist *Chernoe Znamia* group than towards the Anarcho-Syndicalists, who made their best showing in Odessa, a major port and a center of large-scale industry.

The Anarchist-Communists saw their image of the millennium in a romantic mirror that reflected a pre-industrial Russia of agricultural communes and handicrafts cooperatives. On the other hand, the Anarcho-Syndicalists (as well as their pro-syndicalist cousins in the *Khleb i Volia* circle) seemed to be looking simultaneously into time past and time future. The prospect of a new world centered around industrial production did not repel them in the least; indeed, at times they exhibited an almost futuristic devotion to the cult of the machine. Theirs was the Westernizers' admiration of technological progress, in contrast to the Slavophile longing of the Anarchist-Communists for an irretrievable age that perhaps had never existed in the first place.[52] At the same time, however, the Anarcho-Syndicalists did not yield to an uncritical worship of mass production. Deeply influenced by Bakunin and Kropotkin, they anticipated the danger that man might become trapped in the gears and levers of a centralized industrial apparatus. They too looked backward for a way out, to a decentralized society of labor organizations in which the workers of the world could truly be the masters of their own fate. But the Golden Age of local self-determination was not destined to be realized. For in the end, the centralized state and centralized industrialism, the two most powerful forces of modern times, would crush the anarchist dissenters in their path.

[52] It is noteworthy that those syndicalists who remained inside Russia (Novomirskii, for example) were more apt to decry the futility of blindly imitating Western models than their comrades who spent long years abroad.

4 · ANARCHISM AND ANTI-INTELLECTUALISM

Hereditary bondsmen! Know ye not
Who would be free themselves must strike the
blow?
LORD BYRON

Most Russian anarchists harbored a deep-seated distrust of rational systems and of the intellectuals who constructed them. While inheriting the Enlightenment's belief in the inherent goodness of man, they generally did not share the faith of the *philosophes* in the powers of abstract reason.[1] Anti-intellectualism existed in varying degrees throughout the movement. Least evident in Kropotkin's mild and bookish *Khleb i Volia* group, it was particularly strong among the terrorists of *Beznachalie* and *Chernoe Znamia*, who belittled book learning and ratiocination and exalted instinct, will, and action as the highest measures of man. *"Im Anfang war die Tat,"* an aphorism of Goethe's, adorned the masthead of the journal *Chernoe Znamia* in 1905—"In the beginning there was the deed."[2]

The anarchists firmly rejected the notion that society is governed by rational laws. So-called scientific theories of history and sociology, they maintained, were artificial contrivances of the human brain, serving only to impede the natural and spontaneous impulses of mankind. The doctrines of Karl Marx bore the brunt of their criticism. Bidbei, the leader of the *Beznachalie* group, assailed "all these 'scientific' sociological systems concocted in the socialist or pseudo-anarchist kitchen, which have nothing in common with the genuine scientific creations of Darwin, Newton, and Galileo."[3] In the same spirit, Abram Grossman of the *Chernoe Znamia* group attacked the impersonal rationalism of Hegel and his Marxist disciples:

[1] Anarchism was an expression of the "pragmatic revolt" against political and social theory manifested in Europe around the turn of the century. See W. Y. Elliott, *The Pragmatic Revolt in Politics* (New York, 1928); and H. Stuart Hughes, *Consciousness and Society: the Reconstruction of European Social Thought, 1890-1930* (New York, 1958).

[2] *Chernoe Znamia*, No. 1, December 1905, p. 1.

[3] Bidbei, *O Liutsifere*, p. 10.

An idea must not be left to pure understanding, must not be apprehended by reason alone, but must be converted into feeling, must be soaked in "the nerves' juices and the heart's blood." Only feeling, passion, and desire have moved and will move men to acts of heroism and self-sacrifice; only in the realm of passionate life, the life of feeling, do heroes and martyrs draw their strength. . . . We do not belong to the worshipers of "all that is real is rational"; we do not recognize the inevitability of social phenomena; we regard with skepticism the scientific value of many so-called laws of sociology.[4]

To gain an understanding of man and society, Grossman advised, one should ignore the *a priori* "laws" of the sociologists and turn instead to the empirical data of psychology.

The anti-intellectualism of the Russian anarchists was rooted in four radical traditions of the nineteenth century. The first, of course, was anarchism itself, the doctrines of Godwin, Stirner, and Proudhon, but most important by far for the Russian anarchist movement, the doctrines of Bakunin; the second (paradoxically, since the Marxists were the principal target of the Russian anarchists) was a single strand of Marxist thought; Russian Populism of the 1870's was the third; and the last, the syndicalist movement which emerged in France towards the end of the century.

Mikhail Bakunin, it has been noted, rejected "*a priori* ideas or preordained, preconceived laws" in favor of his own "purely instinctive" doctrines.[5] In his view, it would have been utter folly to work out rational projects for the future, since, as he put it, "we consider purely theoretical reasoning fruitless."[6] What mattered to ordinary men and women was not words but deeds. "Teach the people?" he once asked. "That would be stupid. . . . We must not teach the people, but incite them to revolt."[7]

[4] A———, *Burevestnik*, No. 4, 30 October 1906, p. 3.

[5] Bakunin, *Oeuvres*, I, 91; Steklov, *Mikhail Aleksandrovich Bakunin*, I, 189.

[6] Steklov, *Mikhail Aleksandrovich Bakunin*, III, 455.

[7] *Pis'ma M. A. Bakunina*, p. 471.

Bakunin extended his distrust of abstract theories to the intellectuals who spun them. He deprecated the "scientific" system-builders—above all, the Marxists and Comteans—who lived in an unreal world of musty books and thick journals and thus understood nothing of human suffering. Their so-called science of society was sacrificing real life on the altar of scholastic abstractions.[8] Bakunin did not wish to shed the fictions of religion and metaphysics merely to replace them with what he considered the new fictions of pseudo-scientific sociology. He therefore proclaimed a *"revolt of life against science,* or rather, *against the rule of science."*[9] The mission of science was not to govern men but to rescue them from superstition, drudgery, and disease. "In a word," Bakunin declared, "science is the guiding compass of life, but not life itself."[10]

Although Bakunin himself believed that the intellectuals would play an important role in the revolutionary struggle, he warned that all too many of them, in particular his Marxist rivals, had an insatiable lust for power. In 1872, four years before his death, Bakunin speculated on the shape the Marxist "dictatorship of the proletariat" would assume if ever inaugurated: "That would be the rule of *scientific intellect,* the most autocratic, the most despotic, the most arrogant, and the most contemptuous of all regimes. There will be a new class, a new hierarchy of genuine or sham savants, and the world will be divided into a dominant minority in the name of science, and an immense ignorant majority."[11] In one of his major works, *Gosudarstvennost' i anarkhiia* (Statehood and Anarchy), published the following year, Bakunin elaborated upon this dire prophecy in a most striking passage:

According to the theory of Mr. Marx, the people not only must not destroy [the state] but must strengthen it and place it at the complete disposal of their benefactors, guardians, and teachers—the leaders of the Communist party, namely Mr. Marx and his friends, who will proceed to liberate [mankind] in their own way. They will concentrate the reins of government in a strong hand, because the ignorant people require an exceedingly firm guardianship; they will

[8] Bakunin, *Oeuvres,* III, 92.
[9] *Ibid.,* III, 95.   [10] *Ibid.,* III, 89.   [11] *Ibid.,* IV, 477.

establish a single state bank, concentrating in its hands all commercial, industrial, agricultural, and even scientific production, and then divide the masses into two armies—industrial and agricultural—under the direct command of state engineers, who will constitute a new privileged scientific-political estate.[12]

According to Bakunin, the followers of Karl Marx and of Auguste Comte as well were "priests of science," ordained in a new "privileged church of the mind and superior education."[13] With great disdain, they informed the common man: "You know nothing, you understand nothing, you are a blockhead, and a man of intelligence must put a saddle and bridle on you and lead you."[14]

Bakunin maintained that education was as great an instrument of domination as private property. So long as learning was preempted by a minority of the population, he wrote in 1869 in an essay called *Integral Instruction*, it could be effectively used to exploit the majority. "The one who knows more," he wrote, "will naturally dominate the one who knows less." Even if the landlords and capitalists were eliminated, there was a danger that the world "would be divided once again into a mass of slaves and a small number of rulers, the former working for the latter as they do today."[15] Bakunin's answer was to wrest education from the monopolistic grasp of the privileged classes and make it available equally to everyone; like capital, education must cease to be "the patrimony of one or of several classes" and become "the common property of all."[16] An integrated education in science and handicrafts (but not in the hollow abstractions of religion, metaphysics, and sociology) would enable all citizens to engage in both manual and mental pursuits, thereby eliminating a

[12] Bakunin, *Izbrannye sochineniia*, I, 237.
[13] Venturi, *Roots of Revolution*, pp. 432-433.
[14] Eugene Pyziur, *The Doctrine of Anarchism of Michael A. Bakunin* (Milwaukee, 1955), p. 141.
[15] Bakunin, *Oeuvres*, v, 135.
[16] *Ibid.*, v, 144. On this point, Bakunin may well have been influenced by Gracchus Babeuf, with whose work he was familiar. In his journal, *Le Tribun du Peuple*, 30 November 1795, Babeuf wrote that "education is a monstrosity when it is unequal, when it is the exclusive inheritance of one group of society . . . it easily succeeds in strangling, deceiving, stripping, and enslaving."

major source of inequality. "Everyone must work, and everyone must be educated," Bakunin averred, so that in the good society of the future there would be "neither workers nor scientists, but only men."[17]

At the close of the century, Peter Kropotkin developed Bakunin's concept of the "whole" man in his book, *Fields, Factories, and Workshops*. At some length, Kropotkin described the "integrated" community in which everyone would perform both mental and manual labor and live in blissful harmony. Like Bakunin, Kropotkin distrusted those who claimed to possess superior wisdom or who preached so-called scientific dogmas.[18] The proper function of the intellectuals, he believed, was not to order the people about, but to help them prepare for the great task of emancipation; "and when men's minds are prepared and external circumstances are favorable," Kropotkin declared, "the final rush is made, not by the group that initiated the movement, but by the mass of people. . . ."[19]

A second source of anti-intellectualism among the younger generation of Russian anarchists was Marxist literature, an ironical fact considering Bakunin's and Kropotkin's strong suspicions of the Social Democrats. Though the Marxists were the very intellectuals whose political ambitions and "scientific" theories aroused the deepest hostilities of the anarchists, the latter found themselves in full accord with one basic idea that appeared frequently in Marx's writings, namely that the working class must liberate itself through its own efforts instead of depending on some outside savior to do the job. In the *Communist Manifesto* of 1848, Marx and Engels wrote that "all previous movements were movements of minorities, or in the interests of minorities," whereas "the proletarian movement is the self-conscious independent movement of the immense majority."[20] Two years later, in 1850, Marx developed this theme in an address to the central committee of the Commu-

[17] *Ibid.*, v, 145.
[18] Kropotkin, *Modern Science and Anarchism*, p. 86.
[19] Kropotkin, "Revolutionary Government," in *Kropotkin's Revolutionary Pamphlets*, p. 247.
[20] Karl Marx and Frederick Engels, *Selected Works* (2 vols., Moscow, 1962), I, 44.

nist League, when he called on the workingmen of Europe to launch a "revolution in permanence," in order to establish their own proletarian government in the form of municipal councils or workers' committees.[21] To more than a few Russian anarchists who read these bold words a half-century later, it seemed (though with little justification) that Marx had departed from his rigid scheme of historical stages for a radical plan of revolt very close to their own, a plan which aimed to achieve the stateless society all at once, and through the efforts of the dispossessed masses themselves. Bidbei, for one, would see fit to incorporate the watchword of "permanent revolution" into the credo of his *Beznachalie* group in 1905.[22]

A Marxist slogan that had an even stronger impact on the Russian anarchist movement was the famous sentence in Marx's preamble to the bylaws of the newly founded First International in 1864: "The emancipation of the working class must be accomplished by the working class itself."[23] The anarchists interpreted this proclamation as an appeal for a social revolt by the masses themselves, with the object of annihilating rather than merely capturing the state. Marx's ringing sentence in the rules of 1864 was to appear again and again in Russian anarchist literature, sometimes accompanied by a stanza from the *Internationale* bearing an identical message:

> Il n'est pas de sauveurs suprêmes:
> Ni dieu, ni césar, ni tribun.
> Producteurs, sauvons-nous nous mêmes,
> Décrétons le salut commun![24]

That Marxists and anarchists should use these same slogans reflected a common faith in a mass uprising—as against a Blanquist *coup d'état*—which Marx shared with Bakunin in spite of their bitter feud within the First International, and which afterwards served as a point of contact between anarchists and anti-authoritarian socialists, who alike attached

[21] *Ibid.*, I, 106-117.
[22] *Listok gruppy Beznachalie*, No. 1, April 1905, p. 2.
[23] Marx and Engels, *Selected Works*, I, 386.
[24] See, for example, *Khleb i Volia*, No. 15, February 1905, p. 2; No. 23, October 1905, p. 7; and *Golos Anarkhista*, No. 1, 11 March 1918, p. 2.

very great importance to the spontaneity and initiative of the masses.

The anti-intellectualism of the Russian anarchists was also influenced by the strong antagonism toward intellectuals and politicians that developed within the rank and file of European labor during the second half of the nineteenth century. This hostility, which stemmed from the belief that the intellectuals were a separate, soft-handed breed whose interests had little in common with those of workingmen at the bench, was so intense among the Proudhonists that they opposed the entry of nonworkers into the General Council of the First International and generally objected to the presence of educated bourgeois in the labor movement.[25] In France, the determination of factory workers to rely solely on their own forces— *ourvriérisme* as it was called—was manifested everywhere, transcending all political differences. The ultra-radical Allemanists, for example, flatly excluded the "white-handed" from their ranks,[26] and the reformist unions, while not quite so inimical to intellectuals *per se*, were nonetheless wary of radical ideologies which, if acted upon, might endanger the concrete gains of several decades. Nor had the revolutionary syndicalists any use for self-seeking politicians. Nothing could be gained from political agitation, they insisted; parliament was a nest of fraud and compromise, and all partial reforms were illusory, their main effect being the removal of the labor movement's revolutionary sting. Capitalism could be eliminated—and the proletariat thereby liberated—only through the direct industrial action of the workers' unions themselves.

Mistrust deepened when a number of prominent socialists entered parliament and the government. In 1893, the election to the French Chamber of Deputies of the Marxist chieftain Jules Guesde and of Édouard Vaillant, a well-known Blanquist, convinced many workers that their politically minded leaders were being bought off by the enemy. A greater shock came in 1899, when Alexandre Millerand accepted the post

[25] Franz Mehring, *Karl Marx: Geschichte seines Lebens* (Leipzig, 1918), p. 520; Kropotkin, *Memoirs*, p. 281.

[26] Alexandre Zévaès, *Histoire du socialisme et du communisme en France de 1871 à 1947* (Paris, 1947), pp. 202-206.

of Minister of Commerce in René Waldeck-Rousseau's government, the first socialist to serve in a "bourgeois" cabinet. Militant factory hands vented their bitterness the following year at a congress of the CGT in Paris. "All politicians are betrayers," declared one speaker, and another warned his comrades to close their eyes to the meretricious allurements of the middle-class intellectuals and "count exclusively on the enthusiasm of the workers."[27] Fernand Pelloutier, the foremost syndicalist leader, drew a sharp distinction between the "Millerandism" of the politically oriented socialists and the undiluted revolutionism of his syndicalist followers, who were "rebels at all times, men truly without a god, without a master, and without a country, the irreconcilable enemies of all despotism, moral or collective—the enemies, that is, of laws and dictatorships, including the dictatorship of the proletariat."[28] This anti-political bias became the official policy of the CGT in 1906, when the Charter of Amiens affirmed the complete independence of the French trade union movement from all political entanglements.[29]

Pelloutier himself was no grimy proletarian, but a well-scrubbed and well-educated journalist of middle-class upbringing, who had adopted the workers' cause as his own, becoming an enormously effective union leader, trusted and admired by the rank and file of the CGT. Pelloutier devoted his energies to the practical affairs of labor organization and direct action, relegating ideological pursuits to those intellectuals who, in his estimation, were not genuinely concerned with the daily struggle of the workers for a better life. The labor unions, he declared, "don't give a hoot for theory, and their empiricism . . . is worth at least all the systems in the world, which last as long and are as accurate as predictions in the almanac."[30] Ideologies and utopias never came from manual workers, he maintained, but were dreamed up by middle-class intellectuals who "have sought the remedies for our ills in their own ideas,

[27] Levine, *Syndicalism in France*, pp. 101-102.
[28] Fernand Pelloutier, *Histoire des bourses du travail* (Paris, 1902), p. ix.
[29] Louis, *Histoire de mouvement syndical*, I, 263.
[30] Lorwin, *The French Labor Movement*, p. 33.

burning the midnight oil instead of looking at our needs and at reality."[31]

Such theorists of syndicalism as Georges Sorel, Hubert Lagardelle, and Édouard Berth acknowledged that the practical syndicalist movement owed them very little. Indeed, Sorel and Lagardelle readily conceded that they had learned far more from the active unionists than they had taught them.[32] "Burning the midnight oil," they worked out a philosophy which put the moral value of direct action on a much higher plane than its economic results. No great movement, Sorel maintained, had ever succeeded without its "social myth." In the present instance, the general strike was the "myth" that would inspire the working class to deeds of heroism and sustain it in its daily skirmishes with the bourgeoisie.[33] The general strike was an action slogan, a poetic vision, an image of battle capable of rousing the masses to concerted action and of imbuing them with a powerful sense of moral uplift.[34]

Sorel's high-flown notions were largely ignored by the militants of the syndicalist movement—Victor Griffuelhes, Émile Pouget, Georges Yvetot, and Paul Delesalle. Griffuelhes, general secretary of the CGT after Pelloutier's premature death in 1901, when asked by a parliamentary commission whether he had studied Sorel, answered wryly: "I read Alexandre Dumas."[35] A shoemaker by trade and a crusty union activist, Griffuelhes accused the bourgeois intellectuals, who in his judgment knew nothing of the tribulations of factory life, of trying to lure the workers with abstract formulas in order to catapult themselves into positions of privilege and authority. "If one reflects too much," he once remarked, "one never does anything."[36] In spite of his Blanquist antecedents, which led him to emphasize the place of a "conscious minority" in the labor movement, Griffuelhes despised the educated men who aspired to leadership in the unions or in public life. "Among the union activists," he wrote in 1908, "there is a feeling of

[31] *Ibid.*, p. 18.
[32] Levine, *Syndicalism in France*, p. 155.
[33] Georges Sorel, *Reflections on Violence* (Glencoe, 1950), p. 48.
[34] *Ibid.*, pp. 89-90, 200-201.
[35] Édouard Dolléans, *Histoire du mouvement ouvrier* (2 vols., Paris, 1936-1946), II, 126-128.
[36] Elliott, *The Pragmatic Revolt in Politics*, p. 122.

violent opposition to the bourgeoisie. . . . They want passion-ately to be led by workers."[37]

Nowhere in Europe was there greater hostility towards the educated classes than in the villages of mother Russia. The Populist students who descended into the countryside during the 1870's ran into an invisible barrier that separated them from the ignorant *narod*. Bakunin regarded as futile any at-tempt to teach the dark people and his young disciple Nechaev ridiculed the "unasked-for teachers" of the peasantry, whose learning only sapped them of their life-giving "popular juices."[38] After the fiasco of the 1870's, the pitiful failure of the students to communicate with the rural folk led some dis-illusioned Populists to abandon the education which they thought was dividing them from the masses. Others wondered whether the education gap could be bridged at all, whether the Populist philosopher Nikolai Mikhailovskii was not right when he observed that the literate few must "inevitably en-slave" the toiling majority.[39]

Nor was the situation greatly improved when the peasants came to the city to work in the factories, for they brought their suspicion of the intellectuals with them. One laborer in St. Petersburg bitterly complained that "the intelligentsia had usurped the position of the worker." It was all right to accept books from the students, he said, but when they begin to teach you nonsense you must knock them down. "They should be made to understand that the workers' cause ought to be placed entirely in the hands of the workers themselves."[40] Although these remarks were aimed at the Populist Chaikovskii circle

[37] Lorwin, *The French Labor Movement*, p. 29. The same hostility towards politicians and intellectuals was displayed in many countries besides France. On England, Germany, and the United States, respec-tively, see Bertrand Russell, *Proposed Roads to Freedom* (New York, 1919), p. 81n; Peter Gay, *The Dilemma of Democratic Socialism* (New York, 1952), pp. 126-128; and Paul F. Brissenden, *The I.W.W.: a Study of American Syndicalism* (2nd edn., New York, 1957), pp. viii-ix.

[38] Venturi, *Roots of Revolution*, pp. 371-372.

[39] Arthur P. Mendel, *Dilemmas of Progress in Tsarist Russia* (Cam-bridge, Mass., 1961), p. 23. Cf. the similar observations by the Populist writers Kablits and Vorontsov, in Richard Pipes, "*Narodnichestvo*: A Semantic Inquiry," *Slavic Review*, XXIII (September 1964), 449-453.

[40] Venturi, *Roots of Revolution*, pp. 539, 800.

of the 1870's, the same attitude persisted in succeeding decades toward both the Populists and the Marxists, who were
competing for the allegiance of the emerging class of industrial
workers. In 1883, Georgii Plekhanov, the "father" of Russian
Social Democracy, felt constrained to pledge that the Marxian
dictatorship of the proletariat would be "as far removed from
the dictatorship of a group of *raznochintsy* revolutionists as
heaven is from earth."[41] He assured the workers that Marx's
disciples were selfless men, whose mission was to raise the
class consciousness of the proletariat so that it could become
"an independent figure in the arena of historical life, and not
pass eternally from one guardian to another."[42]

Notwithstanding repeated assurances of this sort, many factory workers eschewed the doctrinaire revolutionism of Plekhanov and his associates and bent their efforts to the task of
economic and educational self-improvement. They began to
manifest a tendency (in which they were joined by a number
of sympathetic intellectuals) which later acquired the label of
"economism," a rough equivalent of *ouvriérisme* in France.
The average Russian workman was more interested in raising
his material level than in agitating for political objectives;
he was wary of the revolutionary slogans floated by party
leaders who seemed bent on pushing him into political ad-
ventures that might satisfy their own ambitions while leaving
the situation of the workers essentially unchanged. Political
programs, wrote a leading spokesman of the "economist" point
of view, "are suitable for intellectuals going 'to the people,' but
not for the workers themselves. . . . And it is the defense of the

[41] G. V. Plekhanov, *Sochineniia* (24 vols., Leningrad, 1923-1927),
II, 77. *Raznochintsy* was the term which designated the "men of different
classes" (except the nobility) who made up the Russian intelligentsia in
the latter part of the nineteenth century.

[42] *Ibid.* Cf. Plekhanov's address to the Second International in Paris
in July 1889: "The strength and selflessness of our revolutionary *ideolo-
gists* might suffice in a struggle against the tsar as an individual, but
would not be enough to triumph over tsarism as a political system. In the
opinion of the Russian Social Democrats, therefore, the task of our
revolutionary intelligentsia amounts to the following: it must master the
views of contemporary scientific socialism, spread them among the
workers, and with the aid of the workers capture the stronghold of the
autocracy by storm. The revolutionary movement in Russia can triumph
only as a revolutionary movement of the workers. There is no other way,
nor can there be!" *Ibid.*, IV, 54.

workers' interests . . . that is the whole content of the labor movement." The intelligentsia, he added, quoting Marx's celebrated preamble to the bylaws of the First International, tended to forget that "the liberation of the working class must be the task of the workers themselves."[43]

Underlying the anti-intellectualism of the "economists" was the conviction that the intelligentsia looked upon the working class simply as a means to a higher goal, as an abstract mass predestined to carry out the immutable will of history. According to the "economists," the intellectuals, instead of bringing their knowledge to bear on the concrete problems of factory life, were inclined to lose themselves in ideologies that had no relation to the true needs of the workers. Emboldened by the Petersburg textile strikes of 1896 and 1897, which were organized and directed by local workmen, the "economists" urged the Russian laboring class to remain self-sufficient and reject the leadership of self-centered professional agitators. As one bench worker in the capital wrote in an "economist" journal in 1897, "The improvement of our working conditions depends on ourselves alone."[44]

The anti-political and anti-intellectual arguments of Bakunin and the "economists" made a deep impression on a Polish Marxist named Jan Waclaw Machajski. Born in 1866 in Busk, a small town near the city of Kielce in Russian Poland, he was the son of an indigent clerk, who died when Machajski was a child, leaving a large and destitute family. Machajski attended the *gimnaziia* in Kielce and helped support his brothers and sisters by tutoring the schoolmates who boarded in his mother's apartment. He began his revolutionary career in 1888 in the student circles of Warsaw University, where he had enrolled in the faculties of natural science and medicine. Two or three years later, while attending the University of Zurich, he abandoned his first political philosophy

[43] S. N. Prokopovich, "Otvet na broshiuru Aksel'roda 'K voprosu o sovremennykh zadachakh i taktika russkikh sotsial-demokratov'," in Plekhanov, *Sochineniia*, XII, 501-502.

[44] Peterburzhets, *Ocherk peterburzhskogo rabochego dvizheniia*, p. 81. On the tensions that existed between labor and the intelligentsia in St. Petersburg, see Richard Pipes, *Social Democracy and the St. Petersburg Labor Movement, 1885-1897* (Cambridge, Mass., 1963).

(a blend of socialism and Polish nationalism) for the revolutionary internationalism of Marx and Engels. Machajski was arrested in May 1892 for smuggling revolutionary proclamations from Switzerland into the industrial city of Lodz, which was then in the throes of a general strike. In 1903, after nearly a dozen years in prison and Siberian exile, he escaped to Western Europe, where he remained until the outbreak of the 1905 Revolution.[45]

During his long banishment in the Siberian settlement of Viliuisk (in Iakutsk province), Machajski made an intensive study of socialist literature and came to the conclusion that the Social Democrats did not really champion the cause of the manual workers, but that of a new class of "mental workers" engendered by the rise of industrialism. Marxism, he maintained in his major work, *Umstvennyi rabochii* (The Mental Worker), reflected the interests of this new class, which hoped to ride to power on the shoulders of the manual workers. In a so-called socialist society, he declared, private capitalists would merely be replaced by a new aristocracy of administrators, technical experts, and politicians; the manual laborers would be enslaved anew by a ruling minority whose "capital," so to speak, was education.[46]

[45] Machajski's wife, Vera, has left a handwritten account of her husband's life up to the time of his escape from Aleksandrovsk prison in 1903. The manuscript is in the private collection of Max Nomad in New York City. On Machajski's life, see also Nomad, *Dreamers, Dynamiters, and Demagogues*, p. 104; *Bol'shaia Sovetskaia Entsiklopediia* (65 vols., Moscow, 1926-1947), XIII (1929), 64-66; A. Shetlikh, "Pamiati V. K. [Vatslav Konstantinovich] Makhaiskogo," *Izvestiia*, 24 February 1926, p. 4; and P. A. [Petr Arshinov], "Pamiati V. K. Makhaiskogo," *Delo Truda*, No. 11, April 1926, pp. 5-8.

[46] A. Vol'skii [pseudonym of Machajski], *Umstvennyi rabochii* (3 vols. in 1, Geneva, 1904-1905), II, 41-42. A good exposition of Machajski's ideas is presented by a former disciple, Max Nomad, in *Aspects of Revolt* (New York, 1959), chapter 5, and *Rebels and Renegades* (New York, 1932), pp. 206-208. Another able summary is Marshall S. Shatz, "Anti-Intellectualism in the Russian Intelligentsia: Michael Bakunin, Peter Kropotkin, and Jan Waclaw Machajski," unpublished essay, The Russian Institute, Columbia University (1963), pp. 52-81. Also see Ivanov-Razumnik, *Chto takoe makhaevshchina?* (St. Petersburg, 1908); N. Syrkin, *Makhaevshchina* (Moscow and Leningrad, 1931); P. A. Berlin, *Apostoly anarkhii: Bakunin—Kropotkin—Makhaev* (Petrograd, n.d. [1917]), pp. 28-31; D. Zaitsev, "Marksizm i makhaevshchina," *Obrazovanie*, 1908, No. 3, pp. 35-71; M. Ravich-Cherkasskii, *Anarkhisty* (Kharkov, 1929), pp. 47-60; and L. Kulczycki, *Anarkhizm v Rossii* (St. Peters-

According to Machajski, the radical intelligentsia aimed not at the achievement of a classless society, but merely to establish itself as a privileged stratum. It was small wonder that Marxism, rather than advocating an immediate revolt against the capitalist system, postponed the "collapse" until a future time when economic conditions had sufficiently "matured." With the further development of capitalism and its increasingly sophisticated technology, the "mental workers" would grow strong enough to establish their own rule. Even if the new technocracy were then to abolish private ownership of the means of production, Machajski said, the "professional intelligentsia" would still maintain its position of mastery by taking over the *management* of production and by establishing a monopoly over the specialized knowledge needed to operate a complex industrial economy.[47] The managers, engineers, and political officeholders would use their Marxist ideology as a new religious opiate to becloud the minds of the laboring masses, perpetuating their ignorance and servitude.

Machajski suspected every left-wing competitor of seeking to establish a social system in which the intellectuals would be the ruling class. He even accused the anarchists of Kropotkin's *Khleb i Volia* group of taking a "gradualist" approach to revolution no better than that of the Social Democrats, for they expected the coming revolution in Russia not to go further than the French Revolution of 1789 or 1848. In Kropotkin's projected anarchist commune, Machajski held, "only the possessors of civilization and knowledge" would enjoy true freedom.[48] The "social revolution" of the anarchists, he insisted, was not really meant to be a "purely workers' uprising," but was in fact to be a "revolution in the interests of the intellec-

burg, 1907), pp. 80-90. There is a brief but interesting summary of Machajski's views by his wife: "Ian-Vatslav Makhaiskii, 1866 27/xii-1926 19/ii," manuscript in Nomad's private collection.

[47] Jan Waclaw Machajski, "An Unfinished Essay in the Nature of a Critique of Socialism," unpublished manuscript (written in Paris in 1911), pp. 16-17.

[48] A. Vol'skii, *Bankrotstvo sotsializma XIX stoletiia* (n.p. [Geneva], 1905), p. 30; *Umstvennyi rabochii*, iii, part 2, pp. 9-24; *Burzhuaznaia revoliutsiia i rabochee delo* (n.p. [Geneva], 1905), p. 25.

tuals." The anarchists were "the same socialists as all the others, only more passionate ones."[49]

What then was to be done to avoid this new form of enslavement? In Machajski's view, as long as inequality of income persisted and the instruments of production remained the private property of a capitalist minority, and as long as scientific and technical knowledge remained the "property" of an intellectual minority, the multitudes would continue to toil for a privileged few. Machajski's solution assigned a key role to a secret organization of revolutionaries called the Workers' Conspiracy (*Rabochii Zagovor*), similar to Bakunin's "secret society"[50] of revolutionary conspirators. Presumably, Machajski himself was to be at the head. The mission of the Workers' Conspiracy was to stimulate the workers into "direct action"— strikes, demonstrations, and the like—against the capitalists with the immediate object of winning economic improvements and jobs for the unemployed. The "direct action" of the workers was to culminate in a general strike which, in turn, would trigger off a worldwide uprising, ushering in an era of equal income and educational opportunity. In the end, the pernicious distinction between manual and mental labor would be obliterated, together with all class divisions.[51]

Machajski's theories provoked passionate discussions within the various groups of Russian radicals. In Siberia, where Machajski hectographed the first part of *Umstvennyi rabochii* in 1898, his critique of Social Democracy "had a great effect upon the exiles," as Trotsky, who was among them, recalled in his autobiography.[52] By 1901, copies of *Umstvennyi rabochii* were circulating in Odessa, where "Makhaevism" was beginning to attract a following. In 1905, a small group of *Makhaevtsy*, calling itself the Workers' Conspiracy, was formed in St. Petersburg. Despite Machajski's criticism of the anarchists, a number of them were drawn to his creed. For a time, Olga Taratuta and Vladimir Striga of *Chernoe Znamia* were associated with a society in Odessa known as the Intransigents (*Neprimirimye*), which included both anarchists and

---

[49] *Rabochii Zagovor*, No. 1, September-October 1907, p. 75.
[50] Bakunin, *Gesammelte Werke*, III, 35-38, 82.
[51] *Rabochii Zagovor*, No. 1, pp. 58-63; *Umstvennyi rabochii*, I, 30.
[52] Leo Trotzki, *Mein Leben* (Berlin, 1930), p. 125.

Makhaevtsy; and the Petersburg *Beznachal'tsy* contained a few disciples of Machajski.[53] If some anarchist writers took Machajski to task for seeing everything as a clever plot of the intelligentsia,[54] more than a few, as Nikolai Rogdaev admitted, found in his doctrines "a fresh and vivifying spirit" in contrast to "the stifling atmosphere of the socialist parties, saturated with political chicanery."[55]

Bakuninism, Populism, Syndicalism, Makhaevism—and, ironically, even Marxism itself—nourished the anti-intellectualism of the Russian anarchists and furnished them with slogans which they used to combat their socialist rivals. The influence of Bakunin was perhaps stronger than any other. Bakunin's spirit pervaded the scathing attack on the Social Democrats with which Bidbei opened one of his pamphlets. The leader of *Beznachalie* denounced "the insatiable plunderers and cheap men of ambition, all the geniuses and pigmies of Caesarism, all the pitiful cads and lackeys, and all sorts of vampires and bloodsuckers of the people" who were flocking to join the Social Democratic party.[56] The Russian Marxists, he continued, were "worshipers in the cult of servility," whose unquenchable thirst for discipline was driving them to establish an "all-Russian centralization of power . . . the autocracy of Plekhanov and Co."[57] Bidbei condemned the fact that Marx's followers, like their teacher, considered the peasants and vagabonds amorphous elements of society, lacking the necessary class consciousness to be an effective revolutionary force. Had not the recent peasant disturbances in Poltava and Kharkov provinces amply demonstrated the fighting capacity of the rural population, he asked. And "who, if not the vagabond, can be the demon-*accoucheur* of history? From where, if not from the dismal slums, can seep the noxious poison of

---

[53] *Buntar'*, No. 1, 1 December 1906, pp. 30-31; *Al'manakh*, p. 7; Syrkin, *Makhaevshchina*, pp. 7-8, 65; Gorev, in *Obshchestvennoe dvizhenie v Rossii*, III, 525; Genkin, *Krasnaia Letopis'*, 1927, No. 1, pp. 186-190; *Byloe*, 1918, No. 9, pp. 171-172; *Bol'shaia Sovetskaia Entsiklopediia*, XIII, 66. Machajski's chief popularizer was an SR Maximalist named Evgenii Lozinskii. See his *Chto zhe takoe, nakonets, intelligentsiia?* (St. Petersburg, 1907).

[54] *Burevestnik*, No. 10-11, March-April 1908, p. 31.

[55] *Ibid.*, No. 8, November 1907, p. 9.

[56] Bidbei, *O Liutsifere*, p. 1.   [57] *Ibid.*, p. 7.

derision for the whole callous and cold code of shameful bourgeois morality?"[58] If the socialists would only dispense with
their drawn-out phases of revolutionary struggle and recognize
the awful might of the dark masses, they would see that the
"great day of retribution" was approaching (Bidbei was writing in 1904), that the spirit of pan-destruction was awakening
in the hearts of the oppressed, that Russia stood "on the eve
of a great social tempest."[59]

The words of Bakunin also echoed in the repeated attacks
launched by the *Khlebovol'tsy* against the notion of a "proletarian dictatorship." The only dictatorship the Social Democrats envisioned, declared Kropotkin, was the dictatorship of
their own party.[60] A young associate of Kropotkin's with
strong Tolstoyan leanings, Ivan Sergeevich Vetrov (Knizhnik),
elaborated on this point by defining a political party as "a
state in miniature," with its own bureaucratic hierarchy and
its own circulars and decrees. The Marxists, said Vetrov,
aimed to use this octopus of authority to satisfy "their appetite
for absolute political power."[61] According to the journal of
the *Khleb i Volia* group, Plekhanov, Martov, and Lenin were
the "priests, Magi, and shamans" of the modern age.[62] Their
"dictatorship of the proletariat" was an intrinsically evil concept, for, as Orgeiani once put it, "revolutionary government
always plays an anti-popular role."[63]

Orgeiani, whose denunciation of the Social Democrats reflected the influence of the French syndicalists as well as of
Bakunin and Machajski, feared that the socialist leaders meant
to use the burgeoning labor movement to fulfill their own
designs. The labor movement, he said, was divided into two

[58] *Ibid.,* pp. 11-24.
[59] *Ibid.,* pp. 27-28. Cf. A. Bidbei, *O revoliutsii i o kazarmennykh dobrodeteliakh gospod Tuporylovykh* (n.p. [Paris?], 1904), another vicious
attack on the Social Democrats. (Tuporylov—"Hard-Snout"—was a
pseudonym of Tsederbaum-Martov, the Menshevik leader.)
[60] *Listki "Khleb i Volia",* No. 1, 30 October 1906, p. 5.
[61] I. Vetrov, *Anarkhizm: ego teoriia i praktika* (St. Petersburg, 1906),
p. 31. Knizhnik-Vetrov later abandoned revolutionary anarchism for a
modified form of Tolstoyanism which advocated a decentralized parliamentary republic. See I. S. Knizhnik, *Podgotovka k uchreditel'nomu
sobraniiu* (Petrograd, 1917).
[62] *Khleb i Volia,* No. 17, May 1905, p. 7.
[63] K. Orgeiani, *O revoliutsii i revoliutsionnom pravitel'stve* (London,
1905), p. 14.

camps: the workmen who produced goods and the intellectuals who were out to dominate the workers by "using the privilege of knowledge."[64] If the socialist intellectuals would see fit to put their superior learning at the disposal of the rank and file workers, they could perform an invaluable service to the revolutionary movement. But the socialists, brought up in "the Jacobin tradition" of ordering others about, were likely to persist in their will to power, thus compelling the workers to liberate themselves by their own efforts "from God, the state, and the lawyers—especially the lawyers."[65] Orgeiani and his fellow pro-syndicalists in Geneva must have been immensely pleased with a report in 1904 that the factory workers of Chernigov province were beginning to look upon the anarchist movement as "a workers' organization, not under the tutelage of the intelligentsia, but in which the proletariat can in complete freedom manifest its own revolutionary initiative."[66] This was precisely the attitude that Orgeiani, Korn, and Raevskii hoped to see develop within Russia's emergent working class. They wanted the industrial workers to know that "the Social Democrats view the workers' unions as an aid in the political struggle, whereas the anarchists view them as the natural organs of direct struggle with capitalism, and as the components of the future order."[67]

The pro-syndicalists of the *Khleb i Volia* group reserved a measure of disdain for the handful of Russian intellectuals who also called themselves syndicalists but repudiated the anarchist label. According to Maksim Raevskii, these men—L. S. Kozlovskii, V. A. Posse, and A. S. Nedrov (Tokarev) were the most important—in effect were "quasi-Marxists," who, in their splendid isolation from the practical workers' movement, had swallowed the jejune theories of "Sorel and Co."[68] Former

[64] Orgeiani, *O rabochikh soiuzakh*, p. 5; *Listki "Khleb i Volia,"* No. 9, March 1907, pp. 2-5.

[65] Orgeiani, *O rabochikh soiuzakh*, pp. 4-5. Though apparently influenced by Machajski, Orgeiani rejected his belief that the intelligentsia comprised a separate class with its own ideology, and denied that mental labor was easier to perform than manual labor, as Machajski affirmed. Orgeiani, *Ob intelligentsii* (London, 1912), pp. 10-31.

[66] *Khleb i Volia*, No. 12-13, October-November 1904, p. 8.

[67] *Listki "Khleb i Volia,"* No. 1, 30 October 1906, p. 8.

[68] Raevskii, *Burevestnik*, No. 8, November 1907, p. 4.

Social Democrats, Raevskii added, these self-styled syndicalist thinkers were endeavoring to found "a new school of socialism" by linking "the revolutionary forms of the labor movement with the old theories of Marx."[69] Maria Korn joined the attack, arguing that revolutionary syndicalism was firmly anchored in the anarchist tradition and thus could hardly constitute an offshoot of Marxian socialism, as Kozlovskii and the others believed.[70] These "neo-Marxist" theorists, she said, by embracing a moribund ideology, had divorced themselves from the "practical labor movement . . . deeply rooted in the very revolutionary instincts" of the working class.[71]

An examination of the writings of the "neo-Marxist" syndicalists reveals a curious similarity between their views and those of their anarchist critics.[72] Kozlovskii, for example, who bore the brunt of the anarchist onslaught, fully agreed that syndicalism was a movement of factory workers and not of intellectuals. He assailed Lenin's *Chto delat'?* (What Is To Be Done?) for its plan to commission officers from the intelligentsia to lead the working class in the revolutionary struggle. Syndicalism demanded "great selflessness" from the intellectuals, Kozlovskii asserted; they were to act as "helper, not leader" of the industrial workers.[73] Moreover, the dictatorship of the proletariat was a dangerous concept which could "only

[69] Raevskii, *ibid.*, No. 12, July 1908, pp. 5-7; No. 15, March 1909, p. 24.

[70] Korn, *Revoliutsionnyi sindikalizm i sotsialisticheskie partii*, pp. 3-6, and *Revoliutsionnyi sindikalizm i anarkhism*, pp. 6-9. Cf. Zabrezhnev's review of Kozlovskii's *Ocherki sindikalizma vo Frantsii*, in *Listki "Khleb i Volia"*, No. 16, 7 June 1907, pp. 4-6.

[71] Korn, *Revoliutsionnyi sindikalizm i anarkhizm*, p. 11; *Khleb i Volia* (Paris), No. 1, March 1909, p. 31. Cf. Korn, *Rabochii Mir*, No. 1, February 1914, pp. 3-5. A similar argument was presented a decade later by Aleksei Borovoi, an Anarchist-Individualist who had come to support the syndicalist position: "Theory does not subjugate the movement, but in the movement theories are born and pass away." Syndicalism, he said, was not a rational utopia but the spontaneous expression of proletarian self-consciousness, emerging directly from life itself. A. Borovoi, *Anarkhizm* (Moscow, 1918), pp. 55-58.

[72] Their principal works are L. S. Kozlovskii, *Ocherki sindikalizma vo Frantsii* (Moscow, 1907), and *Sotsial'noe dvizhenie v sovremennoi Frantsii* (Moscow, 1908); A. Nedrov, *Rabochii vopros* (St. Petersburg, 1906); and the series of books published by V. A. Posse under the general title of *Biblioteka rabochego* (n.p. [St. Petersburg], 1905-1906).

[73] Kozlovskii, *Sotsial'noe dvizhenie*, pp. xvi-xviii.

mean the dictatorship of the *leaders* of the proletariat, the dictatorship of a provisional revolutionary government, which one associates with bourgeois revolutions."[74] Kozlovskii likened the Social Democratic party to a religious sect, with its evangels, catechisms, and cathedrals—an obscurantist church in which absolute truths were affirmed and heresies condemned. The socialist leaders were "permeated with the spirit of authority" and aimed to "educate the masses in the cult of the teachers—the apostles—of socialism."[75] In the coming revolution, Kozlovskii declared, the masses should not duplicate the past error of following political leaders. This time the workers, through their own initiative, should seize the means of production and inaugurate a libertarian society of autonomous producers' associations.[76]

In view of the large area of agreement between Kozlovskii's ideas and their own, it seems surprising that Raevskii and Korn should have subjected him to such withering abuse. Were they not intellectuals themselves, as guilty as Kozlovskii of "burning the midnight oil" at their paper-cluttered writing tables? Part of their animosity stemmed from Kozlovskii's praise of the syndicalist theories of Georges Sorel, whom they regarded as an ambitious interloper. Kozlovskii once observed that Sorel's writings, though flawed by unsystematic organization, were nevertheless the work of "a profound and original thinker, a writer of colossal erudition."[77] If this encomium was merely irksome to the syndicalists of *Khleb i Volia*, they had stronger reasons for the icy reception they gave Kozlovskii. His refusal to join the anarchist movement or even to acknowledge the anarchist origins of revolutionary syndicalism was an intolerable affront to them. Worse still, his pretension of being the prophet of a novel doctrine[78] made him a new competitor for the allegiance of the working class.

Like the exiles of Kropotkin's circle, Daniil Novomirskii, the Odessa Anarcho-Syndicalist, denounced the non-anarchist proponents of syndicalism as intellectuals who had never

---

[74] Kozlovskii, *Ocherki sindikalizma vo Frantsii*, p. vi.
[75] *Ibid.*, pp. 76-78.   [76] *Ibid.*, pp. vi-x.
[77] Kozlovskii, *Sotsial'noe dvizhenie*, p. xxix. Lenin, it may be noted in passing, thought Sorel a "well-known muddlehead" (*izvestnyi putanik*). Lenin, *Sochineniia*, XIII, 239.
[78] Kozlovskii, *Ocherki sindikalizma vo Frantsii*, pp. iii, 81.

wielded a hammer or scythe, men who put abstract ideas above living human beings. Kozlovskii and his sympathizers, Novomirskii declared, wished to draw the active labor movement into a Russian form of "Lagardellism,"[79] a type of syndicalism rooted in Marxist theory and still friendly to Social Democracy. Novomirskii's own writings compounded all the elements of anti-intellectualism discernible in the Russian anarchist movement—Bakunin's hatred of government and politicians, Marx's exaltation of the proletariat, the syndicalist call for direct action by the workers, and Machajski's suspicion of "mental workers." (Novomirskii, after all, was a convert from Social Democracy, an anarchist and a syndicalist, and based in Odessa, an early center of Makhaevism.) That he was deeply influenced by Bakunin and Machajski is evident from the following passage in his journal, *Novyi Mir* (The New World): "Which class does contemporary socialism serve in fact and not in words? We answer at once and without beating around the bush: *Socialism is not the expression of the interests of the working class, but of the so-called raznochintsy, or déclassé intelligentsia.*"[80] The Social Democratic party, said Novomirskii, was infested with "political crooks . . . new exploiters, new deceivers of the people."[81] The long-awaited social revolution would prove to be a farce, he warned, should it fail to annihilate, together with the state and private property, yet a third enemy of human liberty: "That new sworn enemy of ours is *the monopoly of knowledge*; its bearer is *the intelligentsia.*"[82] Although Novomirskii believed, with the French syndicalists, that a "conscious minority" of far-sighted "pathfinders" was needed to stir the laboring masses into action,[83] he cautioned the workers not to look for saviors outside their own class. Selfless men simply did not exist—"not in the dark clouds of the empty sky, nor in the luxurious palaces of the tsars, nor in the chambers of the wealthy, nor in any parliament."[84] The proletariat must go it alone, he said.

[79] D. N., *Listki "Khleb i Volia,"* No. 17, 21 June 1907, p. 5.
[80] *Novyi Mir*, No. 1, 15 October 1905, p. 6.
[81] *Ibid.*, p. 10.
[82] D. I. Novomirskii, *Chto takoe anarkhizm?* (n.p., 1907), p. 37.
[83] *Novyi Mir*, No. 1, 15 October 1905, pp. 4, 10.
[84] *Ibid.*, p. 8.

"The liberation of the workers must be the task of the working class itself."[85]

A common hostility towards the intelligentsia was not enough to hold the anarchists together during the decade between the two Russian revolutions. Riven by factional disputes and subjected to Stolypin's stern measures of repression, the anarchist movement in the Tsarist Empire rapidly faded away. The relative prosperity of the years following the 1905 upheaval proved highly uncongenial to ultra-radical philosophies, which thrive in times of misery and despair. In 1906, Russian industry began to recover from the devastating effects of the revolution. Although wage levels remained low and the government narrowly circumscribed the activity of the newly formed labor unions, the over-all situation of the working class gradually improved and the number of strikes fell off sharply. In the countryside a note of hope was sounded with the remarkable growth of peasant cooperatives and the introduction of Stolypin's sweeping land reform, designed to break up the antiquated peasant commune and create in its place a class of sturdy farmers loyal to the Tsar. It was true that the bulk of the population—both rural and urban—remained impoverished and that there was widespread discontent over the Tsar's refusal to countenance a genuine constitutional government; nevertheless, the forces of unrest were decidedly on the wane.

For several years after the Revolution of 1905, the anarchists were targets of a tireless manhunt by the tsarist police. The more fortunate escaped to Western Europe and America. Hundreds of others were either executed after summary trials or made to serve long terms in prison or exile, where many fell victim to scurvy and consumption. They passed the time by reading and writing, meditating and hoping that the next revolution would not be long in coming. One inmate of the Peter-Paul fortress in the capital studied Esperanto, which many anarchists regarded as the universal tongue of the future;[86] eventually he became

[85] *Ibid.*

[86] See E. Chapelier and G. Marin, *Anarchists and the International Language, Esperanto* (London, 1908), a report to the International Congress of Anarchists at Amsterdam, August 1907. The Amsterdam Congress decided, however, that further study was required before Esperanto could be adopted as the official international language. See

fluent in the language, but complained that, owing to the dank air of his cell, his lungs had become seriously infected, making it difficult for him to speak at all.[87] A few, like German Sandomirskii, the Kievan Anarchist-Communist, filled the long days of confinement by recording their impressions of life in prison and exile,[88] while others thought only of escape. One *Chernoznamenets* who shared a Siberian prison cell with Egor Sazonov, the SR youth who had assassinated Viacheslav Pleve in 1904, succeeded in fleeing to the United States, along the same route Bakunin had taken 50 years earlier.[89]

The anarchists who had emigrated to the West lamented the fate of their comrades languishing in Russian jails or martyred on the gallows or before the firing squad. The Brotherhood of Free Communists (*Bratstvo Vol'nykh Obshchinnikov*), a group of Paris expatriates headed by Apollon Karelin, reviled the tsarist regime as "another medieval Inquisition," and likened the *Okhrana* (political police) to the *oprichniki* who had brought swift death to the real and imaginary enemies of Ivan the Terrible. Tsar Nicholas himself was the "crowned hangman," responsible for the slaughter of thousands of high-minded young men and women. "Eternal glory to the deceased! Eternal shame to the hangmen!"[90] In 1907, the émigrés organized an Anarchist Red Cross to aid their imprisoned confreres. Headquarters were established in New York and London (the latter under the direction of Kropotkin, Cherkezov, Rudolf Rocker, and Alexander Schapiro), with branches in the major cities of Western Europe and North America.[91] At scores of lectures and banquets, the Anarchist

---

Résolutions approuvées par le Congrès Anarchiste tenu à Amsterdam, Août 24-31, 1907 (London, 1907), p. 12.

[87] *Golos Ssyl'nykh i Zakliuchennykh Russkikh Anarkhistov*, No. 1, November 1913, p. 6.

[88] G. B. Sandomirskii, *V nevole: ocherki i vospominaniia* (3rd edn., Moscow, 1923).

[89] M. Berezin, *Fun keyten tsu frayhayt* (New York, 1916).

[90] "Protest" of the *Bratstvo Vol'nykh Obshchinnikov* (leaflet, Paris, n.d.), Columbia Russian Archive.

[91] Boris Yelensky, *In the Struggle for Equality: the Story of the Anarchist Red Cross* (Chicago, 1958); *P. A. Kropotkin i ego uchenie*, p. 336; *Anarkhist*, No. 1, 10 October 1907, pp. 11-13. Yelensky was secretary of the Anarchist Red Cross in the United States. See also *V Pomoshch'—Der Hilf-Ruf* (London, 1911-1912), organ of the Anar-

Red Cross collected money and clothing to send to the prisoners in Russia, and circulated petitions to protest the repressive policies of the Imperial government.[92]

At the same time, the exiled anarchists in Geneva, Paris,
London, and New York busied themselves with preparations
for the next revolution. A small band of surviving *Cher-
noznamentsy* revived their journal *Buntar'* in Geneva, while
Kropotkin's followers in London launched a successor to
Khleb i Volia called the *Listki "Khleb i Volia"* (Leaflets of
"Bread and Liberty"). In Paris, a group of Russian Anarchist-
Communists was formed, with perhaps 50 active members.
Occasionally, Kropotkin would cross the channel to attend
its gatherings in Maria Korn's apartment.[93] The Paris group,
in conjunction with a small circle of Polish anarchists, sponsored rallies to commemorate the anniversaries of the Paris
Commune and the Haymarket Square tragedy, and, in 1914,
the centenary of Bakunin's birth. The speakers at these meetings included Korn, Orgeiani, Rogdaev, Zabrezhnev, and
Karelin, as well as such prominent French anarchists and syndicalists as Sébastien Faure and Georges Yvetot.[94] During these
years, Maria Korn found time to study biology and psychology
at the Sorbonne; in 1915, she was awarded a doctorate in
natural science, having completed a thesis on "Physiological
and Psychical Reactions of Fish."[95]

The most important anarchist journal of the postrevolution-
ary period, *Burevestnik*, was founded in Paris in 1906. *Burevestnik* (The Stormy Petrel) was the title of Maksim Gorky's
celebrated poem, the last line of which appeared on the masthead: "Let the storm burst forth more strongly." Under the

---

chist Red Cross in London, published in Russian and Yiddish. An
Anarchist Red Cross was also established inside Russia in 1906 or 1907.

[92] See, for example, *Golos Ssyl'nykh i Zakliuchennykh Russkikh
Anarkhistov* (organ of the Anarchist Red Cross of New York), No. 1,
November 1913, p. 7; No. 2, October 1914, pp. 15-16. Kropotkin
vehemently condemned the repressions in a report to the British Parliament: Prince Kropotkin, *The Terror in Russia* (London, 1909).

[93] Knizhnik, *Krasnaia Letopis'*, 1922, No. 4, p. 42.

[94] The announcements of some of the rallies are in the Bund Archives
and the Columbia Russian Archive.

[95] *Delo Truda*, No. 75, March-April 1933, p. 8; *Freedom* (New York),
18 March 1933, p. 2.

joint editorship of Nikolai Rogdaev, a Kropotkinite since 1900 and one of the Russian delegates to the Amsterdam Congress of 1907,[96] and Maksim Raevskii, an articulate champion of syndicalism, *Burevestnik* generally followed the *Khleb i Volia* line, although Abram Grossman was allowed to register his anti-syndicalist views in its pages. In New York City, *Burevestnik* had a Kropotkinian, pro-syndicalist counterpart, *Golos Truda* (The Voice of Labor), which was established in 1911 as the organ of the Union of Russian Workers of the United States and Canada. *Golos Truda* often published articles by the Paris anarchists, notably Rogdaev, Korn, Orgeiani, and Zabrezhnev. When Raevskii came to America during World War I, he was appointed editor, and, under his supervision, *Golos Truda* became an avowedly Anarcho-Syndicalist publication.

For all their bustling activity, the anarchists found life in exile frustrating and demoralizing, and their efforts to maintain a semblance of unity were poisoned by incessant quarrels and intrigues. A year before the war, Karelin's Brotherhood of Free Communists split asunder amid dark accusations of its leader's "dictatorial" behavior.[97] Squabbles and recriminations plagued the other circles as well. In December 1913, however, hopes for a general reconciliation arose when a conference of Russian anarchists met in Paris to help arrange a new International Congress, the first since the Amsterdam Congress of 1907. After drawing up an agenda which included the momentous issues of terrorism, syndicalism, nationalism, and antimilitarism, the participants announced that the Congress would assemble in London the following August.[98] At the headquar-

[96] Rogdaev served as a propagandist in Briansk, Nezhin, and Ekaterinoslav in 1903, when the anarchist movement in Russia was born, and fought behind the barricades in the Moscow uprising of December 1905. N. Makhno, "Nad svezhei mogiloi t. N. Rogdaeva," *Probuzhdenie*, No. 52-53, November-December 1934, pp. 21-31. In 1909, he brought together an invaluable collection of documents and personal reminiscences of the movement from 1903 to 1908: *Al'manakh: sbornik po istorii anarkhicheskogo dvizheniia v Rossii.*

[97] The Columbia Russian Archive houses a number of leaflets and declarations arising out of this controversy.

[98] "K tovarishcham" (manuscript, Paris, 1914), Columbia Russian Archive; A. Kochegarov (Karelin), "Po povodu predstoiashchego mezhdunarodnogo s"ezda anarkhistov-kommunistov," *Golos Truda* (New York), 1 January 1914, pp. 3-4.

ters of the London Anarchist Federation, Alexander Schapiro, who was designated secretary of the forthcoming gathering, threw himself into making preparations for the event.[99] "The Congress promises to be a great success," he wrote with obvious excitement to a colleague in Austria, "delegates coming from as far as Brazil and Argentine."[100] Peter Kropotkin agreed to deliver the welcoming address to anarchist representatives expected from 17 countries. But on 1 August war broke out, and the Congress was cancelled.

As if the old controversies over terror and syndicalism were not enough, the coming of World War I touched off new polemics which very nearly delivered the *coup de grâce* to the European anarchist movement. The new dispute began when Kropotkin blamed Germany for the war and came out in support of the Entente. Kropotkin's action was prompted by the fear that the triumph of German militarism and authoritarianism might prove fatal to social progress in France, the revered land of the great revolution and the Paris Commune. He urged every man "who cherishes the ideals of human progress" to help crush the German "invasion" of Western Europe.[101] As the bulwark of statism, the German Empire blocked Europe's path toward the decentralized society of Kropotkin's dreams.

Kropotkin's espousal of the Allied cause won the approval of some of the most eminent anarchists in Europe; in 1916, Varlaam Cherkezov, Jean Grave, Charles Malato, Christian Cornelissen, James Guillaume, and ten others joined him in signing the "Manifesto of the Sixteen," which set forth their "defensist" position.[102] Yet, notwithstanding the enormous prestige of these names, the majority of anarchists throughout

[99] See the *Bulletin du Congrès Anarchiste International*, No. 1, May 1914, and No. 2, July 1914, edited by Schapiro in London.

[100] Alexander Schapiro to Rudolf Grossmann, 13 July 1914, Ramus Archive.

[101] Peter Kropotkin, "A Letter on the Present War," *Freedom* (London), October 1914, pp. 76-77; Lebedev, *P. A. Kropotkin*, pp. 70-71; *P. A. Kropotkin i ego uchenie*, pp. 161-166. According to Kropotkin's daughter, his hostility towards Germany was so intense that he sorely regretted that his age prevented him from joining the French army. Interview with Princess Alexandra Kropotkin, New York City, 10 March 1965.

[102] *P. A. Kropotkin i ego uchenie*, pp. 341-343, contains the "Manifesto of the Sixteen."

the world remained faithful to their antimilitarist and anti-patriotic heritage, rallying behind such "internationalists" as Errico Malatesta, Emma Goldman, Alexander Berkman, Ferdinand Domela Nieuwenhuis, Rudolf Rocker, and Sébastien Faure. As they saw it, the war was a capitalist struggle for power and profit, with the masses serving as cannon fodder. Hence it was absurd to regard a victory for either side as preferable.[103] In Geneva, a group of angry "internationalists," including Grossman-Roshchin, Aleksandr Ge, and Orgeiani (Kropotkin's disciple since the movement's inception),[104] branded the champions of the Allied war effort as "Anarcho-Patriots." If Germany's appetite for Belgian territory was a cause of the war, they asked, did England not insist on maintaining its vast naval supremacy? Was France without guilt in its insatiable quest for empire? And what of Russia's eternal lust for the Straits? Only one type of warfare was acceptable to true anarchists, the "internationalist" wing maintained, and this was the social revolution which would destroy the avaricious bourgeoisie and its institutions of oppression. "Down with the war! Down with tsarism and capitalism! Long live the brotherhood of free men! Hail the worldwide social revolution!"[105]

[103] "Zaiavlenie-Protest," typewritten declaration of Russian anarchists in Paris, Columbia Russian Archive; *Nabat* (Geneva), No. 5, April 1916, pp. 1-8. The latter includes protests against the war from anarchists in such far-flung countries as the United States, Bulgaria, and Australia.

[104] Maria Korn, it may be noted, remained loyal to Kropotkin on the war issue.

[105] "Otvet," leaflet of the Geneva Group of Anarchist-Communists (1916), Columbia Russian Archive; *Put' k Svobode*, No. 1, May 1917, pp. 8-11; cf. the protest of the Zurich Group of Anarchist-Communists, and Roshchin's leaflet, "Trevozhnyi Vopros," both in the Columbia Russian Archive, and Alexandre Ghé, *Lettre ouverte à P. Kropotkine* (Lausanne, 1916). For a lengthier "anarchist-internationalist" critique of Kropotkin, Cherkezov, and Korn, see A. Ge, *Put' k pobede* (Lausanne, 1917). The Bolshevik attacks on Kropotkin and his "defensist" sympathizers were, of course, more venomous. "The foremost anarchists of the entire world," wrote Lenin in *Socialism and the War*, "have disgraced themselves no less than the opportunists by their social chauvinism (in the spirit of Plekhanov and Kautsky) in the war." Lenin, *Sochineniia*, XVIII, 204-205. According to Trotsky, the "superannuated anarchist" Kropotkin had disavowed everything he had been teaching for almost half a century, without foreseeing "how a conquering France would humble herself before American bankers." Leon Trotsky, *The History of the Russian Revolution* (3 vols. in 1, Ann Arbor, 1957), I, 230; II, 179.

The issue of the war effort caused an almost fatal split in the anarchist camp. Yet, paradoxically, the war itself, with its pulverizing effect on the Russian government and economy, spurred the revival of the movement, which had been showing new signs of life since 1911. An account of the anarchist re-awakening in Moscow and its environs was left by a young participant named V. Khudolei, who would continue to play a significant role in the years to come.[106] In 1911, a dozen students of the Moscow Commercial Institute organized an anarchist circle. They set about comparing the various forms of anarchism, using as their texts the leaflets and manifestoes still intact from the days of the revolution, as well as Kropotkin's *Conquest of Bread, Mutual Aid,* and *Memoirs of a Revolutionist,* and works by Bakunin, Stirner, Tucker, and others. In the end, the youths rejected individualist anarchism for Kropotkin's communal and pro-syndicalist brand, and in 1913 christened themselves the Moscow Group of Anarchist-Communists.

The new group began corresponding with *Golos Truda* in New York and with leading anarchists and syndicalists in Western Europe. Before long, the students were distributing proclamations in the factories of nearby Tula and Briansk, where they succeeded in forming tiny cells of two or three members each. They also carried literature to the textile centers northeast of Moscow and made contact with at least one new group, located in the town of Kineshma, near Ivanovo-Voznesensk, the Russian Manchester. The Kineshma circle was headed by none other than Nikolai Romanov (Bidbei, until his arrest the leader of the Petersburg *Beznachal'tsy*), who had escaped from Siberia and was now preaching his violent creed under the *nom de guerre* of Stenka Razin. Bidbei circulated anarchist literature through the cotton mills and instigated several strikes, but his group was soon rounded up by the police. Bidbei was never heard from again.[107]

[106] V. Khudolei, "Anarkhicheskie techeniia nakanune 1917 g.," in *Mikhailu Bakuninu*, pp. 314-322.

[107] It is possible (though not likely) that this Nikolai Romanov was not in fact Bidbei. According to Maria Korn, Bidbei remained in prison after 1906 until liberated by the February Revolution of 1917. Max Nettlau, "Anarchistische Ideen in Russland und ihr Verhältnis zu den revolutionären Bewegungen," handwritten manuscript, p. 310 (reverse side), Nettlau Archive.

The war issue split the Moscow anarchists into two hostile groups. Unlike their colleagues abroad, however, most of the Muscovites remained loyal to Kropotkin and his "defensist" associates. The antimilitarist minority followed the example of other disillusioned Kropotkinites by forsaking the *Khleb i Volia* school for Anarcho-Syndicalism. When anarchist cells sprang up in the large factories of the Zamoskvorechie district and within three Moscow trade unions (the printers, leather workers, and railwaymen), the syndicalists supplied them with leaflets calling for the transformation of the "imperialist" war into a social revolution. During the autumn of 1916, the antimilitarists planned a street demonstration with black banners, but their efforts were foiled by the police.

Despite this setback, the anarchist tide was rising swiftly. Russia's ramshackle war machine had suffered a series of disasters which undermined the morale of the troops—many of whom were being sent to the front without arms—and produced extensive disaffection at home. The bureaucracy, that mainstay of the empire, crumbled under the incompetent leadership of Rasputin's appointees. The overtaxed system of transportation was breaking down. In the cities, supplies of food and fuel dwindled to precarious levels, and in the villages, the peasants were beginning to stir, grieved by the senseless slaughter of their uniformed sons. Radical slogans reappeared and grumbling was audible everywhere. By the end of 1916, a second storm was gathering.

PART II · 1917

5 · THE SECOND STORM

Strike dead, strike dead all monks and priests,
destroy all governments of the world,
especially ours!
A DUTCH ANABAPTIST, 1535

In the last week of February 1917, strikes and bread riots broke out in Petrograd. Mobs surged through the streets of the capital in angry demonstrations against the government. Troops were summoned to restore order, but they disregarded the commands of their officers to fire on the unruly crowds and fraternized with them instead. The forces of law and order quickly melted away. In the midst of the turbulence, soviets of workers' deputies, modeled on the prototypes of 1905, appeared throughout the city. On 2 March, a committee of the recently prorogued Fourth Duma organized a predominantly liberal Provisional Government. That same day, Nicholas II was persuaded to abdicate, bringing to an end more than three centuries of Romanov rule.

What was most striking about the February Revolution was its elemental character. It was, as the former director of the Tsar's police observed, "a purely spontaneous phenomenon, and not at all the fruit of party agitation."[1] No revolutionary vanguard led the workers and housewives into the streets of Petrograd; political ideologies and radical groups were momentarily lost in the chaotic outbreak of a hungry people protesting the lack of bread and the unremitting sufferings of the war. To the ill-starred Aleksandr Kerenskii, future premier of the Provisional Government, it appeared as if the whole population had been carried away by "a sense of unlimited freedom, a liberation from the most elementary restraints essential to every human society."[2]

The dreams of the Russian anarchists seemed at last to be coming true. A dozen years after the 1905 "prologue," a second storm had broken, bearing all the earmarks of the long-awaited "social" revolution. Russian radicalism, at a low ebb

[1] General E. K. Klimovich, in *Padenie tsarskogo rezhima* (7 vols., Leningrad, 1924-1927), I, 98.
[2] Quoted in David Shub, *Lenin* (New York, 1948), p. 189.

since the repressions of Stolypin, quickly revived. When news of the revolt reached the anarchist émigrés, their excitement knew no bounds. "The sun has arisen," wrote Iuda Roshchin in Geneva, "and has dispersed the black clouds. The Russian people have awakened! Greetings to revolutionary Russia! Greetings to the fighters for the happiness of the people!"[3] The Provisional Government, on assuming the reins of authority, declared a general amnesty for all political offenders. Roshchin and his comrades in exile made plans to return to their homeland as soon as possible. Meanwhile, inside the defunct empire, Daniil Novomirskii, Olga Taratuta, and hundreds of other anarchists were released from forced labor camps and from the prisons in which they had been languishing for a decade or more.

It was not long before vigorous groups of anarchists emerged anew in the cities of Russia. In Petrograd, a few Anarchist-Communist circles composed of workers and intellectuals had already been revived during the past five years and, on the eve of the revolution, could boast a total membership of about 100;[4] anarchist cells in three large munitions plants—the Metal Factory in the Vyborg district, the Pipe Factory on Vasilii Island, and the huge Putilov Metal Works in the southwestern corner of the city—participated in the February demonstrations that brought the old regime to dust, their members carrying black banners embroidered with the slogan, "Down with authority and capitalism!"[5] Within a few weeks after the collapse of tsarism, anarchist groups dotted the working-class sectors of the capital and its suburbs. The heaviest concentrations occurred in the Vyborg district, situated in the northern part of the city, and at the port and naval base of Kronstadt in the Gulf of Finland, where anarchist workmen were joined by a considerable number of sailors of the Baltic Fleet.

As in Petrograd, the anarchist groups which sprang up in other large cities attracted their membership largely from the

[3] I. Roshchin, "Privet svobode," *Put' k Svobode*, No. 1, May 1917, pp. 1-2. Cf. the reaction of the anarchist émigrés in the United States, described in Joseph Cohen, *Di Yidish-anarkhistishe bavegung in Amerike* (Philadelphia, 1945), pp. 335-336.

[4] *Mikhailu Bakuninu*, p. 322.

[5] Gorev, *Anarkhizm v Rossii*, pp. 103-107.

working class. In Moscow, for example, anarchist units were formed among the bakers and the workers in the food industry,[6] augmenting the groups which had appeared before the revolution among the leather workers, printers, and railroad hands. During March, a Moscow Federation of Anarchist Groups was created which claimed about 70 members.[7] In the south, anarchist circles were organized in the factories of Kiev, Kharkov, Odessa, and Ekaterinoslav, and by mid-year the miners of the Donets Basin had adopted as their platform the preamble to the constitution of the syndicalist Industrial Workers of the World: "The working class and the employing class have nothing in common. There can be no peace so long as hunger and want are found among millions of working people and the few, who make up the employing class, have all the good things of life. Between these two classes a struggle must go on until the workers of the world, organized as a class, take possession of the earth and the machinery of production, and abolish the wage system."[8] As the year advanced, however, the composition of the movement changed somewhat, for each new month brought a growing number of intellectuals back from prison and exile.

Throughout 1917—in contrast to 1905, when anarchism was strongest in the border regions—the movement centered in Petrograd, no longer the headquarters of a despotic government, but the very eye of the revolutionary storm. Until the summer months, when the syndicalists arrived in force from their American and West European sanctuaries, most of the anarchist organizations of "Red Peter" adhered to the Anarchist-Communist persuasion. The local Anarchist-Communist groups in the capital and its environs soon joined together to form a loose-knit Petrograd Federation of Anarchists. By May, the Federation had launched its first newspaper, *Kommuna* (The Commune), to be succeeded in the fall by *Svobodnaia Kommuna* (The Free Commune) and *Burevestnik* (The Stormy Petrel). The goal of the Petrograd Federa-

---

[6] *Ibid.*, p. 105.

[7] *Mikhailu Bakuninu*, p. 321.

[8] John Reed, *Ten Days that Shook the World* (New York, 1960), p. 68. The text of the preamble is in Joyce Kornbluh, ed., *Rebel Voices: An I.W.W. Anthology* (Ann Arbor, 1964), pp. 12-13.

tion, as the names of its newspapers suggest, was to transform the city into an egalitarian commune, patterned after an idealized image of the Paris Commune of 1871. In place of the indiscriminate killings and holdups perpetrated by the Anarchist-Communist terrorists of the previous decade, the Federation called for systematic "expropriations" carried out on a far broader scale, embracing houses and food, factories and farms, mines and railroads. "Through a social revolution to the anarchist commune," was its motto—a revolution designed to remove government and property, prisons and barracks, money and profits, and usher in a stateless society with a "natural economy."[9] The anarchists of Kronstadt, who published a few numbers of their own local journal, *Vol'nyi Kronshtadt* (Free Kronstadt), issued a dramatic appeal to the oppressed masses the world over to extend the social revolution begun in Russia to their own countries and to emancipate themselves from their masters: "Awaken! Awaken humanity! Disperse the nightmare that surrounds you. . . . Put an end to the foolish craving for earthly and heavenly deities. Say, 'Enough! I have arisen!' And you will be free."[10] In words that echoed the diatribes of their *Beznachalie* forebears, the Kronstadt Anarchist-Communists exhorted the downtrodden multitudes around the globe to take revenge on their oppressors. "Hail anarchy! Make the parasites, rulers, and priests—deceivers all —tremble!"[11]

Much to the dismay of the anarchists, the February Revolution fell short of the principal objective of the social revolution, for although it overthrew the monarchy, it failed to eliminate the state. In their disappointment, some anarchists likened the February rising to a game of musical chairs, in which one ruler took the seat of another. What happened in February? asked an Anarchist-Communist journal in Rostov-on-Don. "Nothing special. In place of Nicholas the Bloody, Kerenskii the Bloody has mounted the throne."[12]

[9] *Svobodnaia Kommuna*, No. 2, 2 October 1917, p. 1; *Kommuna*, No. 6, September 1917, pp. 2-3.
[10] *Vol'nyi Kronshtadt*, No. 2, 12 October 1917, p. 2.
[11] *Ibid.*, p. 4.
[12] *Anarkhist* (Rostov-na-Donu), No. 11, 22 October 1917, p. 3. The date on this journal is misprinted as "1907."

Determined to remove the double yoke of the Provisional Government and private property, the anarchists found themselves making common cause with their ideological adversaries, the Bolsheviks, the only other radical group in Russia pressing for the immediate destruction of the "bourgeois" state. The intense hostility the anarchists had felt for years towards Lenin dissipated rapidly as 1917 moved forward. Impressed by a series of ultra-radical statements Lenin had been making since his return to Russia, many (but by no means all) of them came to believe that the Bolshevik leader had shed the straitjacket of Marxism for a new theory of revolution quite similar to their own.

On 3 April, the day he arrived in Petrograd, Lenin proclaimed to his welcomers that a new era was dawning in Russia, an era which would soon witness the replacement of the new "bourgeois" government by a republic of workers' soviets and the substitution of a popular militia for the army and police. Here was the kernel of a program that few anarchists would have disavowed. Moreover, the anarchists must have noted with approval Lenin's pointed omission of any reference to a Constituent Assembly and his failure to invoke Marxist doctrine in support of his proposals.[13]

In the "April Theses," which Lenin read the following day to a gathering of Social Democrats in the Tauride Palace, he pursued the same unorthodox tack, exempting Russia from an entire phase of history—the prolonged period of "bourgeois democracy" which, according to Marx, necessarily preceded the proletarian revolution. "The peculiarity of the present situation in Russia," Lenin said, "is that it represents a *transition* from the first stage of the revolution, which, owing to the insufficient consciousness and organization of the proletariat, gave power to the bourgeoisie, to its second stage, which will place power in the hands of the proletariat and the poorest strata of the peasantry."[14]

This pronouncement, not materially different from Leon Trotsky's theory of "permanent revolution," a theory Lenin had rejected in 1905, left the moderate Social Democrats thun-

---

[13] N. N. Sukhanov, *The Russian Revolution, 1917* (New York, 1955), pp. 282-284.

[14] Lenin, *Sochineniia*, XX, 78.

derstruck. By repudiating the period of capitalism which, in Marx's system, must precede the socialist revolution, was Lenin, they wondered, abandoning his master's laws of history outright? Did he intend to make a mockery of Marxist philosophy by leaping over whole epochs of social and economic change? To the more orthodox socialists, Lenin's remarks constituted a heretical departure from established doctrine; apparently, they thought, he had taken leave of his senses during his long and trying exile or, even worse, had become an anarchist. I. P. Goldenberg, a veteran Russian Marxist, was moved to declare: "Lenin has now made himself a candidate for one European throne that has been vacant for thirty years—the throne of Bakunin! Lenin's new words echo something old—the superannuated truths of primitive anarchism."[15] Nevertheless, Lenin's newly found "anarchism" had a galvanizing effect on his Bolshevik cohorts, who had been floundering during the weeks prior to his return; as Sukhanov, the left-wing Menshevik chronicler of the revolution, noted, Lenin "shook the dust of Marxism off their feet."[16]

If Lenin's impatience with rigid historical stages, his "maximalist" zeal to push history forward, dismayed many of his fellow Marxists, the anarchists, by and large, reacted affirmatively. The April Theses included an array of iconoclastic propositions that anarchist thinkers had long cherished. Lenin called for the transformation of the "predatory imperialist" war into a revolutionary struggle against the capitalist order. He renounced the idea of a Russian parliament in favor of a regime of soviets modeled after the Paris Commune. He demanded the abolition of the police, the army, and the bureaucracy, and proposed that the salaries of officeholders (all of whom were to be elected and subject to recall at any time) not exceed those of skilled workers.[17] Although Lenin's preoccupation with the seizure of political power gave pause to some anarchists, more than a few found his views sufficiently harmonious with their own to serve as a basis for cooperation. Whatever suspicions they still harbored were for the moment

---

[15] Sukhanov, *The Russian Revolution*, p. 287; I. G. Tsereteli, *Vospominaniia o fevral'skoi revoliutsii* (2 vols. in 1, Paris, 1963), I, 301.
[16] Sukhanov, *The Russian Revolution*, p. 324.
[17] Lenin, *Sochineniia*, XX, 76-83.

put aside. Indeed, one Anarcho-Syndicalist leader who returned to Petrograd during the summer of 1917 was convinced that Lenin intended to inaugurate anarchism by "withering away the state" the moment he got hold of it.[18]

Lenin reaffirmed the anarchistic views of the April Theses in August-September 1917, when he drafted his famous pamphlet, *The State and Revolution*. Once again he traced the lineage of the soviets back to the Paris Commune, an event consecrated in anarchist as well as socialist legend, and called upon the proletariat and poor peasantry to "organize themselves freely into communes," then sweep away the capitalist system and transfer the railroads, factories, and land to the "whole society." Though he mercilessly derided the anarchist "dream" of dissolving the state "overnight," he did say that the state would eventually become "entirely unnecessary," quoting with approval a well-known passage from Friedrich Engels' *Origins of the Family, Private Property, and the State*: "The society that will organize production on the basis of free and equal associations of producers will put the whole state machine where it will then belong: into the Museum of Antiquities, by the side of the spinning wheel and the bronze axe."[19] Lenin declared, "So long as there is a state, there is no freedom; when there is freedom, there will be no state." Nor did he fail to acknowledge "the similarity between Marxism and anarchism (both of Proudhon and Bakunin) . . . on this point."[20]

Thus it happened that, during the eight months that separated the two revolutions of 1917, both the anarchists and the Bolsheviks were bending their efforts toward the same goal, the destruction of the Provisional Government. Though a degree of wariness persisted on both sides, a prominent anarchist noted that on most vital questions there existed "a perfect parallelism" between the two groups.[21] Their slogans were often identical, and there even developed a certain camaraderie between the long-time antagonists, a camaraderie en-

[18] Bertram D. Wolfe, introduction to Reed, *Ten Days that Shook the World*, p. xxxi.

[19] Lenin, *Sochineniia*, XXI, 378, 406, 410; Marx and Engels, *Selected Works*, II, 322.

[20] Lenin, *Sochineniia*, XXI, 406, 436.

[21] Voline, *La Révolution inconnue (1917-1921)* (Paris, 1943), p. 185.

gendered by their common purpose. In October, they were to work hand in hand to divert the locomotive of history onto a new set of rails. When a Marxist lecturer told an audience of factory workers in Petrograd that the anarchists were disrupting the solidarity of Russian labor, an irate listener shouted, "That's enough! The anarchists are our friends!" A second voice, however, was heard to mutter, "God save us from such friends!"[22]

In the turmoil and confusion which followed the February Revolution, groups of militant Anarchist-Communists "expropriated" a number of private residences in Petrograd, Moscow, and other cities. The most important case involved the villa of P. P. Durnovo, which the anarchists considered a particularly suitable target, since Durnovo had been the Governor-General of Moscow during the Revolution of 1905. Durnovo's *dacha* was located in the radical Vyborg district, Petrograd's "Faubourg St. Antoine," as John Reed dubbed it,[23] lying on the north side of the Neva, just beyond the Finland Station. It was here that the anarchists had their staunchest following among the workers of the capital. Anarchists and other left-wing workmen seized the Durnovo villa and converted it into a "house of rest," with rooms for reading, discussion, and recreation; the garden served as a playground for their children. The new occupants included a bakers' union and a unit of people's militia.[24]

The expropriators were left undisturbed until 5 June, when a band of anarchists quartered in the *dacha* attempted to "requisition" the printing plant of a "bourgeois" newspaper, *Russkaia Volia* (Russian Liberty). After occupying the premises for a few hours, the attackers were dislodged by troops sent by the Provisional Government.[25] The First Congress of Soviets, then in session, denounced the raiders as criminals "who

---

[22] V. Polonskii, "Anarkhisty i sovremennaia revoliutsiia," *Novaia Zhizn'*, 15 November 1917, p. 1.

[23] Reed, *Ten Days that Shook the World*, p. 5.

[24] A. Miakin, "Dacha Durnovo" (manuscript, Petrograd, 1917), Columbia Russian Archive.

[25] *Rech'*, 6 June 1917, p. 5; 7 June 1917, p. 4.

call themselves anarchists."[26] On 7 June, P. N. Pereverzev, the Minister of Justice, gave the anarchists 24 hours to evacuate Durnovo's house. The following day, 50 sailors came from Kronstadt to defend the *dacha*,[27] and workers in the Vyborg district left their factories and staged demonstrations against the eviction order. The Congress of Soviets responded with a proclamation calling on the workers to return to their jobs. Condemning the seizure of private dwellings "without the agreement of their owners," the proclamation demanded the liberation of Durnovo's *dacha* and suggested that the workers content themselves with the free use of the garden.[28]

During the crisis, the *dacha* was draped in red and black flags, and armed workers came and went. Numerous meetings were held in the garden. Anarchist speakers urged that all orders and decrees, whether from the Provisional Government or the Soviet, be ignored. A typical argument in the street outside the *dacha* was recorded by a reporter for the Soviet's organ, *Izvestiia*:

"We seized the palace because it was the property of a servant of tsarism."

"And what about *Russkaia Volia*?"

"That's a bourgeois organization. We're against all organizations."

"Against workers' organizations too?"

"In principle, yes. But right now. . . ."

"Comrade, under the socialist order will you fight with the workers' organizations and press?"

"Certainly."

"Even with *Pravda*? You will seize it too?"

"Yes . . . even with *Pravda*. We'll seize it if we find it necessary."[29]

The anarchists remained entrenched in the *dacha*, in defiance of both the Provisional Government and the Petrograd Soviet. Sporadic demonstrations continued for several days, merging

[26] *Izvestiia Petrogradskogo Soveta Rabochikh i Soldatskikh Deputatov*, 7 June 1917, p. 11; 9 June 1917, p. 10.

[27] P. N. Miliukov, *Istoriia vtoroi russkoi revoliutsii* (1 vol. in 3 parts, Sofia, 1921-1923), part I, 213-214.

[28] *Izvestiia*, 9 June 1917, p. 1.   [29] *Ibid.*, p. 11.

with the massive pro-Bolshevik demonstration that occurred
in the capital on the eighteenth (the "June Demonstration"),
during which anarchists broke into a jail in the Vyborg quarter
and liberated seven of the inmates (including three ordinary
criminals and a German spy named Müller), giving some of
them sanctuary in the *dacha*.[30] Pereverzev, the Minister of
Justice, now felt compelled to act. He ordered a raid on the
dacha. When two of the anarchist occupants, a workman
named Asnin and Anatolii Zhelezniakov, a truculent Kronstadt sailor, offered resistance, a scuffle ensued in which Asnin
was mortally wounded by a stray bullet and Zhelezniakov
was taken captive and relieved of several bombs. In all, 60
sailors and workers were arrested and imprisoned in the barracks of the Preobrazhenskii Regiment.[31] The Provisional Government ignored a petition from the Baltic sailors for Zhelezniakov's release, and sentenced him to 14 years at hard labor.
A few weeks later, however, he escaped from his "republican
prison."[32] The following January he was to acquire a measure
of fame as the leader of the armed detachment sent by the
Bolsheviks to disperse the Constituent Assembly.

The demonstration spurred by the affair of Durnovo's
dacha reflected the mounting discontent of the Petrograd working class with the Provisional Government. After three months
in power, the new regime had done little more than its tsarist
predecessor to end the war or to cope with the shortages of
food and housing. The mood of the workers was growing increasingly radical. Trotsky observed that the response of the
masses to the anarchists and their slogans served the Bolsheviks as "a gauge of the steam pressure of the revolution."[33]

[30] *Rech'*, 20 June 1917, p. 4; *Izvestiia*, 20 June 1917, p. 5; Miliukov,
Istoriia vtoroi russkoi revoliutsii, part I, 226; Tsereteli, *Vospominaniia*,
II, 252.

[31] F. Drugov, "Ubiitsa Asnina o svoem krovavom dele," *Probuzhdenie*,
No. 30-31, January-February 1933, pp. 26-29; *Rech'*, 20 June 1917, p. 4;
21 June 1917, p. 4; *Izvestiia*, 20 June 1917, p. 5; 21 June 1917, pp. 4,
9-10.

[32] *Izvestiia*, 26 June 1917, p. 9; *Golos Anarkhii* (Saratov), No. 2, 21
September 1917, p. 1; *Bol'shaia Sovetskaia Entsiklopediia* (2nd edn.,
51 vols., Moscow, 1950-1958), xv, 651. On the Durnovo *dacha* incident,
see also Sukhanov, *The Russian Revolution*, pp. 386-388; Trotsky, *History of the Russian Revolution*, I, 441-456; and W. S. Woytinsky, *Stormy
Passage* (New York, 1961), pp. 290-293.

[33] Trotsky, *History of the Russian Revolution*, I, 425.

By the last week of June, workingmen, soldiers, and sailors in and around the capital were on the point of erupting into open violence. A report to the Minister of Justice noted that the Oranienbaum garrison, an important military establishment situated on the mainland directly south of Kronstadt, was "already cleaning the machine guns" in preparation for a move against the government.[34]

In the latter part of June, Kerenskii ordered an assault on the Galician front, a last-ditch effort to turn the tide of the war in Russia's favor and forestall a popular mutiny at the same time. After some initial gains, German reserves moved up and halted the offensive, forcing the Russians into a disorderly retreat. Shortly before the southwestern front collapsed, shattering what little remained of Russian morale, an abortive insurrection broke out in Petrograd known as the "July Days" (3-5 July).

On 3 July, in Anchor Square, Kronstadt's revolutionary forum, two prominent anarchists addressed the crowd of workers, sailors, and soldiers who had gathered there in anticipation of radical action against the government. The first speaker, Kh. Z. ("Efim") Iarchuk, was a veteran of the movement, one of the founders of the *Chernoe Znamia* group in Bialystok before the Revolution of 1905. In 1913, after a five-year term in Siberian exile, he emigrated to the United States, where he joined the Union of Russian Workers and the staff of its organ, *Golos Truda*. Returning to Russia in the spring of 1917, he came to Kronstadt and was elected to the local soviet, becoming the leader of its influential anarchist faction.[35] The Kronstadt Soviet, a maverick body, pressed for an immediate rising against the Provisional Government, in spite of opposition from the Petrograd Soviet. The Petrograd Committee of the Bolshevik party also considered any rebellion at this time to be premature, the majority of its members fearing that an undisciplined outburst by anarchists and rank-and-file Bolsheviks would be easily crushed by the center and right, causing grave damage to their party.

[34] *Ibid.*, II, 10.
[35] *Goneniia na anarkhizm v Sovetskoi Rossii* (Berlin, 1922), pp. 62-63; *Velikaia Oktiabr'skaia sotsialisticheskaia revoliutsiia: dokumenty i materialy; Revoliutsionnoe dvizhenie v Rossii v iiule 1917 g.—iiul'skii krizis* (Moscow, 1959), p. 91.

Iarchuk's comrade was an outspoken member of the Petrograd Federation of Anarchists named I. S. Bleikhman. A tin-
smith by trade, Bleikhman had spent many years as a political
exile abroad and in Siberia. Released from forced labor after
the February Revolution, he came to Petrograd and at once
became a leading member of the Anarchist-Communist Federation, delivering speeches to factory workers and writing
numerous articles for *Kommuna* and *Burevestnik* under the
pen name of N. Solntsev. By July, he had been elected as a
delegate to the Petrograd Soviet. Iraklii Tsereteli, a leading
Menshevik in the Soviet, remembers Bleikhman as a "comical
figure," small in stature, with a thin, clean-shaven face and
greying hair, uttering in ungrammatical Russian the superficial ideas he had gleaned from anarchist pamphlets.[36]

In Anchor Square, Bleikhman, with his shirt open at the
neck and his curly hair flying out on all sides, exhorted a delegation from the First Machine-Gun Regiment to overthrow the
bungling Provisional Government, just as the tsarist regime
had been overturned in February.[37] He assured the soldiers
that they needed no assistance from political organizations to
fulfill their revolutionary mission, for "the February Revolution also took place without the leadership of a party."[38] He
admonished his listeners to ignore the directives of the Petrograd Soviet, most of whose members, he said, were on the side
of the "bourgeoisie," and he called on the masses to requisition all available supplies, to seize the factories and mines, and
to destroy the government and the capitalist system—at once.[39]
Bleikhman denounced the Provisional Government for perse-
cuting the anarchists of the Durnovo *dacha*. "Comrades," he
told the machine-gunners, "your brothers' blood is now perhaps already flowing. Will you refuse to support your comrades? Will you refuse to come out in defense of the
Revolution?"[40]

Later that day, the First Machine-Gun Regiment raised the

[36] Tsereteli, *Vospominaniia*, I, 166-167. Cf. Trotsky, *History of the
Russian Revolution*, II, 13-14.

[37] *Revoliutsionnoe dvizhenie v Rossii v iiule 1917 g.*, p. 81.

[38] Trotsky, *History of the Russian Revolution*, II, 82.

[39] R. P. Browder and A. F. Kerensky, eds., *The Russian Provisional
Government, 1917* (3 vols., Stanford, 1961), III, 1338-1339.

[40] W. H. Chamberlin, *The Russian Revolution, 1917-1921* (2 vols.,
New York, 1957), I, 172.

standard of rebellion in the capital. Crowds of soldiers, Kronstadt sailors, and workmen erupted into armed demonstrations, demanding that the Petrograd Soviet assume power, though the anarchists among them were more interested in destroying the government than in transferring the reins of authority to the soviets. The following day, 4 July, an angry mob demanded revenge on Pereverzev for ordering the raid on the *dacha*. A group of Kronstadt sailors even tried to kidnap Viktor Chernov, the SR leader and Minister of Agriculture, but Trotsky came to the rescue and managed to free the unfortunate minister before any harm befell him.[41]

To call the July Days "an anarchist creation," as did one speaker at a conference of the Petrograd Federation of Anarchists in 1918,[42] would be a gross exaggeration; nor can the Durnovo *dacha* incident be regarded as more than a single link in the chain of events connecting the June Demonstrations in the capital with the abortive July insurrection. Nevertheless, the role of the anarchists should not be minimized. Together with rank-and-file Bolsheviks and unaffiliated radicals, the anarchists acted as gadflies, goading the soldiers, sailors, and workers into the disorganized rising. But the Petrograd Soviet refused to endorse the premature rebellion, and the government was able to suppress the rioters without much difficulty. The leaders of the Bolshevik party were arrested or forced into hiding, while the remaining anarchists were evicted from Durnovo's house, some of them ending up behind bars. The radical tide momentarily ebbed, affording the Provisional Government a very brief respite.

The Anarcho-Syndicalists returning to Russia during the summer of 1917 were sharply critical of the armed seizure of houses and printing presses carried out by their Anarchist-Communist cousins. They deplored what seemed to be an atavistic revival of the terrorism and "ex's" of 1905. Although they emphatically agreed that the war had to be terminated and the revolution carried forward until the state had been abolished, they rejected random expropriation as a retrogres-

---

[41] *Ibid.*, I, 174.
[42] *Burevestnik*, 11 April 1918, p. 2.

sive step. The immediate task, they argued, was to organize the forces of labor.

By 1917, the Anarcho-Syndicalists had been joined by the majority of Kropotkin's *Khleb i Volia* group, which had split apart over its leader's "defensist" position on the war issue. Though Kropotkin was well aware of the extreme war-weariness of the Russian people, he regarded the defeat of German militarism as a necessary precondition of European progress, and, on the eve of his departure for his homeland, he reaffirmed his support of the Entente. Despite this unpopular gesture, when Kropotkin arrived at the Finland Station in June 1917 after 40 years in exile, he was greeted warmly by a crowd of 60,000, while a military band played the *Marseillaise*, a hymn of revolutionaries everywhere and the anthem of the great French Revolution so close to Kropotkin's heart. Kerenskii offered the venerable libertarian a cabinet post as Minister of Education as well as a state pension, both of which Kropotkin bruskly declined.[43] In August, however, he accepted Kerenskii's invitation to speak before the Moscow State Conference (Plekhanov, the sage of Russian Social Democracy and also a supporter of the war effort, was to be another speaker), a body of former Duma members and representatives of the *zemstva*, municipal governments, business associations, trade unions, soviets, and cooperatives, called together by the new Prime Minister in the hope of bolstering his shaky regime. The Conference welcomed Kropotkin with a standing ovation. In a brief address, he urged a renewed military offensive, summoning the whole nation to rally to Russia's defense.[44]

Kropotkin's "patriotism" continued to alienate him from his former followers; he found himself virtually isolated from the renascent anarchist movement inside Russia. His faithful disciple Maria Korn, who had stood by him even on the war question, remained in the West with her ailing mother.[45] Varlaam Cherkezov, who also shared Kropotkin's "defensism,"

[43] Interview with Princess Alexandra Kropotkin, New York City, 10 March 1965.
[44] S. P. Tiruin, "Ot"ezd P. A. Kropotkina iz Anglii v Rossiiu i ego pis'ma," *Na Chuzhoi Storone* (Prague), 1924, No. 4, pp. 224-231; Lebedev, *P. A. Kropotkin*, p. 72; *P. A. Kropotkin i ego uchenie*, p. 230; Woodcock and Avakumovic, *The Anarchist Prince*, p. 397.
[45] *Delo Truda*, No. 75, March-April 1933, p. 9.

returned to his native Georgia, and had little further contact with his former London associate.[46] Orgeiani, who, like Cherkezov, went back to his Caucasian birthplace, had fallen out with his old mentor over Kropotkin's support of the Allies and had entered the Anarcho-Syndicalist camp.

The first prominent Anarcho-Syndicalist to arrive from foreign exile was Maksim Raevskii, who returned in May on the same boat as Trotsky. Born into a prosperous Jewish family in Nezhin, one of the first centers of the anarchist movement in southwestern Russia, Raevskii (his real name was Fishelev) attended *gimnaziia* in his home town, then went to Germany for his university diploma. Moving to Paris, he became an editor of the influential Kropotkinite periodical *Burevestnik* and engaged in heated polemics with the antisyndicalists and "motiveless" terrorists of the *Chernoe Znamia* and *Beznachalie* groups. At the outbreak of World War I, Raevskii was in New York City, the editor of the pro-syndicalist journal *Golos Truda*, the weekly organ of the Union of Russian Workers of the United States and Canada, a body with about 10,000 members.[47]

Raevskii's ablest collaborators on the editorial board of *Golos Truda* were Vladimir (Bill) Shatov and Vsevolod Mikhailovich Eikhenbaum, known in the movement as "Volin." Shatov, a rotund and affable man, had worked at various jobs in America—machinist, longshoreman, printer; in addition to his duties on the staff of *Golos Truda*, he took an active part in the Union of Russian Workers and the IWW.[48] Volin came from a family of doctors in Voronezh, a city in the black-earth region of central Russia. His younger brother, Boris Eikhenbaum, was to become one of Russia's most distinguished literary critics. In 1905, while a law student at St. Petersburg University, Volin joined the Socialist Revolutionary party and was banished to Siberia for his radical activities. He escaped to the West, and in 1911 was converted to anarchism by the Anarchist-Communist circle in Paris led by A. A. Karelin. When hostilities broke out in Europe, Volin joined the Com-

[46] B. Nikolaevskii, "Varlaam Nikolaevich Cherkezov (1864-1925)," *Katorga i Ssylka*, 1926, No. 4, p. 231.

[47] *Delo Truda*, No. 66, May-December 1931, pp. 22-23.

[48] Emma Goldman, *Living My Life* (2 vols. in 1, New York, 1931), II, 595-596.

mittee for International Action Against the War. Arrested by the French police, he managed to flee once again, reaching the United States in 1916. There he entered the Union of Russian Workers and soon won a place on the staff of *Golos Truda.*[49]

In 1917, aided by the Anarchist Red Cross,[50] Shatov and Volin sailed to Russia by the Pacific route, arriving in Petrograd in July. Once reunited with Raevskii, they replanted *Golos Truda* in the Russian capital. Joining their editorial board was Alexander ("Sanya") Schapiro, an eminent Anarcho-Syndicalist who had only recently returned to his native country from London after an absence of some 25 years. Victor Serge, in his celebrated *Memoirs of a Revolutionary,* aptly described Schapiro as a man "of critical and moderate temper."[51] Schapiro was born in Rostov-on-Don in 1882, the son of a revolutionist who himself was to become an active member of the London Anarchist Federation. Taken to Turkey as a child, Sanya attended the French school in Constantinople. He had the good fortune to be brought up with four languages (Russian, Yiddish, French, and Turkish—he later mastered English and German as well), and by the age of eleven he was reading pamphlets by Kropotkin, Élisée Reclus, and Jean Grave. At sixteen, he entered the Sorbonne in Paris to study biology in preparation for a medical career, but was soon forced to give up his studies for lack of funds. In 1900, Schapiro joined his father in London and worked for many years as a close associate of Kropotkin, Cherkezov, and Rocker in the Anarchist Federation on Jubilee Street. He was elected secretary of the International Anarchist Bureau by the Amsterdam Congress of 1907, and later succeeded Rocker as secretary of the Relief Committee of the Anarchist Red Cross.[52]

[49] Voline, *La Révolution inconnue,* pp. 7-11; Rudolf Rocker, introduction to Voline, *Nineteen-Seventeen: The Russian Revolution Betrayed* (New York, 1954); *Delo Truda-Probuzhdenie,* No. 16, January 1946, pp. 13-19; No. 17, March 1946, pp. 18-19; M. S. (Mollie Steimer), *Freedom* (London), 17 November 1945, p. 2.

[50] Yelensky, *In the Struggle for Equality,* pp. 36-40.

[51] Serge, *Mémoires d'un révolutionnaire,* p. 134.

[52] Rudolf Rocker to Senya and Mollie Fleshin, 12 February 1947, Rocker Archive; Eusebio C. Carbo, "Alexander Schapiro," *L'Adunata dei Refrattari* (New York), 22 March 1947, pp. 3-4; Rocker, *The London Years,* p. 244; *P. A. Kropotkin i ego uchenie,* pp. 335-336.

The youngest member of the *Golos Truda* group, Grigorii Petrovich Maksimov, was to become a widely respected figure in the anarchist movement both in Russia and abroad. Born in 1893 in a peasant village near Smolensk, Maksimov attended an Orthodox seminary in the medieval capital of Vladimir. He completed his studies, but changed his mind about entering the priesthood and enrolled in the St. Petersburg Agricultural Academy. While studying there, he read the works of Bakunin and Kropotkin, and was won over to the anarchist cause. Upon graduating as an agronomist in 1915, Maksimov was drafted into the army to serve in the "imperialist" struggle which he bitterly opposed. He returned to Petrograd at the beginning of 1917 and participated in the February strikes that toppled the tsarist government. In August, he joined the staff of *Golos Truda*, becoming the journal's most prolific contributor.[53]

The first issue of *Golos Truda* appeared in August 1917, under the banner of the Union of Anarcho-Syndicalist Propaganda, which was established as the syndicalist counterpart of the Anarchist-Communist Petrograd Federation. During the summer and fall, the Union set about spreading the gospel of syndicalism among the workingmen of the capital. *Golos Truda* published numerous articles on the French *syndicats*, the *bourses du travail*, and the general strike, the editors soliciting contributions from such former *Khlebovol'tsy* as Orgeiani in Georgia and Vladimir Zabrezhnev in Moscow (both of whom had previously contributed to the New York *Golos Truda* from Paris[54]), as well as from the erstwhile "legal Marxist" Vladimir Posse, who had been propagating syndicalist doctrines (though without the "anarchist" prefix) for more than a decade. The printing establishment of *Golos Truda* brought out Russian editions of important Anarcho-Syndicalist works by

[53] Rudolf Rocker, "Grigorii Petrovich Maksimov," *Delo Truda-Probuzhdenie*, No. 33, July-August 1950, pp. 1-6; *Goneniia na anarkhizm v Sovetskoi Rossii*, pp. 54-55; Rudolf Rocker, introduction to G. P. Maximoff, ed., *The Political Philosophy of Bakunin* (Glencoe, Illinois, 1953); George Woodcock, introduction to G. Maximov, *Constructive Anarchism* (Chicago, 1952).

[54] Cf. G. Maksimov, "Anarkhicheskie gazety i zhurnaly," *Delo Truda*, No. 100, December 1937-February 1938, p. 68.

West European authors.[55] In addition, Volin, Shatov, and Maksimov, despite their heavy editorial duties, found time to deliver innumerable speeches in factories and workers' clubs and at labor rallies in the Cirque Moderne.[56]

The principal goal of the *Golos Truda* group was a revolution "anti-statist in its methods of struggle, syndicalist in its economic content, and federalist in its political tasks," a revolution that would replace the centralized state with a free federation of "peasant unions, industrial unions, factory committees, control commissions, and the like in the localities all over the country."[57] Although the Anarcho-Syndicalists endorsed the soviets as "the only possible form of non-party organization of the 'revolutionary democracy'," the only instruments for effecting the "decentralization and diffusion of power,"[58] they pinned their greatest hopes on the local factory committees. The factory committees, declared *Golos Truda*, would "deliver the decisive and mortal blow to capitalism"; they were "the very best form of workers' organization ever to appear . . . the cells of the future socialist society."[59]

The factory committees arose in Russia as a spontaneous product of the February Revolution—"its flesh and blood," as one labor organizer described them in the spring of 1917.[60] In the midst of the Petrograd strikes and demonstrations, workers gathered in diningrooms and workshops, in labor exchanges and medical-fund offices, with the aim of creating local organizations to represent their vital interests. Throughout the capital, under a variety of names—factory committees, shop committees, workers' councils, councils of elders—committees of workers were organized on the factory and workshop level. It was not long before they were functioning in every industrial

[55] The most significant translations were Christian Cornelissen, *Vpered k novomu obshchestvu*; Georges Yvetot, *Fernand Pellut'e i revoliutsionnyi sindikalizm vo Frantsii*; Yvetot, *Azbuka sindikalizma*; and Émile Pataud and Émile Pouget, *Kak my sovershim revoliutsiiu*.

[56] See, for example, *Golos Truda*, No. 3, 25 August 1917; No. 8, 29 September 1917; No. 9, 6 October 1917; No. 12, 27 October 1917 (in memory of the Chicago martyrs); and No. 19, 18 November 1917.

[57] *Ibid.*, No. 1, 11 August 1917, p. 1.

[58] *Ibid.*, p. 2.

[59] *Ibid.*, p. 4; No. 2, 18 August 1917, p. 1.

[60] *Pervaia rabochaia konferentsiia fabrichno-zavodskikh komitetov* (Petrograd, 1917), p. 37.

center of European Russia, arising first in the larger establishments, then, within a few months, taking hold in all but the very smallest.

From the outset, the workers' committees did not limit their demands to higher wages and shorter hours, though these were at the top of every list; what they wanted, in addition to material benefits, was a voice in management. On 4 March, for example, the workers of the Skorokhod Shoe Factory in Petrograd did, to be sure, call upon their superiors to grant them an eight-hour working day and a wage rise, including double pay for overtime labor; but they also demanded official recognition of their factory committee and its right to control the hiring and firing of labor. In the Petrograd Radiotelegraph Factory, a workers' committee was organized expressly to "work out rules and norms for the internal life of the factory," while other factory committees were elected chiefly to control the activities of the directors, engineers, and foremen.[61] Overnight, incipient forms of "workers' control" over production and distribution appeared in the large enterprises of Petrograd, particularly in the state-owned metallurgical plants, devoted almost exclusively to the war effort and employing perhaps a quarter of the workers in the capital. The slogan of "workers' control" caught on at once and spread from factory to factory, provoking great consternation both within the Provisional Government—which now operated the huge enterprises in which the factory committees were making the greatest commotion—and among private entrepreneurs, who caught a glimpse of the nightmare yet to come.

The slogan of "workers' control" had been invented neither by the Anarcho-Syndicalists nor by the Bolsheviks, nor indeed by any radical group. Rather, as a Menshevik witness later recalled, it was "born of the storms of the revolution,"[62] aris-

[61] A. I. Evzel'man, "Bol'sheviki Petrograda v bor'be za bol'shevizatsiiu profsoiuzov i fabzavkomov v period podgotovki i provedeniia Velikoi Oktiabr'skoi sotsialisticheskoi revoliutsii," dissertation, Moscow State University (1951), pp. 98ff.

[62] Solomon Schwarz, "Betriebsräte und Produktionskontrolle in Russland," in H. Pothoff, ed., *Die sozialen Probleme des Betriebes* (Berlin, 1925), p. 175. Cf. G. V. Tsyperovich, *Sindikaty i tresty v Rossii* (3rd edn., Petrograd, 1920), p. 143; and M. Gordon, *Uchastie rabochikh v organizatsii proizvodstva* (Leningrad, 1927), p. 8.

ing as spontaneously as the factory committees themselves.[63] Political affiliation had little to do with the elemental impulse of the workers to organize local committees or to claim a role in directing their factories and workshops. Like the revolutionary syndicalist movement in France, the factory committees of 1917 were the creation of workers belonging to a variety of leftist parties or to none at all. Before long, however, the more militant workingmen grew impatient with the moderate socialists who supported the Provisional Government and its policy of perpetuating the war and the capitalist system. The overthrow of the tsarist regime in February had stirred up hopes of an immediate cessation of hostilities and of a regeneration of society, hopes that by April or May had turned into bitter disappointment. Whereas in 1905 the Social Democrats—Mensheviks no less than Bolsheviks—had been sufficiently radical to satisfy nearly all elements of the working class, now only the anarchists and Bolsheviks were proclaiming what a growing segment of labor wanted to hear: "Down with the war! Down with the Provisional Government! Control of the factories to the workers!" If, as Lenin remarked, the rank and file of Russian labor stood a thousand times more to the left than the Mensheviks and SR's, and a hundred times more to the left even than the Bolsheviks,[64] then it was the Anarcho-Syndicalists who came closest to their radical spirit. But the Anarcho-Syndicalists were unable to capitalize on this temperamental kinship. They exerted an influence in the factory committees that was disproportionate to their small numbers, but because they repudiated a centralized party apparatus, they were never in a position to dominate the committees or to lead the working class on a broad scale. It was left for the Bolsheviks, equipped not only with a most effective party organization, but also with a conscious will to power that the syndicalists lacked, to capture the allegiance of the workingmen, first in the factory committees and then in the soviets and trade unions.

Although Lenin was quite aware of the syndicalist nature of

[63] "Workers' control," however, had been a slogan of the West European syndicalists and the British Guild Socialists since the turn of the century.
[64] Lenin, *Sochineniia*, xx, 345.

the factory committees and their program of workers' control, he also recognized the potential role of the committees in his party's quest for political power. Lenin was looking forward to "a break-up and a revolution a thousand times more powerful than that of February,"[65] and for this he needed the backing of the factory workers. If he was instinctively suspicious of what Bakunin and Kropotkin called "the creative spirit of the masses," Lenin appreciated full well the people's destructive capabilities. He was therefore content, for the moment, to ride the spontaneous tide of revolt that was undermining the Provisional Government, awaiting the day when the Bolsheviks would seize power, stem the syndicalist tide, and begin to construct a new socialist order. Hence Lenin and his party gave vigorous support to the factory committees and their demand for workers' control in industry. Writing in *Pravda* on 17 May, Lenin explicitly endorsed the slogan of "workers' control," declaring that "the workers must demand the *immediate* realization of control, *in fact* and without fail, *by the workers themselves.*"[66] To the Anarcho-Syndicalists, this was further evidence of Lenin's retreat from Marxist dogma. "The Bolsheviks have separated themselves more and more from their original goals," asserted an Anarcho-Syndicalist journal in Kharkov, "and all the time have been moving closer to the desires of the people. Since the time of the revolution, they have decisively broken with Social Democracy, and have been endeavoring to apply Anarcho-Syndicalist methods of struggle."[67]

So it was that, at labor conferences between May and October, Bolshevik and Anarcho-Syndicalist delegates voted together in support of the factory committees and workers' control. Their most formidable opponents in the labor movement were the Mensheviks. Rigidly adhering to Marx's historical framework, the Mensheviks insisted that a protracted period of "bourgeois-democratic" government—a period in which workers' control had no place—had to follow the February Revolution. "We find ourselves in the bourgeois stage of revolution," declared M. I. Skobelev, the Menshevik Minister of Labor, to the First Conference of Petrograd Factory Commit-

[65] *Leninskii sbornik* (35 vols., Moscow, 1924-1925), IV, 290.
[66] Lenin, *Sochineniia*, XX, 379.
[67] *Rabochaia Mysl'*, No. 8, 3 December 1917; quoted in Gorev, *Anarkhizm v Rossii*, p. 110.

tees in June. "The transfer of enterprises into the hands of the people at the present time would not assist the revolution."[68] Any regulation of industry, moreover, was properly the function of the government, Skobelev argued, and not of autonomous factory committees. The committees, he maintained, could best serve the workers' cause by becoming subordinate units in a statewide network of trade unions; the Russian working class, instead of taking "the path of seizing the factories," would do well to rely on the unions to improve its economic situation within the framework of capitalism.[69]

The Anarcho-Syndicalists, however, had no intention of meekly standing aside while the workers' committees were absorbed by the trade unions. Disenchanted with the unions, especially with those under the thumb of the "gradualist" and "conciliatory" Mensheviks, syndicalist spokesmen began to distinguish sharply between the "bold" factory committees, heirs to the legacy of revolutionary syndicalism, and the "reformist" unions, which, according to Volin of the *Golos Truda* group, were filling "the role of mediator between labor and capital."[70] Thus a leading Anarcho-Syndicalist in Kharkov (Rotenberg was his name) told a gathering of factory-committee representatives at the end of May: "The trade unions are bankrupt all over the world. Don't you laugh! Different methods are needed. When the trade unions want to subjugate the revolutionary committees, we say, Hands off! We will not follow your path. We must finish the struggle with capitalism—so that it ceases to exist."[71] In the same vein, a fellow anarchist delegate, representing the Kharkov Locomotive Works, labeled the unions "the offspring of the bourgeoisie," unsuitable for the new age of the common man just over the horizon: "Right now, in fact, if we want to live, we must take over the factories; but if we want to perish—let us go into the trade unions. But we will not do the latter. In order to improve the situation of the workers, we must take the factories into our own hands."[72] These

[68] *Pervaia rabochaia konferentsiia*, p. 14.
[69] *Ibid.*
[70] *Oktiabr'skaia revoliutsiia i fabzavkomy: materialy po istorii fabrichno-zavodskikh komitetov* (3 vols., Moscow, 1927-1929), I, 233.
[71] Iu. Kreizel', *Iz istorii profdvizheniia g. Khar'kova v 1917 godu* (Kharkov, 1921), p. 50.
[72] *Ibid.*, pp. 49, 52.

were the passionate words of men utterly devoted to their factory committees, men captivated by the vision of a brave new world that they could win only through the local committees. They considered the trade unions vestiges of a moribund capitalist order; the factory committees, being "more alive," as they liked to put it, represented the wave of the future, which would sweep away the "bourgeois" Provisional Government and carry in a glorious new era for the workingman. The factory committee was "revolutionary, militant, bold, energetic, and powerful by virtue of its youth," wrote Grigorii Maksimov in *Golos Truda*, whereas the trade union was "older, cautious, inclined towards compromise, calling itself militant but in reality striving for 'class harmony.' "[73] While the centralized bureaucracy of the unions stifled new ideas, the factory committee was "the *chef d'oeuvre* of the workers' creativity."[74]

The persistent efforts of the Mensheviks to subordinate the workers' committees to the trade unions were successfully resisted by the anarchists and Bolsheviks, both of whom were rapidly gaining ground in the labor movement—particularly the Bolsheviks, with their effective organization and leadership. Without a disciplined organization, the anarchists could scarcely hope to match the Bolshevik recruitment campaign; they could only take consolation in the fact that "the Bolsheviks and not the Mensheviks are everywhere on the rise." For the Bolsheviks, so they thought, had "cast off the scholasticism of their apostle and adopted a revolutionary—that is, anti-Marxist—point of view."[75]

The growth of syndicalism among the Petrograd workers during 1917 was a fact acknowledged even by hostile Menshevik observers.[76] New elections to the factory committees in the summer and autumn months yielded a significant number of Anarcho-Syndicalist members. Typically, a large enterprise might have elected a dozen Bolsheviks, two anarchists, and

[73] *Golos Truda*, No. 1, 11 August 1917, p. 4.
[74] *Ibid.*, No. 10, 13 October 1917, p. 3.
[75] *Ibid.*, No. 8, 29 September 1917, pp. 3-4.
[76] Raphael R. Abramovitch, *The Soviet Revolution, 1917-1939* (New York, 1962), p. 99. Cf. *Velikaia Oktiabr'skaia sotsialisticheskaia revoliutsiia: dokumenty i materialy; Oktiabr'skoe vooruzhennoe vosstanie v Petrograde* (Moscow, 1957), p. 52.

perhaps a few Mensheviks and SR's.[77] Maksimov and Shatov of *Golos Truda* were among the most active members of the Central Council of Petrograd Factory Committees. (Maksimov was elected in June and Shatov in August.) But the chief beneficiaries of the leftward swing of the labor movement were the Bolsheviks, who had expediently appropriated the syndicalist labor program just as they were to appropriate the SR agrarian program in October.

The startling gains of Lenin's party provoked a feeling of uneasiness within the anarchist ranks. More and more anarchists came to believe that their movement required a greater degree of organization, lest the allegiance of the working class be lost completely to their temporary Bolshevik allies. A number of local and provincial conferences were hastily summoned in the hope of remedying the woeful disunity of the movement.[78] In Petrograd, the anarchist cells within the large industrial establishments stepped up their activity, and the local branch of the Union of Anarcho-Syndicalist Propaganda in the Vyborg district opened a workers' club with the aim of enlarging its membership.[79] The Anarcho-Syndicalists of Moscow, who already had established their influence among the bakers, printers, railwaymen, and leather workers, extended it to the postal workers and the workers in the perfume industry as well.[80] In the south, syndicalism took root among the miners

[77] See the figures for the Putilov, Obukhov, and Pipe factories in *Professional'noe dvizhenie v Petrograde v 1917 g.*, ed. A. Anskii (Leningrad, 1928), pp. 272, 276; *Bol'sheviki Petrograda v 1917 godu: khronika sobytii* (Leningrad, 1957), p. 612; *Bol'sheviki v period podgotovki i provedeniia Velikoi Oktiabr'skoi sotsialisticheskoi revoliutsii: khronika sobytii v Petrograde, aprel'-oktiabr' 1917 g.* (Leningrad, 1947), pp. 288, 356, 365; Browder and Kerensky, *The Russian Provisional Government*, III, 1711; *Putilovets na putiakh k Oktiabriu* (Moscow and Leningrad, 1933), p. 85; and M. I. Mitel'man *et al.*, *Istoriia Putilovskogo zavoda, 1789-1917* (3rd edn., Moscow and Leningrad, 1941), p. 501. Of the 167 delegates to the All-Russian Conference of Factory Committees (17-22 October), there were 96 Bolsheviks, 24 SR's, 13 anarchists, and 7 Mensheviks. *Izvestiia TsIK*, 24 October 1917, p. 7.

[78] G. Gorelik, *Anarkhisty v rossiiskoi revoliutsii* (Berlin, 1922), p. 7; *Golos Truda*, No. 10, 13 October 1917, p. 4; *Vol'nyi Kronshtadt*, No. 2, 12 October 1917, p. 4.

[79] *Golos Truda*, No. 6, 15 September 1917, p. 4; No. 9, 6 October 1917, p. 4.

[80] Gorelik, *Anarkhisty v rossiiskoi revoliutsii*, p. 20. A respected Anarcho-Syndicalist, Nikolai Konstantinovich Lebedev, edited the journal

of the Donets Basin and the cement workers and longshore-men of Ekaterinodar and Novorossiisk on the Black Sea.[81]

In the very midst of these organizational efforts, however, a schism developed within the anarchist camp over the question of workers' control. In English, the word "control" implies actual domination over a given procedure, but the Russian connotation is more moderate, suggesting observation or in-spection; the expression "workers' control" (*rabochii kontrol'*) meant something much closer to supervision or surveillance (*nadzor, nabliudenie*) of the employers than to the seizure (*zakhvat*) and management (*upravlenie*) of the factories by the workers themselves. Yet, as one factory-committee leader remarked, there were more than a few radical workmen who confused "control" with "the seizure of the factories."[82]

Most of the proponents of outright confiscation were An-archist-Communists who deplored workers' control as a half-way measure, a timid compromise with the existing order. One Anarchist-Communist delegate at a factory-committee conference in the capital demanded nothing less than "the seizure of the factories and the removal of the bourgeoisie."[83] "Control does not satisfy us," complained another. "We must take production entirely into our own hands and confiscate all the factories."[84] At a congress of Petrograd shipyard work-ers (among whom anarchist influence was exceptionally strong), an impatient delegate called for "the transfer of the management of the factories and ports into the hands of the [workers'] committees." "The committees," he declared, "must be active, not passive, that is, must operate the factories and not merely control their activities."[85] Dissenting from this view, a second speaker contended that "the workers who are

---

of the Moscow Perfume Workers and, with his wife, N. Kritskaia, was the author of a widely read history of the French labor movement, *Istoriia sindikal'nogo dvizheniia vo Frantsii, 1789-1907* (Moscow, 1908).

[81] G. P. Maximoff, *The Guillotine at Work* (Chicago, 1940), p. 366; B. E. [Boris Yelensky], "Fabrichno-zavodskie komitety i ikh rol' v velikoi russkoi revoliutsii," *Golos Truzhenika*, No. 25-26, April-May 1927, pp. 7-9. Yelensky was a key figure among the anarchists in the Novorossiisk factory-committee movement.

[82] *Oktiabr'skaia revoliutsiia i fabzavkomy*, I, 171.

[83] *Ibid.*, II, 176.   [84] *Ibid.*, II, 123.

[85] *Vserossiiskii s"ezd predstavitelei rabochikh zavodov, portov i uchrezhdenii Morskogo vedomstva* (Petrograd, 1917), pp. 1-3.

striving to manage the factories seriously overestimate their strength." But his turned out to be a minority voice, for a special commission of the congress endorsed the appeal for expropriation.[86] At still another workers' conference, a perfervid advocate of expropriation demanded "deeds, not words," then set a personal example by engineering the seizure of the enterprise in which he was employed, the Schlüsselburg Gunpowder Works.[87] It is worth noting that this same workman, Iustin Zhuk by name, had been sentenced in 1909 to an indefinite period of forced labor for robbing a sugar factory near Kiev and killing a watchman.[88]

To the Anarcho-Syndicalists, these speeches reflected the same impetuosity that had ruled out cooperation with the Anarchist-Communists in the past. According to Maksimov, the advocates of "seizure for seizure's sake" belonged to the outmoded and discredited school of banditry and terrorism.[89] While the syndicalists agreed that the workers must ultimately take possession of the factories, they were opposed to immediate confiscation before the workers had been adequately trained for the tasks of management. Maksimov and his colleagues on the staff of *Golos Truda* pressed for "total" workers' control, embracing all plant operations—"real and not fictitious" control over work rules, hiring and firing, hours and wages, and the procedures of manufacture.[90] Only thus could workers' control properly serve as a transitional phase, during which the manual laborers would learn how to be their own bosses. "The control commissions must not be mere checking commissions," an Anarcho-Syndicalist from Odessa told the All-Russian Conference of Factory Committees, which met in Petrograd on the eve of the Bolshevik insurrection, "but must be the cells of the future, which even now are preparing for the transfer of production into the hands of the workers."[91]

In the meantime, the factory-owners of Russia were warn-

[86] *Ibid.*, p. 3.
[87] *Oktiabr'skaia revoliutsiia i fabzavkomy*, II, 121, 180-181; Maximoff, *The Guillotine at Work*, p. 351.
[88] *Anarkhist*, No. 4, September 1909, p. 29.
[89] *Vol'nyi Golos Truda*, No. 4, 16 September 1918, p. 3.
[90] *Golos Truda*, No. 10, 13 October 1917, p. 3.
[91] *Oktiabr'skaia revoliutsiia i fabzavkomy*, II, 180.

ing the Provisional Government that the spread of workers' control had placed the nation's economy in jeopardy. The manufacturers complained that the situation in the factories had already reached a point "exceedingly close to industrial anarchy."[92] They blamed the growing economic chaos on the workers' naive conviction that Russia stood on the verge of a shining new era: "The working class [declared a conference of industrialists in southern Russia], captivated by the alluring prospects depicted by its leaders, anticipates the coming of a Golden Age, but terrible shall be its disappointment, which one cannot but foresee."[93] The workers were indeed becoming impatient for the arrival of their Golden Age. As the workers' committees acquired an increasing measure of power in the factories and mines, their vision of a proletarian paradise grew more distinct. Russia seemed about to realize that "visible dream," as a factory-committee chairman in Petrograd described it, in which the workingmen would "govern themselves without bowing their heads before any authority of the propertied classes."[94]

By October, some form of workers' control existed in the great majority of Russian enterprises. There were even sporadic instances in which factory committees ejected their employers and engineers and then endeavored to run the plants themselves, sending delegations in search of fuel, raw materials, and financial aid from workers' committees in other establishments. The committees that seized the reins of management often boasted that they were maintaining—or even raising—existing levels of production. The workers' committee of a copper foundry in Petrograd, for example, claimed that it had almost doubled the rate of production soon after taking over the enterprise, and a delegate to the First Conference of Petrograd Factory Committees made the fantastic estimate that under committee management his aviation plant had increased output by 200 per cent in a two-month period.[95]

[92] *Rabochee dvizhenie v 1917 godu*, eds. V. L. Meller and A. M. Pankratova (Moscow and Leningrad, 1926), pp. 126-127.
[93] *Ibid.*
[94] *Rabochii kontrol' i natsionalizatsiia promyshlennykh predpriiatii Petrograda v 1917-1918 gg.: sbornik dokumentov* (Leningrad, 1947), p. 181.
[95] *Oktiabr'skaia revoliutsiia i fabzavkomy*, I, 147; *Pervaia rabochaia konferentsiia*, p. 58.

The owners, of course, rejected these claims. The usurpations of the factory committees, they argued, only contributed to the growing economic turmoil:

What would you say [wrote a leading commercial journal after the October Revolution] of people who would establish control over the work of a physician at the very moment that he stops the flow of blood in the act of severing the vessels, or when he is administering artificial respiration to one in a coma? What would you say of the official who assigns a controller to supervise the actions of a person who is saving a drowning man or of a ship's captain during a storm?[96]

The factory committees regarded such indictments as brazen attempts to "sow discord" among the workers.[97] Yet, in truth, workers' control—at least in its more extreme forms—was having a devastating effect on production. Though the committees frequently succeeded in forestalling shutdowns and layoffs, their boasts of raising productivity were greatly exaggerated, to say the least. Not only were they faced with a broken-down transportation system and with grave shortages of essential materials, but their meager technical and administrative knowledge could hardly fill the gap left by the expulsion of engineers and directors. As a result, some committees felt compelled "to go to Canossa," as a Bolshevik trade unionist wrote, and return the job of directing production to the evicted managers.[98] In spite of their lofty intentions, the workers' committees were fostering a kind of "productive anarchy" that might well have caused Marx and Engels to shudder in their graves. And as the revolution of 1917 progressed, a factory inspector reported to the Provisional Government, "anarchy in the factories continues to grow."[99]

Throughout the country, tensions between capital and labor mounted swiftly. Naturally, the workers blamed the perilous condition of Russian industry on the employers, accusing them

[96] Quoted in A. Lozovskii, *Rabochii kontrol'* (Petrograd, 1918), p. 6.
[97] *Bol'sheviki Petrograda v 1917 godu*, p. 577.
[98] Lozovskii, *Rabochii kontrol'*, pp. 33-34.
[99] "Materialy k istorii rabochego kontrolia nad proizvodstvom (1917-1918 gg.)," *Krasnyi Arkhiv*, 1940, No. 6, p. 110.

of launching a frightful war for the sake of reaping huge profits, despite the fact that their shortsighted avarice doomed the industrial machine to eventual breakdown. Labor leaders insisted that workers' control over management was necessary to prevent shutdowns, lockouts, and large-scale dismissals. For their part, the manufacturers countered that they were forced to curtail production or even to close up shop by the reckless interference of unqualified workmen in the production process, compounded by severe shortages of fuel and raw materials. The arguments on both sides had merit, but no words could bridge the wide gulf between the contending classes. Together, World War I and the domestic class war were carrying the Russian economy and the Provisional Government to the edge of disaster.

6 · THE OCTOBER INSURRECTION

*The bosses are often swine, but there'll always be
bosses, won't there? What's the good of racking
your brains to try and make sense out of it?*
GRANDPA BONNEMORT, ZOLA's *Germinal*

The anarchists set themselves apart from all other radical
groups in Russia by their implacable opposition to the state in
any form. Faithfully they cleaved to Bakunin's dictum that
every government, no matter who controls it, is an instrument
of oppression. Nor did they exclude the "dictatorship of the proletariat" from this indictment, despite the fact that it was a
basic tenet of their Bolshevik allies. Though the anarchists
shared Lenin's determination to destroy the Provisional Government, Bakunin's warnings about the power-hungry Marxists
lingered in their thoughts.

Their latent suspicions of the "socialist-careerists"[1] rose to
the surface in early September, after the Bolshevik party won
majorities in both the Petrograd and Moscow Soviets.
Svobodnaia Kommuna, organ of the Petrograd Federation of
Anarchists, recollected the oft-repeated allegation of Bakunin
and Kropotkin that the so-called dictatorship of the proletariat
really meant "the dictatorship of the Social Democratic party."[2]
Every revolution of the past, the journal reminded its readers,
simply yielded a new set of tyrants, a new privileged class, to
lord it over the masses; let us hope, it declared, that the people
will be wise enough not to let Kerenskii and Lenin become
their new masters—"the Danton and Robespierre" of the Russian Revolution.[3]

The fears of the Petrograd Federation were shared by the
Union of Anarcho-Syndicalist Propaganda. "At the top,"
wrote Volin, the new editor-in-chief of *Golos Truda* (Raevskii
unexpectedly stepped down in August after the first issue, and

[1] *Golos Truda*, No. 11, 20 October 1917, p. 3.
[2] *Svobodnaia Kommuna*, No. 2, 2 October 1917, p. 2. In 1917, the
"Social Democratic party" still officially embraced both the Mensheviks
and the Bolsheviks; the latter changed their name to the Communist
party in March 1918.
[3] *Ibid.*

thenceforth assumed a passive role in the movement), there would always sit the "obtuse politicians, empty chatterboxes, shameless renegades, and wretched cowards, who have no faith in the free range and creativity of the masses."[4] With the Bolshevik victories in the Petrograd and Moscow Soviets fresh in their minds, the Anarcho-Syndicalist leaders began to fear that the soviets might be reduced to vehicles of political power. The soviets, as the syndicalists viewed them, were nonpolitical bodies, chosen directly in the localities, without the use of party lists. Their function was to handle such matters as housing, food distribution, job placement, and education, thus resembling, in some respects, the French *bourses du travail*. In the very first issue of *Golos Truda*, Raevskii underscored the fact that the soviets had sprung spontaneously from the midst of the working people, not "from the brain of this or that party leader"; the Russian people, he wrote, would not permit them to fall under the dominion of professional revolutionaries, as Lenin apparently desired, judging from his "semi-Blanquist" statements in *What Is To Be Done?* The Bolshevik slogan "All power to the soviets," said Raevskii, was acceptable to the syndicalists only if it signified the "decentralization and diffusion of power," not the transfer of authority from one group to another.[5]

But how was political coercion, with its sundry guises and shapes, to be avoided? Only by achieving "complete decentralization and the very broadest self-direction of local organizations," answered Alexander Schapiro for the *Golos Truda* group.[6] This would entail the total destruction of the state, root and branch, and the prevention of any new government from rising in its place. In other words, the Russian Revolution had to become a true social revolution. The first step, an anarchist speaker told a workers' conference in September, was to launch an immediate general strike. There were no "laws of history," he declared, to hold the people back, no predetermined revolutionary stages, as the Social Democrats maintained. Marx's disciples—both Mensheviks and Bolsheviks—were deceiving the working class with "promises of God's

---

[4] *Golos Truda*, No. 9, 6 October 1917, p. 1.
[5] *Ibid.*, No. 1, 11 August 1917, p. 2. Cf. *Vol'nyi Kronshtadt*, No. 3, 23 October 1917, p. 1.
[6] *Golos Truda*, No. 5, 8 September 1917, p. 1.

reign on earth hundreds of years from now." There was no reason to wait, he cried. The workers must take direct action —not after more centuries of painful historical development, but right now! "Hail the uprising of the slaves and the equality of income!"[7]

To the anarchists, no less abhorrent than the prospect of a "proletarian dictatorship" was that of a Russian parliament. In their eyes, the vote was merely a device to prevent the individual from governing himself. "I am an individual," declared a Rostov anarchist in October 1917, echoing a pronouncement of Max Stirner's, "and there is no authority higher than my 'I'."[8] (Similarly, Proudhon had taught that universal suffrage was "counterrevolution.")[9] When the State Duma was elected in 1906, the anarchists had made it a target of vituperation and abuse.[10] Now in 1917, with a Constituent Assembly in the offing, their attitude was as contemptuous as before. Popular sentiment was strongly in favor of the Assembly, so much so that even the Bolsheviks—hardly admirers of parliamentary democracy—thought it prudent to pay lip service to it.[11] But the anarchists, never in the habit of mincing words, denounced the forthcoming parliament as a shameless fraud.

A widely read anarchist critique of representative government came from the pen of Apollon Karelin, a noted Anarchist-Communist of scholarly temper. According to Karelin, democracy, in practice, was tantamount to "plutocracy." For even if the workers were given the franchise, he argued, the political parties would continue to nominate the candidates for parliament; and since the party leaders would select only businessmen, professionals, and semi-educated workers seeking

[7] *Oktiabr'skaia revoliutsiia i fabzavkomy*, II, 23.

[8] *Anarkhist* (Rostov), No. 11, 22 October 1917, p. 2. "For me, nothing is higher than myself (*Mir geht nichts über mich*)," wrote Stirner in his most famous work, *Der Einzige und sein Eigenthum* (Leipzig, 1845), p. 8.

[9] P.-J. Proudhon, *Idées révolutionnaires* (Paris, 1849), p. 23; quoted in Nomad, *Aspects of Revolt*, p. 142.

[10] See, for example, A. Grossman, "Est' li u nas soiuzniki?" *Burevestnik*, No. 2, 20 August 1906, pp. 3-5; *Al'manakh*, p. 56; and "Pered vyborami v 4-iu Dumu," *Rabochii Mir*, No. 2, 1 September 1912, pp. 1-2.

[11] In private, Lenin expressed disdain for the Constituent Assembly, but his views remained unpublished until several years after the revolution. Lenin, *Sochineniia*, XXI, 329.

greener pastures outside the factory, ordinary manual laborers would never have representatives of their own in the parliamentary system. In any case, he added, representative government was essentially authoritarian, for it deprived the individual of the right to exercise his free will.[12]

Parliamentary democracy was rejected on similar grounds by two anarchist workmen in speeches to a conference of Petrograd factory committees. The first speaker took the Bolsheviks to task for supporting the Constituent Assembly, which was certain to be dominated by "priests and landlords."[13] Only pure workers' organizations, he declared, only factory committees and soviets could protect the interests of the industrial proletariat. His comrade emphatically seconded these remarks. Observing that the lists of candidates for the Constituent Assembly contained few workingmen, he protested that the Assembly was bound to be monopolized by "capitalists and intellectuals." "The intellectuals," he warned, "in no case can represent the interests of the workers. They know how to twist us around their fingers, and they will betray us." The working class, he thundered, can triumph only through "direct combat." "The liberation of the workers is the task of the workers themselves!"[14]

During September and October, as the elections to the Constituent Assembly drew near, anarchist spokesmen poured forth a veritable torrent of invective on the subject of representative government. The Russian people, wrote Schapiro in *Golos Truda*, must awaken to the fact that no parliament can break the path toward liberty, that the good society can be realized only through "the abolition of all power, which only impedes and smothers revolutionary creativity."[15] A few days before the October Revolution, Bill Shatov developed this theme, displaying his considerable oratorical gifts before the All-Russian Conference of Factory Committees. Political power in any shape, he began, was "not worth a rotten egg."

[12] A. Kochegarov (Karelin), *Polozhitel'nye i otritsatel'nye storony demokratii s tochki zreniia anarkhistov-kommunistov* (Geneva, n.d.), pp. 1-4; Karelin, *Gosudarstvo i anarkhisty* (Moscow, 1918). Cf. *Pis'mo anarkhista bratu rabochemu* (Moscow, 1917), p. 11.

[13] *Oktiabr'skaia revoliutsiia i fabzavkomy*, II, 127.

[14] *Ibid.*, II, 128.

[15] *Golos Truda*, No. 4, 1 September 1917, p. 3.

The Russian Revolution, at bottom, was not a struggle for mastery among rival political parties, but an economic conflict to determine who would be the "boss" in industry and agriculture. So long as the capitalists owned the factories, Shatov went on, the workers would remain their slaves, even if a parliamentary republic were instituted. "I repeat, he declared, "political power can give us nothing." Preparations for the Constituent Assembly were a waste of precious energy; besides, dividing the workers into political factions would only destroy their class solidarity. Instead, the workers must get ready to take over the factories, and the peasants the land. "We must create economic organizations. We must be prepared, so that on the day after the revolution we can set industry in motion and operate it."[16]

Given this powerful animus against parliamentary government, it seems symbolic that an anarchist should have led the detachment that dispersed the Constituent Assembly in January 1918, ending its life of a single day. On orders from the new Bolshevik government, it was the Kronstadt sailor Zhelezniakov, now commandant of the Tauride palace guard, who unseated Viktor Chernov with the minatory announcement, "The guard is tired."[17]

At the end of September, *Golos Truda* published a letter from an irate woman, a citizen of Petrograd. She declared that she was fed up with mere talk of overthrowing the Provisional Government and demanded direct action, without further ado. When will the "endless stream of paper and words" cease to flow? she asked. "Down with words! Down with resolutions! Long live the deed! Long live the creative work of the toiling people!"[18]

The writer was perhaps unaware that, for several weeks, anarchists, Bolsheviks, left SR's, and other left-wing elements had been arming themselves for an assault on Kerenskii's

[16] *Oktiabr'skaia revoliutsiia i fabzavkomy*, II, 165-166.
[17] Voline, *La Révolution inconnue*, p. 211; *Goneniia na anarkhizm v sovetskoi Rossii*, p. 18; Gorelik, *Anarkhisty v rossiiskoi revoliutsii*, p. 15; Alexander Berkman, *The Bolshevik Myth (Diary 1920-1922)* (New York, 1925), p. 116; Maximoff, *The Guillotine at Work*, p. 352; *Golos truzhenika*, No. 9-10, July-August 1925, p. 21.
[18] *Golos Truda*, No. 8, 29 September 1917, p. 4.

regime. The buildup began at the end of August, when General Kornilov, attempting a *coup d'état*, advanced against the capital, forcing Kerenskii to appeal to the left for assistance. The factory committees and labor unions of Petrograd swiftly organized detachments of Red Guards,[19] consisting largely of Bolsheviks but augmented by substantial numbers of anarchists, left SR's, Mensheviks, and other radicals,[20] all thrown together by the immediate threat of counterrevolution. As Kornilov's forces approached the city, railway workers delayed trains, telegraph operators refused to transmit the General's dispatches, and leftist agitators effectively circulated among the insurgents, undermining their morale. Iustin Zhuk, who had supervised the confiscation of the Schlüsselburg Gunpowder Works, sent a bargeload of grenades to the capital, which the Central Council of Petrograd Factory Committees distributed among the laborers of the Vyborg district.[21] Before any blood was shed, however, the Kornilov affair petered out. But Kerenskii's doom had been sealed, for the workers were now armed and consolidated behind the leadership of the extreme left. Ironically, Kornilov's march on Petrograd had paved the way for the overturn of the government by his bitterest enemies.

No sooner had the danger from the right been eliminated than the Provisional Government faced the more serious menace on the left. In the middle of September, Kerenskii, trying desperately to rally the populace behind his faltering regime, summoned representatives from the soviets, cooperatives, trade unions, and local governments to attend a "Democratic Conference" in the capital. The anarchists ridiculed the assembly as a "counterrevolutionary fiasco," the final convulsion of a dying era.[22] The Bolsheviks took part, but as an unruly opposition group; and when the Conference organized a "pre-parliament," at the opening session (7 October), Trotsky and his confederates voted with their feet.

From that moment, events moved swiftly. The Bolsheviks

[19] D. A. Tseitlin, "Fabrichno-zavodskie komitety Petrograda v fevrale-oktiabre 1917 goda," *Voprosy Istorii*, 1956, No. 11, pp. 94-95.

[20] *Velikaia Oktiabr'skaia sotsialisticheskaia revoliutsiia: dokumenty i materialy; Revoliutsionnoe dvizhenie v Rossii v avguste 1917 g.—razgrom Kornilovskogo miatezha* (Moscow, 1959), p. 485.

[21] *Oktiabr'skaia revoliutsiia i fabzavkomy*, II, 48.

[22] *Golos Truda*, No. 7, 22 September 1917, p. 1.

and their allies redoubled their efforts to recruit militiamen and to provide them with arms and ammunition. "In the factories," wrote John Reed, "the committee-rooms were filled with stacks of rifles, couriers came and went, the Red Guard drilled. . . ."[23] In the second week of October, the Petrograd Soviet established a Military-Revolutionary Committee, which, under Trotsky's able leadership, was soon to engineer the overthrow of the Provisional Government. Although the Bolsheviks, with 48 members, predominated, 14 left SR's, and 4 anarchists—Shatov among them[24]—were energetic participants. One of the anarchist members, a worker from the Obukhov Steel Plant, reiterated the familiar demand for "deeds and not words," deeds that would sweep away the capitalists "like scum from the face of the earth."[25] Action was not long in coming. On 25 October, Red Guardsmen, garrison troops, and Kronstadt sailors occupied the key points in the capital, meeting no resistance except at the Winter Palace, headquarters of Kerenskii and his ministers. In sharp contrast to the spontaneous mass revolt of February, a *coup d'état* was carried out by a relatively small number of determined men—"hardly more than 25 or 30 thousand at the most," according to Trotsky.[26] To a great extent, this fact was to determine the character of the aftermath.

The October Revolution inspired a great resurgence of revolutionary idealism and faith in the impending millennium. On the day of the insurrection, the Military-Revolutionary Committee issued a triumphant proclamation "To the Citizens of Russia": "The cause for which the people have been fighting—the immediate proposal of a democratic peace, the abolition of landlords' property rights over the land, workers' control over production, the creation of a Soviet Government—that cause has been won. LONG LIVE THE REVOLUTION OF THE WORKERS, SOLDIERS, AND PEASANTS!"[27] Although the anarchists shared in the jubilation, they were, at the same time,

[23] Reed, *Ten Days that Shook the World*, p. 49.

[24] *Ibid.*, p. 37.

[25] *Oktiabr'skoe vooruzhennoe vosstanie v Petrograde*, p. 235.

[26] Trotsky, *History of the Russian Revolution*, III, 294.

[27] Lenin, *Sochineniia*, XXII, 3; Reed, *Ten Days that Shook the World*, p. 134.

troubled by the announcement of a "Soviet Government." They had assisted the Bolsheviks in the overthrow of Kerenskii's "bourgeois" regime, blindly hoping that the "creative masses" would prevent any new government from taking its place. Disregarding the preachments of Bakunin and Kropotkin against political *coups*, they had taken part in a seizure of power in the belief that power, once captured, could somehow be diffused and eliminated. But now, with the proclamation of a "Soviet Government," their old fears of the "dictatorship of the proletariat" suddenly returned.

The first jolt came on the day after the uprising, when the Bolsheviks created a central Soviet of People's Commissars (*Sovnarkom*), composed exclusively of members of their own party. The anarchists immediately objected, arguing that such a concentration of political power would destroy the social revolution; the success of the revolution, they insisted, hinged on the decentralization of political and economic authority. "We appeal to the slaves," declared *Golos Truda* on the morrow of the insurrection, "to reject any form of domination. We call upon them to create *their own nonparty labor organizations*, freely associated among themselves in the towns, villages, districts, and provinces, helping one another. . . ."[28] The soviets, warned the syndicalist journal, must remain decentralized units, free from party bosses and from so-called people's commissars. If any political group should attempt to convert them into instruments of coercion, the people must be ready to take up arms once more.[29]

Anarchist circles in Petrograd were soon buzzing with talk of "a third and last stage of the revolution," a final struggle between "Social Democratic power and the creative spirit of the masses . . . between the authoritarian and libertarian systems . . . between the Marxist principle and the anarchist principle."[30] There were ominous murmurings among the Kronstadt sailors to the effect that, if the new *Sovnarkom* dared betray the revolution, the cannons that took the Winter Palace would take Smolny (headquarters of the Bolshevik govern-

[28] *Golos Truda*, No. 13, 3 November 1917, p. 1.

[29] *Ibid.*, No. 15, 6 November 1917, p. 1; No. 17, 8 November 1917, p. 1.

[30] Voline, *La Révolution inconnue*, pp. 190-191.

ment) as well.[31] "Where authority begins," exclaimed *Golos Truda*, "there the revolution ends!"[32]

The anarchists received the next shock scarcely a week later. On 2 November, the Soviet government published a "Declaration of the Rights of the Peoples of Russia," which affirmed the "inalienable right" of every nationality to express its self-determination by creating an independent state.[33] For the anarchists, this was a step backwards, a counterrevolutionary retreat from the internationalist and stateless ideal. The editors of *Golos Truda* hastened to predict that the Declaration would soon become "a superfluous paper memorial in the 'History of the Great Russian Revolution!'"[34] N. I. Pavlov, an Anarcho-Syndicalist leader in the Moscow Bakers' Union, reproached the Bolsheviks for contaminating the purity of the revolution with their statist policies, and offered the following manifesto as a remedy for the "party blindness" of Russia's new rulers:

> Hail the imminent social revolution!
> Down with the squabbling of political parties!
> Down with the Constituent Assembly, where parties will again bicker over "views," "programs," "slogans"— and over power!
> Hail the soviets in the localities, reorganized along new, truly revolutionary, labor, and non-party lines![35]

Alarmed by the Bolshevik appetite for power, the anarchists worried lest the new regime should interfere with the autonomy of the factory and shop committees or attempt to curb workers' control over production. The Anarchist-Communists, in particular, had reason to be apprehensive, for Lenin, on the eve of the October uprising, had disputed their contention that the workers should not stop at mere control, but should seize the factories outright: "The key to the matter [Lenin had written in "Will the Bolsheviks Retain State Power?"] will not lie in the confiscation of capitalist property, but in

[31] *Ibid.*, p. 200.
[32] *Golos Truda*, No. 14, 4 November 1917, p. 1.
[33] Reed, *Ten Days that Shook the World*, p. 345.
[34] *Golos Truda*, No. 14, 4 November 1917, p. 1.
[35] *Ibid.*, No. 19, 10 November 1917, p. 4.

statewide, all-embracing workers' control over the capitalists and their supporters. By confiscation alone, you will accomplish nothing, for in that there is no element of organization, of accounting, of distribution."[36] In this passage, Lenin was simply repeating what he had stated shortly after his return to Russia: that workers' control implied control by the soviets and not "the ridiculous passing of the railroads into the hands of the railwaymen or the leather factories into the hands of the leather workers," which would result in anarchy rather than socialism.[37]

If the labor program drawn up by the Bolsheviks immediately after the October *coup* proved too meek for the Anarchist-Communists, the Anarcho-Syndicalists had little cause for displeasure. Indeed, they may well have experienced a mild sense of relief, for the first draft decree on workers' control, set down by Lenin himself, had a strong syndicalist flavor. Published on 3 November, the draft provided for the introduction of workers' control in all enterprises employing five or more workmen or handling a volume of business in excess of 10,000 rubles a year. The factory committee, as the executor of control, was to be given access to all company records and to all stores of materials, tools, and products. Moreover, the decisions of the committee were to be binding on the administration.[38] In its final form, the decree on workers' control made the factory committee the control organ of each industrial enterprise, though the committee was to be responsible to a local council of workers' control, which was subordinated in turn to an All-Russian Council of Workers' Control.[39] In practice, however, real power rested with the individual factory committee, which paid scant attention to the new hierarchy of control organs. The workers' committee, as the Petrograd Council of Factory Committees informed the director of the Urania Electric Factory, was "the supreme boss in the plant."[40]

The effect of the decree was to give powerful impetus to a

[36] Lenin, *Sochineniia*, XXI, 261.
[37] *Ibid.*, XX, 473.
[38] *Ibid.*, XXII, 25-26.
[39] *Sbornik dekretov i postanovlenii po narodnomu khoziaistvu (25 oktiabria 1917 g.-25 oktiabria 1918 g.)* (Moscow, 1918), pp. 171-172.
[40] *Rabochii kontrol' i natsionalizatsiia promyshlennykh predpriiatii Petrograda*, p. 261.

brand of syndicalism in which the workers on the spot rather than the over-all trade union apparatus controlled the instruments of production—a brand of syndicalism bordering on total chaos. Before October, workers' control, though widespread, had generally taken a passive, observational form; instances of actual confiscation or of direct intervention in management were scattered, especially in comparison with the numerous cases of land seizure by the peasants of the black-earth provinces. Once given official sanction, however, workers' control spread apace, assuming a more active shape then previously.

Many workers were convinced that the new decree had delivered the means of production into their hands, and for several months following the revolution, the Russian working class enjoyed a degree of freedom and a sense of power unique in its history. But as more and more workers reached out to claim their birthrights, the country hurtled toward the brink of economic collapse. In issuing the radical decree, Lenin was by no means unaware that it might worsen the already chaotic situation, but he gave tactical priority to cementing the loyalty of the bench workers by promising them the speedy realization of their utopia.

By the end of 1917, effective management was rapidly vanishing from Russian industry.[41] A British trade union delegation visiting Russia in 1924 reported, with characteristic English understatement, that workers' control in 1917 had had "a very bad effect on production." The workingmen, the report said, had been transformed overnight into "a new body of shareholders."[42] A similar observation was made by a Bolshevik commentator early in 1918: the workers, he wrote, considered tools and equipment "their own property."[43] Cases of pillage and theft were not uncommon. W. H. Chamberlin re-

[41] John Maynard, *Russia in Flux* (New York, 1951), p. 223, estimates that, within a few months after the October Revolution, only about one-fifth of the enterprises continued to operate under their old ownership and management. The rest, says Maynard, were about evenly divided between nationalization and workers' control, which in practice were not very different.

[42] *Russia: The Official Report of the British Trades Union Delegation to Russia and Caucasus, Nov. and Dec. 1924* (London, 1925), p. 138.

[43] R. Arskii, in *Izvestiia VTsIK*, 27 March 1918, pp. 1-2.

counts an anecdote about a worker who was asked, "What would you do if you were the director of the factory?" "I should steal a hundred rubles and run away," he replied.[44] Individual factory committees sent "pushers" (*tolkachi*) into the provinces to purchase fuel and raw materials, sometimes for outrageous prices. Often they refused to share available supplies with other factories in direst need. Local committees raised wages and prices indiscriminately, and on occasion cooperated with the owners in return for special "bonuses."[45]

If the British trade union delegation simply stated that workers' control had had "a very bad effect" on production, a more vivid assessment was provided by another English observer, a reporter for the *Manchester Guardian*, traveling in Russia during 1917 and 1918:

> It is no exaggeration to say that during November, December, and the greater part of January something approaching anarchy reigned in the industries of Northern Russia. . . . There was no common industrial plan. Factory Committees had no higher authority to which to look for direction. They acted entirely on their own and tried to solve those problems of production and distribution which seemed most pressing for the immediate future and for the locality. Machinery was sometimes sold in order to buy raw materials. The factories became like anarchistic communes . . . anarcho-syndicalist tendencies began to run riot.[46]

In a most revealing admission, the famous Russian-American anarchists Emma Goldman and Alexander Berkman, visiting Petrograd industrial establishments in 1920 (they had been deported from the United States in December 1919), noted that the Laferm Tobacco Factory was in reasonably good

[44] Chamberlin, *The Russian Revolution*, I, 416.

[45] Pankratova, *Fabzavkomy v bor'be za sotsialisticheskuiu fabriku*, p. 238; *Rabochii kontrol' i natsionalizatsiia promyshlennykh predpriiatii Petrograda*, pp. 284-285; T. Shatilova, *Fabzavkomy i profsoiuzy v 1917-1918 gg.* (Leningrad, 1927), p. 17; I. A. Gladkov, *Ocherki sovetskoi ekonomiki, 1917-1920 gg.* (Moscow, 1956), pp. 49-52; S. O. Zagorsky, *La République des soviets* (Paris, 1921), p. 19.

[46] M. Philips Price, *My Reminiscences of the Russian Revolution* (London, 1921), p. 212.

working order only "because the former owner and manager himself was still in charge."[47]

The anarchic situation in the factories seemed a nightmare not only to the manufacturers, but to many intellectuals and workers as well. Trade unionists, whether members of the Bolshevik or the Menshevik faction, advocated state control over industry. Union spokesmen condemned the factory committees for their selfish absorption in the needs of their own enterprises, their "fanatical patriotism" in their "own hut";[48] they warned that the "local pride" of the individual committees might damage the national economy beyond repair and result in "the same sort of atomization as under the capitalist system."[49] "Workers' control," wrote a Bolshevik labor leader in the metal workers' journal, "is an anarchistic attempt to achieve socialism in one enterprise, but actually leads to clashes among the workers themselves, and to the refusal of fuel, metal, etc. to one another."[50] In a similar manner, the Menshevik-dominated Printers' Union disdained the "anarcho-syndicalist illusions" of the less skilled and less sophisticated workmen in other industries, who could not see beyond the gates of their own factories.[51] The Anarcho-Syndicalists of *Golos Truda* were frequently charged with inspiring this parochial outlook and "cottage-industry mentality" (*kustarnichestvo*) by their stubborn rejection of central authority, both economic and political.[52]

While the trade unionists attacked workers' control from the right as a syndicalist illusion, the Anarchist-Communists on the left damned it as a compromise with the capitalist system, and continued to clamor for the outright expropriation of the factories, mines, ports, and railroads by the workers on the spot. So long as the capitalist framework remained, wrote

[47] Goldman, *Living My Life*, II, 791.
[48] *Moskovskii Metallist*, No. 6, 29 November 1917, pp. 18-22.
[49] R. Arskii, "Professional'nye soiuzy i zavodskie komitety," *Vestnik Narodnogo Komissariata Truda*, 1918, No. 2-3, p. 125; *Protokoly 1-go vserossiiskogo s"ezda professional'nykh soiuzov tekstil'shchikov i fabrichnykh komitetov* (Moscow, 1918), p. 30; *Oktiabr'skaia revoliutsiia i fabzavkomy*, I, 230.
[50] Ia. Boiarkov, "Rabochii kontrol' ili regulirovanie promyshlennosti?" *Metallist*, No. 6, 30 November 1917, p. 3.
[51] Lozovskii, *Rabochii kontrol'*, pp. 77-79.
[52] See, for example, *Oktiabr'skaia revoliutsiia i fabzavkomy*, I, 215.

Apollon Karelin in *Burevestnik* (the newspaper of the Petrograd Federation of Anarchists), the worker was a worker and
the boss was the boss; a token role in managing production or
a reduction in working hours could not alter the fundamental
master-slave relationship.[53] More extreme measures were required, declared *Burevestnik*. It was necessary to demolish the
bourgeois world completely, and inaugurate entirely new forms
of labor, "rooted in freedom rather than slavery."[54] The working
masses were exhorted to unfurl the black banner of anarchism
and mount the barricades against the new government of "can-
nibals and man-eaters." "Expose the lie of the Constituent
Assembly, the nonsense of 'control over production,' and the
harm and danger of state centralization," *Burevestnik* exclaimed, "and summon all the oppressed to the Social Revolution."[55] Rumblings of discontent were audible again in
Ekaterinoslav, a center of anarchist violence during the early
years of the century. In December, the Anarchist-Communists
circulated an incendiary manifesto among the factory workers
of the city:

> You have not arisen for the purpose of safeguarding
> someone else's welfare, for the purpose of controlling pro-
> duction belonging not to you but to your enemy—the capi-
> talist. Or are you his watchdog?
> All production to the workers!
> Down with socialist control!
> Down with the Constituent Assembly!
> Down with all authority!
> Down with private property!
> Hail the Anarchist Commune and with it Peace, Liberty,
> Equality, and Fraternity![56]

The Bolsheviks, of course, had no intention of placing their
seal of approval on the random seizure of factories. Nor did
they intend to tolerate workers' control—even in the limited
sense of bookkeeping and inspection—for an indefinite period.
Lenin had legalized workers' control in order to consolidate

[53] A. Karelin, "Zametka o sindikalizme," *Burevestnik*, 21 November
1917, pp. 2-3.
[54] *Ibid.*, p. 1.   [55] *Ibid.*
[56] *Ibid.*, 3 December 1917, p. 2.

the support of the working class behind his insecure regime, but he could hardly allow the workers to wreck the Russian economy and his new government in the process. Determined to forestall a new kind of "anarchy of production," he initiated a series of measures designed to bring the workers' committees under state control and to place the regulation of industry in the hands of a central authority.

As his first move, on 1 December, Lenin created the Supreme Economic Council (*Vesenkha*), assigning it the mission of working out "a plan for the regulation of the economic life of the country."[57] The new body absorbed the All-Russian Council of Workers' Control and laid plans for the over-all regulation of the national economy. Although the syndicalist tide could not be stemmed overnight—indeed, local control by workers' committees was to flourish until the summer of 1918 —an important step had been taken towards the "statization" (*ogosudarstvlenie*) of economic authority.

Before the regulation of the economy could be transferred to the government, it was necessary to curb the unbridled freedom of the industrial workers. Thus the official cry was raised for "iron discipline" in the factories and mines,[58] and the trade unions, which Lenin until now had given a back place to the factory committees, were chosen to bring order to the chaotic proletarian world. It was to be the mission of the unions, as an Odessa Anarcho-Syndicalist (Piotrovskii) had earlier prophesied, to "devour" the factory committees and to convert workers' control into state control.[59]

Decisive measures to "statize" the Russian labor movement were taken at the First All-Russian Congress of Trade Unions, which met in Petrograd from 7 to 14 January 1918, immediately following the dissolution of the Constituent Assembly. Of the 416 voting delegates representing some 2,500,000 trade union members, the Bolsheviks commanded a large majority— 273, not counting the 21 left SR's who voted with them. The

[57] *Natsionalizatsiia promyshlennosti v SSSR: sbornik dokumentov i materialov, 1917-1920 gg.* (Moscow, 1954), p. 499.

[58] *Izvestiia VTsIK*, 27 October 1917, p. 2; *Metallist*, No. 7, 16 December 1917, p. 2; *Rabochii kontrol' i natsionalizatsiia promyshlennykh predpriiatii Petrograda*, pp. 264-265; *Natsionalizatsiia promyshlennosti v SSSR*, p. 189.

[59] *Oktiabr'skaia revoliutsiia i fabzavkomy*, II, 191.

Mensheviks had 66 delegates, while the Anarcho-Syndicalists —who had generally shunned the unions in favor of the factory committees—had only 6.[60] The remaining delegates consisted of 10 right SR's, 6 Maximalists, and 34 nonparty workmen.[61]

The debates at the Congress centered on the nature of the Russian Revolution. In a lengthy address, Iulii Martov set forth the Menshevik view that Russia was undergoing a "bourgeois-democratic" revolution, in which "the fundamental preconditions for the achievement of socialism" were absent.[62] His colleague Cherevanin elaborated upon this theme at a later session of the Congress. Russia was a comparatively backward country, he declared, and "the more backward countries, from the Marxist point of view, are the least able to pass on to socialism." On this question and many others, Cherevanin said, his party and the Anarcho-Syndicalists held "diametrically opposite points of view."[63] The well-known Marxist scholar D. B. Riazanov, though a recent convert to Bolshevism, found himself in general agreement with the Menshevik speakers on this point. His statement that "we do not as yet have the preconditions for socialism" was greeted by applause from the right and center of the hall. Socialism, after all, could not be achieved "overnight," said Riazanov, echoing a phrase in Lenin's *The State and Revolution.*[64]

Mensheviks joined Bolsheviks in upbraiding the anarchists for their premature efforts to inaugurate a stateless society. By pressing for "industrial federalism" at this time, declared the Bolshevik trade-unionist Lozovskii, the Anarcho-Syndicalists were engaging in an "idyllic" quest for the "bluebird of happiness"; a realistic appraisal of the current situation in the factories clearly indicated that Russia required "the centralization of workers' control" in conformity with a general plan.[65]

[60] The unions in which the Anarcho-Syndicalists had a significant influence were the bakers, the river transport, dock, and shipyard workers, the Donets miners, the food-industry workers, the postal and telegraph workers, and, to a lesser degree, the metal and textile workers and the railwaymen.

[61] *Pervyi vserossiiskii s"ezd professional'nykh soiuzov, 7-14 ianvaria 1918 g.* (Moscow, 1918), p. 338.

[62] *Ibid.,* p. 82.　　　　　　[63] *Ibid.,* pp. 200, 225.

[64] *Ibid.,* pp. 26-27. Lenin, quoting a passage from Engels' *Anti-Dühring,* had accused the anarchists of naively desiring to abolish the state "overnight." Lenin, *Sochineniia,* XXI, 410.

[65] *Ibid.,* pp. 192, 229.

A Menshevik delegate deplored the fact that an "anarchist wave" in the shape of factory committees and workers' control was "sweeping over our Russian labor movement."[66] Joining in these strictures, Riazanov advised the factory committees to "commit suicide" by becoming "an integral element" of the trade union structure.[67]

The half-dozen Anarcho-Syndicalist delegates fought a desperate battle to preserve the autonomy of the committees. It was "absurd," exclaimed Grigorii Maksimov, to maintain that Russia was in the bourgeois stage of revolutionary development. Thanks to the factory committees, capitalism as well as autocracy had already been "seized by the throat." The present revolution was "clearing the way towards the realization of the ultimate goal, when the proletariat will be completely free, when there will be neither groans nor inequality." Maksimov claimed that he and his fellow Anarcho-Syndicalists were "better Marxists" than either the Mensheviks or the Bolsheviks —a declaration which caused a great stir in the hall.[68] He was alluding, no doubt, to Marx's appeal for the liberation of the working class by the workers themselves, for a permanent revolution that would replace the state with a libertarian society modeled on the Paris Commune.

Excitement in the Congress reached a climax when Bill Shatov characterized the trade unions as "living corpses," and urged the working class "to organize in the localities and create a free new Russia, without a God, without a tsar, and without a boss in the trade union."[69] When Riazanov protested Shatov's vilification of the unions, Maksimov rose to his comrade's defense, dismissing Riazanov's objections as those of a white-handed intellectual who had never worked, never sweated, never felt life.[70] Another Anarcho-Syndicalist dele-

---

[66] *Ibid.*, p. 48. [67] *Ibid.*, p. 235.
[68] *Ibid.*, pp. 55, 82-86, 213-214.
[69] *Ibid.*, pp. 101-102. Similarly, at the First Congress of Textile Unions and Factory Committees held later in January, a delegate (probably an anarchist) spoke of "the dead trade unions" and declared that "it is impossible to have centralized organizations every time." *Protokoly 1-go vserossiiskogo s"ezda tekstil'shchikov*, p. 38. Lozovskii observed that the Anarcho-Syndicalists had "created a whole theory that the trade unions have died." Lozovskii, *Rabochii kontrol'*, pp. 35-36.
[70] *Pervyi vserossiiskii s"ezd professional'nykh soiuzov*, pp. 237, 240.

gate, Laptev by name, reminded the gathering that the revolution had been made "not only by the intellectuals, but by the masses"; therefore, it was imperative for Russia "to listen to the voice of the working masses, the voice from below. . . ."[71]

But the Bolshevik leaders felt that it was no longer expedient to listen to the destructive voice from below. The time was ripe, they believed, to align themselves with the proponents of state control over industry, a central economic plan, and a statewide apparatus of trade unions. During the spring and summer, when Lenin's goal was to topple the Provisional Government, he had joined forces with the anarchists—particularly the Anarcho-Syndicalists—in support of the factory committees and workers' control. Now that the Bolshevik revolution had been secured, he abandoned the forces of destruction for those of centralization and order, siding with the trade unionist advocates of state control. Consequently, the First Congress of Trade Unions, with its overwhelming Bolshevik majority, voted to transform the factory committees into primary union organs.[72] The Bolshevik leadership, however, parted company with those trade unionists who demanded that the unions remain "neutral" organizations, that is, unions existing independently of the government. Trade union neutrality was labeled a "bourgeois" idea, an anomaly in a workers' state.[73]

With the "statization" of the unions and the conversion of the factory committees into local union cells (if only on paper, at first), the committees became "state institutions," as Lenin desired.[74] Furthermore, the Congress emphasized that workers' control did not mean the local "transfer of the enterprises into the hands of the workers," but was "inseparably tied to a general system of regulation," operating under an over-all economic plan. The "centralization of workers' control" was made the task of the trade unions.[75] In effect, the workers' committees had been ordered to commit suicide—as Riazanov had suggested—by leaping into the jaws of the union apparatus. Thus was Piotrovskii's fearful prophecy that the trade unions would "devour" the factory committees borne out.

Though disheartened by these reverses, the anarchists did

[71] *Ibid.*, p. 50.　　[72] *Ibid.*, p. 374.　　[73] *Ibid.*, p. 364.
[74] Lenin, *Sochineniia*, XXII, 50.
[75] *Pervyi vserossiiskii s'ezd professional'nykh soiuzov*, pp. 369-370.

not consider themselves defeated, nor did they abandon their search for the Golden Age. Their bitter charge that the Bolsheviks were a caste of self-seeking intellectuals who had betrayed the masses rang forth louder than ever. The anarchists insisted that it was the masses (as Laptev had told the Trade Union Congress) who had made the revolution in the first place, that Lenin and his party had merely ridden to power on the spontaneous tide from below.

Here was the outcry of frustrated idealists, who feared that the good society was being snatched from their grasp. And, indeed, it was a protest with a kernel of truth. The Bolshevik feat lay not in making the revolution, but in slowing it down and diverting it into Communist channels, or, as Maksimov was to write 20 years later, in forcing it into the "Procrustean bed" of Marxism.[76] The extraordinary achievement of the Bolsheviks lay in checking the elemental drive of the Russian masses towards a chaotic utopia.

[76] Maximoff, *The Guillotine at Work*, p. 346. Cf. Emma Goldman, *Living My Life*, II, 826: "Yet as a matter of fact the Russian Revolution had been *à la Bakunin*, but it had since been transformed *à la Karl Marx*."

7 · THE ANARCHISTS AND THE BOLSHEVIK REGIME

*While men are gazing up to Heaven, imagining
after a happiness, or fearing a Hell after they are
dead, their eyes are put out, that they see
not what is their birthright.*

GERRARD WINSTANLEY

Ever since its inception at the turn of the century, the Russian anarchist movement—if, indeed, so disorganized a phenomenon can properly be called a "movement"—was plagued by rancorous internal disputes over doctrine and tactics. All efforts to achieve unity were in vain. Perhaps this was inevitable, for the anarchists by nature were inveterate nonconformists who stubbornly resisted organizational discipline. They seemed fated to remain in an atomized condition, a congeries of disparate individuals and groups—syndicalists and terrorists, pacifists and militants, idealists and adventurers.

Factional strife had contributed greatly to the decline of Russian anarchism in the years following the Revolution of 1905, and had nearly delivered the *coup de grâce* to the movement during the war. By 1917, however, many anarchist leaders evinced a strong determination to avoid the quarrels of the past. While aware of the formidable obstacles to unity inherent in the anarchist creed, they nevertheless endeavored to set aside their differences and rally behind the common banner of stateless communism. In this ambition, they were encouraged by the rapid growth of anarchist federations in virtually every large Russian city from Odessa to Vladivostok. If a measure of cooperation was possible on the local level, why not on a national scale as well?

The first step towards unification was taken in July 1917, when an Anarchist Information Bureau was established to summon an All-Russian Conference. Towards the end of the month, representatives from a dozen cities gathered in Kharkov and for five days discussed such vital matters as anarchism's role in the factory committees and trade unions, and the means of converting the "imperialist" war into a worldwide social revolution. Before dispersing, the delegates assigned the Information Bureau the mission of arranging an All-Russian Congress.[1]

In order to gauge the strength of the movement and to determine the degree of interest in a nationwide gathering, the Information Bureau sent questionnaires to anarchist organizations throughout the country. The many replies which soon reached Kharkov reflected overwhelming support for such a congress at the earliest feasible date. Each response included a brief description of the anarchist circles in the particular area, the extent of their activities, and, in some cases, a list of their publications.[2] A valuable profile of the movement was thus obtained. In most locations, the anarchist groups fell into three categories: Anarchist-Communists, Anarcho-Syndicalists, and individualist anarchists. The anarchists in smaller towns often made no clear-cut distinction between Anarchist-Communism and Anarcho-Syndicalism, the two persuasions coalescing into a single Federation of Anarchists or of Anarchist-Communists-Syndicalists. Here and there, groups of Tolstoyans preached the gospel of Christian nonviolence, and though they had few ties with the revolutionary anarchists, their moral impact on the movement was considerable. As for the individualists, some were peaceable and others prone to violence, but all repudiated the territorial communes of the Anarchist-Communists as well as the workers' organizations of the Anarcho-Syndicalists; only unorganized individuals, they believed, were safe from coercion and domination and thus capable of remaining true to the ideals of anarchism. Taking their cue from Stirner and Nietzsche, they exalted the ego and the will and, in some cases, exhibited a distinctly aristocratic style of thought and action.[3] Anarchist-individualism attracted a following of Bohemian artists and intellectuals, and

[1] *Revoliutsionnoe Tvorchestvo*, No. 1-2, January-February 1918, p. 106.

[2] *Biulleten' Osvedomitel'nogo Biuro Anarkhistov v Rossii*, No. 3, 15 December 1917, pp. 2-8; *Bezvlastie* (Kharkov), No. 1, March 1918, pp. 14-15.

[3] "Nietzsche," wrote Emma Goldman, "was not a social theorist but a poet, a rebel and innovator. His aristocracy was neither of birth nor of purse; it was of the spirit. In that respect, Nietzsche was an anarchist, and all true anarchists were aristocrats." *Living My Life*, I, 194.

occasional lone-wolf bandits. Their obsessive quest for pure individual liberty either reduced itself to a form of philosophical solipsism or took the more active shape of revolutionary heroism or sheer banditry, with death as the ultimate form of self-affirmation, the ultimate escape from the constricting fabric of organized society.[4]

At the end of 1917 and the beginning of 1918, anarchist publications announced that the All-Russian Congress was imminent,[5] but the pernicious divisiveness within the movement reasserted itself, and the scheduled meeting never took place. The broadest gathering that could be mustered was a Conference of Anarchists of the Donets Basin, which met in Kharkov on 25 December 1917, and again on 14 February 1918 in the city of Ekaterinoslav. The Conference founded a weekly periodical, *Golos Anarkhista* (The Anarchist Voice), and elected a Bureau of Anarchists of the Donets Basin, which sponsored lectures in southern Russia by such prominent figures as Iuda Roshchin, Nikolai Rogdaev, and Petr Arshinov.[6] Later in 1918, the Anarcho-Syndicalists were to hold two All-Russian Conferences in Moscow, and an All-Russian Congress of Anarchist-Communists would assemble in the same city; but never was there to be a national congress embracing both major wings of the movement, let alone the lesser groups.

The Petrograd Federation of Anarchist Groups, which linked together a variety of Anarchist-Communist circles and clubs in and around the capital, was the most important city-wide organization to appear in Russia during 1917. By November, seven months after the Federation was created, the circulation of its daily newspaper (*Burevestnik*) exceeded 25,000 readers, located chiefly in the Vyborg district, at Kronstadt, and in the working class suburbs of Obukhovo and Kolpino.[7] Continuing the policies laid down by *Kommuna* and

[4] An extremely valuable list of anarchist groups, clubs, journals, and printing establishments active at the beginning of 1918 is in *Revoliutsionnoe Tvorchestvo*, No. 1-2, pp. 138-142.

[5] See, for example, *Burevestnik*, 17 January 1918, p. 4.

[6] *Golos Anarkhista*, No. 1, 11 March 1918, pp. 7-8; Gorelik, *Anarkhisty v rossiiskoi revoliutsii*, pp. 37-38.

[7] Of this figure, not more than a few thousand actually considered themselves anarchists, the rest being radicals of various stripes. In 1917-

Svobodnaia Kommuna, Burevestnik exhorted the homeless and destitute to seize private residences[8] and pressed for the expropriation of private property in general. (Bleikhman, writing under the pen name of N. Solntsev, was a tireless advocate of the confiscation of homes and factories.) Its editors by no means abandoned the cry for a "social revolution" when the Bolsheviks took power; in fact, the Paris Commune, once invoked as the ideal form of society to replace the Provisional Government, now became *Burevestnik's* answer to Lenin's dictatorship. The workers of Petrograd were told to "reject the words, orders, and decrees of the commissars," and to create their own libertarian commune after the model of 1871.[9] At the same time, the newspaper had no less scorn for the "parliamentary fetishism" of the Kadets (Constitutional Democrats), SR's, and Mensheviks,[10] and it jubilantly greeted the dissolution of the Constituent Assembly in January 1918 as a great step towards the anarchist millennium.[11]

Within the Petrograd Federation, two loosely-knit groups, led by men of sharply dissimilar temperament, exerted a powerful influence over the rest, and almost monopolized the pages of *Burevestnik*. The first was headed by Apollon Andreevich Karelin (who frequently wrote under the name of Kochegarov), an intellectual noted for his humanity and erudition, "a splendid old man," as Victor Serge described him.[12] His bearded and bespectacled face suggested the benign and scholarly nature of Prince Kropotkin. One of his associates, Ivan Kharkhardin, aptly likened him to a "Biblical patriarch."[13]

Karelin was born in St. Petersburg in 1863, the son of an artist of aristocratic lineage and a schoolmistress who was related to the novelist and poet Lermontov. He was taken to

---

1918, the total number of active anarchists in Russia (excluding the Tolstoyans and Makhno's peasant movement in the Ukraine) was in the neighborhood of 10,000, a figure augmented by many thousands of close sympathizers.

[8] See, for example, *Burevestnik*, 28 November 1917, p. 1; 3 December 1917, p. 1; and 17 January 1918, p. 4.

[9] *Ibid.*, 9 April 1918, p. 2.

[10] *Ibid.*, 15 November 1917, p. 1.

[11] *Ibid.*, 16 January 1918, pp. 1-2.

[12] Serge, *Mémoires d'un révolutionnaire*, p. 134.

[13] I. Kharkhardin, "Iz vospominanii o A. A. Kareline," *Probuzhdenie*, No. 1, April 1927, p. 11.

Nizhnii Novgorod as a child and there received his *gimnaziia* training. In 1881, when Alexander II was assassinated by the Peoples Will, Karelin, who was eighteen at the time, was arrested as a participant in the radical student movement and sent to the Peter-Paul fortress in Petersburg. He was released when his parents appealed for clemency, and permitted to study law at Kazan University. Once again, however, he joined a Populist circle and engaged in illegal propaganda activity, which doomed him to long periods of "prison and exile, exile and prison," in the words of one of his future disciples.[14] In 1905, Karelin fled from Siberia and spent the dozen years between the two Russian revolutions in Paris. There he formed an anarchist circle of Russian exiles known as the Brotherhood of Free Communists, which published anarchist literature, organized lectures and seminars, and attracted a considerable following (which included the future Anarcho-Syndicalist leader, Volin). Returning to Petrograd in August 1917, Karelin soon gained wide allegiance among the Anarchist-Communists of the capital.[15]

Karelin devoted his energies largely to sober, if unoriginal, analyses of political and economic questions. In a concise and even-tempered style, he presented the Anarchist-Communist case against workers' control,[16] and wrote numerous articles and pamphlets attacking parliamentary government.[17] At meeting halls and workers' clubs throughout the city, Karelin delivered lectures on such subjects as "How to arrange a life for the toilers without authority or parliaments."[18] A pamphlet on the agrarian question that he had published in London in 1912 (following very closely Kropotkin's writings on territorial communes) was still widely read as a succinct statement of the

[14] A. A. Solonovich, "Pamiati A. A. Karelina," *ibid.*, p. 5.
[15] A. A. Karelin, *Vol'naia zhizn'* (Detroit, 1955), pp. 9-20; E. Z. Dolinin, *V vikhre revoliutsii* (Detroit, 1954), pp. 267-271; *Delo Truda*, No. 12, May 1926, pp. 15-16; *Delo Truda-Probuzhdenie*, No. 68, December 1963, p. 26. Dolinin, Solonovich, Kharkhardin, and Khudolei were Karelin's principal disciples during the years following the Revolution of 1917.
[16] *Burevestnik*, 21 November 1917, pp. 2-3.
[17] Kochegarov, *Polozhitel'nye i otritsatel'nye storony demokratii;* Kochegarov, *Gosudarstvo i anarkhisty*.
[18] *Burevestnik*, 19 December 1917, p. 1; 26 January 1918, p. 2.

Anarchist-Communist position on the subject.[19] The first step, according to Karelin, was to distribute all the land to those capable of working it. This was also a page from the SR land program, which Lenin borrowed in November 1917 when he transferred the land of the nobility, church, and crown to the custody of peasant committees. The Bolshevik decree of February 1918 nationalizing the land, however, fundamentally conflicted with the ultimate goal envisioned by Karelin: a federation of autonomous communes, in which the concept of ownership—whether private or state—would be abolished and members rewarded according to their needs.

If Karelin was heir to the moderate Anarchist-Communist tradition of Kropotkin's *Khleb i Volia* group, then the leaders of the second influential faction within the Petrograd Federation, the brothers A. L. and V. L. Gordin, were the successors to the ultra-radical *Beznachal'tsy*. Their choice of *Beznachalie* as the title of a periodical they published briefly in 1917 was by no means fortuitous; both in style and temperament, the Gordins were direct descendants of Bidbei and Rostovtsev, and exponents of the passionate and erratic variety of Russian anarchism founded by Bakunin. The superficial but fascinating essays which they produced in great quantity were marked by a degree of anti-intellectualism unmatched even in the diatribes of their forebears. Take, for example, the following proclamation printed in enormous letters across the front page of *Burevestnik* early in 1918:

UNEDUCATED ONES! DESTROY THAT LOATHSOME CULTURE WHICH DIVIDES MEN INTO "IGNORANT" AND "LEARNED." THEY ARE KEEPING YOU IN THE DARK. THEY HAVE PUT OUT YOUR EYES. IN THIS DARKNESS, IN THE DARKNESS OF THE NIGHT OF CULTURE, THEY HAVE ROBBED YOU.[20]

Hardly a day passed without a similar tirade by the Gordin brothers. Their rejection of contemporary European culture was as sweeping as their output was inexhaustible. The neologisms that adorned their articles and pamphlets were samples

---

[19] A. Kochegarov, *Zemel'naia programma anarkhistov-kommunistov* (London, 1912).

[20] *Burevestnik*, 27 January 1918, p. 1.

of the new language they planned to construct to suit the post-bourgeois world of the future. The compulsive character of their work lends credence to the caustic observation of a contemporary Marxist scholar that the Gordins were suffering from an extreme case of "graphomania."[21] Still and all, their poems and manifestoes make absorbing reading and, for all their prolixity, are not without occasional flashes of insight.

In 1917, the Gordin brothers founded a society of Anarchist-Communists which they called the Union of the Oppressed Five (*Soiuz Piati Ugnetennykh*), with branches in Petrograd and Moscow. The "Oppressed Five" referred to those categories of humanity which endured the greatest hardships under the yoke of Western civilization: "worker-vagabond," national minority, woman, youth, and individual personality. Five basic institutions—the state, capitalism, colonialism, the school, and the family—were held responsible for their sufferings. The Gordins worked out a philosophy which they called "Pan-Anarchism" and which prescribed five remedies for the five baneful institutions that tormented the five oppressed elements of modern society. The remedies for the state and capitalism were, simply enough, statelessness and communism; for the remaining three oppressors, however, the antidotes were rather more novel: "cosmism" (the universal elimination of national persecution), "gyneantropism" (the emancipation and humanization of women), and "pedism" (the liberation of the young from "the vise of slave education").[22]

Anti-intellectualism lay at the heart of the Pan-Anarchist creed. Borrowing a leaf from Bakunin, the brothers Gordin focused their criticism on book learning, the "diabolical weapon" by which the educated few dominated the unlettered masses. They applied Ockham's razor to all *a priori* theories and scholastic abstractions, particularly those of religion and science. Religion was "the fruit of fantasy" and science "the fruit of intellect"; both were mythical inventions of the human brain: "The rule of heaven and the rule of nature—angels, spirits, devils, molecules, atoms, ether, the laws of God-Heaven and the laws of Nature, forces, the influence of one body on

[21] Gorev, *Anarkhizm v Rossii*, pp. 106-107.
[22] Brat'ia Gordiny, *Manifest pananarkhistov* (Moscow, 1918), pp. 4, 20-25.

another—all this is invented, formed, created by society."[23] The Gordins wished to liberate man's creative spirit from the shackles of dogma. For them, science—by which they meant all rational systems, natural science and social science alike— constituted the new religion of the middle class. The greatest fraud of all was Marx's theory of dialectical materialism. "Marxism," they declared, "is the new scientific Christianity, designed to conquer the *bourgeois* world by deceiving the people, the proletariat, just as Christianity deceived the feudal world."[24] Marx and Engels were "the Magi of scientific socialist black-magic."[25]

Despite the immediate threat of Marxism, the Gordin brothers were ebulliently optimistic about the future. "The Gods of Europe are dying," they wrote, victims in a "struggle between two cultures." Religion and science, outmoded and weak, were retreating before the new and vigorous forces of labor and technology. "The culture of Europe is perishing, religion and science are disappearing from the face of the earth, and only Anarchy and Technics shall rule the earth."[26] Confident that the traditional book learning used by the ruling classes to dominate the toiling masses was obsolete, the Gordins advised mothers to stop sending their sons into the church or the university. Soon a new type of education would be introduced, emancipating the children of the world from "white-handedness (*beloruchestvo*), pitiful intellectualizing, and criminal dehumanization."[27] Boys and girls would no longer be compelled to study social and natural "laws" out of books, but would receive a "pantechnical" education stressing inventiveness and practical aptitude, technical skill and muscle power, rather than the power of abstract reasoning. The great task ahead, the Gordins declared, was not to theorize but to

[23] *Ibid.*, pp. 5-7.
[24] *Burevestnik*, 10 April 1918, p. 3.
[25] Brat'ia Gordiny, *Manifest pananarkhistov*, p. 60.
[26] *Burevestnik*, 10 April 1918, pp. 1-3; 11 April 1918, p. 3. A similar declaration (probably drafted by the Gordins) was adopted by the Northern Regional Congress of Anarchists, held in Briansk in August 1918: "Religion and science are the culture of the oppressors; technics and labor are the culture of the oppressed." *Rezoliutsii s''ezda, imevshego mesto v gorode Brianske s 6-go po 11-oe avgusta 1918 g.* (Moscow, 1918), p. 5.
[27] Brat'ia Gordiny, *Manifest pananarkhistov*, p. 28.

create, not merely to dream utopia with our minds but to build it with our hands. And this was the mission of the oppressed five—"The liberation of the oppressed is the task of the oppressed themselves."[28]

In March 1918, when the Bolsheviks moved the seat of government from Peter the Great's vulnerable "window on the West" back to the forest interior of old Muscovy, the leading anarchists of Petrograd lost no time in transferring their headquarters to the new capital. Moscow, now the focal point of the revolution, quickly became the center of the anarchist movement. The Anarcho-Syndicalists immediately began printing *Golos Truda* in Moscow, and the Anarchist-Communist organ, *Burevestnik*, which continued to appear in Petrograd for several more months (it was finally closed down in May), soon took a back place to *Anarkhiia* (Anarchy), the daily newspaper of the Moscow Federation of Anarchist Groups. Before very long, the Moscow Federation had supplanted its Petrograd counterpart as the leading Anarchist-Communist organization in the country.

Formed in March 1917, the Moscow Federation made its headquarters in the old Merchants' Club, which was confiscated by a band of anarchists in the wake of the February Revolution and rechristened the "House of Anarchy." The Federation contained a sprinkling of syndicalists and individualists among its predominantly Anarchist-Communist membership. Its foremost members in the spring of 1918, apart from Apollon Karelin and the Gordin brothers (who had moved to Moscow from Petrograd), included German Askarov, the keen polemicist of anti-syndicalism during the years following the Revolution of 1905 who had edited the émigré journal *Anarkhist* under the name of Oskar Burrit; Aleksei Borovoi, a professor of philosophy at Moscow University, a gifted orator and the author of numerous books, pamphlets, and articles which attempted to reconcile individualist anarchism with the doctrines of syndicalism;[29] Vladimir Bar-

[28] *Ibid.*, pp. 30-48.
[29] Borovoi's most important works were *Obshchestvennye idealy sovremennogo obshchestva* (Moscow, 1906); *Istoriia lichnoi svobody vo Frantsii* (Moscow, 1910); *Anarkhizm* (Moscow, 1918); and *Lichnost' i*

mash, a trained agronomist and a leading participant in the Moscow anarchist movement during the 1905 revolt who had acquired a measure of notoriety by wounding a district attorney in 1906 and by escaping from Moscow's Taganka prison two years later;[30] and Lev Chernyi (P. D. Turchaninov), a well-known poet, the son of an army colonel, and the proponent of a brand of Anarchist-Individualism known as "associational anarchism," a doctrine derived largely from Stirner and Nietzsche, which called for the free association of independent individuals.[31] Chernyi served as the Federation's secretary, while Askarov was a principal editor of its organ, *Anarkhiia*. The Federation devoted its energies chiefly to the dissemination of anarchist propaganda among the poorer classes of Moscow. At clubs established in the industrial districts of Presnia, Lefortovo, Sokolniki, and Zamoskvorechie, Apollon Karelin and Abba Gordin conducted animated discussions among the workmen. By and large, the Federation eschewed "ex's" and other illegal activities, except for the seizure of private homes, of which Lev Chernyi was an especially vociferous advocate.

During the early months of 1918, the anarchists of Moscow and other cities kept up their barrage of criticism against the Soviet government. Ever since the October Revolution, their grievances had been rapidly accumulating: the creation of the Council of People's Commissars (*Sovnarkom*), the "nationalistic" Declaration of the Rights of the Peoples of Russia, the formation of the Cheka, the nationalization of the banks and of the land, the subjugation of the factory committees—in short, the erection of a "commissarocracy (*komissaroderzhavie*), the ulcer of our time," as the Kharkov Anarchist-Communist Association acridly described it.[32] According to an

---

obshchestvo v anarkhistskom mirovozzrenii (Petrograd and Moscow, 1920).

[30] *Buntar'*, No. 1, 1 December 1906, p. 29; *Volna*, No. 28, April 1922, pp. 14-15.

[31] L. Chernyi, *Novoe napravlenie v anarkhizme: assosiatsionnyi anarkhizm* (Moscow, 1907; 2nd ed., New York, 1923). Dolinin, *V vikhre revoliutsii*, pp. 389-408, minimizes Chernyi's debt to Stirner and Nietzsche. Cf. F. Kraemer, "Associational Anarchism," *The Road to Freedom*, II, No. 5, March 1926, p. 3, and No. 6, April 1926, pp. 2-3.

[32] *Bezvlastie*, No. 1, March 1918, p. 1.

anonymous anarchist pamphlet of this period, the concentration of authority in the hands of the *Sovnarkom*, Cheka, and *Vesenkha* (Supreme Economic Council), had cut short all hope for a free Russia: "Bolshevism, day by day and step by step, proves that state power possesses inalienable characteristics; it can change its label, its 'theory,' and its servitors, but in essence it merely remains power and despotism in new forms."[33] The Anarchist-Communists of Ekaterinoslav recalled the message of the *Internationale* that there was no savior of the people, "not God, nor the Tsar, nor any tribune," and exhorted the masses to liberate themselves by replacing the Bolshevik dictatorship with a new society "on the basis of equality and free labor."[34] Similarly, in the Siberian city of Tomsk, the anarchists called for the ouster of Russia's new "hierarchy" of tyrants and the inauguration of a stateless society organized "from below."[35] "Laboring people!" exclaimed an Anarchist-Communist journal in Vladivostok, "Trust only in yourselves and in your organized forces!"[36]

The reaction of the Anarcho-Syndicalists to the new regime was equally bitter. In the *Golos Truda* group, Volin condemned the Bolsheviks for their "statization" of industry,[37] while Maksimov went even further, declaring that it was no longer possible, in good conscience, to support the soviets. The slogan "All power to the soviets," he explained, though never entirely acceptable to the anarchists, had been a "progressive" call to action in the period before the October insurrection; at that time, the Bolsheviks, unlike the "defensists" and "opportunists" who infested the socialist camp, constituted a revolutionary force. But since the October *coup*, Maksimov continued, Lenin and his party had abandoned their revolutionary role for that of political boss and had transformed the soviets into repositories of state power. So long as the soviets remained vehicles of authority, he concluded, every anarchist was in duty bound to combat them.[38]

[33] *Velikii opyt* (n.p., n.d. [1918]).
[34] *Golos Anarkhista*, No. 1, 11 March 1918, pp. 2-3.
[35] *Buntovshchik*, No. 1, 7 April 1918, p. 1.
[36] *Chernoe Znamia*, No. 5, 12 March 1918, p. 1.
[37] Volin, *Revoliutsiia i anarkhizm* (n.p., 1919), p. 96.
[38] G. Lapot' (Maksimov), *Sovety rabochikh soldatskikh i krest'ianskikh deputatov i nashe k nim otnoshenie* (New York, 1918).

The stream of obloquy from the anarchist press reached an unprecedented level in February 1918, when the Bolsheviks resumed their peace negotiations with the Germans at Brest-Litovsk. Anarchists joined with other "internationalists" of the left—left SR's, Menshevik Internationalists, left Communists—to protest against any accommodation with German "imperialism." To Lenin's contention that the Russian Army was too exhausted to fight any longer, the anarchists replied that professional armies were obsolete in any case and that the defense of the revolution was now the mission of the popular masses organized in partisan detachments. At a meeting of the Soviet Central Executive Committee on 23 February, Aleksandr Ge, a leader of the Anarchist-Communist faction, spoke out vehemently against the conclusion of a peace treaty: "The Anarchist-Communists proclaim terror and partisan warfare on two fronts. It is better to die for the worldwide social revolution than to live as a result of an agreement with German imperialism."[39] Both the Anarchist-Communists and Anarcho-Syndicalists argued that bands of guerrilla fighters, organized spontaneously in the localities, would harass and demoralize the invaders, ultimately destroying them just as Napoleon's army had been destroyed in 1812. At the end of February, Volin of *Golos Truda* sketched this strategy in vivid terms: "The whole task is to hold on. To resist. Not to yield. To fight. To wage relentless partisan warfare—here and there and everywhere. To advance. Or falling back, to destroy. To torment, to harass, to prey upon the enemy."[40] But the appeals of Volin and Ge fell on deaf ears; on 3 March, the Bolshevik delegation signed the treaty of Brest-Litovsk.

The terms of the treaty were even harsher than the anarchists had feared. Russia ceded to Germany more than a quarter of its arable land and of its total population, and three-quarters of its iron and steel industry. Lenin insisted that the

[39] *Pravda*, 25 February 1918, p. 2. Ge was a fervent "internationalist" throughout the war and the author of a lengthy critique of "defensism," *Put' k pobede* (Lausanne, 1917). Before coming to Moscow, he had been a member of the Karelinist faction of the Petrograd Federation of Anarchists and a frequent contributor to *Burevestnik*.

[40] Volin, *Revoliutsiia i anarkhizm*, p. 127. Cf. *Golos Anarkhista*, No. 2, 18 March 1918, p. 1; *Vestnik Anarkhii*, No. 10, 14 July 1918, p. 1; and *K Svetu*, No. 3, 24 February 1919, pp. 3-4.

agreement, severe as it was, provided a desperately needed breathing spell which would enable his party to consolidate the revolution and then carry it forward. For the outraged anarchists, however, the treaty was a humiliating capitulation to the forces of reaction, a betrayal of the worldwide revolution. It was indeed an "obscene peace," they said, echoing Lenin's own description.[41] To pay so staggering a price in territory, population, and resources, declared Volin, was a "shameful" act.[42] When the Fourth Congress of Soviets convened on 14 March to ratify the treaty, Aleksandr Ge and his fellow anarchist delegates (there were 14 in all) voted in opposition.[43]

The dispute over the treaty of Brest-Litovsk brought into relief the growing estrangement between the anarchists and the Bolshevik party. With the overthrow of the Provisional Government in October 1917, their marriage of convenience had accomplished its purpose. By the spring of 1918, the majority of anarchists had become sufficiently disillusioned with Lenin to seek a complete break, while the Bolsheviks, for their part, had begun to contemplate the suppression of their former allies, who had outlived their usefulness and whose incessant criticisms were a nuisance the new regime no longer had to tolerate. The anarchists, moreover, beyond their irritating verbal assaults, were beginning to present a more tangible danger. Partly in preparation for the anticipated guerrilla war against the Germans, and partly to discourage hostile maneuvers by the Soviet government, the local clubs of the Moscow Federation of Anarchists had been organizing detachments of "Black Guards" (the black banner was the anarchist emblem), arming them with rifles, pistols, and grenades. From their headquarters in the House of Anarchy, the leaders of the Federation tried to impose a measure of discipline on the Black Guardsmen and to limit the activities of the local clubs to the distribution of propaganda and the "requisitioning" of private residences. This proved to be an impossible task; once armed, a number of groups and isolated individuals succumbed to the temptation of carrying out "expropriations," and, adding

---

[41] *Bol'shevistskaia diktatura v svete anarkhizma* (Paris, 1928), p. 10.
[42] Voline, *La Révolution inconnue*, pp. 212-213.
[43] *Izvestiia VTsIK*, 17 March 1918, p. 2; Lenin, *Sochineniia*, XXII, 618.

insult to injury, they sometimes acted in the name of the Federation. On 16 March, the Federation felt constrained to issue a public repudiation of "ex's" committed under its banner: "The Moscow Federation of Anarchist Groups," announced the front page of *Anarkhiia*, "declares that it does not condone any seizures for personal gain or for personal profit in general, and that it will take every step to combat such manifestations of the bourgeois spirit."[44] The following day, in a tacit admission that members of the Black Guards had been guilty of lawless deeds, *Anarkhiia* prohibited all Guardsmen from embarking on any mission without an order signed by three members of the Black Guard staff and unless accompanied by a staff member.[45]

After the stubborn anarchist campaign against the treaty of Brest-Litovsk, the formation of armed guards and their underworld excursions came as the last straw. The Bolshevik leadership decided to act. A convenient pretext was provided on 9 April, when a band of Moscow anarchists stole an automobile belonging to Colonel Raymond Robins, the representative of the American Red Cross and a sympathetic contact with the United States government.[46] Some Bolsheviks, as Trotsky admitted, were most reluctant to suppress the anarchists, who had helped "in our hour of revolution."[47] Nevertheless, on the night of 11-12 April, armed detachments of the Cheka raided 26 anarchist centers in the capital. Most of the anarchists surrendered without a fight, but in the Donskoi Monastery and in the House of Anarchy itself, Black Guardsmen offered fierce resistance. A dozen Cheka agents were slain in the struggle, about 40 anarchists were killed or wounded, and more than 500 were taken prisoner.[48]

[44] *Anarkhiia*, 16 March 1918, p. 1.

[45] *Ibid.*, 17 March 1918, p. 1.

[46] In January 1918, the Petrograd anarchists had already disturbed relations with the American government by threatening Ambassador David Francis with harm if the United States did not release Tom Mooney (unjustly condemned for a bombing incident in San Francisco) and Alexander Berkman (arrested in New York City for agitation against the draft law). George F. Kennan, *Russia Leaves the War* (Princeton, 1956), pp. 356, 403.

[47] *Ibid.*, p. 176.

[48] *Izvestiia VTsIK*, 13 April 1918, p. 3, and 16 April 1918, pp. 3-4; *Papers Relating to the Foreign Relations of the United States, 1918:*

In the wake of the raids, *Anarkhiia* was temporarily shut down by the government. From Petrograd, however, *Burevestnik* scathingly denounced the Bolsheviks for entering the camp of "the Black Hundreds generals, the counterrevolutionary bourgeoisie": "You are Cains. You have killed your brothers. You are also Judases, betrayers. Lenin has built his October throne on our bones. Now he is resting and arranging for 'breathing spells' on our dead bodies, the bodies of anarchists. You say the anarchists have been suppressed. But this is only our July 3-6. Our October is still ahead."[49] When Aleksandr Ge lodged a protest with the Central Executive Committee of the Soviets, his Bolshevik colleagues assured him that they were rounding up criminal elements only and not truly "ideological" (*ideinye*) anarchists.[50] Shortly afterwards, the Cheka carried out similar arrests in Petrograd—Bleikhman was one of those detained, notwithstanding his membership in the Petrograd Soviet—and extended their raids into the provinces as well.[51] In May, *Burevestnik, Anarkhiia, Golos Truda*, and other leading anarchist periodicals were closed down, in most cases permanently.

The breathing spell that Lenin won at Brest-Litovsk proved to be of brief duration. By summertime, the Bolshevik government had been plunged into a life-and-death struggle with its enemies, both foreign and domestic. Whatever semblance of law and order had remained after the two revolutions of 1917 now broke down completely. Terrorism reared its head in every corner of the land. Radical SR's launched a grim campaign of assassination against prominent state officials, just as they had done in the days of Nicholas II. (Heretofore, the anarchists, by contrast, had generally aimed their bombs and

---

Russia (3 vols., Washington, 1931), I, 497; William Hard, *Raymond Robins' Own Story* (New York and London, 1920), pp. 76-81.

[49] James Bunyan and H. H. Fisher, eds., *The Bolshevik Revolution, 1917-1918: Documents and Materials* (Stanford, 1934), p. 584. "Our July 3-6" refers, of course, to the abortive July Days in 1917, which were followed three months later by the successful October insurrection.

[50] Maximoff, *The Guillotine at Work*, p. 389.

[51] *Ibid.*, pp. 396-404; *Izvestiia*, 16 April 1918, p. 4. Repression was particularly severe in the Volga town of Samara, where anarchists and SR Maximalists had gained control of the soviet.

pistols at lesser targets—policemen, district attorneys, Cossacks, army officers, factory owners, watchmen.) In June 1918, an SR terrorist assassinated Volodarskii, a high-ranking Bolshevik in Petrograd. The following month, two left SR's murdered the German Ambassador, Count Mirbach, in the hope of forcing a renewal of the war. At the end of August, Mikhail Uritskii, head of the Petrograd Cheka, was the victim of SR bullets, and a young SR in Moscow named Fanya ("Dora") Kaplan shot and severely wounded Lenin himself. The attempt on Lenin's life struck some anarchists as analogous to the assassination in 1904 of the reactionary Minister of the Interior, Viacheslav Pleve;[52] Kaplan, they remarked sympathetically, wished "to slay Lenin before he could slay the Revolution."[53]

The anarchists, too, resorted once more to their terrorist ways. Groups of *Chernoznamentsy* and *Beznachal'tsy* sprang up again, as did small bands of hard-core desperadoes which operated under such names as "Hurricane" and "Death,"[54] and were strongly reminiscent of the Black Raven and Hawk groups of the previous decade. As in the years following the 1905 uprising, the south provided particularly fertile soil for anarchist violence. One fanatical circle in Kharkov, known as the Anarcho-Futurists, conjured up the ghosts of Bidbei and Rostovtsev by proclaiming "Death to world civilization!" and urging the dark masses to take up their axes and destroy everything in sight.[55] Anarchists in Rostov, Ekaterinoslav, and Briansk broke into city jails and liberated the prisoners.[56] Fiery manifestoes incited the populace to revolt against its new masters. The following appeal was issued by the Briansk Federation of Anarchists in July 1918:

ARISE PEOPLE!
THE SOCIAL-VAMPIRES ARE DRINKING YOUR BLOOD!
THOSE WHO EARLIER CRIED OUT FOR LIBERTY,
FRATERNITY, AND EQUALITY ARE CREATING TERRIBLE
VIOLENCE!

[52] *Vol'nyi Golos Truda*, No. 4, 16 September 1918, p. 2.
[53] Goldman, *Living My Life*, II, 745.
[54] *Izvestiia VTsIK*, 13 April 1918, p. 3.
[55] *K Svetu*, No. 5, 14 March 1919, p. 1.
[56] Iakovlev, *Russkii anarkhizm v velikoi russkoi revoliutsii*, pp. 10, 47-56.

THE SHOOTING OF PRISONERS IS OCCURRING NOW
WITHOUT TRIAL OR INVESTIGATION AND EVEN
WITHOUT THEIR "REVOLUTIONARY" TRIBUNAL. . .

THE BOLSHEVIKS HAVE BECOME MONARCHISTS. . .

PEOPLE! THE GENDARME'S BOOT IS CRUSHING ALL
YOUR BEST FEELINGS AND DESIRES. . .

THERE IS NO FREE SPEECH, NO FREE PRESS, NO FREE
HOUSING. EVERYWHERE THERE ARE ONLY BLOOD,
MOANS, TEARS, AND VIOLENCE. . .

YOUR ENEMIES SUMMON HUNGER TO HELP THEM
IN THEIR STRUGGLE WITH YOU. . .

ARISE THEN PEOPLE!

DESTROY THE PARASITES WHO TORMENT YOU!

DESTROY ALL WHO OPPRESS YOU!

CREATE YOUR HAPPINESS YOURSELVES . . . DO NOT
TRUST YOUR FATE TO ANYONE . . .

ARISE PEOPLE! CREATE ANARCHY AND THE
COMMUNE![57]

The south was the spawning ground for a host of anarchist
"battle detachments" patterned after those of the 1905 period.
Their avowed purpose was the destruction of would-be counterrevolutionaries, whether Russian "Whites," Bolsheviks,
Ukrainian nationalists, or German troops carrying out the
treaty of Brest-Litovsk. The Black Sea Partisan Detachment
in Simferopol and the M. A. Bakunin Partisan Detachment
in Ekaterinoslav sang of the new "era of dynamite" that
would greet oppressors of every stripe:

> Dear to us is the legacy of Ravachol
> And the last speech of Henry,
> For the slogan "Commune and Liberty"
> We are ready to lay down our lives!
>
> Down with the noise of church-bells!
> We shall sound a different alarm
> With explosions and groans in the land
> We shall build our own harmony![58]

[57] *Vestnik Anarkhii*, No. 10, 14 July 1918, p. 1.
[58] M. N. Chudnov, *Pod chernym znamenem (zapiski anarkhista)*
(Moscow, 1930), pp. 53ff.

True to their word, the anarchist bands of the south inaugurated a tumultuous era of explosions and "expropriations," though their daring exploits were not always motivated by selfless revolutionary ideals.

Over the next two years, Moscow also endured a rash of anarchist violence. Victor Serge reports that, in the summer of 1918, the Black Guardsmen who had survived the Cheka raids of the preceding months, contemplated the armed seizure of the capital, but Aleksei Borovoi and Daniil Novomirskii talked them out of it.[59] Many of them, however, sought refuge from Bolshevik persecution in the underworld. Lev Chernyi, secretary of the Moscow Federation of Anarchists, helped form an "underground group" in 1918, and the following year joined an organization called the Underground Anarchists (*Anarkhisty Podpol'ia*), founded by Kazimir Kovalevich, a member of the Moscow Union of Railway Workers, and by a Ukrainian anarchist named Petr Sobolev. Though based in the capital, the Underground Anarchists established ties with the battle detachments of the south. In the fall of 1919, they published two numbers of an incendiary leaflet called *Anarkhiia* (not to be confused with the organ of the Moscow Federation, shut down by the government the previous year), the first of which denounced the Bolshevik dictatorship as the worst tyranny in human history. "Never has there been so sharp a division between oppressors and oppressed as there is now," it declared.[60] A few days before these words were printed, the Underground Anarchists struck their heaviest blow against the "oppressors." On 25 September, together with a number of left SR's (both groups were seeking revenge for the arrests of their comrades), they bombed the headquarters of the Moscow Committee of the Communist Party in Leontiev Street, while a plenary meeting was in session. The explosion killed 12 members of the Committee and wounded 55 others, including Nikolai Bukharin, the eminent Bolshevik theorist and editor of *Pravda*, Emelian Iaroslavskii, who later was to write a short history of Russian anarchism, and Iu. M. Steklov, editor of *Izvestiia* and future biographer of

[59] Serge, *Mémoires d'un révolutionnaire*, p. 85.
[60] *Anarkhiia*, No. 1, 29 September 1919; quoted in Iakovlev, *Russkii anarkhizm v velikoi russkoi revoliutsii*, p. 49.

Bakunin.[61] Elated by their success, the Underground Anarchists triumphantly announced that the blast was the signal for an "era of dynamite" that would terminate only when the new despotism had been utterly destroyed.[62]

But their exultation was soon cut short. The bombing, though at once disavowed by the most prominent anarchist leaders, triggered a massive wave of new arrests. The Underground Anarchists were the first to be hunted down. A group of them blew themselves up in a "requisitioned" *dacha* after their leaders, Kovalevich and Sobolev, had been shot by the police.[63] The Cheka cast a wide net for political offenders, trying hundreds of them in three-man summary courts. The parallel between these courts and the military tribunals created after the Revolution of 1905 was not lost on the anarchists, who compared the Cheka agents to Stolypin's "hangmen."[64] Bolshevik spokesmen maintained that, with the survival of the revolution at stake, it was imperative to snuff out violent opposition from every quarter. No anarchists, they insisted, were being arrested merely for their beliefs, but only for criminal deeds. "We do not persecute Anarchists of ideas," Lenin assured Alexander Berkman several months after the Leontiev Street bombing, "but we will not tolerate armed resistance or agitation of that character."[65] Unfortunately for the "ideological" anarchists, the Cheka did not bother to run its prisoners through a catechism of anarchist doctrine before meting out retribution.

With the flare-up of terrorism in 1918, the old debate between the syndicalists and the terrorists over the efficacy of violent action was revived. The young syndicalist Maksimov,

---

[61] *Pravda*, 6 November 1919, p. 1; *25-e sentiabria 1919 goda: pamiati pogibshikh pri vzryve v Leont'evskom pereulke* (Moscow, 1925), pp. 117, 201-203. According to Abba Gordin, it was Sobolev who threw the bomb. A. Gordin, *Zikhroynes un kheshboynes* (2 vols., Buenos Aires, 1955-1957), I, 237-246.

[62] *Anarkhiia*, No. 2, 23 October 1919; quoted in Iakovlev, *Russkii anarkhizm*, p. 50.

[63] Maximoff, *The Guillotine at Work*, p. 359; *Goneniia na anarkhizm v Sovetskoi Rossii*, pp. 31-33.

[64] *Nabat*, 7 July 1918; quoted in Maximoff, *The Guillotine at Work*, p. 423.

[65] Berkman, *The Bolshevik Myth*, pp. 91, 142-147.

with a mixture of exasperation and contempt, condemned the
Anarchist-Communists for returning to the discredited tactics
of assassination and "expropriation." Terrorism was a gross
distortion of anarchist principles, he argued, dissipating revolutionary energy while doing nothing to eliminate social injustice. At the same time, Maksimov scorned the sedentary
"Manilovs" in the Anarchist-Communist camp (Manilov was
a day-dreaming landowner in Gogol's *Dead Souls*), romantic
visionaries who pined for pastoral utopias, oblivious of the
complex forces at work in the modern world. It was time to
stop dreaming of the Golden Age, he declared. It was time to
"organize and act!"[66]

By the time Maksimov's injunction appeared in print, he
and his colleagues had already begun to carry it out. At the
end of August 1918, the Anarcho-Syndicalists held their First
All-Russian Conference in Moscow with the aim of organizing their forces and adopting a common platform. The delegates attacked the Bolshevik dictatorship on a broad front
and approved a battery of resolutions condemning Lenin's
political and economic programs. On the political side, the
syndicalists demanded that the *Sovnarkom* be abolished at
once and replaced by a federation of "free soviets," chosen
directly in the factories and villages, without "political chatterboxes gaining entry through party lists and turning [the
soviets] into a talking-shop."[67] Furthermore, although the Conference endorsed the military struggle against the Whites, it
called for the arming of the workers and peasants to super-
sede the outmoded standing army.

The resolutions on economic questions amounted to a
blanket rejection of the Bolshevik program of "war communism." In the agricultural sector, the Anarcho-Syndicalists
warned that the land policies of the new regime would lead to
the renewed "enserfment" of the peasantry by the *kulaks* and
the state. To avert this fate, they advocated the equalization
of land allotments and the gradual formation of autonomous
peasant communes. They also demanded the immediate cessation of grain requisitions by the state, proposing that the job

[66] *Vol'nyi Golos Truda*, No. 4, 16 September 1918, p. 3.
[67] *Vmesto programmy: rezoliutsii I i II Vserossiiskoi konferentsii anarkhistov-sindikalistov* (Berlin, 1922), p. 12.

of distributing food be turned over to worker-peasant organizations. In industry, the syndicalists accused the government
of betraying the working class with its suppression of workers'
control in favor of such capitalist devices as one-man management, labor discipline, and the employment of "bourgeois"
engineers and technicians. By forsaking the factory committees—"the beloved child of the great workers' revolution"—
for those "dead organizations," the trade unions, and by sub-
stituting decrees and red tape for industrial democracy, the
Bolshevik leadership was creating a monster of "state capitalism," a bureaucratic Behemoth, which it ludicrously called
"socialism." The twin evils of political dictatorship and "state
capitalism" could be removed only through an "immediate and
radical revolution" by the workers themselves.[68]

The charge that the Bolshevik party had introduced "state
capitalism" rather than proletarian socialism became a major
theme in anarchist criticism of the Soviet regime. In April
1918, Lenin admitted that the economic chaos in Russia had
compelled him to jettison "the principles of the Paris Commune," which had served as his guidelines in the April Theses
and *The State and Revolution.*[69] By shedding these hallowed
principles, the anarchists maintained, Lenin had sacrificed the
self-determination of the working class on the altar of centralized authority; he had simply reintroduced the old system
of exploitation in new dress. Under Bolshevik rule, declared
the journal of the Briansk Federation of Anarchists, the Russian state had become "some sort of amazing machine, a
mighty web of lace that acts as a judge, manages school affairs
and makes sausages, builds houses and collects taxes, directs
the police and cooks soup, digs coal and lets men languish in
jail, assembles troops and sews garments. . . ."[70]

The most penetrating anarchist critique of "state capitalism"
appeared in a new syndicalist journal, *Vol'nyi Golos Truda*
(The Free Voice of Labor), established in August 1918 (at
the time of the First Conference of Anarcho-Syndicalists) as
the successor to the suppressed *Golos Truda.* The journal's
editors—Grigorii Maksimov, M. Chekeres (Nikolai Dolenko),

[68] *Ibid.*, pp. 11-14.
[69] Lenin, *Sochineniia*, XXII, 447.
[70] *Vestnik Anarkhii*, No. 10, 14 July 1918, p. 3.

and Efim Iarchuk—were in the left wing of Anarcho-Syndicalism, men of a militant stamp, whose philosophy was an
acerbic blend of Bakuninism and revolutionary syndicalism, in
the tradition of Novomirskii's South Russian Group of Anarcho-Syndicalists of the 1905 period.

The attack on "state capitalism" in *Vol'nyi Golos Truda*
took the form of a lengthy article entitled "Paths of Revolution" and signed by a certain "M. Sergven." One suspects—
judging from content and style—that the author was Maksimov. The article began with a severe indictment of the "dictatorship of the proletariat" that Lenin and his confederates
claimed to have instituted after overthrowing the Provisional
Government. The Bolshevik Revolution, the author asserted,
had merely resulted in the substitution of state capitalism for
private capitalism; one big owner had taken the place of many
small ones. By means of "a whole bureaucratic system and a
new 'statized' morality," the Soviet government had enserfed
the working masses all over again. The peasants and factory
workers now found themselves under the heel of "a new class
of administrators—a new class born largely from the womb of
the intelligentsia." What had taken place in Russia, the article
went on, resembled the earlier revolutions in Western Europe:
no sooner had the oppressed farmers and craftsmen of England and France removed the landed aristocracy from power
than the ambitious middle class stepped into the breech and
erected a new class structure with itself at the top; in a similar
manner, the privileges and authority once shared by the Russian nobility and bourgeoisie had passed into the hands of a
new ruling class, composed of party officials, government
bureaucrats, and technical specialists.

At this point, the author of "Paths of Revolution" made a
remarkable departure from the usual condemnation of the Bolsheviks as betrayers of the working class. Lenin and his followers, wrote Sergven, were not necessarily cold-blooded
cynics who, with Machiavellian cunning, had mapped out the
new class structure in advance to satisfy their personal lust for
power. Quite possibly, they were motivated by a genuine con-
cern for human suffering. Yet, he added plaintively, even the
loftiest intentions must founder when centralized power is introduced. The division of society into administrators and work-

ers follows inexorably from the centralization of authority. It cannot be otherwise: management implies responsibility, which, in turn, implies special rights and advantages. Once the functions of management and labor are separated, the former assigned to a minority of "experts" and the latter to the untutored masses, all possibility of dignity and equality is destroyed.

Under the centralized rule of Lenin and his party, the article concluded, Russia had entered a period of state capitalism rather than socialism. State capitalism was "the new dam before the waves of our social revolution." And those who believed that the working class was so huge and powerful that it could crash through the dam failed to recognize that the new class of administrators and officeholders constituted a most formidable opponent. In the hour of revolution, Sergven lamented, the Anarcho-Syndicalists—who, unlike the Marxists, truly believed that the liberation of the working class was the task of the workers themselves—were too poorly organized to keep the rebellion from being diverted into nonsocialist and nonlibertarian channels. The Russian people began the revolution spontaneously, without orders from any central authority. They tore political power to shreds and scattered the shreds over the immense countryside. But those scattered shreds of power poisoned the local soviets and committees. The goddess "Dictatorship" appeared again in the new garb of *Ispolkoms* and *Sovnarkoms*, and the revolution, failing to recognize who she was, warmly embraced her. So it was that the Russian Revolution had come to be locked in the arms of centralized state power, which was squeezing out its life's breath.[71]

The expression "state capitalism" was used by the anarchists to designate the pernicious concentration of political and economic power in the hands of the Bolshevik government; it was meant to suggest that the state (that is, the Bolshevik party, assisted by thousands of bureaucrats) had become the boss and exploiter in place of a multiplicity of private entrepreneurs. The term "capitalism," however, as normally de-

[71] M. Sergven, "Puti revoliutsii," *Vol'nyi Golos Truda*, No. 4, 16 September 1918, pp. 1-2. For other anarchist assaults on "state capitalism," see Volin, *Revoliutsiia i anarkhizm*, p. 96; *Bezvlastie*, No. 8, 1 September 1921, p. 1; and *Pochin*, No. 2, 5-20 March 1923, p. 1.

fined, applies to an economic system characterized by private ownership, the profit motive, and a free market, and thus had but little relevance to the situation in Russia. It is worth noting that a second article in the same issue of *Vol'nyi Golos Truda* described the Soviet system as a form of "state communism"—that is, *centralized* communism imposed from above as distinguished from *anarchist* communism organized freely from below on the basis of true equality. The author, a leader of the Moscow Bakers' Union named Nikolai Pavlov, demanded the immediate transfer of the factories and land to a loose federation of "free cities" and "free communes." The anarchists, he averred, firmly opposed centralized authority of any sort.[72] That Lenin's government should view both epithets —"state capitalism" and "state communism"—with disfavor was hardly any surprise. Immediately after the two articles appeared, *Vol'nyi Golos Truda* was shut down.

During its brief existence, *Vol'nyi Golos Truda* repeatedly stressed the urgency of organizational reform within the syndicalist movement. More specifically, the journal called for the formation of an All-Russian Confederation of Anarcho-Syndicalists capable of redirecting the Russian Revolution onto decentralized rails.[73] Its appeal soon bore fruit. When the Second All-Russian Conference of Anarcho-Syndicalists convened in Moscow at the end of November 1918, the question of organization appeared at the head of the agenda. The delegates endorsed the proposal to create a nationwide confederation, and further recommended that ties with foreign anarchist groups be strengthened. The Conference, moreover, resolved to increase the dissemination of syndicalist propaganda among the factory workers, with "decentralization" as the watchword in both politics and economics. Although the delegates admitted that the state could not be abolished "today or tomorrow," they wished to replace the Bolshevik Leviathan with a "confederation of free soviets," which would serve as a bridge to the stateless society of the future. In the economic sector, the Conference demanded the "general expropriation of the

[72] N. Pavlov, "Svobodnaia kommuna i vol'nyi gorod," *Vol'nyi Golos Truda*, No. 4, pp. 2-3.
[73] *Ibid.*, p. 3.

expropriators—including the state," followed by the "syndicalization" of industrial production.[74]

Having approved *Vol'nyi Golos Truda*'s idea of an All-Russian Confederation of Anarcho-Syndicalists, the Conference proceeded to choose two editors of the defunct journal, Grigorii Maksimov and Efim Iarchuk, to be secretary and treasurer of an Executive Bureau charged with organizing the Confederation. Little can be said, however, about the Anarcho-Syndicalist Confederation, apart from the fact that it enjoyed at least a nominal existence after the November Conference. There is scant evidence that the Executive Bureau had much success in coordinating the activities of the clubs and circles that made up the syndicalist movement, or in appreciably enlarging their membership and influence in the factory committees and trade unions. Nor did the Bureau make any genuine progress in healing the rift with the Anarchist-Communists. Early in 1919, a handful of prominent anarchists from both wings of the movement (most notable were Nikolai Pavlov and Sergei Markus of the syndicalists and Vladimir Barmash, German Askarov, and I. S. Bleikhman of the Anarchist-Communists) made a feeble attempt at unity by founding the Moscow Union of Anarcho-Syndicalists-Communists. But this venture, like all its predecessors, ended in dismal failure. The single achievement of the Moscow Union was the publication of a new journal called *Trud i Volia* (Labor and Liberty), which chastised the Bolshevik regime for "statizing the human personality" and issued appeals for direct action "to destroy every authoritarian or bureaucratic system."[75] In May 1919, after its sixth number, *Trud i Volia* was, quite predictably, shut down.

The deepening of the Civil War of 1918-1921 threw the anarchists into a quandary over whether to assist the Bolsheviks in their internecine struggle with the Whites. Ardent libertarians, the anarchists found the repressive policies of the Soviet government utterly reprehensible; yet the prospect of a

---

[74] *Vmesto programmy*, pp. 21-23.
[75] *Trud i Volia*, No. 5, 7 May 1919, p. 1; No. 6, 20 May 1919, p. 2. The journal also issued a few separate pamphlets, for example, *Kakie nuzhny poriadki* (Moscow, 1919?).

White victory seemed even worse. Any opposition to Lenin's regime at this time might tip the balance in favor of the counterrevolutionaries; on the other hand, active support, or even benevolent neutrality, might enable the Bolsheviks to entrench themselves too deeply to be ousted later.

The acrimonious debates provoked by this dilemma served to widen the fissures in the anarchist camp. A variety of opinion soon emerged, ranging from active resistance to the Bolsheviks, through passive neutrality, to eager collaboration. Some anarchists even joined the Communist party. In the end, a large majority gave varying degrees of support to the beleaguered regime. The Anarcho-Syndicalists, for the most part, collaborated openly, and those among them who persisted in criticizing the "dictatorship of the proletariat" (in particular, the left-wing syndicalists of *Vol'nyi Golos Truda*) refrained from active resistance, deferring the "third revolution" until the greater evil on the right could be eliminated. Even among the more hostile Anarchist-Communists, a majority threw in their lot with Lenin's party. But here there were more dissenters. A large segment maintained a grudging and rather malevolent neutrality, and a few Anarchist-Communist groups, even in these precarious circumstances, would deny the Bolsheviks any quarter, issuing venomous appeals (as did the Briansk Federation) for the immediate overthrow of the "Social-Vampires" or (in the case of the Underground Anarchists) launching a campaign of terrorism against Communist party officials.

These militant Anarchist-Communists had the utmost contempt for their "renegade" colleagues—"Soviet anarchists," they labeled them—who had succumbed to the blandishments of the "pseudo-Communists." The lion's share of abuse was reserved for the Anarcho-Syndicalists. The syndicalists at heart had always believed in "centralism first and foremost," declared their detractors, and now were shamelessly revealing their true colors as purveyors of "hucksterism rather than revolutionism . . . accepting party cards from the Bolsheviks for a few crumbs at the statist table."[76] As for those anarchists who considered themselves "sober realists" in contrast to

[76] *Svoboda* (Kiev), No. 1, September 1919, p. 28.

the "utopian dreamers" who stubbornly refused to cooperate with the state—they were nothing more than "Anarcho-Bureaucrat" Judases, traitors to the cause of Bakunin and Kropotkin. "Anarchism," proclaimed the irreconcilables, "must be purged of this watery mixture of Bolshevism in which it is being dissolved by the Anarcho-Bolsheviks and Anarcho-Syndicalists."[77]

Lenin himself was so impressed by the zeal and courage of the "Soviet anarchists" that, in August 1919, at the climax of the Civil War, he was moved to remark that many anarchists were "becoming the most dedicated supporters of Soviet power."[78] Bill Shatov was an outstanding case in point. Throughout the Civil War period, Shatov served Lenin's government with the same energy he had displayed as a member of the Military-Revolutionary Committee at the time of the October insurrection. As an officer in the Tenth Red Army during the autumn of 1919, he played an important role in the defense of Petrograd against the advance of General Iudenich.[79] In 1920, he was summoned to Chita by Aleksandr Krasnoshchekov, a radical with anarchist affiliations, to become Minister of Transport in the Far Eastern Republic.[80] Several years later, he was again sent to the East, this time to supervise the construction of the Turk-Sib Railroad.[81]

Frequently castigated as an "Anarcho-Bolshevik" and a "Soviet anarchist,"[82] Shatov attempted to justify his position to

[77] *Burevestnik*, 10 April 1918, p. 1; *K Svetu*, No. 1, 2 February 1918, p. 3.

[78] Lenin, *Sochineniia*, XXIV, 437.

[79] Serge, *Mémoires d'un révolutionnaire*, p. 96.

[80] Henry K. Norton, *The Far Eastern Republic of Siberia* (London, 1923), pp. 184-185; E. H. Carr, *The Bolshevik Revolution, 1917-1923* (3 vols., New York, 1951-1953), I, 355-356; Maynard, *Russia in Flux*, p. 298. That Shatov served as an important official in Siberia has been disputed by some survivors of the anarchist movement. Krasnoshchekov, Prime Minister of the Far Eastern Republic, was recalled to Moscow in 1921; charged with embezzlement in 1924, he was subsequently shot. Interview with Boris Yelensky, *Freie Arbeiter Stimme*, New York City, 6 September 1963; Carr, *The Bolshevik Revolution*, II, 357n.

[81] Serge, *Mémoires d'un révolutionnaire*, p. 96.

[82] *Anarkhicheskii Vestnik*, No. 1, July 1923, pp. 56-72; No. 7, May 1924, p. 35; *Rabochii Put'*, No. 2-3, March-April 1923, pp. 15-16. Iuda Roshchin and German Sandomirskii were also principal targets of criticism. Generally speaking, the "Anarcho-Bolshevik" epithet was used in 1917 and early 1918, while "Soviet anarchist" came into vogue during the Civil War.

Alexander Berkman and Emma Goldman shortly after their arrival in Russia in January 1920: "Now I just want to tell you that the Communist State in action is exactly what we anarchists have always claimed it would be—a tightly centralized power still more strengthened by the dangers of the Revolution. Under such conditions, one cannot do as one wills. One does not just hop on a train and go, or even ride the bumpers, as I used to do in the United States.[83] One needs permission. But don't get the idea that I miss my American 'blessings.' Me for Russia, the Revolution, and its glorious future."[84] The anarchists, said Shatov, were "the romanticists of the revolution." But one could not fight with ideals alone, he hastened to add. At the moment, the chief task was to defeat the reactionaries.[85] "We anarchists should remain true to our ideals," he told Berkman, "but we should not criticize at this time. We must work and help to build."[86]

Shatov was but one of many well-known anarchists who fought in the Red Army.[87] More than a few died in action, including Iustin Zhuk and Anatolii Zhelezniakov, whose entire careers had been marked by violence and rebellion.[88] (Zhelezniakov, commander of an armored train, was killed near Ekaterinoslav in July 1919 by the shell-fire of Denikin's artillery.) Aleksandr Ge of the Soviet Central Executive Committee was sabered to death by White troops in the Caucasus, where he was serving as a high official of the Cheka.[89]

Other prominent figures in the anarchist movement held government posts during the Civil War period. Alexander

[83] Before World War I, Shatov did, in fact, ride the rails from one end of the United States to the other, traveling as a lecturer and organizer for the Union of Russian Workers of the United States and Canada. See his letter to *Golos Truda* (New York), 1 August 1913, p. 7.

[84] Goldman, *Living My Life*, II, 729.

[85] *Ibid.*, II, 730-731.

[86] Berkman, *The Bolshevik Myth*, pp. 35-36.

[87] See Gorelik, *Anarkhisty v rossiiskoi revoliutsii*, pp. 37-40; and Voline, *La Révolution inconnue*, pp. 234-235.

[88] *Bol'shevistskaia diktatura v svete anarkhizma*, p. 8; *Goneniia na anarkhizm v Sovetskoi Rossii*, p. 53; Gorelik, *Anarkhisty v rossiiskoi revoliutsii*, p. 16; *The Russian Revolution and the Communist Party* (Berlin, 1922), pp. 18-19; Augustin Souchy, *Wie lebt der Arbeiter und Bauer in Russland und der Ukraine?* (Berlin, n.d. [1921?]), p. 22; *Golos Truda*, December 1919, pp. 50-51.

[89] Victor Serge, *L'An I de la révolution russe* (Paris, 1930), p. 255.

Schapiro of *Golos Truda* and German Sandomirskii, a leading Kiev Anarchist-Communist who had been banished to Siberia after the Revolution of 1905, took positions in Chicherin's Commissariat of Foreign Affairs.[90] Aleksei Borovoi became a commissar in the medical administration,[91] and Nikolai Rogdaev was placed in charge of Soviet propaganda in Turkestan.[92] In 1918, after *Golos Truda* was shut down, Volin left Moscow for the south, where he fought against the Whites; he worked for a time in the Soviet Department of Education in Voronezh and Kharkov, but refused the post of educational director for the whole Ukraine.[93] Vladimir Zabrezhnev (once a member of Kropotkin's *Khleb i Volia* group in London) actually joined the Communist party and became secretary of *Izvestiia* in Moscow.[94] Daniil Novomirskii also entered the Communist party and was made an official of the Comintern after its formation in 1919.[95] With Trotsky's help, Maksim Raevskii, the former editor of *Golos Truda* in New York and Petrograd, secured a nonpolitical job in the government. (He had become acquainted with Trotsky when the two men traveled to Russia on the same boat in May 1917.)[96]

Waclaw Machajski (who had returned to Russia in 1917) was also given a nonpolitical post of minor importance, namely that of technical editor for *Narodnoe Khoziaistvo* (later *Sotsialisticheskoe Khoziaistvo*), the organ of the Supreme Economic Council.[97] Machajski remained, however, sharply critical of Marxism and its adherents. In the summer of 1918, he published a single issue of a journal called *Rabochaia*

[90] Serge, *Mémoires d'un révolutionnaire*, p. 134.

[91] *Probuzhdenie*, No. 68-69, March-April 1936, p. 32.

[92] Serge, *Mémoires d'un révolutionnaire*, p. 134. Alexander Berkman, "Diary: Russia, 1919-1921," entry of 8 March 1920, handwritten manuscript, Berkman Archive. Berkman describes Rogdaev as a "fine fellow, intelligent, sincere, active. Broad vision and objective judgment." A much shortened version of Berkman's diary was published in 1925 as *The Bolshevik Myth*.

[93] *Ibid;* Maximoff, *The Guillotine at Work*, p. 619; *Anarkhicheskii Vestnik*, No. 7, May 1924, p. 18; Rocker, introduction to Voline, *Nineteen-Seventeen*.

[94] Knizhnik, *Krasnaia Letopis'*, 1922, No. 4, p. 35; *P. A. Kropotkin i ego uchenie*, p. 337.

[95] Serge, *Mémoires d'un révolutionnaire*, p. 134.

[96] Nomad, *Dreamers, Dynamiters, and Demagogues*, pp. 163-164.

[97] N. Baturin, "Pamiati 'makhaevshchiny,'" *Pravda*, 2 March 1926, p. 2; Syrkin, *Makhaevshchina*, p. 6.

Revoliutsiia (The Workers' Revolution), in which he censured the Bolsheviks for failing to order the total expropriation of the bourgeoisie or to improve the economic situation of the working class. After the February Revolution, wrote Machajski, the workers had received a rise in wages and an eight-hour day, but after October, their material level had been raised "not one whit!"[98] The Bolshevik insurrection, he continued, was nothing but "a counterrevolution of the intellectuals." Political power had been seized by the disciples of Marx, "the petty bourgeoisie and the intelligentsia . . . the possessors of the knowledge necessary for the organization and administration of the whole life of the country." And the Marxists, in accordance with their prophet's religious gospel of economic determinism, had chosen to preserve the bourgeois order, obliging themselves only "to prepare" the manual workers for their future paradise.[99] Machajski enjoined the working class to press the Soviet government to expropriate the factories, equalize incomes and educational opportunity, and provide jobs for the unemployed. Yet, as dissatisfied as he was with the new regime, Machajski grudgingly accepted it, at least for the time being. Any attempt to overthrow the government, he said, would benefit only the Whites, who were a worse evil than the Bolsheviks.[100]

Needless to say, it was not the Raevskiis and Machajskis whom Lenin had in mind when he spoke of "dedicated supporters of Soviet power." Rather, it was the Shatovs and Zhelezniakovs, the Ges and Novomirskiis—anarchist leaders who threw their wholehearted support behind the Bolshevik regime when it was threatened by the Whites. This category also included Iuda Roshchin, a leader of *Chernoe Znamia* in 1905, who was now moving headlong towards the Communist camp. Roshchin welcomed the formation of the Third International in 1919, and hailed Lenin as one of the great figures of the modern age. According to Victor Serge, Roshchin even tried to work out an "anarchist theory of the dictatorship of the proletariat."[101] In the meantime, until such a theory could be formulated, he called for a *rapprochement* with the Bol-

[98] *Rabochaia Revoliutsiia*, No. 1, June-July 1918, p. 4.
[99] *Ibid.*, pp. 9, 12, 25.   [100] *Ibid.*, p. 6.
[101] Serge, *Mémoires d'un révolutionnaire*, p. 134.

sheviks on the grounds of sheer expediency. Speaking before a group of Moscow anarchists in 1920, he urged his comrades to cooperate with Lenin's party: "It is the duty of every Anarchist to work whole-heartedly with the Communists, who are the advance guard of the Revolution. Leave your theories alone, and do practical work for the reconstruction of Russia. The need is great, and the Bolsheviks welcome you."[102] Most members of the audience greeted the speech with jeers and catcalls, and wrote Roshchin off as another loss to the "Soviet anarchists."[103] But Alexander Berkman, who was present at the meeting, recalled with candor that Roshchin's words sent a sympathetic thrill through him.[104]

Roshchin by no means stood alone in his endeavors to reconcile the disparate doctrines of anarchism and Bolshevism. Indeed, in Moscow alone, two sizeable groups of fellow-traveling Anarchist-Communists were organized with the object of forging links of amity and cooperation with the "proletarian dictatorship." Apollon Karelin was the guiding spirit of the first group, and the Gordin brothers of the second, perpetuating a division that first emerged in the Petrograd Federation of Anarchists during 1917. (While agreeing on many vital issues, Karelin and the Gordins differed too sharply in temperament and tactics to work harmoniously in the same organization.)

In 1918, Karelin became a "Soviet anarchist" in a literal sense, winning a seat in the Soviet Central Executive Committee. His pro-Soviet organization of anarchists, established in the spring of that year,[105] was known rather pretentiously as the All-Russian Federation of Anarchist-Communists. The new Federation undertook to coax the militant anti-Bolsheviks into cooperating with the government. Karelin argued that a Soviet dictatorship was a practical necessity in order to stave off the forces of reaction; moreover, from the standpoint of theory, it was acceptable as a transitional phase on the road towards a free anarchist society. In defending the Soviet government,

[102] Berkman, *The Bolshevik Myth*, p. 68.
[103] See B. S., *Otkrytoe pis'mo I. Grossmanu-Roshchinu (otvet sovetskim "anarkhistam")* (Moscow?, 1920).
[104] Berkman, *The Bolshevik Myth*, p. 68.
[105] *Probuzhdenie*, No. 1, April 1927, p. 10.

declared *Vol'naia Zhizn'* (Free Life), the Federation's journal from 1919 to 1921, the new group was defending not the principle of authority, but the revolution itself.[106] *Vol'naia Zhizn'* claimed to represent all varieties of anarchist opinion— Anarchist-Communist, Anarcho-Syndicalist, Anarchist-Individualist, and even Tolstoyan. In reality, it took an Anarchist-Communist (yet pro-Soviet) line, criticizing syndicalism as a narrow doctrine[107] and virtually ignoring the individualist and religious schools of anarchist thought.

The second pro-Bolshevik organization of Anarchist-Communists in Moscow, the Universalists, was formed in 1920 by the Gordin brothers, together with German Askarov, who, like Karelin, was a member of the Soviet Central Executive Committee. For the most part, the views of the Universalists were the same as those of Karelin's All-Russian Federation. They urged all anarchists to assist the Red Army in every way possible and to repudiate terrorism and other actions hostile to the government. A temporary dictatorship, the Universalists maintained, was a necessary stage in the transition to stateless communism.[108]

It is difficult to understand how the Gordins were able to make the leap from their rabidly anti-Marxist theory of Pan-Anarchism to Anarcho-Universalism, a doctrine which endorsed the "dictatorship of the proletariat." Perhaps they were allured by the mystique of Bolshevik power. Perhaps they had come to regard the Bolsheviks—whose emphasis on revolutionary will seemed to imply a rejection of economic determinism—as apostates from the Marxist creed. Or possibly they simply considered Lenin a lesser evil than Admiral Kol-

[106] *Vol'naia Zhizn'*, No. 2, November 1919, pp. 4-7. Preceding *Vol'naia Zhizn'* as the organ of Karelin's Federation was *Svobodnaia Kommuna* (Moscow, 1918), not to be confused with the journal of the same name published by the Petrograd Federation of Anarchists in 1917.

[107] V. Khrustalev, "Protiv sindikalizma," *Vol'naia Zhizn'*, No. 13-14, April 1921, pp. 2-3.

[108] Iakovlev, *Russkii anarkhizm v velikoi russkoi revoliutsii*, pp. 74-81; Maximoff, *The Guillotine at Work*, pp. 455-458; A. L. Gordin, *Ot iuridicheskogo anarkhizma k fakticheskomu* (Moscow, 1920); A. Gordin, "Anarkho-Universalizm," *Burevestnik* (New York), No. 3-4, December 1921-January 1922, pp. 32-40; Gordin, *Zikhroynes un kheshboynes*, II, 308-312. Unfortunately, I have not been able to locate any copies of the group's journal, *Universal*, which Askarov edited.

chak.[109] In any case, by 1920 the White armies were retreating on all fronts, and the Universalists and their fellow "Soviet anarchists," having supported the winning side, were soon to reap their rewards.

[109] It may be noted that the beliefs of the Universalists were on many points similar to those of the ultra-radical offshoot of the Socialist Revolutionaries, the SR Maximalists, who split in 1920, the majority entering the Communist party. See G. Nestroev, *Maksimalizm i bol'shevizm* (Moscow, 1919); Soiuz S-R Maksimalistov, *O rabochem kontrole* (Moscow, 1918) and *Trudovaia sovetskaia respublika* (Moscow, 1918); and the journal *Maksimalist* (Moscow, 1918-1921).

8 · THE DOWNFALL OF
RUSSIAN ANARCHISM

*Despotism has passed from the palaces of the
kings to the circle of a committee. It is neither
the royal robes nor the scepter nor the crown
that makes kings hated, but ambition and tyranny. In my country, there has only been
a change in dress.*

JEAN VARLET, *Explosion*, 1793

For centuries, the Ukraine had provided a haven for runaway
serfs, brigands, rebels, and other fugitives from the persecutions of the tsarist government and privileged aristocracy. Nor
did this tradition cease with the disappearance of the monarchy. In 1918, when the new Bolshevik regime began in
earnest to suppress its political opponents, the anarchists of
Petrograd and Moscow flocked to the "wild fields" of the
southland, to seek asylum in a region which, 15 years earlier,
had been a cradle of their movement.

Upon reaching the Ukraine, the refugees from the north
lost no time in linking up with the large number of their fellow
anarchists who had returned from prison and exile after the
February Revolution. Kharkov, where an abortive attempt to
unify the movement had been made in 1917, became the base
of a new drive to weld the disparate anarchist groups into a
coherent revolutionary force. The product of this drive was the
Nabat (Tocsin) Confederation of Anarchist Organizations,
which, by the fall of 1918, had established headquarters in
Kharkov, as well as flourishing branches in Kiev, Odessa,
Ekaterinoslav, and other major cities of the Ukraine. The Confederation sponsored the formation of a Union of Atheists,
and soon could boast of an extensive youth movement
throughout the south.[1]

[1] *Nabat* (Kharkov), No. 15, 12 May 1919, p. 3; *Biulleten' Initsiativnoi
Gruppy Anarkhistskoi Molodezhi Ukrainy "Nabat,"* No. 1, April 1919;
Biulleten' Kievskoi Gruppy Anarkhistskoi Molodezhi (Kiev, 1920). On
the *Nabat* groups and their activities, see P. Rudenko, *Na Ukraine:
povstanchestvo i anarkhicheskoe dvizhenie* (Buenos Aires, 1922), pp.
19-27.

Volin, the former editor of the syndicalist newspaper *Golos Truda*, was a guiding spirit of the new association. He viewed *Nabat* as the embodiment of what he termed "united anarchism" (*edinyi anarkhizm*), that is, a single organization embracing Anarchist-Communists, Anarcho-Syndicalists, and individualist anarchists, while guaranteeing a substantial measure of autonomy for every participating group and individual. But Volin's efforts to bind together the heterogeneous strands of anarchism ended abruptly when, by a curious paradox, most of his own syndicalist comrades refused to join *Nabat*. The dissenters considered "united anarchism" a vague and ineffectual formula of unification, and feared that the Anarchist-Communists would become the dominant partners in the new confederation.[2]

Besides Volin, the most prominent leaders of the *Nabat* movement were two veteran anarchists, Aron Baron and Petr Arshinov. Baron's history as an anarchist dated from the Revolution of 1905, when he was banished to Siberia for participating in the uprising. He escaped to the United States, however, and spent the early years of World War I in Chicago, where he and his wife, Fanya, were once arrested and beaten by the police for fomenting a mass demonstration against unemployment. Returning to Russia in 1917, Baron soon became a popular lecturer and writer in the Ukraine, and was elected by the bakers' union of Kiev as its representative in the city soviet. After the Bolshevik insurrection, he and Fanya moved to Kharkov and helped launch the *Nabat* movement. Besides his post in the Confederation's secretariat, Baron served with Volin as co-editor of the journal *Nabat*.[3]

Petr Andreevich Arshinov had been a Bolshevik before converting to anarchism in 1906. A metal worker in an industrial suburb of Ekaterinoslav, he dispensed anarchist propaganda in his factory and organized an anarchist cell among his workmates.[4] In addition to his role as an agitator, Arshinov also engaged in terrorist exploits which ultimately led to his arrest

[2] *Delo Truda-Probuzhdenie*, No. 16, January 1946, p. 16.

[3] *Volna*, No. 28, April 1922, pp. 12-14; *Goneniia na anarkhizm v Sovetskoi Rossii*, pp. 36-37. The *Nabat* journal appeared in a number of Ukrainian cities during the Civil War, including Kharkov, Elizavetgrad, Odessa, and Guliai-Pole.

[4] P. A. Arshinov, *Dva pobega (iz vospominanii anarkhista 1906-9 gg.)* (Paris, 1929).

and imprisonment. He managed to flee the country, but soon returned to Russia only to be taken into custody again, this time for smuggling anarchist literature across the Austrian border. For 7 years he languished in a Moscow prison until freed in the political amnesty granted by the Provisional Government after the February Revolution. Following a period of active participation in the Moscow Federation of Anarchists, Arshinov returned to his native Ekaterinoslav, joined the Bureau of Anarchists of the Donets Basin (he served as editor of its journal, *Golos Anarkhista*), and lectured to the miners and factory workers as he had done a decade before.[5]

Of the younger members of the *Nabat* Confederation, perhaps the most outstanding were Senya Fleshin, Mark Mrachnyi (Klavanskii), and Grigorii Gorelik (called "Anatolii" by his comrades). Fleshin, born in Kiev in 1894, worked in the offices of Emma Goldman's *Mother Earth* in New York City during the war, then returned to Russia in 1917, settling in Kharkov.[6] Mrachnyi was an energetic member of the anarchist student movement in Kharkov. He entered *Nabat* shortly after its formation and was entrusted with setting up a clandestine printing press in Siberia under the Confederation's auspices, a mission which he apparently carried out successfully.[7] The third young recruit, Gorelik, returned to Russia from American exile in 1917, and served as secretary of the Donets Anarchist Bureau before joining the *Nabat* organization.[8]

Also on the roster of *Nabat* leaders was Nikolai Dolenko, a self-educated peasant from Poltava province.[9] Under the name of M. Chekeres, he had contributed numerous articles to the most important anarchist periodicals during the war years, including the New York *Golos Truda* and the fervently antimilitarist publication in Geneva, *Put' k Svobode*, edited by Roshchin and Orgeiani. More recently, as we have seen, he worked with Maksimov and Iarchuk as an editor of *Vol'nyi*

[5] *Goneniia na anarkhizm v Sovetskoi Rossii*, p. 48.

[6] *Letters from Russian Prisoners* (London, 1925), p. 104; Emma Goldman, *My Disillusionment in Russia* (Garden City, New York, 1923), p. 166; *Bulletin of the Joint Committee for the Defense of Revolutionists Imprisoned in Russia*, No. 1, October 1923.

[7] *Goneniia na anarkhizm v Sovetskoi Rossii*, pp. 57-58.

[8] *Ibid.*, pp. 51-52; Gorelik, *Anarkhisty v rossiiskoi revoliutsii*, p. 38.

[9] *Goneniia na anarkhizm v Sovetskoi Rossii*, p. 52.

Golos Truda in Moscow. Lastly, there was Olga Taratuta, the Ekaterinoslav terrorist and perhaps the most famous of the *bezmotivniki* involved in the bombing of the Café Libman in Odessa in 1905. Released from Kiev's Lukianovskaia prison in March 1917, a tired and subdued woman in her late forties, she at first remained aloof from her former associates and confined herself to working for the Red Cross in Kiev. But in 1920, her ire aroused by the Cheka's relentless persecution of the anarchists, she returned to the fold, joining both the *Nabat* Confederation and the Anarchist Black Cross, which Apollon Karelin had founded to assist anarchists jailed or exiled by the Communists.[10]

In November 1918, the *Nabat* Confederation gathered in the town of Kursk for its first general conference. In contrast with Karelin's All-Russian Federation of Anarchists in Moscow, the *Nabat* group had little use for the Bolshevik "dictatorship of the proletariat" or for any other "transitional stage" that might precede the inauguration of the stateless society. The Russian Revolution, proclaimed the Conference, was only the "first wave" of the worldwide social revolution, which was destined to continue until it had replaced the capitalist order with a free federation of urban and rural communes. And yet, however critical they were of the Soviet dictatorship, the delegates considered the Whites an even greater evil and resolved to oppose them by organizing their own partisan detachments, which would operate outside the official framework of the Red Army. In the economic sphere, the Confederation favored anarchist participation in nonparty soviets, in factory committees free from trade union domination (the unions were branded as an "outmoded form of workers' organization"), and in committees of poor peasants. Finally, the Conference reemphasized the need to create durable federations of anarchist groups on the district, city, and national levels, and to attain a greater degree of solidarity within the movement as a whole.[11]

The same issues dominated the First *Nabat* Congress, which met in Elizavetgrad five months later, in April 1919. Writing

[10] *Ibid.*, p. 44; *Volna*, No. 28, pp. 11-12.
[11] *Pervaia konferentsiia anarkhistskikh organizatsii Ukrainy "Nabat": deklaratsii i rezoliutsii* (Buenos Aires, 1922), pp. 13-27.

in the Confederation's journal shortly before the Congress opened, Senya Fleshin set the tone of the gathering when he chastised the Communists for erecting a "Chinese wall between themselves and the masses."[12] The Congress, echoing Fleshin's protest, deplored the fact that the once free and spontaneous workers' committees of revolutionary Russia had been absorbed by the trade unions, a "purely official, administrative-political, and even police apparatus of the new boss-exploiter, the state."[13] The soviets, too, had been transformed by the Bolsheviks into instruments of state authority, declared the delegates, who called for their replacement by nonpolitical committees of every sort—factory and peasant committees, house and block committees, and cultural-educational committees. The delegates also turned their fire upon their own comrades, roundly condemning both "Soviet anarchism" and the Pan-Anarchism of the Gordin brothers. Moreover, they attacked the "factional narrowness" of the Anarcho-Syndicalists (who had refused to join the Confederation) and rejected a proposal to send a delegation to the Third All-Russian Conference of Anarcho-Syndicalists, scheduled to take place in the near future.[14] These unsparing assaults on fellow anarchist groups, of course, scarcely contributed towards *Nabat*'s main objective of achieving unity within the movement.

On one critical point, however, the *Nabat* Confederation found itself in full agreement with the majority of its anarchist cousins: namely, that the most pressing task of the anarchist movement was to defend the revolution against the White onslaught, even if this should mean a temporary alliance with the Communists. Just as the Kursk Conference had done the previous year, however, the Elizavetgrad Congress resolved to boycott the Red Army, denouncing it as an authoritarian organization, directed "from above" in typical militarist fashion. *Nabat* pinned its hopes instead on a "partisan army" organized spontaneously among the revolutionary masses themselves.[15]

[12] *Nabat* (Kharkov), No. 9, 23 March 1919, p. 3.
[13] *Rezoliutsii pervogo s"ezda Konfederatsii anarkhistskikh organizatsii Ukrainy "Nabat"* (Buenos Aires, 1923), p. 24; *Nabat*, No. 14, 5 May 1919, p. 4.
[14] *Rezoliutsii pervogo s"ezda*, pp. 14-32. The Third Anarcho-Syndicalist Conference never met.
[15] *Ibid.*, p. 18.

And, as the most likely nucleus of such a "partisan army," the leaders of the Confederation looked to the guerrilla band operating in the Ukraine under the command of Nestor Makhno.

Nestor Ivanovich Makhno was born in 1889, the youngest son of a poor peasant couple in the large Ukrainian settlement of Guliai-Pole, situated in Ekaterinoslav province between the Dnieper River and the Sea of Azov.[16] He was barely a year old when his father died, leaving five small boys to the care of their mother. As a child of seven, Makhno was put to work tending cows and sheep for the local peasantry, and later found employment as a farm laborer and as a worker in a foundry.[17] In 1906, at the age of seventeen, he joined an Anarchist-Communist group in Guliai-Pole. He was brought to trial two years later for participating in a terrorist adventure which claimed the life of a district police officer. The court doomed him to be hanged, but because of his youth Makhno's sentence was commuted to an indefinite period of forced labor in the Butyrki prison in Moscow.[18] Makhno proved to be a recalcitrant inmate, unable to accept the discipline of prison life, and during the nine years of his detention he was often placed in irons or in solitary confinement. In 1910, when Petr Arshinov entered Butyrki after his arrest for smuggling anarchist literature into Russia, the two rebels became fast friends. Arshinov, older and better educated than the semi-literate peasant boy from Guliai-Pole, taught Makhno the elements of anarchist doctrine and confirmed him in the faith of Bakunin and Kropotkin.

Makhno and Arshinov were released from prison under the Provisional Government's amnesty in March 1917. Arshinov remained in Moscow, becoming an active member of the Moscow Federation of Anarchists, while Makhno returned to his native village in the Ukraine. There he at once assumed a leading role in community affairs. He helped organize a union of farm laborers and served as its chairman; before long, he

[16] Guliai-Pole, which is conventionally described as a "village," had a population of about 30,000 and boasted several factories and schools.

[17] Makhno is often portrayed as a village schoolmaster, but Volin notes that there is no evidence to support this: *La Révolution inconnue*, p. 523. For an excellent account of Makhno's career, see David Footman, *Civil War in Russia* (London, 1961), pp. 245-302.

[18] P. Arshinov, *Istoriia makhnovskogo dvizheniia (1918-1921 gg.)* (Berlin, 1923), pp. 48-50; I. Teper, *Makhno* (Kiev, 1924), p. 22.

was elected chairman of the local union of carpenters and metal workers and also of the Guliai-Pole Soviet of Peasants' and Workers' Deputies. In August 1917, as head of the Soviet, Makhno recruited a small band of armed peasants and set about expropriating the estates of the neighboring gentry and distributing the land to the poor peasants. From that time, the villagers began to regard him as a new Stenka Razin or Pugachev, sent to realize their ancient dream of land and liberty.[19]

Makhno's activities, however, came to an abrupt halt the following spring, when the Soviet government signed the treaty of Brest-Litovsk and a large force of German and Austrian troops marched into the Ukraine. Makhno shared the indignation of his fellow anarchists at this unforgivable compromise with German "imperialism," but his band of partisans was too weak to offer effective resistance. Forced into hiding, he made his way to the Volga River, then proceeded northwards, wandering from town to town until, in June 1918, he arrived in Moscow, where many of the leading Russian anarchists were concentrated.

During his short visit to the capital, Makhno had an inspiring audience with his idol, Peter Kropotkin. They spoke at length about the tangled situation in the Ukraine, but Kropotkin gently declined to give Makhno any concrete advice on what to do once he should return to his native district. "This question involves great risk for your life, comrade," said the old man, "and only you yourself can solve it correctly." As Makhno rose to leave, Kropotkin added: "One must remember, dear comrade, that our struggle knows no sentimentality. Selflessness and strength of heart and will on the way towards one's chosen goal will conquer all."[20] Kropotkin's moral qualities left an indelible impression on Makhno, as they did on all libertarians who came into contact with the gentle prince; and his parting words, so Makhno testifies in his memoirs, helped sus-

---

[19] Arshinov, *Istoriia makhnovskogo dvizheniia*, pp. 50-51; N. Makhno, *Russkaia revoliutsiia na Ukraine (ot marta 1917 g. po aprel' 1918 g.)* (Paris, 1929), pp. 7-20; George Woodcock, *Anarchism: A History of Libertarian Ideas and Movements* (New York, 1962), p. 419.

[20] N. Makhno, *Pod udarami kontr-revoliutsii (aprel'-iiun' 1918 g.)* (Paris, 1936), pp. 106-107.

tain him throughout the Civil War and during the lonely and dismal years that followed.

While in Moscow, Makhno was also received by Lenin, who sounded him out on the attitude of the Ukrainian peasantry towards the new regime, the military situation in the south, and the differences between the Bolshevik and anarchist conceptions of the revolution. "The majority of anarchists think and write about the future," Lenin declared, "without understanding the present. That is what divides us Communists from them." Though the anarchists were "selfless" men, Lenin went on, their "empty fanaticism" blurred their vision of present and future alike. "But I think that you, comrade," he said to Makhno, "have a realistic attitude towards the burning evils of the time. If only one-third of the Anarchist-Communists were like you, we Communists would be ready, under certain well-known conditions,[21] to join with them in working towards a free organization of producers." Makhno retorted that the anarchists were not utopian dreamers but realistic men of action; after all, he reminded Lenin, it was the anarchists and SR's, rather than the Bolsheviks, who were beating back the nationalists and privileged classes in the Ukraine. "Perhaps I am mistaken," answered Lenin, who then offered to help Makhno return to the south.[22]

Makhno came away from the interview feeling the impact of Lenin's forceful personality, but no less hostile to what he derisively termed the "paper revolution" fabricated by socialist intellectuals and bureaucrats.[23] Even the anarchists he met in the Moscow Federation—Borovoi, Roshchin, Gordin, Sandomirskii, and others—struck him as men of books rather than deeds; however impressive their humanity and learning, they seemed mesmerized by their own words and resolutions and devoid of the will to fight for their ideals.[24] Makhno soon left the huge city that was so alien to his peasant temperament, and returned to Guliai-Pole, to the soil from which he drew his strength and which nourished his passion for spontaneity and liberty.

In July 1918, when Makhno arrived in Guliai-Pole, the area

---

[21] Lenin did not elaborate on the "well-known conditions."
[22] *Ibid.*, pp. 126-135. Cf. Footman, *Civil War in Russia*, pp. 252-256.
[23] Makhno, *Pod udarami kontr-revoliutsii*, p. 93.
[24] *Ibid.*, pp. 98-100, 146.

was occupied by Austrian troops and by the militia (*varta*) of their Ukrainian puppet, Hetman Skoropadskii. Still a fugitive, Makhno slipped into the village to find that, in his absence, his mother's house had been burned down and his brother, Emelian, a crippled war veteran, had been shot.[25] Almost overnight, he organized a detachment of partisans and, under the black flag of anarchism, launched a series of daring raids upon the Austro-Hungarians and Hetmanites, and upon the manors of the local nobility. "We will conquer," declared one of his first proclamations to the peasants of the south, "not so that we may follow the example of past years and hand over our fate to some new master, but to take it in our own hands and conduct our lives according to our own will and our own conception of truth."[26]

Extraordinary mobility and a bag of clever tricks constituted Makhno's chief tactical devices. Traveling on horseback and in light peasant carts (*tachanki*) on which machine guns were mounted, his men moved swiftly back and forth across the open steppe between the Dnieper and the Sea of Azov, swelling into a small army as they went, and inspiring terror in the hearts of their adversaries. Hitherto independent guerrilla bands accepted Makhno's command and rallied behind his black banner. Villagers willingly provided food and fresh horses, enabling the *Makhnovtsy* to travel 40 or 50 miles a day with little difficulty. They would turn up quite suddenly where least expected, attack the gentry and military garrisons, then vanish as quickly as they had come. Disguised in uniforms taken from Hetman Skoropadskii's *varta*, they infiltrated the enemy's ranks to learn their plans or to fire on them at point-blank range; on one occasion, Makhno and his retinue, masquerading as Hetmanite guardsmen, gained entry to a landowner's ball and fell upon the guests in the midst of their festivities.[27] When cornered, the *Makhnovtsy* would bury their weapons, make their way singly back to their villages, and take

[25] Arshinov, *Istoriia makhnovskogo dvizheniia*, p. 52. Subsequently, another brother died in battle with Denikin, and a third was shot in Guliai-Pole by the Bolsheviks. Voline, *La Révolution inconnue*, pp. 667-668.

[26] Arshinov, *Istoriia makhnovskogo dvizheniia*, p. 56.

[27] *Ibid.*, pp. 52-56; V. V. Rudnev, *Makhnovshchina* (Kharkov, 1928), pp. 22-23.

up work in the fields, awaiting the next signal to unearth a new cache of arms and spring up again in an unexpected quarter.[28] Makhno's insurgents, in the words of Victor Serge, revealed "a truly epic capacity for organization and combat."[29] Yet they owed much of their success to the exceptional qualities of their commander-in-chief. Makhno was a bold and resourceful leader who combined an iron will with a quick sense of humor, and won the love and devotion of his peasant followers. In September 1918, when he defeated a much superior force of Austrians at the village of Dibrivki, his men bestowed on him the affectionate title of *bat'ko*, their "little father."[30]

When the armistice of November 1918 resulted in the withdrawal of the Central Powers from Russian territory, Makhno managed to seize a large part of their arms and equipment, and next turned his wrath upon the followers of the Ukrainian nationalist leader, Petliura. At the end of December, he succeeded in dislodging the Petliurist garrison from the city of Ekaterinoslav, in an operation of great enterprise and daring. His troops, with their weapons concealed inside their clothing, rode into the central railway station of Ekaterinoslav on an ordinary passenger train; they took the nationalists by complete surprise and drove them out of the city. The next day, however, the enemy reappeared with reinforcements, and Makhno was compelled to flee across the Dnieper and return to his base in Guliai-Pole. The Petliurists, in turn, were evicted by the Red Army shortly afterwards.

During the first five months of 1919, the Guliai-Pole region was virtually free of external political authority. The Austrians, Hetmanites, and Petliurists had all been driven away, and neither the Reds nor the Whites were strong enough as yet to try to fill the void. Makhno took advantage of this lull to attempt to reconstruct society on libertarian lines. In January, February, and April, the *Makhnovtsy* held a series of Regional Congresses of Peasants, Workers, and Insurgents to discuss economic and military matters and to supervise the task of reconstruction.

The question which dominated the Regional Congresses was

[28] Nomad, *Apostles of Revolution*, p. 309.
[29] Serge, *Mémoires d'un révolutionnaire*, p. 135.
[30] Arshinov, *Istoriia makhnovskogo dvizheniia*, pp. 57-58.

that of defending the area from those who might seek to establish their control over it. The Second Congress, which met in Guliai-Pole on 12 February 1919, voted in favor of "voluntary mobilization," which in reality meant outright conscription, as all able-bodied men were required to serve when called up.[31] The delegates also elected a Regional Military-Revolutionary Council of Peasants, Workers, and Insurgents to carry out the decisions of the periodic Congresses. The new Council stimulated the election of "free" soviets in the towns and villages, that is, soviets from which members of political parties were excluded. Although Makhno's intention in setting up these bodies was to do away with political authority, the Military-Revolutionary Council, acting in conjunction with the Regional Congresses and the local soviets, in effect formed a loose-knit government in the territory surrounding Guliai-Pole.

The Military-Revolutionary Council also helped establish anarchistic communes, which had first appeared in the Guliai-Pole region during the 1905 Revolution and had again sprung into being in 1917. Each commune contained perhaps a dozen households with a total of 100 to 300 members. Though only a few actually considered themselves anarchists, the participants operated the communes on the basis of full equality and accepted the Kropotkinian principle of mutual aid as their fundamental tenet. The Regional Congresses of Peasants, Workers, and Insurgents allotted each commune livestock and farm implements confiscated from the neighboring estates of the nobility, and as much land as its members were able to cultivate without hiring additional labor. The first such commune to be organized during this period was named in honor of Rosa Luxemburg, who was admired by the more politically conscious peasants as a martyr in the struggle for liberty and equality.[32]

Like the Military-Revolutionary Council, the Insurgent Army of the Ukraine (as the Makhnovite forces were called)

[31] *Put' k Svobode* (Guliai-Pole), No. 2, 24 May 1919, p. 1; Arshinov, *Istoriia makhnovskogo dvizheniia*, pp. 86-89.
[32] Arshinov, *Istoriia makhnovskogo dvizheniia*, pp. 84-86; Makhno, *Russkaia revoliutsiia na Ukraine*, pp. 172-181. Rosa Luxemburg and Karl Liebknecht, founders of the German Communist party, were shot by right-wing soldiers after the abortive Spartacus uprising of January 1919, while being taken to prison in Berlin.

1. Mikhail Bakunin (International Institute of Social History)

2. Peter Kropotkin (Bund Archives)

Изданіе Анархистовъ-Общинниковъ.

Т. РОСТОВЦЕВЪ.

3. "For Land and Liberty," St. Petersburg, 1905 (Columbia Special Collections)

4. "The Preparation of Bombs," 1905 (Columbia Russian Archive)

5. A *Chernoe Znamia* Meeting, Minsk, 1906
   (Bund Archives)

ГОЛОСЪ

ССЫЛЬНЫХЪ И ЗАКЛЮЧЕННЫХЪ РУССКИХЪ АНАРХИСТОВЪ.

Изданіе Анархическаго Краснаго Креста в Нью-Іоркѣ.

No. 1.   НОЯБРЬ 1913.   No. 1.

КО ВСѢМЪ ДРУЗЬЯМЪ И ТОВАРИЩАМЪ!

Прошло четыре года съ тѣхъ поръ, какъ мы организовались подъ именемъ: „Анархическій Красный Крестъ въ Нью-Іоркѣ", съ цѣлью облегченія невыносимо-тяжелаго положенія нашихъ заключенныхъ товарищей, находящихся въ когтяхъ русской правящей тираніи.

Когда мы оглядываемся на наше прошлое, просматриваемъ отчеты собранныхъ и разосланныхъ нами денегъ, видимъ численный ростъ нашей организаціи и тысячи симпатизирующихъ, сердца которыхъ бьются въ унисонъ съ сердцами нашихъ страдающихъ братьевъ и сестеръ, мы говоримъ себѣ, что работали не напрасно. А когда лишній разъ прочитываемъ кипы писемъ нашихъ товарищей изъ мрачныхъ тюремъ и холодной Сибири, хранящіяся въ нашемъ архивѣ, представляемъ себѣ сколько радостей и надеждъ внесли въ ихъ разбитыя сердца и набольвшія души за истекшіе четыре года, сердца наши, преисполняются радостью за прошлую дѣятельность, — бодростью и вѣрою въ будущее.

Припоминая, какъ ничтожны были наши средства четыре года тому назадъ, мы не можемъ, конечно, не радоваться нашему успѣху. Но, когда мы вспоминаемъ объ условіяхъ, въ которыхъ находятся заключенные, вспоминаемъ страданія и муки томящихся въ неволѣ товарищей, мы не можемъ не сознаться, что наша помощь была очень ничтожна въ сравненіи съ огромнымъ числомъ нуждающихся.

6. Appeal for Imprisoned Anarchists, 1913
(New York Public Library)

7. Bakunin Centenary, Paris, 1914 (Columbia Russian Archive)

8. "The Bourgeois Order," Petrograd, 1917
(New York Public Library)

9. Nestor Makhno in Guliai-Pole (New York
   Public Library)

10. The Funeral of Kropotkin, February 1921
    (New York Public Library)

11. Nikolai Rogdaev (Alexander Berkman Aid Fund)

12. Lev Chernyi (Courtesy of Senya Fleshin)

13. Aron Baron in Siberian Exile, 1925 (Labadie Collection)

14. Volin in Paris (Courtesy of Senya Fleshin)

15. Alexander Schapiro (International Institute of Social History)

16. Grigorii Maksimov in the United States
(Courtesy of John Cherney)

in theory was subject to the supervision of the Regional Congresses. In practice, however, the reins of authority rested firmly with Makhno and his staff of commanders. Despite his efforts to avoid anything that smacked of regimentation, Makhno appointed his key officers (the rest were elected by the men themselves) and subjected his troops to the stern military discipline traditional among the Cossack legions of the nearby Zaporozhie region. Still and all, the Insurgent Army never lost its plebeian character. All of its officers were peasants or, in a few cases, factory or shop workers. One looks in vain for a commander who sprang from the upper or middle classes, or even from the radical intelligentsia.

A self-taught man of action, Makhno was temperamentally poles apart from the intellectuals in the Russian anarchist movement, though he felt a deep respect, if not a sense of awe, for their superior learning, and sought their assistance in teaching his peasant followers the fundamentals of anarchist doctrine. Volin and Aron Baron arrived at his camp in the summer of 1919, after the Bolsheviks had dispersed the *Nabat* Confederation and forced its members into hiding. Together with Petr Arshinov, Makhno's former cellmate, who had joined him several months earlier, they edited the movement's journal, *Put' k Svobode* (Road to Freedom), resumed publication of their suppressed periodical, *Nabat*, and organized a Cultural-Educational Commission which issued leaflets and delivered lectures to the troops.[33] Beyond these activities, the intellectuals planned to open schools modeled after the *Escuela Moderna* of Francisco Ferrer,[34] which had fostered a spirit of independence and spontaneity among the pupils. Moreover, the Cultural-Educational Commission founded an experimental theater and contemplated a program of adult education for the peasants and workers.[35]

A considerable number of Jews held important positions in the Makhnovite movement. Some were intellectuals who, like Aron Baron, served on the Cultural-Educational Commission,

[33] Voline, *La Révolution inconnue*, p. 581; *Delo Truda-Probuzhdenie*, No. 16, January 1946, p. 17.
[34] Ferrer was a respected Spanish libertarian who had been court-martialed and executed in 1909 on a trumped-up charge of fomenting a rebellion in Barcelona.
[35] Voline, *La Révolution inconnue*, pp. 637-638.

but the great majority fought in the ranks of the Insurgent Army, either as members of special detachments of Jewish infantry and artillery, or else within the regular partisan units, alongside peasants and workmen of Ukrainian, Russian, and other national origins. Makhno personally condemned discrimination of any sort, and strove to bridle the virulent anti-Semitic feeling of his peasant followers, a task which proved as difficult as it was to curb their looting and drinking (the latter was complicated by Makhno's own bouts with alcohol). Punishments for anti-Semitic acts were swift and severe: one troop commander was summarily shot after raiding a Jewish town; a soldier met the same fate merely for displaying a poster with the stock anti-Semitic formula, "Beat the Jews, Save Russia!"[36]

In the early months of 1919, as Makhno and his adherents prepared the groundwork for a libertarian society, their relations with the Bolsheviks remained reasonably friendly, at least on the surface. The peasants of Guliai-Pole even shipped a large quantity of grain to the factory workers of Petrograd and Moscow, who were suffering severe shortages of food. The Soviet press extolled Makhno as a "courageous partisan" and a great revolutionary leader. Relations were at their best in March 1919, when Makhno and the Communists concluded a pact for joint military action against the White Army of General Denikin. According to the agreement, the Insurgent Army of the Ukraine became a division of the Red Army, subject to the orders of the Bolshevik Supreme Command but retaining its own officers and internal structure, as well as its name and black banner.[37]

These outward gestures of harmony, however, could not conceal the basic hostility between the two groups. The Communists had little taste for the autonomous status of the Insurgent Army or for the powerful attraction which it exerted on their own peasant recruits; the *Makhnovtsy*, on their side,

[36] *Ibid.*, pp. 673-675; Arshinov, *Istoriia makhnovskogo dvizheniia*, pp. 203-213; Nomad, *Apostles of Revolution*, p. 311. Volin adduces testimony by Elias Tcherikover, an eminent Jewish historian and authority on anti-Semitism in the Ukraine, to the effect that the number of anti-Semitic acts committed by the *Makhnovtsy* was "negligible" in comparison with those committed by other combatants in the Civil War, the Red Army not excepted.

[37] Arshinov, *Istoriia makhnovskogo dvizheniia*, pp. 94-95.

feared that sooner or later the Red Army would attempt to bring their movement to heel. At the beginning of the year, outspoken delegates to the first two Makhnovite Congresses had already accused the Bolshevik party of seeking "to deprive the local soviets of peasants' and workers' deputies of their freedom and autonomy" and of "demanding a monopoly of the Revolution."[38] When a Third Congress was summoned in April, the Red commander in the Dnieper area, Dybenko, banned it as a "counterrevolutionary" gathering. Makhno's Military-Revolutionary Council dispatched an indignant reply: "Have you the right to pronounce counterrevolutionary a people which . . . has thrown off the bonds of slavery and which is now creating its own life according to its own will? Should the masses of revolutionary people remain silent while 'the revolutionists' take away the freedom they have just won?"[39] On 10 April 1919, the Third Congress of Peasants, Workers, and Insurgents met in open defiance of the ban placed upon it. Soviet newspapers now abandoned their eulogies of the *Makhnovtsy* and began to attack them as "kulaks" and "Anarcho-Bandits." In May, two Cheka agents sent to assassinate Makhno were caught and executed. The final breach occurred when the *Makhnovtsy* called a Fourth Regional Congress for 15 June and invited the soldiers in the ranks of the Red Army to send representatives. Trotsky, Commander-in-Chief of the Bolshevik forces, was furious. On 4 June, he banned the Congress and outlawed Makhno. Communist troops carried out a lightning raid on Guliai-Pole and ordered the Rosa Luxemburg Commune and its sister communes dissolved. A few days later, Denikin's forces arrived and completed the job, wiping out what still remained of the communes and liquidating the local soviets as well.

The shaky alliance was hastily resumed that summer, when Denikin's massive drive towards Moscow sent both the Communists and *Makhnovtsy* reeling. During August and September, Makhno's guerrillas were pushed back towards the western borders of the Ukraine. Volin, who took part in the exhausting retreat, recalled in his memoirs that the *Makhnovtsy*, in the face of overwhelming odds, refused to despair. A huge

[38] Quoted in Footman, *Civil War in Russia*, p. 267.
[39] Arshinov, *Istoriia makhnovskogo dvizheniia*, pp. 98-103.

black flag floated over the lead wagon of the Insurgent Army, bearing the slogans "Liberty or Death" and "The Land to the Peasants, the Factories to the Workers."[40] Then, on 26 September 1919, Makhno suddenly launched a successful counterattack at the village of Peregonovka, near the town of Uman, cutting the White General's supply lines and creating panic and disorder in his rear. This was Denikin's first serious reverse in his dramatic advance into the Russian heartland and a major factor in halting his drive towards the Bolshevik capital. By the end of the year, a counteroffensive by the Red Army had forced Denikin to beat a swift retreat to the shores of the Black Sea.[41]

The *Makhnovshchina* reached its crest in the months following the victory at Peregonovka. During October and November, Makhno occupied Ekaterinoslav and Aleksandrovsk for several weeks, and thus obtained his first chance to apply the concepts of anarchism to city life. Makhno's first act on entering a large town (after throwing open the prisons) was to dispel any impression that he had come to introduce a new form of political rule. Announcements were posted informing the townspeople that henceforth they were free to organize their lives as they saw fit, that the Insurgent Army would not "dictate to them or order them to do anything."[42] Free speech, press, and assembly were proclaimed, and in Ekaterinoslav half a dozen newspapers, representing a wide range of political opinion, sprang up overnight. While encouraging freedom of expression, however, Makhno would not countenance any political organizations which sought to impose their authority on the people. He therefore dissolved the Bolshevik "revolutionary committees" (*revkomy*) in Ekaterinoslav and Aleksandrovsk, instructing their members to "take up some honest trade."[43]

Makhno's aim was to throw off domination of every type and to encourage economic and social self-determination. "It is up to the workers and peasants," said one of his proclamations in 1919, "to organize themselves and reach mutual un-

[40] Voline, *La Révolution inconnue*, p. 578.
[41] Arshinov, *Istoriia makhnovskogo dvizheniia*, pp. 134-141.
[42] Voline, *La Révolution inconnue*, p. 599.
[43] *Ibid.*, p. 602; Arshinov, *Istoriia makhnovskogo dvizheniia*, pp. 149-152.

derstandings in all areas of their lives and in whatever manner they think right."[44] In October 1919, an SR speaker who called for effective leadership at a Congress of Workers and Peasants in Aleksandrovsk was greeted with shouts of protest from the *Makhnovtsy*: "We have had enough of your leaders. Always leaders and more leaders. Let us try to do without them for once."[45] When the railroad workers of Aleksandrovsk complained that they had not been paid for many weeks, Makhno advised them to take control of the railway lines and charge the passengers and freight shippers what seemed a fair price for their services.

Makhno's utopian projects, however, failed to win over more than a small minority of workingmen, for, unlike the farmers and artisans of the village, who were independent producers accustomed to managing their own affairs, factory workers and miners operated as interdependent parts of a complicated industrial machine, and were lost without the guidance of supervisors and technical specialists. Furthermore, the peasants and artisans could barter the products of their labor, whereas the urban workers depended on regular wages for their survival. Makhno, moreover, compounded the confusion when he recognized all paper money issued by his predecessors—Ukrainian nationalists, Whites, and Bolsheviks alike. He never understood the complexities of an urban economy, nor did he care to understand them. He detested the "poison" of the cities and cherished the natural simplicity of the peasant environment into which he had been born. In any event, Makhno found very little time to implement his ill-defined economic programs. He was forever on the move, rarely pausing even to catch his breath. The *Makhnovshchina*, in the words of his contemporaries, was a "kingdom on wheels," a "republic on *tachanki*." "As always," wrote Volin of Makhno's projects in Ekaterinoslav and Aleksandrovsk, "the instability of the situation prevented positive work."[46]

At the end of 1919, Makhno received instructions from the Red Command to transfer his army forthwith to the Polish

[44] Voline, *La Révolution inconnue*, pp. 598-599.

[45] *Ibid.*, pp. 610-611; Arshinov, *Istoriia makhnovskogo dvizheniia*, pp. 146-148.

[46] Voline, *La Révolution inconnue*, pp. 578, 603; Rudnev, *Makhnovshchina*, p. 66.

front. The order was plainly designed to draw the *Makhnovtsy* away from their home territory and thus leave it open to the establishment of Bolshevik rule. Makhno refused to budge. He replied that his Insurgent Army was the one truly popular force in the Ukraine and that it would remain there to protect the people's newly won freedom. Trotsky, he said, wanted to replace Denikin's "hordes" with the Red Army and the dispossessed landlords with political commissars.[47] Trotsky's response was firm and unhesitating: he outlawed the *Makhnovtsy* and prepared to move against them. In a desperate attempt to prevent the attack, Makhno's headquarters in Guliai-Pole issued a flood of leaflets appealing to the Bolshevik troops to refuse any order that might disturb the "peaceful settlements" of the Ukraine. The people do not need "commissar-rule," declared the leaflets, but a "free soviet order." "We will answer violence with violence."[48]

There ensued eight months of bitter struggle with losses high on both sides. A severe typhus epidemic augmented the toll of victims. Volin, felled by the disease in the town of Krivoi Rog, was captured by the Red Army and removed to a Moscow prison.[49] Badly outnumbered, Makhno's partisans avoided pitched battles and relied on the guerrilla tactics they had perfected in more than two years of Civil War. In one of their songs, they proclaimed their faith in Makhno's leadership:

> We shall defeat them
> And thrash them in this war.
> We shall take them captive
> To the last commissar.
>
> Hoorah, hoorah, hoorah!
> We march against the foe,
> For *matushka* Galina,
> For *bat'ko* Makhno![50]

In October 1920, Baron Wrangel, Denikin's successor in the south, launched a major offensive, striking northwards from

[47] "Tovarishchi krest'iane!" (leaflet, 3 February 1920), Fedeli Archive.
[48] "Ostanovis'! Prochitai! Porazdumai!" and "Tovarishchi krasnoarmeitsy fronta i tyla," Fedeli Archive.
[49] Voline, *La Révolution inconnue*, p. 635n.
[50] Teper, *Makhno*, p. 78; Rudnev, *Makhnovshchina*, pp. 22-23. Galina was Makhno's wife.

the Crimean peninsula. Once more the Red Army enlisted Makhno's aid, and again an alliance was signed by which the Insurgent Army became a semi-autonomous division under the Bolshevik Command.[51] In return for Makhno's cooperation, the Communists agreed to amnesty all anarchists in Russian prisons and guaranteed the anarchists freedom of propaganda on condition that they refrain from calling for the violent overthrow of the Soviet government.[52] (Hence Volin, once recovered from his bout with typhus, was able to resume publication of *Nabat* in Kharkov and to begin preparations for an All-Russian Congress of Anarchists, which was scheduled to meet there at the end of the year.)

Barely a month later, however, the Red Army had made sufficient gains to assure victory in the Civil War, and the Soviet leaders tore up their agreement with Makhno. Not only had the *Makhnovtsy* outlived their usefulness as a military partner, but as long as the *bat'ko* was left at large, the spirit of primitive anarchism and the danger of a peasant jacquerie—a *Pugachevshchina*—would remain to haunt the unsteady Bolshevik regime. Thus, on 25 November, Makhno's commanders in the Crimea, fresh from their victories over Wrangel's army, were seized by the Red Army and immediately shot. The next day, Trotsky ordered an attack on Makhno's headquarters in Guliai-Pole, while the Cheka simultaneously arrested the members of the *Nabat* Confederation who had assembled in Kharkov for their impending Congress, and carried out raids on anarchist clubs and organizations throughout the country.[53]

During the attack on Guliai-Pole, most of Makhno's staff were captured and imprisoned or simply shot on the spot. The *bat'ko* himself, however, together with the battered remnant of an army which had once numbered in the tens of thousands, managed to elude his pursuers. After wandering over the Ukraine for the better part of a year, the partisan leader, exhausted and still suffering from unhealed wounds, crossed the

[51] In June 1920, Wrangel attempted to strike a bargain with Makhno for common action against the Bolsheviks. But Makhno seized and executed the Baron's unfortunate envoys, just as he had executed his rival guerrilla chieftain, Grigoriev, when the latter came to discuss military cooperation the year before.

[52] Arshinov, *Istoriia makhnovskogo dvizheniia*, pp. 171-173.

[53] Voline, *La Révolution inconnue*, pp. 642-648.

Dniester River into Rumania and eventually found his way to Paris.[54]

Bolshevik harassment of the anarchists had been mounting ever since the Cheka launched its first raids against the Moscow Federation in April 1918. By 1919, the armed detachments of Black Guards and the aggressive bands of guerrilla fighters—forces which might present a military danger to the government—were no longer the only targets of the police; the intellectuals of the Anarcho-Syndicalist and *Nabat* Confederations, armed with nothing more lethal than their pens, were also subjected to frequent arrests and detention, especially the recalcitrants who refused to halt their criticisms of the "betrayals" and "excesses" of Lenin and Trotsky. Grigorii Maksimov noted that, between 1919 and 1921, he was taken into custody no less than six times; even such loyal "Soviet anarchists" as the Gordin brothers and Iuda Roshchin were imprisoned for brief periods.[55]

During the summer of 1920, Emma Goldman and Alexander Berkman vehemently protested the harassment of their comrades to the Second Congress of the Communist International, then meeting in Moscow.[56] Similar complaints were lodged by the Anarchist Black Cross. The Anarcho-Syndicalists urged the foreign syndicalists who had come to Moscow as delegates to the Comintern gathering to use their influence upon the Soviet leadership. This stream of protests, however, failed to prevent Trotsky's "major surgical operation" in the Ukraine during November 1920,[57] when the Red Army raided Makhno's headquarters in Guliai-Pole and the Cheka rounded up the leaders of the *Nabat* Confederation in Kharkov—including Volin, Aron and Fanya Baron, Olga Taratuta, Senya Fleshin, Mark Mrachnyi, Dolenko-Chekeres, and Anatolii Gorelik—and packed them off to the Taganka and Butyrki prisons in Moscow. In the capital, Maksimov and Iarchuk of the Anarcho-Syndicalist Confederation were detained for sev-

[54] Arshinov, *Istoriia makhnovskogo dvizheniia*, pp. 189-200.

[55] Maximoff, *The Guillotine at Work*, p. 361.

[56] Goldman, *Living My Life*, II, 799ff.; *Letters from Russian Prisoners*, p. 249.

[57] G. P. Maksimov, *Za chto i kak bol'sheviki izgnali anarkhistov iz Rossii?* (n.p. [Berlin], 1922), p. 3.

eral weeks.[58] Incensed by this new wave of arrests, Emma Goldman complained bitterly to Anatolii Lunacharskii, the Commissar of Education, and to the feminist Commissar of Welfare, Aleksandra Kollontai, both of whom, as Emma told Angelica Balabanoff, "recognized these abuses but felt it impolitic to protest."[59] Balabanoff, a secretary of the Comintern, then arranged for Emma to meet with Lenin, who reassured her that no anarchists would be persecuted for their beliefs, that only "bandits" and Makhno's insurrectionists were being suppressed.[60]

With the mass arrests of the Anarcho-Syndicalists (who, unlike the *Makhnovtsy*, presented no armed threat to the government), the Bolsheviks hoped to eliminate once and for all their persistent influence among the factory workers. The continuing agitation of the syndicalists, indeed their very presence in the factories, served to remind the workers of the glimpse of freedom they had caught in 1917, the heyday of workers' control.[61] Since that time, as the regime moved towards centralized control over the economy, the syndicalists had been fighting a rearguard action and encouraging the workers to do the same. In March 1920, the Second All-Russian Congress of Food-Industry Workers, meeting in Moscow, adopted a resolution proposed by the Anarcho-Syndicalist Executive Bureau (Maksimov, Iarchuk, and Sergei Markus), which censured the Bolshevik regime for inaugurating "unlimited and uncontrolled dominion over the proletariat and peasantry, frightful centralism carried to the point of absurdity . . . destroying in the country all that is alive, spontaneous, and free."[62] "The so-called dictatorship of the proletariat," the resolution went on, "is in reality the dictatorship over the proletariat by the party and even by individual persons."[63] Maksimov, the author of

[58] Gorelik, *Anarkhisty v rossiiskoi revoliutsii*, p. 46; Berkman, *The Bolshevik Myth*, pp. 280-287; Maximoff, *The Guillotine at Work*, pp. 360-361.

[59] Angelica Balabanoff, *My Life as a Rebel* (New York, 1938), p. 254.

[60] *Ibid.*, p. 255.

[61] Alexander Berkman noted in his diary on 7 March 1920 that the *Golos Truda* bookstore in Moscow was being deluged with requests for literature from every corner of Russia. "Diary: Russia, 1919-1921," Berkman Archive.

[62] *Vmesto programmy*, p. 28.

[63] *Ibid.*

these bold phrases, called for a new society based on nonparty soviets and free labor. Convinced that the factory committees, with the general strike as their weapon, could ultimately bring about economic decentralization in Russia, he tried to organize an underground Federation of Food Workers as the first step towards the formation of a Russian General Confederation of Labor.[64]

Although little came of Maksimov's organizational efforts, his goal of a decentralized labor confederation began to gain favor among the more radical elements in the factories and shops, and even to grip the imagination of an articulate group of dissenters within the Communist party itself. By the end of 1920, under the leadership of the colorful Madame Kollontai and her paramour, Aleksandr Shliapnikov, a former metal worker and now the first People's Commissar of Labor, a "workers' opposition" had taken shape, attracting considerable rank-and-file support in the trade unions and factory committees. The "workers' opposition" was profoundly disturbed by the policies of "war communism." Its adherents particularly deplored the "militarization" of the labor force and the replacement of workers' control by one-man management in the factories. Their mounting criticism of Bolshevik policies reflected the disillusionment of the workers with their new rulers and popular resentment at the apparent drift of the Soviet regime towards a new bureaucratic state. The "workers' opposition" protested that the government economic agencies and the Communist party itself had been inundated with "bourgeois" technicians and other nonproletarian elements. The Bolshevik leaders, declared Kollontai, had no understanding of the needs of bench workers or of life in the workshop. Distrusting the rank and file, they tended to "place more reliance on the bureaucratic technicians, descendants of the past, than in the healthy elemental class creativeness of the working masses."[65] "The basis of the controversy," she said, "is namely this: whether we shall realize communism through the workers or over their heads, by the hands of soviet officials."[66]

Kollontai, Shliapnikov, and their associates demanded that

---

[64] Maximoff, *The Guillotine at Work*, pp. 368-369.
[65] A. Kollontai, *The Workers Opposition in Russia* (Chicago, 1921), pp. 29-30.
[66] *Ibid.*, p. 20.

the administration of the economy be transferred from the government to the factory committees and trade unions, both to be organized into an All-Russian Congress of Producers, freely elected and independent of party control. The creative powers of the factory workers, they argued, should be given free rein, instead of being "crippled by the bureaucratic machine which is saturated with the spirit of routine of the bourgeois capitalist system of production and control."[67] The "workers' opposition," Kollontai concluded, aimed to achieve a genuine proletarian dictatorship rather than the dictatorship of party leaders, for as Marx and Engels proclaimed: "Creation of communism can and will be the work of the toiling masses themselves. Creation of communism belongs to the workers."[68]

Lenin watched the growth of the opposition movement with increasing displeasure. He disputed Kollontai's appeal to the founding fathers in support of her position. Condemning the ideas of the "workers' opposition" as a "syndicalist and anarchist deviation" from the Marxist tradition, he summoned its leaders to submit to party discipline. Lenin, fearing that syndicalist doctrines were "permeating the broad masses," denounced all talk of "industrial democracy" or of an All-Russian Congress of Producers.[69] He firmly denied his earlier contention, in *The State and Revolution*, that ordinary workingmen were capable of running political and economic affairs. "Practical men," he declared, "know that this is a fairy tale."[70]

By the beginning of 1921, Lenin had become sufficiently alarmed by the revival of syndicalist tendencies among the factory workers and among the intellectuals of his own party to take further measures to curb them. Thus he placed on the Index the works of Fernand Pelloutier (the outstanding figure in the French syndicalist movement), and certain writings of Bakunin and Kropotkin as well. Kropotkin, the living symbol of libertarianism, still commanded widespread respect and devotion in Russia. He had come to believe, as he told Emma

[67] *Ibid.*, pp. 22-23; "Tezisy rabochei oppozitsii," *Pravda*, 25 January 1921, pp. 2-3.
[68] Kollontai, *The Workers Opposition*, p. 44.
[69] Lenin, *Sochineniia*, XXVI, 222-233.
[70] *Ibid.*, XXI, 399; XXVI, 103.

Goldman in 1920, that syndicalism alone could furnish the groundwork for the reconstruction of Russia's economy.[71]

Kropotkin had not been personally molested during the raids on the Moscow anarchists in 1918, but in the summer of that year, the old prince was compelled to move to a modest wooden house in the village of Dmitrov, some 40 miles north of the capital. There he spent much of his time writing a book on ethics (which he was never to finish),[72] and receiving a steady stream of visitors, including Volin, Maksimov, Emma Goldman, and Alexander Berkman. Kropotkin was greatly disturbed by the authoritarian methods of the Soviet government. He bitterly opposed the dissolution of the Constituent Assembly as well as the terroristic practices of the Cheka, and likened the party dictatorship imposed by the Bolsheviks to the "Jacobin endeavor of Babeuf."[73] Nevertheless, in an open letter to the workers of Western Europe, he urged them to prevail upon their governments to end the blockade of Russia and abandon their intervention in the Civil War. "Not that there is nothing to oppose in the methods of the Bolshevik government," Kropotkin reiterated. "Far from it! But all foreign armed intervention necessarily strengthens the dictatorial tendencies of the government and paralyzes the efforts of those Russians who are ready to aid Russia, independently of the government, in the restoration of its life."[74]

In May 1919, a year before this declaration, Kropotkin met with Lenin in Moscow to talk over their differences. The discussion was continued in a brief correspondence, in which Kropotkin kept up his attack on the Bolshevik dictatorship. "Russia has become a Revolutionary Republic only in name," he wrote to Lenin in March 1920. "At present it is ruled not by soviets but by party committees. . . . If the present situation should continue much longer, the very word 'socialism' will turn into a curse, as did the slogan of 'equality' for forty years

[71] Goldman, *My Disillusionment in Russia*, p. 158.

[72] P. Kropotkin, *Etika* (Petrograd, 1922). The uncompleted manuscript was published by the *Golos Truda* press.

[73] *P. A. Kropotkin i ego uchenie*, pp. 196-200; *Kropotkin's Revolutionary Pamphlets*, p. 254.

[74] *P. A. Kropotkin i ego uchenie*, p. 197; *Kropotkin's Revolutionary Pamphlets*, p. 253.

after the rule of the Jacobins."[75] But Kropotkin had not lost hope. "I deeply believe in the future," he affirmed in May 1920. "I believe the syndicalist movement . . . will emerge as the great force in the course of the next fifty years, leading to the creation of the communist stateless society."[76]

In January 1921, Kropotkin, nearly eighty years old, fell mortally ill with pneumonia. His old disciple, Dr. Aleksandr Atabekian, who had founded the Anarchist Library in Geneva 30 years before, went to his dying mentor's bedside.[77] Three weeks later, on 8 February 1921, Kropotkin died. His family declined Lenin's offer of a state burial, and a committee of leading Anarcho-Syndicalists and Anarchist-Communists, momentarily united by the death of their great teacher, was set up to arrange a funeral.[78] Lev Kamenev, chairman of the Moscow Soviet, allowed Aron Baron and several other imprisoned anarchists a day's liberty to take part in the procession. Braving the bitter cold of the Moscow winter, 20,000 marched in the cortege to the Novodevichii Monastery, the burial place of Kropotkin's ancestors. They carried placards and black banners bearing demands for the release of all anarchists from prison and such mottoes as "Where there is authority, there is no freedom," and "The liberation of the working class is the task of the workers themselves." A chorus chanted "Eternal Memory." As the procession passed the Butyrki prison, the inmates shook the bars on their windows and sang an anarchist hymn to the dead. Emma Goldman spoke at Kropotkin's graveside, and students and workers placed flowers by his tomb.[79] Kropotkin's birthplace, a large house in the old aristo-

[75] David Shub, "Kropotkin and Lenin," *Russian Review*, XII (October 1953), 232; *Delo Truda*, No. 62-63, January-February 1931, pp. 7-13.

[76] *Anarkhicheskie Organizatsii: Pamiati Petra Alekseevicha Kropotkina*, No. 1, 8-13 February 1921, p. 1.

[77] *Pamiati Petra Alekseevicha Kropotkina*, pp. 108-112; *Goneniia na anarkhizm v Sovetskoi Rossii*, pp. 48-49. After the October Revolution, Atabekian again established his own anarchist press in Moscow, in the teeth of Bolshevik interference.

[78] *Anarkhicheskie Organizatsii*, p. 1.

[79] Interview with Princess Alexandra Kropotkin, 10 March 1965; Woodcock and Avakumovic, *The Anarchist Prince*, pp. 436-437; *Kropotkin's Revolutionary Pamphlets*, p. 29; Emma Goldman, *My Further Disillusionment in Russia* (Garden City, New York, 1924), pp. 63-64; Serge, *Mémoires d'un révolutionnaire*, pp. 137-138; *P. A. Kropotkin i ego uchenie*, p. 320; *Klich Anarkhistov*, May 1921.

cratic quarter of Moscow, was turned over to his wife and comrades to be used as a museum for his books, papers, and personal belongings. Supervised by a committee of scholarly anarchists which included Nikolai Lebedev, Aleksei Solonovich, and Dr. Atabekian, it was maintained by contributions from friends and admirers throughout the world.[80]

The Russian Civil War yielded a grim legacy of famine, industrial collapse, fuel shortages, personal hatred, and political disaffection. It was this bitter harvest which gave rise to the extreme tension in Moscow and Petrograd during the opening weeks of 1921, setting the scene for the Kronstadt rebellion, an event, as Lenin observed, which "lit up reality better than anything else."[81]

Towards the end of February, a sudden wave of strikes swept through the largest factories of Petrograd. Leaflets and proclamations were circulated, some demanding fuel and bread, the elimination of Trotsky's "labor battalions," and the revival of free soviets and factory committees, others calling for freedom of speech, the restoration of the Constitutent Assembly, an end to Cheka terror, and the liberation of SR's, anarchists, and other political prisoners from Communist jails. Before the month was out, delegations of sailors and workmen from the Kronstadt naval base on nearby Kotlin Island had arrived in the capital to join with the strikers in some of their demonstrations. At Kronstadt itself, sympathy meetings were held in Anchor Square—where Bleikhman had delivered his fiery speeches during the July Days of 1917—and on board the battleship *Petropavlovsk*, which lay in the harbor. The actual rebellion erupted early in March at the island base and its surrounding industrial complex. The rising lasted two weeks, until Bolshevik troops and volunteers crossed the frozen ice in the Gulf of Finland and suppressed the insurgents.[82]

[80] *Kropotkin's Revolutionary Pamphlets*, p. 30; N. K. Lebedev, *Muzei P. A. Kropotkina* (Leningrad and Moscow, 1928); "Muzei imeni P. A. Kropotkina," *Probuzhdenie*, No. 15, February 1931, pp. 44-46; Woodcock and Avakumovic, *The Anarchist Prince*, p. 437; Serge, *Mémoires d'un révolutionnaire*, p. 138.

[81] Lenin, *Sochineniia*, XXVI, 291.

[82] A sound discussion of the revolt is George Katkov's "The Kronstadt Rising," *Soviet Affairs*, No. 2, 1959, pp. 9-74. See also Alexander Berk-

Kronstadt had had a history of volatile radicalism reaching back to the Revolution of 1905. The revolt of March 1921, like the earlier uprisings during 1905 and 1917, was a spontaneous affair and not, as often depicted, engineered by the anarchists or, for that matter, by any other single party or group. Its participants, rather, were radicals of all stripes— Bolsheviks, SR's, anarchists, and many with no specific political affiliation. Those anarchists who had played prominent roles in Kronstadt during 1917 were no longer present four years later: the sailor Zhelezniakov, it will be recalled, had been killed by Denikin's army in 1919; Bleikhman had died in Moscow in 1920 or early 1921; and Iarchuk was in Moscow with most of his comrades, who, when not in prison, were under the close surveillance of the Cheka.

Still, the spirit of anarchism, so powerful in Kronstadt during the Revolution of 1917, had by no means disappeared. On the eve of the insurrection, anarchists distributed leaflets among the sailors and workers, bearing the slogan, "Where there is authority, there is no liberty," and reviling the "iron discipline" and "forced labor" imposed on the factory workers by the Bolshevik regime. The leaflets reiterated the familiar anarchist demands for an end to compulsory labor, the restoration of workers' control, the formation of autonomous partisan bands in place of the Red Army, and the inauguration of a true social revolution, one which would usher in the stateless society of free communes.[83] But quite apart from such direct propaganda, the influence of anarchist ideas was much in evidence among the insurgents. Thus, in true anarchist fashion, the rebels lamented that Russia had fallen under the domination of "a small group of Communist bureaucrats," and they cried out for the destruction of the "commissarocracy"

---

man, *The Kronstadt Rebellion* (Berlin, 1922); Berkman, *The Bolshevik Myth*, pp. 291-297; E. Iarchuk, *Kronshtadt v russkoi revoliutsii* (New York, 1923), pp. 52-63; Voline, *La Révolution inconnue*, pp. 425-488; Ida Mett, *La Commune de Cronstadt* (Paris, 1949), pp. 30-58; Robert V. Daniels, "The Kronstadt Revolt of 1921: A Study in the Dynamics of Revolution," *American Slavic and East European Review*, x (December 1951), 241-254; and D. Fedotoff White, *The Growth of the Red Army* (Princeton, 1944), pp. 127-157.

[83] N. A. Kornatovskii, ed., *Kronshtadtskii miatezh: sbornik statei, vospominanii i dokumentov* (Leningrad, 1931), pp. 164-166.

erected by Lenin and Trotsky and their retinue.[84] The workers, they said, had not emancipated themselves from the private capitalists in order to become the slaves of the state.[85] "All power to the soviets," proclaimed the insurrectionists, "but not to the parties."[86] In the rebel journal, they announced that the Kronstadt uprising marked the beginning of the "third revolution," destined to continue until the Russian people were liberated from their new masters: "Here in Kronstadt the first stone of the third revolution has been laid, striking the last fetters from the laboring masses and opening a broad new road for socialist creativity."[87]

The anarchists, elated by the mutiny, hailed Kronstadt as "the second Paris Commune."[88] Even such pro-Soviet groups as the Universalists and Karelin's All-Russian Federation of Anarchists were jubilant, and denounced the government when troops were sent to put down the revolt. Fearing a blood-bath, Alexander Berkman and Emma Goldman, together with two of their comrades, petitioned Zinoviev to allow them to mediate the dispute.[89] But the government was in no mood to consider any accommodation with the insurgents. "The time has come," declared Lenin to the Tenth Party Congress as the rebellion raged in the Finnish Gulf, "to put an end to opposition, to put the lid on it; we have had enough opposition."[90]

Following this pronouncement, the "workers' opposition" (though its adherents had joined their fellow Communists in condemning the Kronstadt revolt) was quickly suppressed. A new wave of political arrests swept the country. Anarchists

[84] *Pravda o Kronshtadte* (Prague, 1921), pp. 66, 102, 110. In October 1918, there was a small mutiny at Kronstadt, the precursor of the 1921 affair, in which the participants (likewise radicals of various hues) demanded the replacement of the "commissarocracy" by a federation of "free soviets." I. Flerovskii, "Miatezh mobilizovannykh matrosov v Peterburge 14 oktiabria 1918 g.," *Proletarskaia Revoliutsiia*, 1926, No. 8 (55), pp. 218-237.

[85] *Pravda o Kronshtadte*, p. 173.

[86] Berkman, *The Kronstadt Rebellion*, p. 25; A. S. Pukhov, *Kronshtadtskii miatezh v 1921 g.* (Leningrad, 1931), p. 77.

[87] *Pravda o Kronshtadte*, pp. 83-84; Berkman, *The Kronstadt Rebellion*, p. 28.

[88] Gorelik, *Anarkhisty v rossiiskoi revoliutsii*, p. 51.

[89] Goldman, *Living My Life*, II, 887; Berkman, *The Bolshevik Myth*, p. 302.

[90] Leonard Schapiro, *The Origin of the Communist Autocracy* (Cambridge, Mass., 1956), p. 316.

were rounded up in Petrograd, Moscow, Kiev, Kharkov, Ekaterinoslav, and Odessa. Those who had been released after their arrest in November 1920, when the backbone of the movement was broken, were taken into custody once again. The Moscow Cheka seized Maksimov and Iarchuk, the secretary and treasurer of the Anarcho-Syndicalist Executive Bureau, and sent them to join their colleagues in the Taganka prison.[91] Most of the surviving book stores, printing offices, and clubs were closed[92] and the few remaining anarchist circles broken up. Even the pacifist followers of Tolstoy were imprisoned or banished. (A number of Tolstoyans had already been shot during the Civil War for refusing to serve in the Red Army.)[93]

Aleksei Borovoi was dismissed from the faculty of Moscow University.[94] In November 1921, the police raided the Universalist Club, a former center of "Soviet anarchism," and shut down its newspaper. Two of its leaders, Vladimir Barmash and German Askarov, both prominent intellectuals and members of the Moscow Soviet, were arrested on charges of "banditry and underground activities."[95] According to Maksimov, the Universalists, who had rejoiced at the outbreak of the Kronstadt insurrection, were succeeded by a more subservient group called the "Anarcho-Biocosmists," which pledged unwavering support of the Soviet government and solemnly declared its intention to launch a social revolution "in interplanetary space but not upon Soviet territory."[96]

[91] Maksimov, *Za chto i kak bol'sheviki izgnali anarkhistov iz Rossii?*, pp. 5-6.

[92] The *Golos Truda* printing establishment and book stores (in Petrograd and Moscow) were a notable exception, surviving until the end of the NEP.

[93] A. Tolstaia, *Otets: zhizn' L'va Tolstogo* (2 vols., New York, 1953), II, 305; Woodcock, *Anarchism*, p. 418.

[94] *Delo Truda*, No. 52-53, September-October 1929, pp. 1-2; Goldman, *Living My Life*, II, 892; Maximoff, *The Guillotine at Work*, p. 595. In early 1921, at the request of the student body of Sverdlov University, Borovoi was scheduled to debate with Bukharin and Lunacharskii on the theme of "Anarchism versus Marxism," but at the last moment the Communists cancelled the meeting.

[95] M. Mrachnyi, "Kto sidit v komm. tiur'makh?," *Volna*, No. 28, April 1922, pp. 14-15; Emma Goldman, *The Crushing of the Russian Revolution* (London, 1922), p. 12; Berkman, *The Bolshevik Myth*, p. 309.

[96] Maximoff, *The Guillotine at Work*, p. 362. In 1923, another

The suppression of the anarchists produced some undesired repercussions. At the same time as the Bolsheviks were filling the cells of Butyrki and Taganka with syndicalists, Universalists, *Makhnovtsy*, and members of the *Nabat* Confederation, they were engaged in a heated competition with the Socialist International in Amsterdam for the allegiance of the syndicalists in Western Europe and North America. In July 1921, the Communists created the Red International of Trade Unions (better known as the Profintern) with the mission of alluring the organized labor movement away from the International Federation of Trade Unions in Amsterdam. But the foreign delegates attending the founding congress of the Profintern in Moscow, already disturbed by the liquidation of Makhno's army and by the suppression of the Kronstadt rising, were stunned anew by the latest wave of anarchist arrests. S. A. Lozovskii, the president of the Profintern, Foreign Minister Chicherin, and Lenin himself repeatedly assured their visitors that "ideological" anarchists were in no way being persecuted. Nevertheless, Goldman, Berkman, and Alexander Schapiro were able to persuade a number of European syndicalists to make representations to Lenin on behalf of their imprisoned Russian comrades.[97] Other Profintern delegates lodged a protest with Feliks Dzerzhinskii, head of the Cheka.[98] To dramatize their plight, the anarchist prisoners in Taganka—Maksimov, Volin, Iarchuk, Barmash, Mrachnyi, among others—staged an eleven-day hunger strike while the Profintern congress was in session.[99]

To add to the government's embarrassment, another commotion arose when, in September 1921, the Cheka shot the

anarchist group called for support of the Soviet government and the Third International. *Pravda*, 7 September 1923, p. 2.

[97] Berkman, *The Bolshevik Myth*, pp. 152-153; Goldman, *Living My Life*, II, 909-914; *Goneniia na anarkhizm v Sovetskoi Rossii*, p. 5; *Anarkhicheskii Vestnik*, No. 5-6, November-December 1923, p. 54; Jean Gaudeaux, *Six mois en Russie bolchéviste* (Paris, 1924), pp. 122-194. Gaudeaux, a French syndicalist, was one of the Profintern delegates who personally protested to Lenin.

[98] Maksimov, *Za chto i kak bol'sheviki izgnali anarkhistov*, p. 14.

[99] Maximoff, *The Guillotine at Work*, pp. 194, 484; *Letters from Russian Prisoners*, p. 252; *Goneniia na anarkhizm v Sovetskoi Rossii*, pp. 57-58; Maksimov, *Za chto i kak bol'sheviki izgnali anarkhistov*, pp. 10-20.

anarchist poet, Lev Chernyi, and Fanya Baron. Chernyi had been active in the Moscow Black Guard and was a member of the Underground Anarchists, the group responsible for the Leontiev Street bombing of the Moscow Communist headquarters in 1919, but he personally had played no part in the incident. Fanya Baron's record as an "ideological" anarchist was untainted by terrorism of any sort.[100] Emma Goldman was so outraged by the executions that she considered making a scene in the manner of the English suffragettes, by chaining herself to a bench in the hall where the Third Comintern Congress was meeting and shouting her protests to the delegates, but she was dissuaded by her Russian friends.[101]

Amid the outcry at home and abroad, Lenin deemed it prudent to relent. That same month, he released those of the better-known anarchist prisoners who had no record of violent opposition to the Soviet government, on condition that they leave the country at once. Maksimov, Volin, Mrachnyi, Iarchuk, and a few others departed for Berlin in January 1922.[102] Meanwhile, Emma Goldman, Alexander Berkman, and Sanya Schapiro, profoundly disheartened by the turn the revolution had taken, had made up their minds to emigrate also. "Grey are the passing days," Berkman recorded in his diary. "One by one the embers of hope have died out. Terror and despotism have crushed the life born in October. The slogans of the Revolution are forsworn, its ideals stifled in the blood of the people. The breath of yesterday is dooming millions to death; the shadow of today hangs like a black pall over the country. Dictatorship is trampling the masses under foot. The Revolution is dead; its spirit cries in the wilderness. . . . I have decided to leave Russia."[103]

[100] A. Gorelik, "Za chto i kak ubili L'va Chernogo," *Probuzhdenie*, No. 23-27, June-October 1932, p. 27; Voline, *La Révolution inconnue*, pp. 289-290; Berkman, *The Bolshevik Myth*, p. 318n; Goldman, *Living My Life*, II, 919; *Anarkhicheskii Vestnik*, No. 1, July 1923, p. 62.

[101] Serge, *Mémoires d'un révolutionnaire*, pp. 168-169.

[102] Maksimov, *Za chto i kak bol'sheviki izgnali anarkhistov*, pp. 20-32; Gorelik, *Anarkhisty v rossiiskoi revoliutsii*, p. 51.

[103] Berkman, *The Bolshevik Myth*, p. 319.

EPILOGUE

Where are those who will come to serve the
masses—not to utilize them for their
own ambitions?

PETER KROPOTKIN

In the wake of the Kronstadt revolt, the Bolsheviks instituted the New Economic Policy, which ended the forced requisitioning of grain and relaxed government controls over agriculture, industry, and trade. Lenin's purpose was to avert further uprisings like Kronstadt by giving his torn and exhausted country a "breathing spell." No respite, however, was accorded the political opposition. Indeed, a campaign was launched to extinguish the smoldering remains of political disaffection. Those anarchist militants who had hitherto eluded the Cheka's net were tracked down and brought before Revolutionary Tribunals, which they faced with the same defiance exhibited by their forebears in Stolypin's courts after the 1905 rebellion. In December 1922, one defendant in Petrograd called his trial a mockery and refused to answer his inquisitors. The Bolsheviks, he declared, had turned their weapons against the bravest defenders of the Revolution because, like all tyrants, they dreaded criticism. "But we do not fear you or your hangmen," he cried. "Soviet 'justice' may kill us, but you will never kill our ideals. We shall die as anarchists and not as bandits."[1]

Anarchist prisoners in the jails of Moscow, Petrograd, and other cities were sent to concentration camps near Archangel in the frozen north or to "political isolators" scattered throughout the country. Reports reaching the West told of the severe conditions they were forced to endure: extreme cold, inadequate food, heavy labor, and the ravages of scurvy and consumption. Only the letters from their families and comrades kept alive a flicker of hope. "I sit and dream of liberty," wrote an inmate of the Iaroslavl "polit-isolator," his health broken by tuberculosis.[2] The ancient monasteries in the town of Suz-

[1] Speeches of the anarchist Machanovskii, Petrograd Revolutionary Tribunal, 13 and 21 December 1922, handwritten manuscript, Fleshin Archive.

[2] A. D. Fedorov to Mark Mrachnyi, 13 January 1926, Fleshin Archive.

dal and on the Solovetskii Islands in the White Sea were converted into prisons for hundreds of political offenders, who
staged demonstrations and hunger strikes to protest their confinement. A few desperate souls resorted to self-immolation,
following the example of the Old Believers who, 250 years
before, had made human torches of themselves while barri-
caded in the Solovetskii Monastery. During the mid-1920's,
the anarchists were removed from Solovetskii and dispersed
among the Cheka prisons in the Ural Mountains or banished
to penal colonies in Siberia.[3]

The anarchists who had been allowed to leave Russia lost
no time in organizing committees to aid their imprisoned comrades. Berkman, Goldman, Schapiro, Volin, Mrachnyi, Maksimov, Yelensky, and Senya and Mollie Fleshin applied their
energies to relief work. The files of their organizations—most
notably the Joint Committee for the Defense of Revolutionists Imprisoned in Russia (Berlin, 1923-1926), the Relief
Fund of the International Working Men's Association for
Anarchists and Anarcho-Syndicalists Imprisoned or Exiled in
Russia (Berlin and Paris, 1926-1932), and the Alexander
Berkman Aid Fund, active in Chicago to this day—bulge
with letters and dossiers of incarcerated anarchists, their
names followed by such grim annotations as "beaten in Butyrki," "repeated hunger strikes," "killed in prison," "shot by
Kiev Cheka," "beaten for resisting forced feeding," and "fate
unknown."[4] The émigrés spared no effort to maintain a
steady flow of relief parcels and messages of encouragement
to their confreres in Russia. Their success in alleviating the
hunger, boredom, and despair of the prisoners was quite remarkable, considering the restrictions on relief activities imposed by the Soviet government. Their letters and parcels,
in the words of the recipients, were "a godsend," "a breath
of fresh air in this stifling atmosphere."[5] However, the effort
and expense involved in organizing protest meetings, raising

[3] *Bulletin of the Joint Committee for the Defense of Revolutionists
Imprisoned in Russia*, January-February 1925; November-December
1925; *Delo Truda*, No. 22, March 1927, pp. 13-14; Maximoff, *The
Guillotine at Work*, pp. 225, 298; David Dallin and Boris Nicolaevsky,
Forced Labor in Soviet Russia (New Haven, 1947), p. 172.

[4] Fleshin and Berkman Archives.

[5] Fleshin Archive.

funds, issuing bulletins, writing letters, sending packages, and the like, did not fail to take their toll on the aging anarchists in the West, sapping them of their physical strength and keeping them in perpetual poverty. "Often I think that we revolutionists are like the capitalistic system," observed Emma Goldman, herself a tireless relief worker. "We drain men and women of the best that is in them and then stand quietly by to see them end their last days in destitution and loneliness."[6]

In the meantime, death was silencing the old guard of the movement. Vladimir Zabrezhnev, the former Kropotkinite who joined the Communist party after the October Revolution, died in Moscow in 1920, while serving as secretary of the government newspaper, *Izvestiia*.[7] A few months later, I. S. Bleikhman succumbed to a lung ailment which had been seriously aggravated during a term of forced labor in a Bolshevik prison.[8] Kropotkin's death in February 1921 was followed in December by the death of his estranged pupil, Gogeliia-Orgeiani, in his native Caucasus.[9] Varlaam Cherkezov, another Georgian and close associate of Kropotkin's during the early years of the movement, returned to his former sanctuary in London and died there in 1925, in his eightieth year.[10] In 1926, Waclaw Machajski succumbed to a heart attack in Moscow,[11] and Apollon Karelin died of a cerebral hemorrhage, having witnessed the destruction of his All-Russian Federation of Anarchists and the arrest and banishment of his most able disciples, Kharkhardin, Solonovich, and Khudolei.[12]

This dark chronicle of prison, banishment, and death was only occasionally brightened by better tidings. Olga Taratuta, beaten by her jailers in Butyrki, afflicted by scurvy in the Orel "polit-isolator," and finally sent into Siberian exile, was sud-

[6] Emma Goldman to Max Nettlau, 14 January 1933, Nettlau Archive.

[7] Knizhnik, *Krasnaia Letopis'*, 1922, No. 4, p. 35.

[8] Fleshin Archive; *Goneniia na anarkhizm v Sovetskoi Rossii*, p. 49. Bleikhman was not shot by the Communists, as Tsereteli asserts in his memoirs: *Vospominaniia*, I, 167.

[9] *P. A. Kropotkin i ego uchenie*, pp. 333-334.

[10] Nikolaevskii, *Katorga i Ssylka*, 1926, No. 4, pp. 230-231; M. Korn, "Pamiati V. N. Cherkezova," *Delo Truda*, 1925, No. 5, pp. 3-5; *Delo Truda-Probuzhdenie*, No. 48, March-June 1955, pp. 17-18.

[11] Baturin, *Pravda*, 2 March 1926, p. 2; Syrkin, *Makhaevshchina*, p. 6.

[12] Karelin, *Vol'naia zhizn'*, p. 13; *Probuzhdenie*, No. 1, April 1927, p. 48; *Bulletin of the Joint Committee*, January-February 1925; November-December 1925.

denly paroled and allowed to return to Kiev.[13] A number of former "Soviet anarchists"—Karelinites, Universalists, and Anarcho-Syndicalists—were released from prison and placed under police surveillance. In 1924, Abba Gordin, the Universalist leader, was permitted to emigrate to the United States. His brother, V. L. Gordin, though a convert to Bolshevism, was seized in 1925 and locked up in a psychiatric ward.[14] According to a reliable source, he fled to America and became, *mirabile dictu*, a Protestant missionary. (The Gordins were sons of a rabbi.)[15]

A modicum of peaceful anarchist activity was permitted to continue throughout the NEP period. The *Golos Truda* bookshops and publishing house remained open, and brought out several volumes of Bakunin's writings (a project begun in 1919), as well as a number of new works, including a valuable collection of anarchist reminiscences edited by Aleksei Borovoi.[16] At the same time, Borovoi and his colleagues on the Kropotkin Museum Committee, notably Atabekian and Lebedev, were allowed to pursue their work unmolested by the authorities. In 1927, these and other prominent anarchists (Rogdaev, Barmash, Askarov, and Lidiia Gogeliia among them), apparently with the blessings of the Moscow Soviet, issued a public protest against the execution of Sacco and Vanzetti, a *cause célèbre* of radicals and libertarians throughout the world.[17]

For the remnants of the movement living in foreign exile, small groups of aging and disheartened men and women scattered over Europe and America, there remained the bitterness of having seen the Russian Revolution turn into the very op-

[13] Fleshin Archive; *Delo Truda*, No. 33-34, February-March 1928, pp. 3-4. Taratuta's subsequent history is unknown; she probably died in Siberia during Stalin's purge of 1935-1938.

[14] Serge, *L'An I de la révolution russe*, p. 254; *Delo Truda*, No. 5, October 1925, p. 10.

[15] S. Simon, "Di shafn fun Aba Gordin," lecture to the 74th Anniversary Banquet of the *Freie Arbeiter Stimme*, New York City, 17 January 1965.

[16] M. A. Bakunin, *Izbrannye sochineniia* (5 vols., Petrograd and Moscow, 1919-1922); *Mikhailu Bakuninu, 1876-1926: ocherki istorii anarkhicheskogo dvizheniia v Rossii*, ed., A. A. Borovoi (Moscow, 1926).

[17] *Delo Truda*, No. 32, January 1928, pp. 7-8.

posite of all their hopes; at best, as a sympathetic student of anarchism recently observed, there could be the melancholy consolation that their forefather Bakunin, looking at Marxian socialism a half-century earlier, had prophesied it all.[18] "The long years of the 'building of socialism,'" declared the Federation of Russian Anarchist-Communist Groups of the United States and Canada, "justifies in full Bakunin's statement that 'socialism without liberty is slavery and bestiality.'"[19] In Berlin and Paris, in New York and Buenos Aires, the embittered survivors kept up their vitriolic attacks on the Bolshevik dictatorship. They branded Lenin "the Torquemada, Loyola, Machiavelli, and Robespierre of the Russian Revolution," and condemned his party as "new kings" who were trampling the banner of liberty underfoot.[20] They scorned the NEP as a cynical maneuver to restore the bourgeois system, a reactionary compromise with the capitalists, technical specialists, and rich peasants. The expatriates vowed never to abandon the struggle to throw off "the yoke of the statist Communist party . . . the yoke of the intelligentsia and bourgeoisie"; they would not rest until both "private and state capitalism" had been reduced to rubble and superseded by factory committees and free soviets, the organizations from below suppressed by the Bolsheviks after the October Revolution.[21] "Let us fight on," proclaimed Grigorii Maksimov, "and our slogan shall be 'The Revolution is dead! Long live the Revolution!'"[22]

Although the various anarchist factions in emigration criticized the Soviet regime in much the same terms and usually cooperated with one another in relief work, the old divisions persisted. On arriving in Berlin, the main center of the exiles during the early twenties, Arshinov and Volin of the *Nabat* Confederation founded a monthly journal called *Anark-*

[18] Woodcock, *Anarchism*, p. 418.

[19] *Our Position* (Chicago?, 1934?), p. 1. The quotation appears in Bakunin, *Oeuvres*, I, 59.

[20] Maximoff, *The Guillotine at Work*, p. 17; Volin, in *Anarkhicheskii Vestnik*, No. 3-4, September-October 1923, p. 3.

[21] *Osvobozhdenie Profsoiuzov* (Paris), No. 1, November 1928, pp. 1-2. Cf. *Manifest protesta anarkhistov-kommunistov protiv bol'shevistskogo pravitel'stva k proletariatu vsego mira* (New York, 1922).

[22] Maximoff, *The Guillotine at Work*, p. 23.

hicheskii Vestnik (The Anarchist Herald),[23] while the syndicalists, led by Maksimov, Iarchuk, and Schapiro, launched their own periodical, *Rabochii Put'* (The Workers' Way), on the presses of the German organ, *Der Syndikalist.* Yet both groups recognized that, unless they remedied the disorganization which had plagued them from the very start, the anarchists could scarcely hope to survive as a movement, much less solve the complex social problems of the twentieth century. More than a few grudgingly admitted the truth of Karl Radek's contention that the romanticism of the anarchists and their instinctive hostility towards organization prevented them from facing the realities of contemporary industrial society, with its expanding population and its intricate division of labor, and doomed them to failure and defeat.[24]

The Anarcho-Syndicalists were particularly sensitive to strictures of this kind, since they had always prided themselves on their modern outlook: unlike the quixotic Anarchist-Communists, they insisted, they did not pine for a bygone age of primitive agricultural communes, but looked forward to a decentralized industrial society incorporating the latest advances in science and technology. Ruefully acknowledging that their movement in Russia had failed for want of an effective organization,[25] the syndicalist exiles resolved to join forces with their colleagues of other nations and provide the working class with an alternative to the politically-oriented labor internationals in Moscow and Amsterdam. In December 1922-January 1923, Anarcho-Syndicalists from a dozen countries (including the Russian expatriates) met in Berlin and founded a new workers' international which they christened the International Working Men's Association, claiming it to be the true successor to its namesake of 1864-1876.

The founding congress of the "Anarcho-Syndicalist" International, as the IWMA was commonly known, focused its attention on the meaning of the Bolshevik Revolution for the

[23] Anatolii Gorelik parted company with the other *Nabat* leaders and emigrated to Buenos Aires, where a new *Golos Truda* group had been formed in 1919. He died there in 1956. *Delo Truda-Probuzhdenie*, No. 54, May-October 1957, p. 35; No. 56, June 1958, pp. 23-25.

[24] K. Radek, *Anarkhisty v sovetskoi Rossii* (Petrograd, 1918), p. 2.

[25] *Rabochii Put'*, No. 1, March 1923, pp. 1, 8; No. 6, August 1923, pp. 1-2.

workingman. The delegates viewed it as an event of enormous significance, for it had brought into sharp relief the differences between state socialism, which leads inevitably to the subjugation of the working class, and revolutionary syndicalism, which preserves the liberty and self-reliance of the masses. Cherishing their libertarian heritage, the syndicalists pledged themselves to remain faithful to the slogan of the First International: "THE EMANCIPATION OF THE WORKING CLASS MUST BE THE THE TASK OF THE WORKERS THEMSELVES."[26] They called upon the workingmen of the world to wage a daily struggle to improve their situation within the existing capitalist framework, until the time was ripe to launch a "general insurrectional strike." This would be the signal for the social revolution that would sweep away the bourgeois order and usher in a free society, organized "from below upwards" and "unhampered by State, army, police, or exploiters and oppressors of any kind." The centralized state would be abolished in favor of a "free system of councils," linked together by a General Confederation of Labor. "The government of men," affirmed the platform of the Anarcho-Syndicalist International, echoing Saint-Simon and Engels, would be replaced by "the administration of things." For the state, whether constitutional democracy or proletarian dictatorship or any other form, would "always be the creator of new monopolies and new privileges: it could never be an instrument of liberation."[27]

Alexander Schapiro and Grigorii Maksimov played important roles in the formation of the Berlin International, but its guiding spirit and its leader for many years was Rudolf Rocker, former head of the London Anarchist Federation. In 1932, threatened by the rising influence of the Nazi party, the International moved to Amsterdam, and four years later it was shifted again to Madrid, so as to be at the scene of the Spanish Civil War, in which the syndicalist confederation (CNT) had assumed a major role. Franco's victory compelled the syndicalists to move their headquarters to Stockholm in 1939. There the IWMA was kept alive by the syndicalist Sverige Arbetares Central, until its final move to Toulouse after World

[26] *The International Working Men's Association, I.W.M.A.: Its Policy, Its Aims, Its Principles* (n.p., 1933), p. 8. This pamphlet was written by Alexander Schapiro.
[27] *Ibid.,* pp. 7-9.

War II, where it still survives, more than 40 years after its creation.

Within the Anarchist-Communist wing of the movement, the loudest advocate of organizational reform was Petr Arshinov. On reaching Berlin in 1922, he founded the Group of Russian Anarchist-Communists Abroad, which moved to Paris three years later and began to publish its own journal, *Delo Truda* (Labor's Cause). Arshinov attributed the downfall of the Russian anarchists to their perpetual state of disarray. The only hope for a revival of the movement, according to the "Organizational Platform" issued by his *Delo Truda* group in 1926, lay in the formation of a General Union of Anarchists with a central executive committee to coordinate policy and action.[28] The strongest support for this plan came from Arshinov's old jailmate and pupil, Nestor Makhno, also living in Paris, a fretful and dejected consumptive, for whom alcohol was the only escape from the alien world into which he had been flung. "Nestor is a sick man," wrote Alexander Berkman in 1926, "yet must work in a factory very hard and at a dog's wages, can't even live on them with his wife and baby, though his wife also works. And similarly the others. It is hell."[29]

Makhno, as it turned out, was the only prominent anarchist willing to subscribe to the Organizational Platform. Volin broke with Arshinov over it and, together with Senya Fleshin and several other dissenters, published a scathing reply the following year. Arshinov and his supporters, they argued, grossly exaggerated the organizational defects of the movement. Their call for a central committee not only clashed with the basic anarchist principle of local initiative, but was a clear reflection of their leader's "party spirit." (Arshinov's opponents rarely failed to point out that he had been a Bolshevik before joining the anarchists in 1906.) What the *Delo Truda* group sought to create, in short, was an anarchist *party* whose mission was to lead the masses rather than to assist them in preparing their

[28] *Organizatsionnaia platforma vseobshchego soiuza anarkhistov (proekt)* (Paris, 1926).

[29] Alexander Berkman to Ben Capes, 22 February 1926, Berkman Archive.

own revolution.[30] "Alas," wrote Mollie Fleshin, "the entire spirit of the 'platform' is penetrated with the idea that the masses MUST BE POLITICALLY LED during the revolution. There is where the evil starts, all the rest . . . is mainly based on this idea. It stands for an Anarchist Communist Workers' Party, for an army . . . for a system of defense of the revolution which will inevitably lead to the creation of a spying system, investigators, prisons and judges, consequently, a TCHEKA."[31]

Arshinov responded to these attacks by reproaching "Volin and Co." for embroiling the anarchists in yet another sterile controversy. He insisted that nothing in his proposals even remotely conflicted with the ideals of anarchism, so long as compulsion was conscientiously avoided and a decentralized organizational structure preserved.[32] Makhno, rushing to his companion's defense, suggested that Volin, who had fallen into the hands of the Reds in 1919 while serving in the Insurgent Army of the Ukraine, had not been captured, as was generally thought, but had defected to the Communists.[33] Makhno's allegation, in turn, drew the fire of Alexander Berkman, Emma Goldman, and Errico Malatesta, who now joined in the criticism of the Organizational Platform.[34] In a letter to the anarchist archivist and historian, Max Nettlau, Berkman lashed out at Makhno as the possessor of "a militarist temperament," and entirely in Arshinov's power. As for Arshinov himself, "his whole psychology is Bolshevik," wrote Berkman, "he is a most arbitrary and tyrannical, domineering nature. This throws some light on the program also." "The trouble with most of our people," Berkman lamented, "is that they

---

[30] *Otvet neskol'ko russkikh anarkhistov na organizatsionnuiu platformu* (Paris, 1927). A critic in the United States charged Arshinov with employing "Jesuit methods" in order to fulfill his self-appointed role of "savior" of the Russian anarchist movement. M. I. Suk, "Kritika 'Organizatsionnoi Platformy,' " *Probuzhdenie*, No. 8, June 1929, pp. 57-61.

[31] Mollie Fleshin to Comrade Ginev, 30 November 1927, Fleshin Archive.

[32] P. Arshinov, *Novoe v anarkhizme (K chemu prizyvaet organizatsionnaia platforma)* (Paris, 1929), p. 23.

[33] N. Makhno, *Makhnovshchina i ee vcherashnie soiuzniki-bol'sheviki (Otvet na knigu M. Kubanina "Makhnovshchina")* (Paris, 1928), pp. 41-43.

[34] For Malatesta's reaction, see *Probuzhdenie*, No. 11, March 1930, pp. 11-14.

will not see that Bolshevik *methods* cannot lead to liberty, that methods and issues are in essence and effects identical."[35] In 1930, Arshinov's opponents, who had labeled his platform an "Anarcho-Bolshevik deviation" and had repeatedly accused him of propagating "party anarchism," felt themselves vindicated when Arshinov defected to the Soviet Union and rejoined the party which he had quit for anarchism a quarter-century before. Shortly thereafter, his journal, *Delo Truda*, was transferred to the United States and Grigorii Maksimov became its new editor.[36]

Thus once again the anarchists demonstrated their congenital inability to subordinate personal differences to the good of the movement. Even inside Russia, where only a handful of anarchists remained at liberty, bitter factional disputes arose among the members of the Kropotkin Museum Committee. "There is again a skirmish between two groups of our Comrades," wrote Kropotkin's widow to Max Nettlau in 1928. "Both strive to be master in . . . the Museum, while none of them have taken part in the building of that institution. I hope that none of them will be masters while I am alive, and something will have to be done to secure the safety of the Museum when I am no more there."[37] There seemed to be no end to the squabbling. Berkman expressed his dismay in a letter to Senya and Mollie Fleshin: "I consider it terrible that our movement, everywhere, is degenerating into a swamp of petty personal quarrels, accusations, and recriminations. There is too much of this rotten thing going on, particularly in the last couple of years." Emma Goldman added a postscript: "Dear children. I agree entirely with Sasha. I am sick at heart over the poison of insinuations, charges, accusations in our ranks.

[35] Alexander Berkman to Max Nettlau, 28 June 1927, Berkman Archive. Alexander Schapiro's position in the controversy is of considerable interest. "I oppose Archinoff *much more than you do*," he wrote Emma Goldman on 24 April 1928. "Yet, I consider that he is thoughtful, that he is stubborn, that he sticks to his guns, and that HE KNOWS WHAT HE WANTS: these are qualities flagrantly lacking among many of our friends to whom our personal sympathies instinctively go." Goldman Archive.

[36] *Delo Truda-Probuzhdenie*, No. 16, January 1946, p. 18.

[37] Sophie Kropotkin to Max Nettlau, 4 December 1928, Nettlau Archive.

If that will not stop there is no hope for a revival of our movement."[38]

At the end of the twenties, Stalin inaugurated a new era of totalitarian rule in Russia. What little activity had been permitted the anarchists during the NEP came to an abrupt and violent end. In 1929, the *Golos Truda* bookshops in Leningrad and Moscow were closed permanently as a fresh round of arrests and persecutions began. Anarchists who had already served out long terms at hard labor were once more banished to Siberia or to other remote and forbidding locations. Within a very few years, Atabekian, Askarov, Barmash, Borovoi, and many of their comrades had perished in prison or exile.[39] According to Victor Serge, a certain Fishelev—very likely Maksim Raevskii, the well-known syndicalist and former editor of *Burevestnik* and *Golos Truda*—was arrested for publishing the platform of the Trotskyite opposition.[40] However, Raevskii apparently was released, for he is reported to have died in Moscow of heart failure in 1931, while sitting at his writing table.[41] Nikolai Rogdaev, Raevskii's old companion and co-editor of *Burevestnik*, died in Tashkent the following year; exiled there after completing a long sentence in the Suzdal "polit-isolator," he collapsed from a cerebral hemorrhage "in a street named, by a mocking coincidence, Sacco-Vanzetti."[42]

The "Soviet anarchists" who remained at their government posts during the NEP grew increasingly disillusioned with the policies of the new regime. Daniil Novomirskii, a Communist since 1919, came to view the NEP as an unforgivable

[38] Alexander Berkman to Senya and Mollie Fleshin, 28 September 1928, Fleshin Archive.
[39] *Bulletin of the Relief Fund of the International Working Men's Association for Anarchists and Anarcho-Syndicalists Imprisoned or Exiled in Russia*, November-December 1929; *Delo Truda*, No. 50-51, July-August 1929, pp. 1-3; No. 52-53, September-October 1929, pp. 1-2; *Probuzhdenie*, No. 43-44, February-March 1934, pp. 44-45; *Goneniia na anarkhizm v Sovetskoi Rossii*, pp. 35-36; Maximoff, *The Guillotine at Work*, p. 339; Serge, *Russia Twenty Years After*, p. 86; Aleksei Borovoi to Senya Fleshin, 14 October 1931, Fleshin Archive.
[40] Serge, *Mémoires d'un révolutionnaire*, p. 243.
[41] *Delo Truda*, No. 66, May-December 1931, pp. 22-23.
[42] *Man: A Journal of the Anarchist Ideal and Movement* (San Francisco), II, No. 6-7, June-July 1934, p. 121; *Delo Truda*, No. 74, December 1932-February 1933, p. 2.

retreat from the goals of the revolution. He turned in his party card and sought escape in the world of scholarship, becoming a contributor to the *Large Soviet Encyclopedia*.[43] German Sandomirskii, though he remained in the foreign ministry during the first years of the NEP, also turned to scholarly pursuits, editing a collection of documents on the Geneva Conference of 1922 and writing a lengthy study of Italian fascism.[44] Afterwards, he devoted more and more of his time to the Kropotkin Museum. Though passed over by the GPU in 1929, these former anarchists were marked men. In 1936, Novomirskii and his wife were swept up in the great purge and vanished into the dark world of Siberian concentration camps. Sandomirskii and Bill Shatov, notwithstanding their loyal service to the government, were also exiled to Siberia, where they are believed to have been shot.[45]

The syndicalist leader, Efim Iarchuk, who had left Russia in 1922, experienced a change of heart and appealed for permission to return. With Bukharin's help he was readmitted in 1925 and joined the Communist party.[46] Iarchuk and Petr Arshinov, who took the same path five years later, both disappeared in the purge. Aron Baron, after 18 years in prison and exile, was unexpectedly set free in 1938, but after settling in Kharkov was seized by the police and never heard from again.[47] Finally, Iuda Roshchin, profoundly disturbed by Stalin's rise to power, is thought to have escaped the latter's wrath by dying a natural death just before the purge began.[48] The endless chain of arrests and deportations deprived the Kropotkin Museum of the remaining few who had dedicated

[43] Serge, *Russia Twenty Years After*, p. 88; *Mémoires d'un révolutionnaire*, p. 171.

[44] G. B. Sandomirskii, ed., *Materialy genuezskoi konferentsii* (Moscow, 1922); *Fashizm* (2 vols., Moscow, 1923).

[45] *Probuzhdenie*, No. 56-57, March-April 1935, p. 48; No. 70-71, May-June 1936, p. 48; Serge, *Russia Twenty Years After*, pp. 87-88; Maximoff, *The Guillotine at Work*, pp. 351n., 619.

[46] *Delo Truda*, No. 7-8, December 1925-January 1926, pp. 15-16; *Goneniia na anarkhizm v Sovetskoi Rossii*, pp. 62-63; Maximoff, *The Guillotine at Work*, pp. 348, 409.

[47] Fanya Avrutskaia to Mark Mrachnyi, 7 December 1926, Fleshin Archive; Maximoff, *The Guillotine at Work*, p. 8.

[48] Nomad, *Dreamers, Dynamiters, and Demagogues*, p. 35; Serge, *Mémoires d'un révolutionnaire*, p. 210.

themselves to its upkeep. Soon after the death of Kropotkin's widow in 1938, the Museum was closed.[49]

In the meantime, the movement in emigration was also dying out. Anarchist weeklies became monthlies, and monthlies became quarterlies, their pages often filled up with articles written many decades earlier by Bakunin, Kropotkin, and Malatesta. The aging anarchists continued to celebrate Bakunin's birthday and the Paris Commune of 1871. They mourned the Chicago martyrs, the anniversary of Kropotkin's death, and the execution of Sacco and Vanzetti. They denounced Stalin and his bloody deeds. They excoriated Hitler and the fascists, but considered a popular front with the communists and socialists "absolutely impossible."[50] For a brief time, they could exult in the dramatic role of the anarchists in the Spanish Civil War and hope that their cause had gained a new lease on life.[51] But the defeat of the left in Spain sounded the knell of the movement. Afterwards, there was little left but despair.

One by one, the survivors saw their old friends into the grave. Maria Goldsmit-Korn, who had remained in Paris when her comrades returned to Russia in 1917, took poison 15 years later in a state of depression brought on by her mother's death.[52] "The old guard is passing away," Alexander Berkman wrote despondently in 1935, "and there are almost none of the younger generation to take its place, or at least to do the work that must be done if the world is ever to see a better day."[53] The following year Berkman shot himself to death in

[49] Serge, *Mémoires d'un révolutionnaire*, p. 298; Woodcock and Avakumovic, *The Anarchist Prince*, p. 437; *Delo Truda-Probuzhdenie*, No. 26, September 1948, p. 5. Nikolai Lebedev, secretary of the Museum for several years, had died in August 1934. *Probuzhdenie*, No. 56-57, March-April 1935, p. 48.

[50] *Our Position*, p. 4.

[51] *Na pomoshch' ispanskim bortsam* (New York, 193?); "Ispanskaia grazhdanskaia voina," *Probuzhdenie*, No. 74-75, September-October 1936, pp. 1-2.

[52] *Delo Truda*, No. 74, December 1932-February 1933, pp. 1-2; *Freedom* (New York), 18 March 1933, p. 2; Alexander Berkman to Mollie Fleshin, 13 February 1933, Berkman Archive.

[53] Alexander Berkman to Pierre Ramus (Rudolf Grossmann), 21 August 1935, Berkman Archive.

Nice.[54] Four years later, Emma Goldman collapsed and died in Toronto, while on a lecture tour. Her body was removed to Chicago and buried in the Waldheim Cemetery, near the graves of the Haymarket Square martyrs.[55]

Volin, Schapiro, and Maksimov lived on through the war, aggrieved by the deaths of their comrades in Russia and in the West. In September 1945, Volin died of tuberculosis in Paris. His body was cremated and his ashes interred in the Père-Lachaise Cemetery, not far from the grave of Nestor Makhno, who had succumbed to the same disease a decade earlier.[56] Sanya Schapiro, after editing the Parisian anarchist journal, *La Voix du Peuple*, for a number of years, emigrated to New York, where he died of heart failure in 1946.[57] "The best brains of the movement are passing out one after another," wrote Mollie Fleshin after Schapiro's death, "and though I am far from being a pessimist, yet I have a feeling as if the movement itself is passing out. . . ."[58]

Grigorii Maksimov had left Berlin for Paris in 1924, and then came to the United States the next year. He settled in Chicago, where he worked as a paperhanger by day and spent his evenings editing *Golos Truzhenika* (The Laborer's Voice), a Russian-language periodical of the IWW which appeared until 1927. When Petr Arshinov defected to the Soviet Union, Maksimov assumed the editorship of *Delo Truda*, whose headquarters were thereupon shifted from Paris to Chicago. Under his supervision, *Delo Truda* quickly became the most important journal of the Russian émigrés, pro-syndicalist in its

[54] *Probuzhdenie*, No. 72-73, July-August 1936, p. 1; *Man*, IV, No. 7, July 1936, p. 1; *Fraye Arbeter Shtime*, 3 July 1936, p. 1. For a different version of Berkman's death, see Nomad, *Dreamers, Dynamiters, and Demagogues*, pp. 207-208.

[55] Richard Drinnon, *Rebel in Paradise: A Biography of Emma Goldman* (Chicago, 1961), pp. 300, 313.

[56] Rocker, introduction to Voline, *Nineteen-Seventeen*; Voline, *The Revolution Betrayed*, p. 216; M. S. (Mollie Steimer Fleshin), in *Freedom* (London), 17 November 1945, p. 2; *Fraye Arbeter Shtime*, 7 December 1945, p. 6.

[57] Rudolf Rocker to Senya and Mollie Fleshin, 12 February 1947, Rocker Archive; Carbo, *L'Adunata dei Refrattari*, 22 March 1947, pp. 3-4. In New York, Schapiro edited a monthly journal called *New Trends*, which ceased to appear a few months before his death.

[58] Mollie Fleshin to Rudolf and Milly Rocker, 16 March 1947, Fleshin Archive.

general outlook but open to contributions from anarchists of every hue, following a tradition set by the Paris *Burevestnik* and New York *Golos Truda* between the Revolutions of 1905 and 1917.

Maksimov made a new attempt to reconcile the differences between the Anarchist-Communists and Anarcho-Syndicalists, possibly aware that their angry disputes stemmed less from conflicting doctrines than from differences of temperament and personality. His own "social credo," which he published in 1933,[59] was an amalgam of the two traditions, closely resembling the pro-syndicalist variety of Anarchist-Communism advocated by Kropotkin and his school. In Maksimov's vision of the good society, agricultural cooperatives were to serve as transitional forms during the gradual evolution towards communism (Maksimov scorned the brutal methods used in Stalin's drive to collectivize Soviet farming), while industrial management would be turned over to workers' committees and federations of labor. Eventually, every workman would enjoy a four- or five-hour working day and a four-day week. The distribution of food and manufactured goods was to be handled by house and consumer committees. Courts of law would be supplanted by voluntary arbitration boards; prisons would be abolished and their functions absorbed by the schools, hospitals, and institutions of public welfare; and professional armies were to be disbanded and the mission of defense assigned to a people's militia.[60] In Maksimov's view, the Anarcho-Syndicalist International provided an admirable organizational instrument to achieve all this, for the IWMA, in contrast to the Comintern, truly adhered to the slogan of the First International that "the liberation of the working class is the task of the workers themselves."[61] The centralization of authority, he wrote, must lead inexorably—as it had in Soviet Russia—to the "bureaucratization of the entire industrial apparatus, to the emergence of an official class, to the removal of the producers from the administration of the social economy,

[59] G. P. Maksimov, *Moe sotsial'noe kredo* (Chicago, 1933).
[60] Maximov, *Constructive Anarchism*, pp. 28ff., 145.
[61] Maksimov, *Moe sotsial'noe kredo*, p. 13.

to the strangling of independent activity on the part of the workers, and to economic crisis."[62]

Maksimov stayed on as editor when *Delo Truda* merged with the Detroit anarchist publication, *Probuzhdenie*, in 1940. Though extremely busy with editorial chores, he found time to publish a strong indictment of the terror in Russia entitled *The Guillotine at Work*, and labored over a collection of Bakunin's writings, until his heart gave out in 1950.[63] His edition of Bakunin appeared three years later.[64]

Of the major figures in the Russian anarchist movement, now only Abba Gordin was left. Having emigrated to the United States in 1924, he continued to produce a seemingly endless stream of books, essays, and poems, in several languages. He became a co-editor of the *Freie Arbeiter Stimme,* a Yiddish anarchist journal in New York, and published his own periodical, *The Clarion*, devoted to wordy attacks on the evils of contemporary society. By the early thirties, Gordin had come to regard nationalism rather than class conflict as the driving force of modern history. The class, he wrote, is "a flimsy, artificial super-structure erected upon a shaky, shifting foundation of occupation," while the roots of the nation are deeply "grounded in biology, racial elements being involved, and psychology, in its concrete form of a national tongue."[65] Turning back to his own national heritage, Gordin founded the Jewish Ethical Society, which attracted a small but loyal following.[66]

In 1940, Gordin published a long-winded but interesting critique of Marxism, which he had been evolving for more than two decades. Marxist doctrine, he wrote, harking back to his Pan-Anarchist Manifesto of 1918, was "a hybrid born of quasi-religion and pseudo-science." The laws for which Marx claimed scientific validity were nothing but a shameless

[62] Maximov, *Constructive Anarchism*, p. 102.

[63] Woodcock, introduction to *Constructive Anarchism*; Rocker, *Delo Truda-Probuzhdenie*, No. 33, July-August 1950, pp. 1-6. Rocker himself died in New York in 1958.

[64] G. P. Maximoff, ed., *The Political Philosophy of Bakunin: Scientific Anarchism* (Glencoe, Ill., 1953).

[65] A. Gordin, "Instead of a Program," *The Clarion*, I, No. 2, 1932, p. 2.

[66] S. Simon, "Aba Gordin—der mentsh un denker," *Fraye Arbeter Shtime*, 1 October 1964, pp. 3, 6.

"violation of history"; moreover, Marx's narrow-minded doctrine of class struggle between workers and owners ignored the cleavage that also existed between workers and managers. Echoing Machajski, Gordin declared that Marxian socialism was not the ideology of manual workers but of "a privileged class of politico-economic organisateurs."[67] In a passage strongly reminiscent of Bakunin's *Statehood and Anarchy*, Gordin described the consequences of what he regarded as the managerial revolution of the Bolsheviks: "Pretty soon . . . and the iron-clad dams will be installed! Before long, and the sites upon which the torn down edifices stood, will be graced, after the wreck and debris have been cleared away, with palatial palaces and sumptuous temples. The king is dead—long live the king! The old laws have been outlawed, former authorities banished in order to make elbowroom for the newcomers. . . ."[68] During the late 1950's, the old anarchist, drawn by the magnet of Hebrew culture, emigrated to Israel, where he died in 1964.[69]

The Russian anarchists, despite their tangled history of personal quarrels and factional strife, shared a common determination to bring about a stateless society in which no man would be master over his brother. For more than two decades, during a tumultuous period spanning two great revolutions, the anarchists consistently denounced the state (autocracy and "proletarian dictatorship" alike) and property (both private and public) as the twin sources of oppression and suffering in Russia. Inspired by Bakunin and Kropotkin, they protested against the growing political and economic centralization of Russian society, with its de-humanizing tendencies and its progressive encroachments on individual liberty. They would brook no compromise with centralized power. In their eyes, it was futile to seek partial improvements from the holders of authority; the most they could expect would be occasional crumbs from "the statist table," whether tsarist or communist. Piecemeal reform, moreover, was incapable of eliminating the basic evils

[67] Abba Gordin, *Communism Unmasked* (New York, 1940), pp. 45-68, 158.
[68] *Ibid.*, p. 121.
[69] Simon, *Fraye Arbeter Shtime*, 1 October 1964, p. 6.

of government and capitalism—state capitalism as well as private. For the anarchists, the only hope of rescuing the mass of disinherited working people from everlasting bondage lay in demolishing the state and the capitalist system. Theirs was an apocalyptical vision of violent change, a vision of wholesale destruction and resurrection. From the rubble of the old order would emerge a Golden Age, without government, without property, without hunger or want, a shining era of freedom in which men would direct their own affairs without interference from any authority.

For many anarchists, the Golden Age meant a return to an earlier simplicity that had existed before the centralized state and large-scale manufacture began to transform human beings into faceless automatons. They yearned to recapture the direct human relationships of the agricultural commune and handicrafts cooperative, the *obshchina* and *artel'*, and thereby restore the primitive bliss of medieval Russia, when, supposedly, there was "neither Tsar nor state" but only "land and liberty."[70] The society of the future, then, was to be patterned after the society of the past: a federation of small communities, free from authority and compulsion, whose members were joined by the ties of cooperative effort and mutual aid. In such a society, the toiler in the field and factory would regain the dignity of being his own master, and no longer be treated as chattel or as a marketable commodity.

But how was it possible to recapture the freedom and simplicity of pre-industrial Russia in an age of expanding mass production? How could the personal values of the small communal society be preserved in an impersonal world of large factories and rapidly growing cities? A small number of anarchists tried to resolve the dilemma by exhorting the workers to destroy their machines and factories, in the manner of the Luddites, and revive the moribund world of handicrafts production. The great majority, however, welcomed scientific and technological progress with open arms, inheriting from Peter Kropotkin, and from William Godwin before him, the belief that machinery would relieve men of drudgery and fatigue, allow time for leisure and cultural pursuits, and remove for-

[70] *Vol'naia Volia*, 1903, No. 1.

ever the stigma traditionally attached to manual labor. To spurn mechanized industry simply because it had been born of the capitalist system, wrote a Petrograd Anarcho-Syndicalist in 1917, would be the greatest folly; in the world of the future, millions of people would live happily in large cities and work in modern factories made of steel and concrete, while parks would satisfy man's need to be close to nature.[71] The old culture of Europe was dying, declared the Gordin brothers in 1918, and "only Anarchy and Technics shall rule the earth."[72]

In this new industrial milieu, the values of the small society would be retained by means of the factory committee. The pro-syndicalists saw the factory committee as an urban counterpart of the *obshchina* and *artel'*, as the present-day expression of man's natural propensity toward mutual aid. "In the factory committees," declared a female textile worker at a labor conference in 1918, "one can perceive, though not fully developed, the embryo of socialist communes."[73] In a similar vein, Emma Goldman once observed that the autonomous workers' council "is the old Russian *mir* in an advanced and more revolutionary form. It is so deeply rooted in the people that it sprang naturally from the Russian soil as flowers do in the fields."[74] By creating a federation of urban factory committees and rural communes, the anarchists hoped to attain the best of two worlds, the simple world of the past and the mechanized world of the future. They sought to incorporate the latest technical advances into a decentralized social system free from the coercive features of capitalism, a system in which the working class would no longer be reduced to an obedient army of puppets manipulated from above. To achieve industrialism while preserving the self-determination of the individual, the anarchists believed, would be to combine the worthiest elements of the socialist and liberal traditions. For socialism without liberty, as Proudhon and Bakunin had taught, is the worst form of slavery.

The anarchists discarded the conventions of bourgeois civi-

[71] *Golos Truda*, No. 6, 15 September 1917, pp. 3-4.

[72] *Burevestnik*, 10 April 1918, pp. 1-3.

[73] *Protokoly 1-go Vserossiiskogo s"ezda professional'nykh soiuzov tekstil'shchikov i fabrichnykh komitetov*, p. 44.

[74] Emma Goldman to Max Nettlau, 12 December 1922, Nettlau Archive.

lization in the hope of achieving a complete transvaluation of values, a radical transformation of human nature and of the relationship between the individual and society. Yet, if they repudiated the social dogmas of their time as artificial, abstract, and far removed from real life, their own approach to building the good society could hardly be called pragmatic or empirical. Visionary utopians, the anarchists paid scant attention to the practical needs of a rapidly changing world; they generally avoided careful analysis of social and economic conditions, nor were they able or even willing to come to terms with the inescapable realities of political power. For the religious and metaphysical gospels of the past, they substituted a vague messianism which satisfied their own chiliastic expectations; in place of complex ideologies, they offered simple action-slogans, catchwords of revolutionary violence, poetic images of the coming Golden Age. By and large, they seemed content to rely on "the revolutionary instincts of the masses" to sweep away the old order and "the creative spirit of the masses" to build the new society upon its ashes. "Through a Social Revolution to the Anarchist Future!" proclaimed a group of exiles in South America; the practical details of agriculture and industry "will be worked out afterwards" by the revolutionary masses.[75] Such an attitude, though it sprang from a healthy skepticism towards the ideological "blueprints" and "scientific laws" of their Marxist adversaries, could be of little help in setting a course of action designed to revolutionize the world.

Russian anarchism never became a creed of the mass of peasants and industrial workers. Though it drew some support from the working class, anarchism was destined to remain, for the most part, a dream of small groups of individuals who had alienated themselves from the mainstream of contemporary society: conscience-stricken noblemen like Bakunin, Kropotkin, Cherkezov, and Bidbei; apostate seminarians like Kolosov of the *Beznachalie* group or the Anarcho-Syndicalist leader, Maksimov; members of ethnic minorities like Gogeliia-Orgeiani, Grossman-Roshchin, and the Gordin brothers; peasant guerrillas like Nestor Makhno and his followers; and

---

[75] *"Deklaratsiia" gruppy russkikh anarkhistov sodeistviia "Delu Truda": prakticheskie zadachi anarkhizma v sovremennuiu epokhu* (Buenos Aires, 1930), p. 13.

déclassé intellectuals like Volin and Lev Chernyi. The success of the Bolshevik Revolution deprived the anarchists of much of their support, both within the rank and file of the labor movement and among the intellectuals, many of whom accepted the jobs held out to them by the new regime and thus became "Soviet anarchists." The majority, however, remained true to their faith. They continued to shower abuse upon the premises and consequences of "scientific" socialism. Again and again, they warned that political power is evil, that it corrupts all who wield it, that government of any kind stifles the revolutionary spirit of the people and robs them of their freedom.

These anarchists were fated to be rejected, reviled, and, finally, stamped out or driven into exile. Those who survived, though they suffered periods of disillusionment and despair, retained their idealism to the end. If they were failures by material standards, within their small circles they found personal warmth, camaraderie, and high-minded devotion to a common cause; moreover, by liberating themselves from the conventions of a world they detested, perhaps they even attained as individuals some measure of the "higher order" they so desperately craved for all mankind. At the same time, they clung tenaciously to the hope that ultimately their ideals would triumph for humanity as a whole. "All Russia is dark in the long arctic night," wrote Grigorii Maksimov in 1940. "But the morning is inevitable. And Russia's dawn will be a dawn of the toiling people of the whole world. We joyously greet its approach."[76]

---

[76] Maximoff, *The Guillotine at Work*, p. 337.

CHRONOLOGY OF
PRINCIPAL EVENTS*

1876	1 July	Death of Bakunin
1892		Anarchist Library founded in Geneva
1903		Kropotkinites establish *Khleb i Volia* in Geneva; *Chernoe Znamia* groups appear inside Russia
1905	9 January	"Bloody Sunday" Spread of anarchist movement in Russia
	April-July	Bidbei publishes *Listok gruppy Beznachalie* in Paris
	October	General strike in Russian cities
	13 October	Formation of Petersburg Soviet
	17 October	October Manifesto
	November-December	Anarchists bomb Hotel Bristol in Warsaw and Café Libman in Odessa
	6-17 December	Moscow uprising
1906	January	*Chernoe Znamia* Conference in Kishinev
	July	*Burevestnik* founded in Paris
	September	Novomirskii forms South Russian Group of Anarcho-Syndicalists Stolypin's "pacification": arrests and trials of anarchists
1907	27 April	Conference of Urals Groups of Anarchist-Communists
	August	International Congress of Anarchists in Amsterdam Anarchist Red Cross established in Western Europe and the United States
1911		*Golos Truda* founded in New York First signs of anarchist revival in Russia

* Dates, as in the text, are given in the old style.

1914	1 August	World War I begins
		Debates between "defensist" and antimilitarist anarchists
1917	February	February Revolution
	2 March	Abdication of Tsar; formation of Provisional Government
	March	Amnesty of political prisoners
	March	Formation of Petrograd and Moscow Federations of Anarchist-Communist Groups
	30 May-3 June	First Conference of Petrograd Factory Committees
	June	Kropotkin returns to Russia
	June	Durnovo *dacha* imbroglio
	18 June	"June Demonstrations"
	3-5 July	"July Days"
	18-22 July	Conference of Anarchists in Kharkov
	August	*Golos Truda* reestablished in Petrograd
	24-28 August	Kornilov affair
	October	Formation of Military-Revolutionary Committee: four anarchist members
	17-22 October	All-Russian Conference of Factory Committees
	25 October	October Revolution
	14 November	Decree on workers' control
	25 December	First Conference of Anarchists of Donets Basin
1918	6 January	Dispersal of Constituent Assembly
	7-14 January	First All-Russian Congress of Trade Unions
	14 February	Second Conference of Anarchists of Donets Basin
	3 March	Treaty of Brest-Litovsk
	12 March	Government moves from Petrograd to Moscow
	11-12 April	Cheka raids on Moscow anarchists

	spring	Karelin founds All-Russian Federation of Anarchists
	6-11 August	Northern Regional Congress of Anarchists
	25 August–1 September	First All-Russian Conference of Anarcho-Syndicalists
	12-16 November	First Conference of *Nabat* Confederation
	25 November–1 December	Second All-Russian Conference of Anarcho-Syndicalists
	25 December	All-Russian Congress of Anarchist-Communists
1919	23 January	First Regional Congress of Peasants, Workers, and Insurgents (*Makhnovtsy*)
	12 February	Second Regional Congress of Peasants, Workers, and Insurgents
	2-7 April	First Congress of *Nabat* Confederation
	10 April	Third Regional Congress of Peasants, Workers, and Insurgents
	25 September	Underground Anarchists bomb Communist headquarters in Moscow
	26 September	Makhno routs Denikin's forces at Peregonovka
	20 October	Regional Congress of Peasants and Workers in Aleksandrovsk
1920	August	Gordin brothers found Anarcho-Universalists
	26 November	Communist raids on Makhno's headquarters at Guliai-Pole; arrest of *Nabat* Confederation
1921	8 February	Death of Kropotkin
	13 February	Kropotkin's funeral in Moscow
	1-17 March	Kronstadt uprising
		Suppression of anarchists in Russia
1922	January	Group of anarchist leaders deported from Russia

1922	25 December–	
	2 January 1923	International Working Men's Association (Anarcho-Syndicalist International) founded in Berlin
1926		Karelin dies in Moscow
1929		Arrest of surviving anarchists in Russia
1934		Makhno dies in Paris
1935-1938		Stalin's purge: Novomirskii, Sandomirskii, Shatov, and others perish
1939		Kropotkin Museum closed
1945		Volin dies in Paris
1946		Schapiro dies in New York
1950		Maksimov dies in Chicago
1964		Abba Gordin dies in Israel

ANNOTATED BIBLIOGRAPHY

ARCHIVES

Archive of Russian and East European History and Culture, Columbia University. Contains an outstanding collection of leaflets of the 1905 period. In addition, there are proclamations and manuscripts of the émigré groups in Paris, Geneva, and Zurich between 1905 and 1917, and a manuscript on the Durnovo *dacha* affair.

Bund Archives of the Jewish Labor Movement, New York City. Rich in Yiddish and Russian materials, mostly on the 1905 period.

International Institute of Social History, Amsterdam. Houses the archives of Senya Fleshin, Max Nettlau, Alexander Berkman, Emma Goldman, Boris Yelensky, Pierre Ramus, and Ugo Fedeli. These contain files of the anarchist relief committees, letters from anarchist prisoners in Russia, and an immense correspondence among the anarchists in exile. Leaflets and proclamations of Makhno's Insurgent Army of the Ukraine are in the Fedeli Archive. The Institute also possesses a unique collection of photographs.

Labadie Collection, University of Michigan. Numerous pamphlets (most of them from the post-1917 period) and a small number of manuscripts and photographs.

Max Nomad, private collection, New York City. Manuscripts, letters, and publications of Jan Waclaw Machajski and his wife.

Dissertations and other unpublished works are listed in the next section.

BOOKS, PAMPHLETS, AND ARTICLES

Abramovitch, Raphael R. *In tsvey revolutsies.* 2 vols., New York, 1944.

———. *The Soviet Revolution, 1917-1939.* New York, 1962.

Adams, Arthur E. *Bolsheviks in the Ukraine: the Second Campaign, 1918-1919.* New Haven and London, 1963.

Adler, Georg. *Anarkhizm.* St. Petersburg, 1906.

Al'manakh: sbornik po istorii anarkhicheskogo dvizheniia v Rossii. Ed. N. Rogdaev. Paris, 1909. An indispensable collection of reminiscences and studies of the Russian anarchist movement from 1903 to 1908 by leading participants; perhaps the single most important work on the 1905 period.

Anarkhiia po Prudonu. Kiev, 1907.

"Di Anarkhisten bay der arbayt," *Folk-Tsaytung*, Vilna, 24 and 28 May 1906.

Anarkhizm i khuliganstvo. St. Petersburg, 1906.

Anisimov, S. "Sud i rasprava nad anarkhistami-kommunistami," *Katorga i Ssylka*, 1932, No. 10, pp. 129-176. The trial of the Ekaterinoslav terrorists described by an attorney for the defense.

An—skii, *Chto takoe anarkhizm?* St. Petersburg, 1907.

Antologiia russkoi sovetskoi poezii. 2 vols., Moscow, 1957.

Anweiler, Oskar, *Die Rätebewegung in Russland, 1905-1921.* Leiden, 1958. A pioneering study of the soviets.

Arshinov, P. A. *Dva pobega (iz vospominanii anarkhista 1906-9 gg.).* Paris, 1929. Reminiscences of Arshinov's early years in the anarchist movement.

———. *Istoriia makhnovskogo dvizheniia (1918-1921 gg.).* Berlin, 1923. A valuable history of Makhno's movement by one of his closest associates.

———. *Novoe v anarkhizme (K chemu prizyvaet organizatsionnaia platforma).* Paris, 1929. A reply to the critics of his "Organizational Platform."

Arskii, R. "Professional'nye soiuzy i zavodskie komitety," *Vestnik Narodnogo Komissariata Truda*, 1918, No. 2-3, pp. 122-128.

B. S. *Otkrytoe pis'mo I. Grossmanu-Roshchinu (Otvet sovetskim "anarkhistam").* Moscow?, 1920. An attack on "Soviet anarchism."

Bakunin, M. A. *Gesammelte Werke.* 3 vols., Berlin, 1921-1924.

———. *Izbrannye sochineniia.* 5 vols., Petrograd and Moscow, 1919-1922.

———. *Oeuvres.* 6 vols., Paris, 1895-1913.

———. *Pis'ma M. A. Bakunina k A. I. Gertsenu i N. P. Ogarevu.* Ed. M. P. Dragomanov. Geneva, 1896.

———. *Sobranie sochinenii i pisem, 1828-1876.* Ed. Iu. M. Steklov. 4 vols., Moscow, 1934-1936.

Balabanoff, Angelica. *My Life as a Rebel.* New York, 1938.

Baron, Salo W. *The Russian Jew under Tsars and Soviets.* New York, 1964.

Baron, Samuel H. *Plekhanov: The Father of Russian Marxism.* Stanford, 1963.

Bel'skii, T. "Ob elementakh anarkhii v russkoi revoliutsii," in *Politicheskoe polozhenie i takticheskie problemy.* Moscow, 1906, pp. 82-98.

Berezin, M. *Fun keyten tsu frayhayt.* New York, 1916. Memoirs of an Anarchist-Communist who escaped from Siberia to New York on the eve of World War I.

———. *Kontr-revoliutsionery li my?* n.p., n.d. [Chicago?, 1918?]

Berkman, Alexander. *The "Anti-Climax": The Concluding Chapter of My Russian Diary "The Bolshevik Myth."* Berlin, 1925.

———. *The Bolshevik Myth (Diary 1920-1922).* New York, 1925. An absorbing diary by the famous Russian-American anarchist. The full manuscript (with much additional material of importance) is in the Berkman Archive.

———. *The Kronstadt Rebellion.* Berlin, 1922. A brief but significant account of the uprising from the anarchist point of view. Also published in German.

———. *Now and After: The ABC of Communist Anarchism.* New York, 1929. Also published as *What Is Communist Anarchism?*

———. *The Russian Tragedy (a Review and an Outlook).* Berlin, 1922.

Berlin, Isaiah. "Herzen and Bakunin on Individual Liberty," in Ernest J. Simmons, ed., *Continuity and Change in Russian and Soviet Thought,* Cambridge, Mass., 1955, pp. 473-499.

Berlin, P. A. *Apostoly anarkhii: Bakunin—Kropotkin—Makhaev.* Petrograd, n.d. [1917?]

Bernstein, E. *Anarkhizm.* St. Petersburg, 1907.

Bidbei, A. [Nikolai Romanov]. *O Liutsifere, velikom dukhe vozmushcheniia, "nesoznatel'nosti," anarkhii i beznachaliia.* n.p. [Paris?], 1904. A vitriolic attack on the Social Democrats by the leader of the *Beznachalie* group.

———. *O revoliutsii i o kazarmennykh dobrodeteliakh gospod Tuporylovykh.* n.p. [Paris?], 1904.

Billington, James H. *Mikhailovsky and Russian Populism.* London, 1958.

Bogrov, V. *Dmitrii Bogrov i ubiistvo Stolypina.* Berlin, 1931.

Bol'shaia sovetskaia entsiklopediia. 1st edn., 65 vols., Moscow, 1926-1947.

Bol'sheviki Petrograda v 1917 godu: khronika sobytii. Leningrad, 1957.

Bol'sheviki v period podgotovki i provedeniia Velikoi Oktiabr'skoi sotsialisticheskoi revoliutsii: khronika sobytii v Petrograde, aprel'-oktiabr' 1917 g. Leningrad, 1947.

Bol'shevistskaia diktatura v svete anarkhizma: desiat' let sovetskoi vlasti. Paris, 1928. An acerbic critique of the Bolshevik regime by an anarchist group in Paris.

Borovoi, A. A. *Anarkhizm.* Moscow, 1918. A thoughtful study of anarchist doctrine by a prominent individualist anarchist.

———. *Istoriia lichnoi svobody vo Frantsii.* Moscow, 1910.

———. *Lichnost' i obshchestvo v anarkhistskom mirovozzrenii.* Petrograd and Moscow, 1920. An attempt to reconcile individualist anarchism with the tenets of Anarchist-Communism and Anarcho-Syndicalism.

———. *Obshchestvennye idealy sovremennogo obshchestva.* Moscow, 1906. An early statement of the Anarchist-Individualist position.

———, ed. *Mikhailu Bakuninu, 1876-1926: ocherk istorii anarkhicheskogo dvizheniia v Rossii.* Moscow, 1926. An invaluable collection of essays on the Russian anarchist movement from its nineteenth-century origins until the 1920's; one of the most important works on the subject.

——— and N. Lebedev, eds. *Sbornik statei posviashchennyi pamiati P. A. Kropotkina.* Petrograd and Moscow, 1922.

——— and N. Otverzhennyi, *Mif o Bakunine.* Moscow, 1925.

Brissenden, Paul F. *The I.W.W.: A Study of American Syndicalism.* 2nd edn., New York, 1957.

Browder, R. P. and A. F. Kerensky, eds. *The Russian Provisional Government, 1917.* 3 vols., Stanford, 1961.

Brupbacher, Fritz. *Marx und Bakunin: ein Beitrag zur Geschichte der Internationalen Arbeiterassoziation.* Berlin, 1922.

Bugaev, B. N. "Na perevale," *Vesy,* 1906, No. 8, pp. 52-54.

Bukharin, N. I. *Anarchismus und wissenschaftlicher Kommunismus.* Hamburg, 1920? A Bolshevik view of anarchist doctrine.

Bukhbinder, N. A. *Istoriia evreiskogo rabochego dvizheniia v Rossii.* Leningrad, 1925.

Bunyan, James and H. H. Fisher, eds. *The Bolshevik Revolution, 1917-1918: Documents and Materials.* Stanford, 1934.

Burgin, H. *Di Geshikhte fun der yidisher arbayter bavegung in Amerike, Rusland un England.* New York, 1915.

Carbo, Eusebio C. "Alexander Schapiro," *L'Adunata dei Refrattari,* 22 March 1947, pp. 3-4.

Carmichael, Joel. *A Short History of the Russian Revolution.* New York, 1964.

Carr, Edward Hallett. *The Bolshevik Revolution, 1917-1923.* 3 vols., New York, 1951-1953.

———. *Michael Bakunin.* London, 1937. The standard biography in English.

Chamberlin, W. H. *The Russian Revolution, 1917-1921.* 2 vols., New York, 1957.

Chapelier, E. and G. Marin. *Anarchists and the International Language, Esperanto.* London, 1908. A report to the International Congress of Anarchists in Amsterdam, August 1907.

Chego dobivaiutsia Anarkhisty-Kommunisty. Iaroslavl, n.d.

Cherevanin, N. [F. A. Lipkin]. "Dvizhenie intelligentsii," in *Obshchestvennoe dvizhenie v Rossii v nachale XX-go veka,* eds. L. Martov, P. Maslov, and A. Potresov, 4 vols., St. Petersburg, 1909-1914, I, 259-290.

Cherkezov, V. N. *Concentration of Capital: A Marxian Fallacy.* London, 1911.

———. *Doktriny marksizma: nauka-li eto?* Geneva, 1903. An early critique of Marxism by a respected Russian anarchist, exiled in London.

———. *Nakonets-to soznalis'! Otvet k Kautskomu.* Tiflis, 1907.

———. *Pages of Socialist History.* New York, 1902.

Chernoe znamia. St. Petersburg, 1906. A collection of articles by Kropotkin, Malatesta, and other leading anarchists.

Chernov, V. M. *The Great Russian Revolution.* New Haven, 1936.

Chernyi, L. [P. D. Turchaninov]. *Novoe napravlenie v anarkhizme: assotsiatsionnyi anarkhizm.* 2nd edn., New York, 1923. The credo of "associational anarchism," a brand of Anarchist-Individualism, by its originator. (1st edn., Moscow, 1907).

———. *O klassakh.* Moscow, 1924.

Chertkov, V. G. *Protiv vlasti*. Christchurch, England, 1905. By the leading disciple of Tolstoy.

Chikagskaia drama, 1-go Maia, 1886-go goda. 2nd edn., New York, 1916.

Chto nam delat' v armii? (*Mysli ofitsera*). n.p., 1903. One of the earliest antimilitarist tracts by the Russian anarchists.

Chudnov, M. N. *Pod chernym znamenem* (*Zapiski anarkhista*). Moscow, 1930. Memoirs of an anarchist guerrilla who fought in the Ukraine during the Civil War.

Ciliga, Anton. *The Kronstadt Revolt*. London, 1942.

Cohen, J. *Di yidish-anarkhistishe bavegung in Amerike*. Philadelphia, 1945.

Cole, G. D. H. *A History of Socialist Thought*. 5 vols. in 7, London, 1953-1960.

Congrès anarchiste tenu à Amsterdam Août 1907. Paris, 1908.

Dallin, David and Boris Nicolaevsky. *Forced Labor in Soviet Russia*. New Haven, 1947.

Daniels, Robert V. *The Conscience of the Revolution: Communist Opposition in Soviet Russia*. Cambridge, Mass., 1960.

————. "The Kronstadt Revolt of 1921: A Study in the Dynamics of Revolution," *American Slavic and East European Review*, x (December 1951), 241-254.

Dave, Victor and Georges Yvetot. *Fernand Pellut'e i revoliutsionnyi sindikalizm vo Frantsii*. St. Petersburg, 1920.

David, Henry. *The History of the Haymarket Affair*. New York, 1936.

"Deklaratsiia" gruppy russkikh anarkhistov sodeistviia "Delu Truda": prakticheskie zadachi anarkhizma v sovremennuiu epokhu. Buenos Aires, 1930.

Doklady Mezhdunarodnomu revoliutsionnomu rabochemu kongressu 1900-go goda. London, 1902.

Dolinin (Moravskii), E. Z. *V vikhre revoliutsii*. Detroit, 1954. A collection of essays and sketches by a disciple of Apollon Karelin.

Dolléans, Édouard. *Histoire du mouvement ouvrier*. 2 vols., Paris, 1936-1946.

Dr. Leo (pseud.). *Pochemu i kak my priblizhaemsia k anarkhii?* Berlin, n.d.

Driker, N. *Anarkhizm i sindikalizm* (*Doklad prednaznachennyi dlia Vserossiiskogo S"ezda Anarkhistov*). Kiev, n.d.

Drinnon, Richard. *Rebel in Paradise: A Biography of Emma Goldman.* Chicago, 1961.

Dubnow, S. M., *History of the Jews in Russia and Poland.* 3 vols., Philadelphia, 1916-1920.

―――― and G. Ia. Krasnyi-Admoni, eds. *Materialy dlia istorii antievreiskikh pogromov v Rossii.* 2 vols., Petrograd, 1919-1923.

Dubnov-Erlikh, S. *Garber-bund un bershter-bund.* Warsaw, 1937.

Dunin, A. A. "Graf L. N. Tolstoi i tolstovtsy v Samarskoi gubernii," *Russkaia Mysl',* 1912, No. 11, pp. 156-166.

25-e sentiabria 1919 goda: pamiati pogibshikh pri vzryve v Leont'evskom pereulke. Moscow, 1925. Materials on the bombing of the Moscow Committee of the Communist Party.

Edel'shtadt, D. *Anarkhizm kommunizm.* New York, 1917.

Ekonomicheskoe polozhenie Rossii nakanune Velikoi Oktiabr'-skoi sotsialisticheskoi revoliutsii: dokumenty i materialy, mart-oktiabr' 1917. 2 vols., Moscow, 1957.

Elliott, William Y. *The Pragmatic Revolt in Politics.* New York, 1928.

Eltzbacher, Paul. *Der Anarchismus.* Berlin, 1900.

Evzel'man, A. Ia. "Bol'sheviki Petrograda v bor'be za bol'she-vizatsiiu profsoiuzov i fabzavkomov v period podgotovki i provedeniia Velikoi Oktiabr'skoi sotsialisticheskoi revoliutsii," dissertation, Moscow State University, 1951.

Fabzavkomy i profsoiuzy: sbornik statei. Moscow, 1925.

Fedotoff White, D. *The Growth of the Red Army.* Princeton, 1944.

Fin, Ia. *Fabrichno-zavodskie komitety v Rossii.* Moscow, 1922.

Fischer, Louis. *The Life of Lenin.* New York, 1964.

Flerovskii, I. "Miatezh mobilizovannykh matrosov v Peterburge 14 oktiabria 1918 g.," *Proletarskaia Revoliutsiia,* 1926, No. 8, pp. 218-237.

Florinsky, Michael T. *The End of the Russian Empire.* New Haven, 1931.

Footman, David. *Civil War in Russia.* London, 1961. Contains an excellent chapter on Makhno.

Frank, H. *Anarkho-sotsialistishe ideyen un bavegungen bay Yidn.* Paris, 1951.

――――. "Di Bialystoke tkufe fun der ruslendisher anarkhistisher bavegung," in *Geklibene shriftn*, New York, 1954, pp. 388-411.

———. *Natsionale un politishe bavegungen bay Yidn in Bialystok*. New York, 1951.

Friedmann, Aurel. *Das anarcho-kommunistische System des Fürsten Peter Kropotkin*. Cologne, 1931.

Gaudeaux, Jean. *Six mois en Russie bolchéviste*. Paris, 1924. By a French syndicalist delegate to the First Profintern Congress.

Gay, Peter. *The Dilemma of Democratic Socialism*. New York, 1952.

Ge (Ghé), A. *Lettre ouverte à P. Kropotkine*. Lausanne, 1916. Takes sharp issue with Kropotkin's stand on the war.

———. *Put' k pobede*. Lausanne, 1917. A sweeping attack on the anarchist "defensists."

Genkin, I. I. "Anarkhisty: iz vospominanii politicheskogo katorzhanina," *Byloe*, 1918, No. 9, pp. 163-183.

———. *Po tiur'mam i etapam*. Petrograd, 1922. Incorporates the material in the preceding article; a valuable source of information on the *Beznachal'tsy*.

———. "Sredi preemnikov Bakunina," *Krasnaia Letopis'*, 1927, No. 1, pp. 170-205.

Georgievskii, E. *Sushchnost' anarkhizma*. Odessa, n.d.

Di Geshikhte fun Bund. Eds. G. Aronson *et al.* 2 vols., New York, 1962. The principal source of information on the Jewish Bund.

Geyer, Dietrich. *Lenin in der russischen Sozialdemokratie: Die Arbeiterbewegung im Zarenreich als Organisationsproblem der revolutionären Intelligenz, 1890-1903*. Cologne, 1962.

Girard, A. *Idei revoliutsionnogo anarkhizma sredi Frantsuzskogo proletariata*. Moscow, 1917.

Gladkov, I. A. *Ocherki sovetskoi ekonomiki, 1917-1920 gg.* Moscow, 1956.

Goldman, Emma. *Anarchism and Other Essays*. New York, 1910. A Russian translation of the first five essays was published in Petrograd in 1921.

———. *The Crushing of the Russian Revolution*. London, 1922.

———. *Living My Life*. New York, 1931. A memorable autobiography, with much material on the Russian anarchists.

―――. *My Disillusionment in Russia.* Garden City, New York, 1923.

―――. *My Further Disillusionment in Russia.* Garden City, New York, 1924.

Goneniia na anarkhizm v Sovetskoi Rossii. Berlin, 1922. Contains capsule biographies of leading Russian anarchists; an important source on the suppression of the anarchists after 1917.

Gordin, Abba. *Communism Unmasked.* New York, 1940.

―――. *Ot iuridicheskogo anarkhizma k fakticheskomu.* Moscow, 1920.

―――. *Zikhroynes un kheshboynes.* 2 vols., Buenos Aires, 1955-1957.

Gordiny, Brat'ia [A. L. and V. L. Gordin]. *Manifest pananarkhistov.* Moscow, 1918.

Gordon, M. *Uchastie rabochikh v organizatsii proizvodstva.* Leningrad, 1927.

Gorelik, A. [Grigorii Gorelik]. *Anarkhisty v rossiiskoi revoliutsii.* Berlin, 1922. Brief history of the anarchists in the revolution by a member of the *Nabat* Confederation; tends to exaggerate the anarchists' role.

―――. *Vospitanie v sovetskoi Rossii.* Buenos Aires, 1923.

Gorev, B. I. [B. I. Gol'dman]. *Anarkhizm v Rossii (Ot Bakunina do Makhno).* Moscow, 1930. A brief history by a Social Democrat; the best work of its kind in Russian.

―――. "Apoliticheskie i antiparlamentskie gruppy (anarkhisty, maksimalisty, makhaevtsy)," in *Obshchestvennoe dvizhenie v Rossii v nachale XX-go veka,* III, 473-534.

Gray, Alexander. *The Socialist Tradition: Moses to Lenin.* London, 1946.

Grossman-Roshchin, I. "Dumy o bylom (Iz istorii belostotskogo anarkhicheskogo 'chernoznamenskogo' dvizheniia)," *Byloe,* 1924, No. 27-28, pp. 172-182.

―――. *Iskusstvo izmeniat' mir.* Moscow, 1930.

―――. *Kharakeristika tvorchestva P. A. Kropotkina.* Moscow and Petrograd, 1921.

Guillaume, James. *L'Internationale: documents et souvenirs (1864-1878).* 4 vols., Paris, 1905-1910.

Hagadah shol peysakh. Vilna [London], 1886. An illegal pamphlet in the form of a prayerbook, smuggled into Russia by anarchists in London.

Haimson, Leopold H. *The Russian Marxists and the Origins of Bolshevism*. Cambridge, Mass., 1955.

Hans, Nicholas. *History of Russian Educational Policy, 1701-1917*. London, 1931.

Harcave, Sidney. *First Blood: The Russian Revolution of 1905*. New York, 1964.

Hard, William. *Raymond Robins' Own Story*. New York and London, 1920.

Hershberg, A. S. *Pinkos Bialystok*. 2 vols., New York, 1950. A useful chronicle of the events in Bialystok, including the activities of the anarchists during the 1905 period.

Herzen, A. I. *"Kolokol": izbrannye stat'i A. I. Gertsena, 1857-1869*. Geneva, 1887.

Hughes, H. Stuart. *Consciousness and Society: The Reconstruction of European Social Thought, 1890-1930*. New York, 1958.

Iakovlev, Ia. A. *Les "Anarchistes Syndicalistes" russes devant le tribunal du prolétariat mondial*. Moscow, 1921.

―――. *Russkii anarkhizm v velikoi russkoi revoliutsii*. Moscow, 1921. A polemical study by a Bolshevik writer.

Iarchuk, E. *Kronshtadt v russkoi revoliutsii*. New York, 1923. By a prominent anarchist who was active in Kronstadt during 1917.

Iaroslavskii, E. E. *Anarkhizm v Rossii*. Moscow, 1937. Probably the worst history of the anarchists. There is a widely distributed English translation.

The International Working Men's Association, I.W.M.A.: Its Policy, Its Aims, Its Principles, n.p., 1933. A basic document.

Istoriia grazhdanskoi voiny v SSSR. 4 vols., Moscow, 1935-1959.

Itkin, M. L. "Bor'ba petrogradskikh proletariata pod rukovodstvom partii Lenina-Stalina za rabochii kontrol' v promyshlennosti v 1917 godu (fevral'-oktiabr')," dissertation, Leningrad State University, 1953.

Iushkevich, P. *Teoriia i praktika sindikalizma*. St. Petersburg, 1907.

Ivaniukov, I. I. *Chto takoe anarkhizm?* 2nd edn., St. Petersburg, 1906.

Ivanov-Razumnik [R. V. Ivanov]. *Chto takoe makhaevshchina?* St. Petersburg, 1908. A perceptive study of "Makhaevism."

Ivanovich, M. [M. I. Bulgakov]. "Anarkhizm v Rossii," *Sotsial-ist-Revoliutsioner*, 1911, No. 3, pp. 75-94.

Ivanovich, S. *Anarkhisty i anarkhizm v Rossii.* St. Petersburg, 1907.

————. "Anarkhizm v Rossii i bor'ba s nim," *Sovremennyi Mir*, 1906, No. 1, part 2, pp. 1-11.

Joll, James. *The Anarchists.* London, 1964. A stimulating interpretive account of the anarchist movement in the nineteenth and twentieth centuries; well-written and incisive.

Kakie nuzhny poriadki. Moscow, n.d. [1919?]

Kaminski, H.-E. *Michel Bakounine: la vie d'un révolutionnaire.* Paris, 1938.

Karelin, A. A. *Chto takoe anarkhiia?* Moscow, 1923.

————. *Gorodskie rabochie, krest'ianstvo, vlast' i sobstvennost'.* Buenos Aires, 1924.

————. *Gosudarstvo i anarkhisty.* Moscow, 1918. A popular anarchist critique of the state.

————. (A. Kochegarov, pseud.). *K voprosu o kommunizme.* n.p., 1918.

————. *Novoe kratkoe izlozhenie politicheskoi ekonomii.* New York, 1918.

————. *Obshchestvennoe vladenie v Rossii.* St. Petersburg, 1893.

————. (A. Kochegarov, pseud.). *Polozhitel'nye i otritsatel'nye storony demokratii s tochki zreniia anarkhistov-kommunistov.* Geneva, n.d.

————. *Smertnaia kazn'.* Detroit, 1923.

————. *Tak govoril Bakunin.* Bridgeport, Conn., n.d.

————. *Vol'naia zhizn'.* Detroit, 1955. A fairly broad selection of Karelin's writings, with a biographical introduction.

———— (A. Kochegarov, pseud.). *Zemel'naia programma anarkhistov-kommunistov.* London, 1912. A brief exposition of the Anarchist-Communist land program.

Katkov, George. "The Kronstadt Rising," *Soviet Affairs*, No. 2, 1959, pp. 9-74. An intelligent account of the revolt.

Keep, J. L. H. *The Rise of Social Democracy in Russia.* London, 1963. A superb history of the Social Democrats through 1907.

Kenafick, K. J. *Michael Bakunin and Karl Marx.* Melbourne, 1948.

Kennan, George F. *Russia Leaves the War.* Princeton, 1956.

Kharkhardin, I. *Kropotkin, kak ekonomist.* Moscow, 1922.

Khleb i volia: stat'i P. Kropotkina, V. Cherkezova, E. Rekliu, L. Bertoni i drugikh. St. Petersburg, 1906. A collection of articles by eminent anarchists.

Kindersley, Richard. *The First Russian Revisionists.* London, 1962.

Knizhnik, I. S. (I. Vetrov, pseud.). *Anarkhizm: ego teoriia i praktika.* St. Petersburg, 1906.

———— (A. Kratov, pseud.). *Novaia Rossiia i evrei.* Petrograd, 1917.

———— (I. Vetrov, pseud.). *Ocherk sotsial'noi ekonomiki s tochki zreniia anarkhicheskogo kommunizma.* Paris, 1908.

———— (A. Kratov, pseud.). *Podgotovka k uchreditel'nomu sobraniiu.* Petrograd, 1917.

————. "Vospominaniia o Bogrove, ubiitsa Stolypina," *Krasnaia Letopis'*, 1923, No. 5, pp. 287-294.

————. "Vospominaniia o P. A. Kropotkine i ob odnoi anarkhistskoi emigrantskoi gruppe," *Krasnaia Letopis'*, 1922, No. 4, pp. 28-51. A personal memoir about the anarchist émigrés in Paris between the two revolutions; by a member of the colony.

Kollontai, A. *The Workers Opposition.* Chicago, 1921.

Kol'tsov, D. [B. A. Ginzburg]. "Rabochie v 1890-1904 gg.," in *Obshchestvennoe dvizhenie v Rossii v nachale XX-go veka,* I, 183-229.

Korn, M. [M. I. Gol'dsmit]. *Bor'ba s kapitalom i vlast'iu; Nashi spornye voprosy.* London, 1912.

————. *Revoliutsionnyi sindikalizm i anarkhizm; Bor'ba s kapitalom i vlast'iu.* Petrograd and Moscow, 1920. Essays by a leading Kropotkinite and pro-syndicalist.

————. *Revoliutsionnyi sindikalizm i sotsialisticheskie partii.* London, 1907. An important syndicalist pamphlet.

Kornatovskii, N. A., ed. *Kronshtadtskii miatezh: sbornik statei, vospominanii i dokumentov.* Leningrad, 1931.

Kozlovskii, L. S. *Ocherki sindikalizma vo Frantsii.* Moscow, 1906.

————. *Sotsial'noe dvizhenie v sovremennoi Frantsii.* Moscow, 1908.

Kreizel', Iu. B. *Iz istorii profdvizheniia g. Khar'kova v 1917 godu.* Kharkov, 1921.

Krest'ianskoe dvizhenie 1902 goda. Moscow and Petrograd, 1923.

Kritskaia, N. and N. Lebedev. *Istoriia sindikal'nogo dvizheniia vo Frantsii, 1789-1907.* Moscow, 1908.

Kropotkin, P. A. *Der Anarchismus in Russland.* Berlin, 1905.

————. *Buntovskii dukh.* Geneva, 1905.

————. *La Conquête du pain.* Paris, 1892. The Russian translation (1902), issued under the title of *Khleb i volia,* had a great influence on the movement.

————. *Etika.* Petrograd, 1922.

————. *Fields, Factories, and Workshops.* London, 1899. A work of major importance.

————. *The Great French Revolution, 1789-1793.* London, 1909.

————. *Kropotkin's Revolutionary Pamphlets.* Ed. Roger N. Baldwin. New York, 1927. A good collection.

————. "A Letter on the Present War," *Freedom* (London), October 1914, pp. 76-77.

————. *Memoirs of a Revolutionist.* Boston, 1899. A classic.

————. *Modern Science and Anarchism.* New York, 1908.

————. *Mutual Aid: A Factor of Evolution.* London, 1902. Another major work.

————. *Paroles d'un révolté.* Paris, 1885.

————. *Russkaia revoliutsiia.* Geneva, 1905.

————, ed. *Russkaia revoliutsiia i anarkhizm.* London, 1907.

Kubanin, M. *Makhnovshchina.* Leningrad, n.d. [1927].

Kulczycki, L. *Anarkhizm v Rossii.* St. Petersburg, 1907. Also published as *Anarkhizm v sovremennom sotsial'no-politiches-kom dvizhenii v Rossii.*

————. *Sovremennyi anarkhizm: izlozhenie, istochniki, kritika.* St. Petersburg, 1907. A thoughtful study.

Kurchinskii, M. A. *Apostol egoizma: Maks Shtirner i ego filosofiia anarkhii.* Petrograd, 1920.

Lampert, E. *Studies in Rebellion.* London, 1957.

Lane, David. "The Russian Social Democratic Labour Party in St. Petersburg, Tver and Ashkhabad, 1903-1905," *Soviet Studies,* xv (January 1964), 331-344.

Lazarev, E. "Dmitrii Bogrov i ubiistvo Stolypina," *Volia Rossii,* 1926, No. 8-9, pp. 28-65.

Lebedev, N. K. *Elize Rekliu, kak chelovek, uchenyi i myslitel'.* Petrograd, 1920.

———. *Muzei P. A. Kropotkina.* Leningrad and Moscow, 1928. A description of the Kropotkin Museum by its secretary.

———. *P. A. Kropotkin.* Moscow, 1925.

———. *Rabochie soiuzy.* Moscow, 1917.

Lenin, V. I. *Leninskii sbornik.* 35 vols., Moscow, 1924-1945.

———. *Sochineniia.* 2nd edn., 31 vols., Moscow, 1931-1935.

Lenskii, Z. "Natsional'noe dvizhenie," in *Obshchestvennoe dvizhenie v Rossii v nachale XX-go veka,* I, 349-371.

Letters from Russian Prisoners. London, 1925. Material on the Bolshevik repression of political opponents, including the anarchists.

Levin, Sh. *Untererdishe kemfer.* New York, 1946.

Levine, Louis. *Syndicalism in France.* 2nd edn., New York, 1914. Still the best treatment of the subject.

Liashchenko, P. N. *Istoriia narodnogo khoziaistva SSSR.* 2 vols., Leningrad, 1947-1948.

Litvak, A. *Vos geven.* Vilna, 1925.

Lorwin, V. R. *The French Labor Movement.* Cambridge, Mass., 1954.

Louis, Paul. *Histoire du mouvement syndical en France.* 2 vols., Paris, 1947-1948.

Lozinskii, E. Iu. *Chego zhdat russkim rabochim ot vseobshchego izbiratel'nogo prava?* St. Petersburg, 1907.

———. *Chto zhe takoe, nakonets, intelligentsiia?* St. Petersburg, 1907. A Makhaevist treatise.

———. *Itogi parlamentarizma: chto on dal i mozhet li on chto-to dat' rabochim massam?* St. Petersburg, 1907.

———. (E. Ustinov, pseud.). *Sovremennyi anarkhizm: ego konechnye idealy, programma, taktika i nravstvenno-klassovaia sushchnost'.* Geneva, 1905. Also published in Moscow, 1906, under another pseudonym, "Podolianin."

Lozovskii, A. [S. A. Dridzo]. *Anarkho-sindikalizm i kommunizm.* Moscow, 1923. An attack on syndicalism by a Bolshevik trade union official.

———. *Rabochii kontrol'.* Petrograd, 1918.

Lur'e, S. Ia. *Predtechi anarkhizma v drevnem mire.* Moscow, 1926.

Luxemburg, Rosa. *The Mass Strike: The Political Party and the Trade Union.* Detroit, n.d.

Machajski, Jan Waclaw. (A. Vol'skii, pseud.). *Bankrotstvo sotsializma XIX stoletiia.* n.p. [Geneva], 1905.

―――. *Burzhuaznaia revoliutsiia i rabochee delo.* n.p. [Geneva], 1905.

―――. *Umstvennyi rabochii.* 3 vols. in 1, Geneva, 1904-1905. Machajski's *magnum opus.*

―――. "An Unfinished Essay in the Nature of a Critique of Socialism," manuscript photocopy, Paris, 1911.

Maitron, Jean. *Histoire du mouvement anarchiste en France (1880-1914).* Paris, 1951. An authoritative history.

Makhno, N. I. *Makhnovshchina i ee vcherashnie soiuzniki-bol'-sheviki (Otvet na knigu M. Kubanina "Makhnovshchina").* Paris, 1928.

―――. *Pod udarami kontr-revoliutsii (aprel'-iiun' 1918 g.).* Paris, 1936.

―――. *Russkaia revoliutsiia na Ukraine (ot marta 1917 g. po aprel' 1918 god).* Paris, 1929.

―――. *Ukrainskaia revoliutsiia (iiul'-dekabr' 1918 g.).* Paris, 1937. This and the two preceding entries constitute Makhno's recollections of his guerrilla army in the Civil War.

Maksimov (Maximoff, Maximov), G. P. *Beseda s Bakuninym o revoliutsii.* Chicago, 1934.

―――. *Bolshevism: Promises and Reality.* Glasgow, n.d.

―――. *Constructive Anarchism.* Chicago, 1952. Contains the credo of a leading Anarcho-Syndicalist.

―――. *The Guillotine at Work: Twenty Years of Terror in Russia.* Chicago, 1940. An indictment of the suppression of the anarchists, with many supporting documents.

―――. *Moe sotsial'noe kredo.* Chicago, 1933. An English translation of this pamphlet is included in *Constructive Anarchism.*

―――. *"Rassvet": provodnik russkogo fashizma.* Chicago, 1933.

―――― (G. Lapot', pseud.). *Sovety rabochikh soldatskikh i krest'ianskikh deputatov i nashe k nim otnoshenie.* New York, 1918.

―――. *Za chto i kak bol'sheviki izgnali anarkhistov iz Rossii?* n.p. [Berlin?], 1922.

―――, ed. *The Political Philosophy of Bakunin: Scientific Anarchism.* Glencoe, Ill., 1953.

Malia, Martin. *Alexander Herzen and the Birth of Russian Socialism, 1812-1855.* Cambridge, Mass., 1961.

Manifest protesta anarkhistov-kommunistov protiv bol'shevistskogo pravitel'stva k proletariatu vsego mira. New York?, 1922. Also published in English.

Markin, I. V. "Ot rabochego kontrolia nad proizvodstvom k rabochemu upravleniiu promyshlennost'iu (1917-1918 gg., g. Petrograd)," dissertation, Leningrad State Pedagogical Institute, 1950.

Martov, L. [Iu. O. Tsederbaum]. *Politicheskie partii v Rossii.* St. Petersburg, 1906.

Marx, K. and F. Engels. *Kritika ucheniia Shtirnera.* 2 parts, St. Petersburg, 1913.

———. *Selected Works.* 2 vols., Moscow, 1962.

———. *Sviatoe semeistvo.* 2 vols., St. Petersburg, 1906. Translation and notes by Waclaw Machajski. The notes are of great interest.

Masaryk, T. G. *The Spirit of Russia.* 2 vols., London, 1955.

Maslov, P. P. *Agrarnyi vopros v Rossii.* 2 vols., St. Petersburg, 1908.

"Materialy k istorii rabochego kontrolia nad proizvodstvom (1917-1918 gg.)," *Krasnyi Arkhiv,* 1940, No. 6, pp. 106-129.

Matiushenko, A. I. *Ot vorovstva k anarkhizmu.* St. Petersburg, 1908.

Maximoff, Maximov (see Maksimov).

Maynard, Sir John. *Russia in Flux.* New York, 1951.

Mehring, Franz. *Karl Marx: Geschichte seines Lebens.* Leipzig, 1918.

Meijer, J. M. *Knowledge and Revolution: The Russian Colony in Zuerich (1870-1873).* Assen, 1955.

Mendel, Arthur P. *Dilemmas of Progress in Tsarist Russia.* Cambridge, Mass., 1961.

Mett, Ida. *La Commune de Cronstadt: Crépuscule sanglant des Soviets.* Paris, 1949. An anarchist account of the uprising.

Miliukov, P. N. *Istoriia vtoroi russkoi revoliutsii.* 1 vol. in 3 parts, Sofia, 1921-1923.

Mitel'man, M. I., *et al. Istoriia Putilovskogo zavoda, 1789-1917.* 3rd edn., Moscow and Leningrad, 1941.

Mushin, A. *Dmitrii Bogrov i ubiistvo Stolypina.* Paris, 1914.

Na pomoshch' ispanskim bortsam. New York, 193?.

Nacht, S. *Vseobshchaia stachka i sotsial'naia revoliutsiia.* Paris, 1904. Also printed in New York, 1916, under pseudonym of Arnold Roller.

Natsionalizatsiia promyshlennosti v SSSR: sbornik dokumentov, 1917-1920 gg. Moscow, 1954.

Nedrov, A. [A. S. Tokarev]. *Rabochii vopros.* St. Petersburg, 1906.

Nestroev, G. *Maksimalizm i bol'shevizm.* Moscow, 1919.

Nettlau, Max. *Der Anarchismus von Proudhon zu Kropotkin.* Berlin, 1927. Second volume of an encylopedic history of anarchism, of which only three volumes were published. The sequel, which carries the history from 1886 to 1914, is in manuscript form in the International Institute of Social History.

————. *Anarchisten und Sozialrevolutionäre.* Berlin, 1931. Third volume of his history of anarchism.

————. *Bibliographie de L'anarchie.* Brussels, 1897.

————. "Michael Bakunin: eine Biographie," 3 vols., manuscript photocopy, London, 1896-1900. A detailed biography, containing much unique material.

————. "A Memorial Tribute: To Marie Goldsmith and Her Mother," *Freedom* (New York), I, No. 10, 18 March 1933, p. 2.

————. *Der Vorfrühling der Anarchie.* Berlin, 1925. First volume of his history of anarchism.

Nikolaevskii, B. "Varlaam Nikolaevich Cherkezov (1846-1925)," *Katorga i Ssylka,* 1926, No. 4, pp. 222-232.

Nomad, Max. *Apostles of Revolution.* Boston, 1939. Includes valuable studies of Bakunin, Nechaev, and Makhno.

————. *Aspects of Revolt.* New York, 1959.

————. *Dreamers, Dynamiters, and Demagogues.* New York, 1964. Reminiscences of a former disciple of Machajski.

————. *Rebels and Renegades.* New York, 1932.

————. "Reminiscences," *New Politics,* II (Winter 1963), 89-95.

Norton, Henry K. *The Far Eastern Republic of Siberia.* London, 1923.

Novomirskii, D. I. [Ia. Kirillovskii]. *Chto takoe anarkhizm?* n.p., 1907.

————. *Iz programmy sindikal'nogo anarkhizma.* n.p. [Odessa], 1907. The fullest exposition of Novomirskii's Anarcho-Syndicalist views.

―――. *Manifest Anarkhistov-Kommunistov.* n.p., 1905. An English translation was issued in New York in 1921.

Novyi pokhod protiv sotsial' demokratii: dokumenty po delu N. I. Muzilia. Geneva, 1905.

Oktiabr'skaia revoliutsiia i fabzavkomy: materialy po istorii fabrichno-zavodskikh komitetov. 3 vols., Moscow, 1927-1929. The most important source on the factory committees.

Organizatsionnaia platforma vseobshchego soiuza anarkhistov (Proekt). Paris, 1926. A controversial proposal for organizational reform in the anarchist movement.

Orgeiani, K. [G. Gogeliia]. *Kak i iz chego razvilsia Revoliutsionnyi Sindikalizm.* n.p. [London?], 1909. By a leading exponent of syndicalism.

―――. *O rabochikh soiuzakh.* London, 1907.

―――. *O revoliutsii i revoliutsionnom pravitel'stve.* London, 1905. Issued under another pseudonym, K. Iliashvili.

―――. *Ob intelligentsii.* London, 1912.

―――. *Pamiati chikagskikh muchenikov.* Geneva, 1905. By "K. Iliashvili."

Otverzhennyi, N. *Shtirner i Dostoevskii.* Moscow, 1925.

Otvet neskol'kikh russkikh anarkhistov na organizatsionnuiu platformu. Paris, 1927.

Our Position. Chicago?, 1934? Resolutions adopted at the Chicago convention of the Federation of Russian Anarchist-Communist Groups in the United States and Canada, September 1934.

P. A. Kropotkin, 1842-1922: k 80-tiletiiu so dnia rozhdeniia. Moscow, 1922. Articles by members of the Kropotkin Museum Committee.

P. A. Kropotkin i ego uchenie: internatsional'nyi sbornik, posviashchennyi desiatoi godovshchine smerti P. A. Kropotkina. Ed. G. P. Maksimov. Chicago, 1931. An important collection of essays and materials on the Russian anarchist movement.

Padenie tsarskogo rezhima. 7 vols., Leningrad, 1924-1927.

Pamiati Petra Alekseevicha Kropotkina. Petrograd and Moscow, 1921.

Pankratova, A. M. *Fabzavkomy i profsoiuzy v revoliutsii 1917 goda.* Moscow and Leningrad, 1927.

———. *Fabzavkomy Rossii v bor'be za sotsialisticheskuiu fabriku.* Moscow, 1923.

Papers Relating to the Foreign Relations of the United States, 1918: Russia. 3 vols., Washington, 1931.

Pares, Sir Bernard. *The Fall of the Russian Monarchy.* London, 1939.

Pazhitnov, K. A. *Polozhenie rabochego klassa v Rossii.* St. Petersburg, 1906.

Pelloutier, Fernand. *Histoire des bourses du travail.* Paris, 1902. Russian translation, St. Petersburg, 1906.

Pereval (pseud.). *Bezgosudarstvennyi kommunizm i sindikalizm.* n.p., 191?.

Pervaia konferentsiia anarkhistskikh organizatsii Ukrainy "Nabat": Deklaratsii i rezoliutsii. Buenos Aires, 1922.

Pervaia rabochaia konferentsiia fabrichno-zavodskikh komitetov. Petrograd, 1917.

Pervyi vserossiiskii s"ezd professional'nykh soiuzov, 7-14 ianvaria 1918 g. Moscow, 1918.

Peterburzhets [K. M. Takhtarev]. *Ocherk peterburzhskogo rabochego dvizheniia 90-kh godov: po lichnym vospominaniiam.* London, 1902.

Philips Price, M. *My Reminiscences of the Russian Revolution.* London, 1921.

Pipes, Richard. "*Narodnichestvo:* A Semantic Inquiry," *Slavic Review,* XXIII (September 1964), 441-458.

———. *Social Democracy and the St. Petersburg Labor Movement, 1885-1897.* Cambridge, Mass., 1963.

"Pis'ma P. A. Kropotkina k V. N. Cherkezovu," *Katorga i Ssylka,* 1926, No. 4, pp. 7-28.

Pis'mo anarkhista bratu rabochemu. Moscow, 1917.

Pis'mo Vladimira Lapidusa (Strigi). n.p. [Geneva?], 1907. Letter of a leading *Chernoznamenets* shortly before his death from a bomb explosion.

Plekhanov, G. V. *Anarkhizm i sotsializm.* St. Petersburg, 1905. A widely read Marxist critique of anarchism, translated into several languages.

———. *Sochineniia.* 24 vols., Leningrad, 1923-1927.

Pollack, Emanuel. *The Kronstadt Rebellion.* New York, 1959.

Polonskii, V. A. "Anarkhisty i sovremennaia revoliutsiia," *Novaia Zhizn'*, 15 November 1917, p. 1.

————. *Materialy dlia biografii M. Bakunina.* 3 vols., Moscow, 1923-1933.

Posse, V. A. *Kakova dolzhna byt' programma russkikh proletariev?* Geneva, 1905.

————. *Moi zhiznennyi put': dorevoliutsionnyi period (1864-1917 gg.).* Moscow and Leningrad, 1929. Memoirs of a noted "legal Marxist," who became a syndicalist before the Revolution of 1905.

————. *Rabochie stachki: ocherki.* St. Petersburg, 1906. One of a series of pamphlets by Posse under the general title of *Biblioteka rabochego.*

————. *Uchreditel'noe sobranie.* Petrograd, 1917.

————. *Vospominaniia V. A. Posse (1905-1917 gg.).* Petrograd, 1923. A condensed version of *Moi zhiznennyi put'.*

————. *Vseobshchaia stachka.* Geneva, 1903.

Pravda o Kronshtadte. Prague, 1921. An important collection of documents on the Kronstadt revolt.

Prawdin, Michael. *The Unmentionable Nechaev: A Key to Bolshevism.* London, 1961.

Preobrazhenskii, E. A. *Anarkhizm i kommunizm.* 2nd edn., Moscow, 1921.

Professional'noe dvizhenie v Petrograde v 1917 g.: ocherki i materialy. Leningrad, 1928.

Protokoly 1-go Vserossiiskogo s"ezda professional'nykh soiuzov tekstil'shchikov i fabrichnykh komitetov. Moscow, 1918.

Prugavin, A. S. *O L've Tolstom i o tolstovtsakh.* Moscow, 1911.

Pukhov, A. S. *Kronshtadtskii miatezh v 1921 g.* Leningrad, 1931.

Putilovets na putiakh k Oktiabriu: iz istorii "Krasnogo putilovtsa." Moscow and Leningrad, 1933.

Pyziur, Eugene. *The Doctrine of Anarchism of Michael A. Bakunin.* Milwaukee, 1955. A capable exposition of Bakunin's theories.

Rabochee dvizhenie v 1917 godu. Eds. V. L. Meller and A. M. Pankratova. Moscow and Leningrad, 1926.

Rabochii kontrol' i natsionalizatsiia promyshlennykh predpriiatii Petrograda v 1917-1919 gg.: sbornik dokumentov. Leningrad, 1947.

Radek, Karl. *Anarchismus und Räteregierung*. Hamburg, n.d.

———. *Anarkhisty i sovetskaia Rossiia*. Petrograd, 1918.

Radkey, Oliver H. *The Agrarian Foes of Bolshevism*. New York, 1958.

———. *The Sickle under the Hammer*. New York, 1963.

Raevskii, M. [L. Fishelev]. *Anarkho-sindikalizm i "kriticheskii" sindikalizm*. New York, 1919. An important work by the editor of *Golos Truda*.

Rafes, M. *Ocherki po istorii "Bunda."* Moscow, 1923.

———, ed. *Der yidisher arbeter*. 2 vols., Moscow, 1925.

Ramus, Pierre [Rudolf Grossmann]. *Vil'iam Godvin, kak teoretik kommunisticheskogo anarkhizma*. Moscow, 1925.

Rashin, A. G. *Formirovanie promyshlennogo proletariata v Rossii*. Moscow, 1940.

Ravich-Cherkasskii, M. *Anarkhisty*. Kharkov, 1929. One of the better Soviet histories.

Rech' Emilia Anri pered sudom. Geneva, 1898.

Rech' Matreny Prisiazhniuka v Kievskom voenno-okruzhnom sude 19-go iiulia 1908 goda. New York, 1916. Trial speech of a Kiev Anarchist-Individualist.

Reed, John. *Ten Days that Shook the World*. New York, 1960.

Résolutions approuvées par le Congrès Anarchiste tenu à Amsterdam, Août 24-31, 1907. London, 1907. Also published in English and German.

Revoliutsiia 1917 goda: khronika sobytii. 6 vols., Moscow and Leningrad, 1923-1930.

Revoliutsiia 1905-1907 gg. v Rossii: dokumenty i materialy. 16 vols., Moscow and Leningrad, 1955-1963.

Rezoliutsii pervogo s"ezda Konfederatsii anarkhstiskikh organizatsii Ukrainy "Nabat." Buenos Aires, 1923.

Rezoliutsii s"ezda imevshego mesto v gorode Brianske s 6-go po 11-oe avgusta 1918 g. Moscow, 1918.

Rimlinger, Gaston V. "Autocracy and the Factory Order in Early Russian Industrialization," *Journal of Economic History*, xx (March 1960), 67-92.

———. "The Management of Labor Protest in Tsarist Russia, 1870-1905," *International Review of Social History*, v (1960), 226-248.

Robinson, Geroid T. *Rural Russia under the Old Regime*. New York, 1957.

Robitnichii kontrol' i natsionalizatsiia promislovosti na Ukraine: zbirnik dokumentiv i materialiv. Kiev, 1957.

Rocker, Rudolf. *Anarcho-Syndicalism.* London, 1938. The best general work on the subject.

———. *The London Years.* London, 1956. Reminiscences by the leader of the Jewish Federation of Anarchists in London.

Rogdaev, N. [N. I. Muzil']. *Internatsional'nyi kongress anarkhistov v Amsterdame.* n.p., 1907. A report on the Amsterdam Congress by a Russian delegate.

Romanov, F. "Moskovskie tekstil'shchiki ot Fevralia k Oktiabriu," *Voprosy Profdvizheniia,* 1935, No. 7-8, pp. 71-87.

Rostovtsev, T. [N. V. Divnogorskii]. *Nasha taktika.* Geneva, 1907. The tactics of the *Beznachalie* group as presented by a principal member.

———. *Za vsiu zemliu, za vsiu voliu.* n.p., 1905?

Rudenko, P. *Na Ukraine: povstanchestvo i anarkhicheskoe dvizhenie.* Buenos Aires, 1922.

Rudnev, V. V. (V. Bazarov, pseud.). *Anarkhicheskii kommunizm i marksizm.* St. Petersburg, 1906. A Menshevik critique of anarchist communism.

———. *Makhnovshchina.* Kharkov, 1928.

Russell, Bertrand. *Proposed Roads to Freedom.* New York, n.d. [1919].

Russia: the Official Report of the British Trades Union Delegation to Russian and Caucasia, Nov. and Dec., 1924. London, 1925.

The Russian Revolution and the Communist Party. Berlin, 1922. Also in German, 1921. A denunciation of the Bolshevik regime by four Moscow anarchists; smuggled out of Russia in 1921.

Russkaia revoliutsiia i anarkhizm. n.p., 1922.

Sandomirskii, G. B. *Fashizm.* 2 vols., Moscow, 1923.

———. *Plekhanov i anarkhisty.* Moscow, 1918.

———. "Po povodu starogo spora," *Katorga i Ssylka,* 1926, No. 2, pp. 11-34.

———. *Torzhestvo antimilitarizma (K istorii anarkhistskogo dvizheniia).* Moscow, 1920.

———. *V nevole: ocherki i vospominaniia.* 3rd edn., Moscow, 1923. Prison memoirs of a well-known Kiev anarchist.

———, ed. *Materialy genuezskoi konferentsii.* Moscow, 1922.

Sazhin, M. P. "Russkie v Tsiurikhe (1870-1873 gg.)," *Katorga i Ssylka*, 1932, No. 10, pp. 25-78.

Sbornik dekretov i postanovlenii po narodnomu khoziaistvu (25 oktiabria 1917 g.-25 oktiabria 1918 g.). Moscow, 1918.

Scalapino, Robert A. and George T. Yu. *The Chinese Anarchist Movement.* Berkeley, 1961.

Schapiro, Leonard. *The Communist Party of the Soviet Union.* New York, 1960. The best general history.

————. *The Origin of the Communist Autocracy.* Cambridge, Mass., 1956. An outstanding work.

Scheibert, Peter. *Von Bakunin zu Lenin: Geschichte der russischen revolutionären Ideologien, 1840-95.* Part 1, Leiden, 1956.

Schwarz, Solomon. "Betriebsräte und Produktionskontrolle in Russland," in *Die sozialen Probleme des Betriebes*, ed. Heinz Pothoff, Berlin, 1925.

Sefer Biale-Podlaske. Tel Aviv, 1961.

Serge, Victor. *L'An I de la révolution russe.* Paris, 1930.

————. *Mémoires d'un révolutionnaire.* Paris, 1951. There is a good English translation (1963, slightly abridged) of these absorbing reminiscences.

————. *Russia Twenty Years After.* New York, 1937.

Shatilova, T. *Fabzavkomy i profsoiuzy v 1917-1918 gg.* Leningrad, 1927.

Shatz, Marshall S. "Anti-Intellectualism in the Russian Intelligentsia: Michael Bakunin, Peter Kropotkin, and Jan Waclaw Machajski," certificate essay, the Russian Institute, Columbia University, 1963.

Shchepetev, A. "Sovremennyi anarkhizm i klassovaia tochka zreniia," *Russkoe Bogatstvo*, 1907, No. 1, pp. 114-148.

Shliapnikov, A. G. *Sem'nadtsatyi god.* 4 vols., Moscow, 1923-1931.

Shlossberg, D. "Vseobshchaia stachka 1903 g. na Ukraine," *Istoriia Proletariata SSSR*, VII (1931), 52-85.

Shub, David. "Kropotkin and Lenin," *Russian Review*, XII (October 1953), 227-234.

————. *Lenin.* New York, 1948.

Simmons, Ernest J. *Leo Tolstoy.* Boston, 1946.

Soiuz S-R Maksimalistov. *O rabochem kontrole.* Moscow, 1918.

————. *Trudovaia sovetskaia respublika.* Moscow, 1918.

Sorel, Georges. *Reflections on Violence.* Glencoe, Ill., 1950.

Souchy, Augustin. *Wie lebt der Arbeiter und Bauer in Russland und in der Ukraine?* Berlin, n.d., [1921?]

Spektorskii, E. V. "Russkii anarkhizm," *Russkaia Mysl'*, 1922, No. 1-2, pp. 230-253.

Stanislav [A. Vol'skii—A. V. Sokolov]. *Teoriia i praktika anarkhizma.* Moscow, 1906.

Steklov, Iu. M. *Mikhail Aleksandrovich Bakunin: ego zhizn' i deiatel'nost', 1814-1876.* 4 vols., Moscow, 1926-1927. The principal biography in Russian.

Stirner, Max [Johann Kaspar Schmidt]. *Der Einzige und sein Eigenthum.* Leipzig, 1845. An extremely influential book by the German theorist of individualist anarchism.

Strel'skii, P. [V. Iu. Lavrov]. *Novaia sekta v riadakh sotsialistov.* Moscow, 1907.

Sukhanov, N. N. [Himmer]. *The Russian Revolution, 1917.* New York, 1955. Abridged translation of 4 vol. memoirs, *Zapiski o revoliutsii*, Petrograd and Moscow, 1922-1923.

Sviatlovskii, V. V. *Ocherki po anarkhizmu.* Petrograd, 1922.

Svoboda i trud: anarkhizm-sindikalizm. St. Petersburg, 1907. A collection of articles on syndicalism.

Svobodnoe trudovoe vospitanie: sbornik statei. Ed. N. K. Lebedev. Petrograd and Moscow, 1921.

Syrkin, L. N. *Makhaevshchina.* Moscow and Leningrad, 1931.

Taktika, fortifikatsiia i prigotovlenie vzryvchatykh veshchestv. Geneva?, 1907. Rostovtsev's instructions on the preparation of bombs.

Teper (Gordeev), I. *Makhno.* Kiev, 1924.

Tiurin, S. P. "Ot"ezd P. A. Kropotkina iz Anglii v Rossiiu i ego pis'ma," *Na Chuzhoi Storone*, 1924, No. 4, pp. 216-238.

Tokmakoff, George. "Stolypin's Assassin," *Slavic Review*, XXIV (June 1965), 314-321.

Tolstaia, A. *Otets: zhizn' L'va Tolstogo.* 2 vols., New York, 1953.

Treadgold, Donald W. *Lenin and His Rivals: The Struggle for Russia's Future, 1898-1906.* New York, 1955.

Tret'ia vserossiiskaia konferentsiia professional'nykh soiuzov, 3-11 iiulia (20-28 iiunia st. st.) 1917 g. Moscow, 1927.

Trotsky, Leon. *The History of the Russian Revolution.* 3 vols. in 1, Ann Arbor, Mich., 1957.

————. *Mein Leben.* Berlin, 1930.

Trus, A. and J. Cohen. *Breynsk: sefer ha-zikheron.* New York, 1948.

Tseitlin, D. A. "Fabrichno-zavodskie komitety Petrograda v fevrale-oktiabre 1917 goda," *Voprosy Istorii,* 1956, No. 11, pp. 86-97.

Tsereteli, I. G. *Vospominaniia o fevral'skoi revoliutsii.* 2 vols. in 1, Paris, 1963.

Tsyperovich, G. V. *Sindikaty i tresty v Rossii.* 3rd edn., Petrograd, 1920.

Tucker, Benjamin R. *Instead of a Book.* 2nd edn., New York, 1897.

Tugan-Baranovskii, M. I. *Russkaia fabrika v proshlom i nastoiashchem.* 3rd edn., St. Petersburg, 1907.

Ulam, Adam B. *The Bolsheviks.* New York, 1965. A penetrating study.

————. *The Unfinished Revolution.* New York, 1960.

Urussov, S. D. *Memoirs of a Russian Governor.* London and New York, 1908.

Utechin, S. V. "Bolsheviks and their Allies after 1917: The Ideological Pattern," *Soviet Studies,* x (October 1958), 114-135.

————. "The 'Preparatory' Trend in the Russian Revolutionary Movement in the 1880's," *Soviet Affairs,* No. 3, 1962, pp. 7-22.

Velikaia Oktiabr'skaia sotsialisticheskaia revoliutsiia: dokumenty i materialy. 10 vols., Moscow, 1957-1963.

Velikaia Oktiabr'skaia sotsialisticheskaia revoliutsiia: khronika sobytii. 4 vols., Moscow, 1957-1961.

Velikhov, L. *Sravnitel'naia tablitsa russkikh politicheskikh partii.* Petrograd, 1917.

Velikii opyt. n.p., n.d. Anarchist pamphlet criticizing the Bolshevik regime.

Venturi, Franco. *Roots of Revolution.* New York, 1960. A monumental study of the Populist movement.

Vetrov, A. "Proshloe i nastoiashchee anarkhizma," *Fakel,* 1907, vol. 2, 163-190.

Vizetelly, Ernest Alfred. *The Anarchists: their Faith and their Record.* London, 1911.

Vmesto programmy: rezoliutsii I i II Vserossiiskikh konferentsii anarkho-sindikalistov. Berlin, 1922.

Volin (Voline) [V. M., Eikhenbaum]. *Le Fascisme rouge*. Paris, 1934?

————. *Raz"iasnenie*. Paris, 1929.

————. *Revoliutsiia i anarkhizm (sbornik statei)*. Kharkov?, 1919. A selection of Volin's articles and editorials from *Golos Truda*.

————. *La Révolution inconnue (1917-1921)*. An important work by one of Russia's leading anarchists. A large portion of the book has been translated into English: *Nineteen-Seventeen: the Russian Revolution Betrayed* and *The Unknown Revolution* (New York and London, 1954-1955).

————. *Stikhotvoreniia*. Paris, 1927.

————. *La Véritable révolution sociale*. Paris, 1935.

Von Laue, Theodore H. "Factory Inspection under the Witte System, 1892-1903," *American Slavic and East European Review*, XIX (October 1960), 347-362.

————. "Russian Peasants in the Factory, 1892-1904," *Journal of Economic History*, XXI (March 1961), 61-80.

Vseobshchaia stachka na iuge Rossii v 1903 godu: sbornik dokumentov. Moscow, 1938.

Vserossiiskii s"ezd predstavitelei rabochikh zavodov, portov i uchrezhdenii Morskogo vedomstva, 1-i. Petrograd, 1917.

Witte, S. Iu. *Vospominaniia*. 2 vols., Berlin, 1922.

Wolfe, Bertram D. *Three Who Made a Revolution*. New York, 1948.

Woodcock, George. *Anarchism: A History of Libertarian Ideas and Movements*. New York, 1962. A comprehensive and lucid history; the best introduction to the subject.

———— and Ivan Avakumovic. *The Anarchist Prince*. London, 1950. The best biography of Kropotkin.

Woytinsky, W. S. *Stormy Passage*. New York, 1961.

Yarmolinsky, Avrahm. *Road to Revolution*. London, 1957.

Yelensky, Boris. *In the Struggle for Equality: The Story of the Anarchist Red Cross*. Chicago, 1958.

Zabrezhnev, V. *Ob individualisticheskom anarkhizme*. London, 1912.

Zadachi sotsial'noi revoliutsii. n.p. [Paris?], n.d.

Zagorsky, S.O. *La République des Soviets*. Paris, 1921.

Zaiats, S. *Kak muzhiki ostalis' bez nachal'stva.* Moscow, 1906.

Zaiavlenie pered sudom Zhorzha Et'evana. Geneva, 1903.

Zaitsev, D. "Marksizm i makhaevshchina," *Obrazovanie,* 1908, No. 3, pp. 35-71.

Zalezhskii, V. *Anarkhisty v Rossii.* Moscow, 1930. A tendentious study of the Russian anarchists by a Soviet historian.

Zenker, E. V. *Anarkhizm: istoriia i kritika anarkhicheskikh uchenii.* Moscow, 1906.

Zévaès, Alexandre. *Histoire du socialisme et du communisme en France de 1871 à 1947.* Paris, 1947.

BULLETINS, JOURNALS, AND NEWSPAPERS

Amerikanskie Izvestiia. New York, 1920-192?.

Anarkhicheskie Organizatsii: Pamiati Petra Alekseevicha Kropotkina. Moscow, 1921. A single number, 8-13 February, to eulogize the deceased Kropotkin.

Anarkhicheskii Vestnik. Berlin, 1923-1924.

Anarkhiia. Moscow, 1918. Organ of the Moscow Federation of Anarchist Groups. Moscow, 1919. Organ of the Underground Anarchists. Buenos Aires, 1930. Published by the *Delo Truda* group of South America.

Anarkhist. Geneva, 1907; Paris, 1908-1910. Edited by German Askarov. Rostov na/Donu, 1917. Organ of the Don Federation of Anarchist-Communists.

Der Arbayter Fraynd. London, 1885-1960. Organ of the Jewish Federation of Anarchists, edited by Rudolf Rocker and others.

Bez Rulia. Paris, 1908. Only one number appeared (September).

Bezvlastie. Kharkov, 1918. Journal of the Kharkov Association of Anarchists. Luga, 1921. Organ of Luga Anarchists.

Biulleten' Initsiativnoi Gruppy Anarkhistskoi Molodezhi Ukrainy "Nabat." Kharkov?, 1919.

Biulleten' Kievskoi Gruppy Anarkhistskoi Molodezhi. Kiev, 1920.

Biulleten' Osvedomitel'nogo Biuro Anarkhistov Rossii. Kharkov, 1917.

Bulletin du Congrès Anarchiste International. London, 1914. Edited by Alexander Schapiro.

Bulletin of the Joint Committee for the Defense of Revolutionists Imprisoned in Russia. Berlin, 1923-1926.

Bulletin of the Relief Fund of the International Working Men's Association for Anarchists and Anarcho-Syndicalists Imprisoned or Exiled in Russia. Berlin, Paris, 1926-1932.

Buntar'. Paris, 1906; Geneva, 1908-1909. Edited by Iuda Grossman-Roshchin and others.

Buntovshchik. Tomsk, 1918.

Burevestnik. Paris, 1906-1910. Edited by Maksim Raevskii and Nikolai Rogdaev; the outstanding émigré journal of the Russian anarchists during the post-1905 period. Petrograd, 1917-1918. Organ of the Petrograd Federation of Anarchist Groups. Odessa, 1920. New York, 1921-1922.

Chernoe Znamia. Geneva, 1905. Only one number appeared (December); organ of the *Chernoe Znamia* group abroad. Vladivostok, 1918. Organ of the Vladivostok Union of Revolutionary Anarchist-Communists.

The Clarion. New York, 1932-1934. Edited by Abba Gordin.

Delo Truda. Paris, Chicago, New York, 1925-1939. Edited by Petr Arshinov and later by Grigorii Maksimov.

Delo Truda-Probuzhdenie. New York, 1940——. Established by a merger of *Delo Truda* (New York) and *Probuzhdenie* (Detroit); edited by Maksimov until 1950.

Fraye Arbeter Shtime (Freie Arbeiter Stimme). New York, 1890——.

Dos Fraye Vort. Buenos Aires, 1956——.

Glos Rewolucyjny. Warsaw, 1906. Published by the Warsaw Federation of Anarchist Groups "International."

Golos Anarkhii. Saratov, 1917. Organ of the Saratov Free Association of Anarchist Groups.

Golos Anarkhista. Ekaterinoslav, 1918. Edited by Petr Arshinov and others.

Golos iz Podpol'ia. Argentina [Buenos Aires?], 1930-1931.

Golos Ssyl'nykh i Zakliuchennykh Russkikh Anarkhistov. New York, 1913-1914. Organ of the Anarchist Red Cross in New York.

Golos Truda. New York, 1911-1916. Organ of the Union of Russian Workers of the United States and Canada. Petrograd, Moscow, 1917-1918. Organ of the Union of Anarcho-Syndicalist Propaganda. One number, in the form of a journal, was published in Petrograd and Moscow in December 1919.

Golos Truzhenika. Chicago, 1918-1927. An IWW publication. Edited for a time by Maksimov.

Izvestiia VTsIK (earlier *Izvestiia Petrogradskogo Soveta* and *Izvestiia TsIk*). Petrograd, Moscow, 1917——.

K Svetu. Kharkov, 1918-1919. Organ of the Kharkov Association of Anarchists.

Khleb i Volia. Geneva, 1903-1905. The first journal of the Russian anarchist movement. Paris, 1909. One issue appeared (No. 1-2, March-July). New York, 1919. Organ of the Union of Russian Workers.

Klich Anarkhistov. New York, 1921. A single issue (May) as a memorial tribute to Kropotkin.

Kommuna. Kronstadt, 1917. Organ of the Petrograd Federation of Anarchist-Communists.

Listki "Khleb i Volia." London, 1906-1907. A continuation of *Khleb i Volia,* published by the Kropotkin circle.

Listok gruppy Beznachalie. Paris, 1905. Organ of Bidbei's *Beznachalie* group.

Maksimalist. Moscow, 1918-1921. Organ of the Union of SR Maximalists.

Man: A Journal of the Anarchist Ideal and Movement. San Francisco, 1933-1940.

Metallist. Petrograd, 1917-1919.

Molot. Paris, 1912? Organ of the Group of Free Socialists. Only one number appeared.

Moskovskii Metallist. Moscow, 1917-1918.

Mother Earth. New York, 1906-1918. Edited by Emma Goldman.

Nabat. Kharkov, Elizavetgrad, Odessa, Guliai-Pole, 1917-1920. Organ of the *Nabat* Confederation of the Ukraine. Other *Nabats* were published in Geneva, 1916, and Altai, 1920.

Narodnaia Mysl'. n.p., 1950-1953. Mimeographed anarchist monthly.

New Trends. New York, 1945-1946. Edited by Alexander Schapiro.

Novyi Mir. Paris, 1905. Edited by Novomirskii; only one number appeared (15 October).

Novyi Put'. Petrograd, 1917-1918. Monthly journal of the Central Council of Factory Committees.

Osvobozhdenie Profsoiuzov. Paris, 1928.

Pochin. Moscow, 1923.

Pravda. Petrograd, Moscow, 1917———.

Probuzhdenie. Detroit, 1927-1939.

Protiv Techeniia. St. Petersburg, 1907. Edited by Evgenii Lozinskii.

Put' k Svobode. Geneva, 1917. Publication of the Zurich and Geneva Group of Anarchist-Communists (Grossman-Roshchin, Orgeiani, and others); only one number appeared (May). Guliai-Pole, 1919-1920. Organ of Makhno's Insurgent Army of the Ukraine.

Rabochaia Mysl'. New York, 1916-1917. A journal of the Union of Russian Workers. Kharkov, 1917. An Anarcho-Syndicalist publication.

Rabochaia Revoliutsiia. Moscow, 1918. Written by A. Vol'skii (Waclaw Machajski); only one number was issued (June-July).

Rabochee Znamia. Lausanne, 1915.

Rabochii Mir. Zurich, London, 1912-1914.

Rabochii Put'. Berlin, 1923. Anarcho-Syndicalist journal.

Rabochii Zagovor. n.p. [Geneva], 1907. Written by Machajski; one number of 83 pages was published (September-October).

Rassvet. New York, Chicago, 1924-1937.

Rech'. St. Petersburg, 1906-1917.

Revoliutsionnoe Tvorchestvo. Moscow, 1918.

The Road to Freedom. Stelton, New Jersey; New York City, 1924-1932.

Sotsialisticheskii Vestnik. Berlin, Paris, New York, 1921———.

Svoboda. Kiev, 1919. Journal of Kiev Association of Free Anarchists; only one number appeared (September).

Svobodnaia Kommuna. Petograd, 1917. Organ of the Petrograd Federation of Anarchist-Communist Groups.

Svobodnoe Obshchestvo. New York, 1920-1921.

Svobodnoe Slovo. Christchurch, England, 1901-1905. Tolstoyan journal; edited by Vladimir Chertkov.

Der Syndikalist. Berlin, 1918-1933.

Trud i Volia. Moscow, 1919. Organ of the Union of Anarchist-Syndicalist-Communists.

Trudovaia Respublika. London, 1909.

Universal. Moscow, 1920. Organ of the Anarcho-Universalists.

V Pomoshch'—Der Hilf-Ruf. London, 1911-1912. Organ of

the Anarchist Red Cross in London, in Russian and Yiddish; edited by Rocker.

Vestnik Anarkhii. Briansk, 1918. Organ of the Briansk Federation of Anarchists.

Vil'na Gromada. n.p. [New York?], 1922. Organ of Ukrainian Anarchist-Communists.

Volia Ukraini. Newark, New Jersey, 1923.

Volna. n.p. [New York], 1920-1924.

Vol'naia Mysl'. Buenos Aires, 1932.

Vol'naia Volia. Moscow, 1903.

Vol'naia Zhizn'. Moscow, 1919-1921. Organ of Karelin's All-Russian Federation of Anarchist-Communists.

Vol'nyi Golos. Elizavetgrad, 1919.

Vol'nyi Golos Truda. Moscow, 1918. Anarcho-Syndicalist publication, edited by Maksimov and others.

Vol'nyi Kronshtadt. Kronstadt, 1917.

Vol'nyi Rabochii. Odessa, 1906. Published by Novomirskii; one issue appeared (25 December).

Zsherminal. London, 1900-1912. Theoretical monthly of the Jewish Federation of Anarchists; edited by Rocker.

INDEX

agents provocateurs, 18, 47, 53
Aksakov, K. S., 36
Aleksandrovsk, anarchists in, 218-19
Aleshker, L., 67
Alexander II, Tsar, 26; assassination of, 9, 14-15, 62, 175; and Jews, 15-16
Alexander III, Tsar, 15, 17
Alexander Berkman Aid Fund, 235
Allemanists, 97
All-Russian Congress of Anarchists, plans for, 171-73, 221
All-Russian Federation of Anarchist-Communists, 201-202, 207, 230, 236-37
Al'manakh, 115n
Amsterdam, anarchists in, 240
anarchism, doctrines of, 3-4, 18-20, 35-36, 152, 250-53. *See also* anarchist-communism, Anarchist-Communists, Anarcho-Syndicalists, collectivist anarchism, individualist anarchists, Tolstoyans
Anarchist Black Cross, 207, 222
anarchist-communism, 28-32, 82, 194
Anarchist-Communists, 44ff, 56, 89-90, 172ff, 205; and labor movement, 78-79; conference in Urals, 79; in Petrograd, 124-26; criticize workers' control, 147, 164-65; All-Russian Congress of, 171-73; and terrorism, 189-90; cooperate with Bolsheviks, 201-203; in exile, 241-43. *See also* Beznachalie, Chernoe Znamia, Khleb i Volia
Anarchist-Individualists, *see* individualist anarchists
Anarchist Information Bureau, 171-72
Anarchist Library, 38, 227
Anarchist Red Cross, 68n, 113-14, 138
anarchists, 3-4, 46; in Bialystok, 18-21; anti-intellectualism of, 18-19, 45, 91-112; criticize social-

ists, 19; number of, 33-34, 42-43, 68-69n, 173-74n; antecedents, 35-37; revolutionary aims, 44; Amsterdam Congress, 66, 82-84, 112n, 115, 138; and February Revolution, 123ff; criticize Soviet regime, 159-60; conference in Donets Basin, 173; and Constituent Assembly, 174; on "All power to the soviets," 181; condemn Brest-Litovsk treaty, 182-83; arrest of, 184-85, 230-36, 244-45; and terrorism, 186-89; on soviets, 140, 159, 190, 207-208, 224, 238; and Kronstadt rebellion, 228-31; in Civil War, 196-203; in exile, 237-50. *See also* Anarchist-Communists, Anarcho-Syndicalists, individualist anarchists, Tolstoyans
Anarcho-Biocosmists, 231
Anarcho-Futurists, 186
Anarcho-Syndicalists, 56, 72ff, 89-90, 119, 172, 179, 205, 237; and terrorism, 61-63, 135; in France, 73-76, 80-81, 92, 97-100, 111, 142; in 1917, 136ff; Union of Anarcho-Syndicalist Propaganda, 139, 146, 152; on soviets, 140, 153; and workers' control, 141ff, 161-70; influence in trade unions, 167n; at First Congress of Trade Unions, 167-70; All-Russian Conferences of, 173, 190-91, 208; Confederation of, 194-95; Executive Bureau of, 195, 223, 231; arrest of, 222-23; in exile, 239-41
Anarcho-Universalists, *see* Universalists
Anarkhicheskii Vestnik (The Anarchist Herald), 239
Anarkhiia (Anarchy), printing press, 44, 65; newspaper, 179-80, 184; terrorist leaflet, 188
Anarkhist (The Anarchist), 86, 179

Other Paul Avrich Titles on AK Press

The Modern School Movement:
Anarchism And Education In The United States
Paul Avrich
ISBN: 1904859097
416 pages $21.95/£13.95

Between 1910 and 1960 anarchists across
the United States established more than
twenty schools where children might study
in an atmosphere of freedom and self-
reliance in contrast to the formality and discipline of the traditional classroom. These
"Modern Schools," sought to abolish all
forms of authority, and to usher in a new
society based on the voluntary cooperation
of free individuals. Their object, during an
era of war, social ferment, and government
repression, was to create not only a new type of school, but also a new world.
Among the participants were Emma Goldman, Margaret Sanger, Alexander
Berkman, and artist Man Ray. Based on extensive interviews with former pupils
and teachers, the book was nominated for the Pulitzer Prize in Biography.

Anarchist Voices: An Oral History of
Anarchism in America (Unabridged)
Paul Avrich
ISBN: 1904859275
592 pages $28.00/£16.00

In *Anarchist Voices,* Avrich lets anarchists
speak for themselves. This book contains
180 interviews conducted over a period of
30 years. The interviewees were active
between the 1880s and the 1930s and represent all schools of anarchism. Each of the six
thematic sections begins with an explanato-
ry essay, and each interview with a biogra-
phical note. Their stories provide a wealth of personal detail about such anarchist
luminaries as Emma Goldman and Sacco and Vanzetti. This work of impeccable
scholarship is an invaluable resource not only for scholars of anarchism but also
for those studying immigration, ethnic politics, education, and labor history.

Other Titles from AK Press

Books

MARTHA **ACKELSBERG**—*Free Women of Spain*
KATHY **ACKER**—*Pussycat Fever*
MICHAEL **ALBERT**—*Moving Forward: Program for a Participatory Economy*
JOEL **ANDREAS**—*Addicted to War: Why the U.S. Can't Kick Militarism*
JOEL **ANDREAS**—*Adicto a la Guerra: Por qué EEUU no puede librarse del militarismo*
PAUL **AVRICH**—*Anarchist Voices: An Oral History of Anarchism in America (Unabridged)*
PAUL **AVRICH**—*The Modern School Movement: Anarchism and Education in the United States*
PAUL **AVRICH**—*The Russian Anarchists*
ALEXANDER **BERKMAN**—*What is Anarchism?*
ALEXANDER **BERKMAN**—*The Blast: The Complete Collection*
HAKIM **BEY**—*Immediatism*
JANET **BIEHL** & PETER **STAUDENMAIER**—*Ecofascism: Lessons From The German Experience*
BIOTIC BAKING BRIGADE—*Pie Any Means Necessary The Biotic Baking Brigade Cookbook*
JACK **BLACK**—*You Can't Win*
MURRAY **BOOKCHIN**—*Anarchism, Marxism, and the Future of the Left*
MURRAY **BOOKCHIN**—*The Ecology of Freedom: The Emergence and Dissolution of Hierarchy*
MURRAY **BOOKCHIN**—*Post-Scarcity Anarchism*
MURRAY **BOOKCHIN**—*Social Anarchism or Lifestyle Anarchism: An Unbridgeable Chasm*
MURRAY **BOOKCHIN**—*Spanish Anarchists: The Heroic Years 1868–1936, The*
MURRAY **BOOKCHIN**—*To Remember Spain: The Anarchist and Syndicalist Revolution of 1936*
MURRAY **BOOKCHIN**—*Which Way for the Ecology Movement?*
MAURICE **BRINTON**—*For Workers' Power*
DANNY **BURNS**—*Poll Tax Rebellion*
MAT **CALLAHAN**—*The Trouble With Music*
CHRIS **CARLSSON**—*Critical Mass: Bicycling's Defiant Celebration*
JAMES **CARR**—*Bad*
NOAM **CHOMSKY**—*At War With Asia*
NOAM **CHOMSKY**—*Chomsky on Anarchism*
NOAM **CHOMSKY**—*Language and Politics*
NOAM **CHOMSKY**—*Radical Priorities*
WARD **CHURCHILL**—*On the Justice of Roosting Chickens: Reflections on the Consequences of U.S. Imperial Arrogance and Criminality*
WARD **CHURCHILL**—*Since Predator Came*
HARRY **CLEAVER**—*Reading Capital Politically*
ALEXANDER **COCKBURN** & JEFFREY ST. CLAIR (ed.)—*Dime's Worth of Difference*
ALEXANDER **COCKBURN** & JEFFREY ST. CLAIR (ed.)—*The Politics of Anti-Semitism*
ALEXANDER **COCKBURN** & JEFFREY ST. CLAIR (ed.)—*Serpents in the Garden*
DANIEL **COHN-BENDIT** & GABRIEL **COHN-BENDIT**—*Obsolete Communism: The Left-Wing Alternative*
EG SMITH COLLECTIVE—*Animal Ingredients A–Z (3rd edition)*
VOLTAIRINE de **CLEYRE**—*Voltairine de Cleyre Reader*

ALEXANDRE **SKIRDA**—*Facing the Enemy: A History Of Anarchist Organisation From Proudhon To May 1968*

ALEXANDRE **SKIRDA**—*Nestor Mahkno: Anarchy's Cossack*

VALERIE **SOLANAS**—*Scum Manifesto*

CJ **STONE**—*Housing Benefit Hill & Other Places*

ANTONIO **TELLEZ**—*Sabate: Guerilla Extraordinary*

MICHAEL **TOBIAS**—*Rage and Reason*

JIM **TULLY**—*Beggars of Life: A Hobo Autobiography*

TOM **VAGUE**—*Anarchy in the UK: The Angry Brigade*

TOM **VAGUE**—*Televisionaries*

JAN **VALTIN**—*Out of the Night*

RAOUL **VANEIGEM**—*A Cavalier History Of Surrealism*

FRANCOIS EUGENE **VIDOCQ**—*Memoirs of Vidocq: Master of Crime*

MARK J **WHITE**—*An Idol Killing*

JOHN **YATES**—*Controlled Flight Into Terrain*

JOHN **YATES**—*September Commando*

BENJAMIN **ZEPHANIAH**—*Little Book of Vegan Poems*

BENJAMIN **ZEPHANIAH**—*School's Out*

HELLO—*2/15: The Day The World Said NO To War*

DARK STAR COLLECTIVE —*Beneath the Paving Stones: Situationists and the Beach, May '68*

DARK STAR COLLECTIVE —*Quiet Rumours: An Anarcha-Feminist Reader*

ANONYMOUS —*Test Card F*

CLASS WAR FEDERATION —*Unfinished Business: The Politics of Class War*

CDs

MUMIA **ABU JAMAL**—*175 Progress Drive*

MUMIA **ABU JAMAL**—*All Things Censored Vol.1*

MUMIA **ABU JAMAL**—*Spoken Word*

JUDI **BARI**—*Who Bombed Judi Bari?*

JELLO **BIAFRA**—*Become the Media*

JELLO **BIAFRA**—*Beyond The Valley of the Gift Police*

JELLO **BIAFRA**—*The Big Ka-Boom, Part One*

JELLO **BIAFRA**—*High Priest of Harmful*

JELLO **BIAFRA**—*I Blow Minds For A Living*

JELLO **BIAFRA**—*If Evolution Is Outlawed*

JELLO **BIAFRA**—*Machine Gun In The Clown's Hand*

JELLO **BIAFRA**—*No More Cocoons*

NOAM **CHOMSKY**—*An American Addiction*

NOAM **CHOMSKY**—*Case Studies in Hypocrisy*

NOAM **CHOMSKY**—*Emerging Framework of World Power*

NOAM **CHOMSKY**—*Free Market Fantasies*

NOAM **CHOMSKY**—*The Imperial Presidency*

NOAM **CHOMSKY**—*New War On Terrorism: Fact And Fiction*

NOAM **CHOMSKY**—*Propaganda and Control of the Public Mind*

NOAM **CHOMSKY**—*Prospects for Democracy*

NOAM **CHOMSKY** & **CHUMBAWAMBA**—*For A Free Humanity: For Anarchy*

WARD **CHURCHILL**—*Doing Time: The Politics of Imprisonment*

WARD **CHURCHILL**—*In A Pig's Eye: Reflections on the Police State, Repression, and Native America*

WARD **CHURCHILL**—*Life in Occupied America*

WARD **CHURCHILL**—*Pacifism and Pathology in the American Left*

ALEXANDER **COCKBURN**—*Beating the Devil: The Incendiary Rants of Alexander Cockburn*

ANGELA **DAVIS**—*The Prison Industrial Complex*

THE **EX**—*1936: The Spanish Revolution*

NORMAN **FINKELSTEIN**—*An Issue of Justice: Origins of the Israel/Palestine Conflict*

FREEDOM ARCHIVES—*Chile: Promise of Freedom*

FREEDOM ARCHIVES—*Prisons on Fire: George Jackson, Attica & Black Liberation*

FREEDOM ARCHIVES—*Robert F. Williams: Self-Defense, Self-Respect & Self-Determination*

JAMES **KELMAN**—*Seven Stories*

TOM **LEONARD**—*Nora's Place and Other Poems 1965–99*

CASEY **NEILL**—*Memory Against Forgetting*

GREG **PALAST**—*Weapon of Mass Instruction*

CHRISTIAN **PARENTI**—*Taking Liberties: Policing, Prisons and Surveillance in an Age of Crisis*

UTAH **PHILLIPS**—*I've Got To know*

UTAH **PHILLIPS**—*Starlight on the Rails*

DAVID **ROVICS**—*Behind the Barricades: Best of David Rovics*

ARUNDHATI **ROY**—*Come September*

VARIOUS—*Better Read Than Dead*

VARIOUS—*Less Rock, More Talk*

VARIOUS—*Mob Action Against the State: Collected Speeches from the Bay Area Anarchist Bookfair*

VARIOUS—*Monkeywrenching the New World Order*

VARIOUS—*Return of the Read Menace*

HOWARD **ZINN**—*Artists In A Time of War*

HOWARD **ZINN**—*Heroes and Martyrs: Emma Goldman, Sacco & Vanzetti, and the Revolutionary Struggle*

HOWARD **ZINN**—*A People's History of the United States: A Lecture at Reed*

HOWARD **ZINN**—*People's History Project*

HOWARD **ZINN**—*Stories Hollywood Never Tells*

DVDs

NOAM **CHOMSKY**—*Distorted Morality*

ARUNDHATI **ROY**—*Instant Mix Imperial Democracy*

HOWARD **ZINN** & ANTHONY **ARNOVE** (ed.)—*Readings from Voices of a People's History of the United States*

Printed in the USA
CPSIA information can be obtained
at www.ICGtesting.com
JSHW022208140824
68134JS00018B/927